T0226258

Communications in Computer and Information Science   790

Commenced Publication in 2007
Founding and Former Series Editors:
Alfredo Cuzzocrea, Xiaoyong Du, Orhun Kara, Ting Liu, Dominik Ślęzak,
and Xiaokang Yang

More information about this series at http://www.springer.com/series/7899

Armando Eduardo De Giusti (Ed.)

Computer Science – CACIC 2017

23rd Argentine Congress
La Plata, Argentina, October 9–13, 2017
Revised Selected Papers

 Springer

Editor
Armando Eduardo De Giusti ⓘ
Universidad Nacional de La Plata
La Plata
Argentina

ISSN 1865-0929   ISSN 1865-0937 (electronic)
Communications in Computer and Information Science
ISBN 978-3-319-75213-6   ISBN 978-3-319-75214-3 (eBook)
https://doi.org/10.1007/978-3-319-75214-3

Library of Congress Control Number: 2018931377

Printed on acid-free paper

This Springer imprint is published by the registered company Springer International Publishing AG
part of Springer Nature
The registered company address is: Gewerbestrasse 11, 6330 Cham, Switzerland

Preface

Welcome to the selected papers of the XXIII Argentine Congress of Computer Science (CACIC 2017), held in La Plata, Argentina, during October 9–13, 2017. CACIC 2017 was organized by the School of Computer Science of the National University of La Plata (UNLP) on behalf of the Network of National Universities with Computer Science Degrees (RedUNCI)[1].

CACIC is an annual congress dedicated to the promotion and advancement of all aspects of computer science. Its aim is to provide a forum within which the development of computer science as an academic discipline with industrial applications is promoted, trying to extend the frontier of both the state of the art and the state of the practice. The main audience for, and participants of CACIC are seen as researchers in academic departments, laboratories, and industrial software organizations.

CACIC 2017 covered the following topics: intelligent agents and systems; distributed and parallel processing; software engineering; hardware architecture, networks and operating systems; graphic computation, visualization, and image processing; computer technology applied to education; databases and data mining; innovation in software systems; computer security; innovation in computer science education; signal processing and real-time systems.

This year, the congress received 171 submissions. Each submission was reviewed by at least two, and on average 3.1 Program Committee members and/or external reviewers. A total of 132 full papers, involving 476 authors from 69 universities, were accepted. According to the recommendations of the reviewers, 28 of them were selected for this book.

During CACIC 2017, special activities were also carried out, including four plenary lectures, two invited speakers, two discussion panels, and an International School with six courses.

Special thanks to the members of the different committees for their support and collaboration. Also, we would like to thank the local Organizing Committee, reviewers, lecturers, speakers, authors, and all conference attendees. Finally, we want to thank Springer for their support of this publication.

January 2018   Armando De Giusti

---

[1] RedUNCI website: http://redunci.info.unlp.edu.ar.

Organization

The XXIII Argentine Congress of Computer Science (CACIC 2017) was organized by the School of Computer Science of the National University of La Plata (UNLP) on behalf of the Network of National Universities with Computer Science Degrees (RedUNCI).

General Chair

Armando De Giusti — National University of La Plata, Argentina

Editorial Assistant

Enzo Rucci — National University of La Plata, Argentina

Program Committee

Patricia Pesado (RedUNCI Chair)	National University of La Plata, Argentina
Marcelo Estayno (RedUNCI Co-chair)	National University of La Matanza, Argentina
María José Abásolo	National University of La Plata, Argentina
Cluadio Aciti	National University of Buenos Aires Center, Argentina
Hugo Alfonso	National University of La Pampa, Argentina
Jorge Ardenghi	National University of South, Argentina
Marcelo Arroyo	National University of Río Cuarto, Argentina
Hernan Astudillo	Technical University Federico Santa María, Chile
Sandra Baldasarri	University of Zaragoza, Spain
Javier Balladini	National University of Comahue, Argentina
Luis Barvoza	University of Minho, Portugal
Rodolfo Bertone	National University of La Plata, Argentina
Oscar Bria	National University of La Plata, Argentina
Nieves R. Brisaboa	University of La Coruña, Spain
Carlos Buckle	National University of Patagonia San Juan Bosco, Argentina
Alberto Cañas	University of West Florida, USA
Ana Casali	National University of Rosario, Argentina
Silvia Castro	National University of South, Argentina
Antonio Castro Lechtaler	National University of Buenos Aires, Argentina
Alejandra Cechich	National University of Comahue, Argentina
Edgar Chávez	Michoacana University of San Nicolás de Hidalgo, Mexico

Sponsors

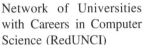

National University of
La Plata (UNLP)

Network of Universities
with Careers in Computer
Science (RedUNCI)

Secretary of University Politics
(SPU)

Ministry of Science, Technology and Productive Innovation (MinCyT)

National Council for
Scientific and Technical
Research (CONICET)

Commission for Scientific
Research Province of Buenos
Aires (CIC)

Trust Fund for the Promotion
of the Software Industry
(FONSOFT)

Engineering Academy of
Buenos Aires

Chamber of Businesses of
Software and Information
Services (CESSI)

POLO IT La Plata

Contents

Intelligent Agents and Systems

Deep Neural Networks for Shimmer Approximation in Synthesized Audio Signal

Mario Alejandro García$^{(\boxtimes)}$ ⓘ and Eduardo Atilio Destéfanis

Universidad Tecnológica Nacional, Córdoba, Argentina
mgarcia@frc.utn.edu.ar

Abstract. Shimmer is a classical acoustic measure of the amplitude perturbation in a signal. This kind of variation in the human voice allows to characterize some properties, not only of the voice itself, but of the person who speaks. During the last years deep learning techniques have become the state of the art for recognition tasks on the voice. In this work the relationship between shimmer and deep neural networks is analyzed. A deep learning model is created. It is able to approximate shimmer value of a simple synthesized audio signal (stationary and without formants) taking the spectrogram as input feature. It is concluded firstly, that for this kind of synthesized signal, a neural network like the one we proposed can approximate shimmer, and secondly, that the convolution layers can be designed in order to preserve the information of shimmer and transmit it to the following layers.

Keywords: Shimmer · Voice quality · Deep learning
Deep neural network · Convolutional neural network

1 Introduction

Shimmer is a classical acoustic measure of the amplitude perturbation of a signal. This kind of variations in the human voice allows to characterize some properties, not only of the voice itself, but on the person who speaks [1].

Shimmer value is associated to voice quality [2–7], state of mind [8–13], age [14] and gender [15] of people. There are many research works that use shimmer (among other measures) with goals ranging from pathologies detection [6,16,17] to the improvement of human-machine interfaces through the estimation of the intensionality of a spoken phrase [18]. Regarding synthesized voices, Yamasaki et al. show in [19] that a certain shimmer level increases the degree of naturalness.

The application of deep learning techniques is the state of the art in automated audio analysis, with the detection of pronounced phonemes and the identification of the person that speaks as main objectives [20–26], but also used to detect emotions, age, gender, etc. [27–33].

Classifiers based on neural networks can be divided into two groups according to the type of input features, those using previously calculated acoustic measures [10,14] and those using raw audio [22,24,25] or spectral data [21–23,28–31,34,35].

© Springer International Publishing AG, part of Springer Nature 2018
A. E. De Giusti (Ed.): CACIC 2017, CCIS 790, pp. 3–12, 2018.
https://doi.org/10.1007/978-3-319-75214-3_1

In [26] a hybrid approach is applied by adding shimmer and other measures to improve the recognition achieved with spectral data. It is important to clarify, for first group of classifiers, that shimmer calculation has a major complication, it depends on the previous detection of the fundamental frequency (f_0) of vocal cords vibration. It is difficult to estimate f_0 in pathological voices [36,37]. The estimation of the actual f_0 value is still a research topic [36–40]. Regarding the second group of classifiers, it is not possible to know whether the outputs are influenced by the shimmer value of the signal.

1.1   Objectives

The objective of this work is to make an estimation of the shimmer value in a synthesized audio signal through a neural model. The neural network must combine convolutional layers and feed forward layers. The inputs of the neural model will be the spectral values of the signal.

Main contributions of developing a neural network that estimates shimmer from spectral features of an audio signal are, on the one hand, the procurement of a f_0 independent shimmer calculation method, and on the other, to answer the question about the extent to which amplitude disturbances of the original audio can influence the output of a deep learning model with raw audio or spectral data input. In other words, how much shimmer information is preserved to the last layers of the model.

1.2   Shimmer Calculation

There are different versions of shimmer. The most important difference between them is the window size (number of f_0 cycles) used for the calculation. Some versions can be seen in [41].

Chosen version of shimmer for this work is the proposed by Klingholz and Martin [42], also known as *Relative Shimmer*.

Relative Shimmer, hereinafter referred to as "shimmer", is a way of measuring cycle-to-cycle amplitude perturbations of the fundamental frequency of a signal. It is shown as a *perturbation/total amplitude* relation.

$$\text{shimmer} = \frac{\frac{1}{N-1} \sum_{i=1}^{N-1} |A_i - A_{i+1}|}{\frac{1}{N} \sum_{i=1}^{N} |A_i|} \qquad (1)$$

where N is the number of periods of f_0 in the signal and A_i is the maximum amplitude into i period.

2   Methods and Materials

2.1   Neural Models

Deep learning models with ascending complexity were generated for problems of shimmer approximation. First, shimmer was approximated for f_0 variable,

k constant and f_{mod} constant. Then, shimmer was approximated for f_0 variable, k variable, and f_{mod} constant. Finally, a model was found to approximate shimmer with f_0, k and f_{mod} variable.

In all cases, spectral audio data (instead of raw audio) were used as input features. There are two reasons, the improvement of training performance due the dimension reduction, and the similarity with human auditory system, where spectral decomposition is performed in the basilar membrane of the cochlea and not by the neurons in auditory cortex [43].

2.2   Data

Audio. Audio data without harmonics was generated. As in [1] the amplitude modulation of human voice was approximated by a sinusoidal wave. The expression of each audio signal $y(t)$ was:

$$y(t) = \frac{1}{1+k} \sin(\alpha + 2t\pi f_0)(1 + k\sin(\beta + 2t\pi f_{\text{mod}})) \qquad (2)$$

where t is time [sec], f_0 is the frequency of vocal fold vibration [Hz], f_{mod} is the modulatory frequency [Hz], k is the constant of the amplitude modulator sensibility, α and β are constant to handle the phase of the signal to be modulated and the modulating signal respectively.

For training, test and validation data generation, random values were taken with uniform distribution. f_0 got values in $[200, 1000]$ Hz range, f_{mod} in $[5, 10]$ Hz, k in $[0, 0.4]$, α and β in $[0, 2\pi]$.

250 ms of audio generated with $f_0 = 200$ Hz, $f_{\text{mod}} = 8$ Hz and $k = 0.4$, are shown in Fig. 1.

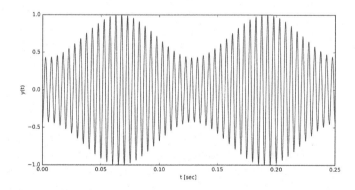

Fig. 1. Generated audio for $f_0 = 200$ Hz, $f_{\text{mod}} = 8$ Hz and $k = 0.4$

Training Data. Three datasets were created to train each model, a training dataset with 2500 elements, a testing dataset with 500 elements and a validation dataset with 500 elements. Each element is composed by shimmer (Eq. (1)) value to be estimated and the spectrogram of generated audio.

Due to the fact that f_0 is known at the time of audio generation, shimmer value can be accurately calculated.

The spectrogram is calculated on 2 s of 44100 samples/sec audio. A $Tukey(0.25)$ window of width $= 256$ was used, which determines a 129×393 (frequency/time) shape structure that contains the signal spectral density.

Figure 2 shows values of the second, third and fourth rows (index 1 to 3) of the spectrogram of signal in Fig. 1.

Spectrograms data and shimmer data were scaled into the range $[0, 1]$.

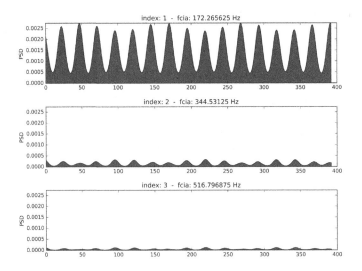

Fig. 2. Three rows with higher average value of Power Spectral Density (PSD) in spectrogram of audio generated with $f_0 = 200$ Hz, $f_{\mathrm{mod}} = 8$ Hz and $k = 0.4$

3 Results

An initial analysis was performed with f_0, f_{mod} and k known data. It was found that a neural network with dense connections is able to calculate shimmer value with high precision if it gets f_0, f_{mod} and k as input features. Optimal structure of this network was empirically found. This is a three layer network, two layers of 20 neurons with $tanh()$ activation function and a linear neuron as output. In next models, convolution layers are used at the initial part of the network, and then, dense layers with 20, 20 and 1 neurons. The function of convolution layers is to calculate f_0, f_{mod} and k values in order to dense layers calculate shimmer.

It was noted that only the first 15 rows of the spectrogram (lower frequencies) would have significant information. Then, only for the scope proposed in this work, the rest of the frequencies were deleted. Spectrogram shape changes from 129×393 to 15×393. This provides a important performance improvement.

3.1 Shimmer Approximation with f_0 Variable

Without harmonics, f_0 calculation from spectrogram is easy, it is enough to obtain the energy average value weighted by the frequency that each spectrogram row represents. As expected, a network such as Fig. 3, where each complete row of the spectrogram is connected to one neuron of an *Average pooling* layer, is able to perform the weighted average of frequencies and calculate the shimmer value in densely connected layers. Tests were performed with f_0 in $[200, 1000]$ Hz range, $k = 0.4$ and $f_{\mathrm{mod}} = 8$ Hz. A satisfactory approximation was achieved, with a mean square error (MSE) $< 10^{-4}$.

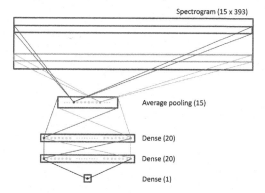

Fig. 3. Shimmer approximation model on signals with f_0 in $[200, 1000]$ Hz range, $f_{\mathrm{mod}} = 8$ Hz and $k = 0.4$. Each neuron in the *Average pooling* layer has a complete frequency of the spectrogram as its visual field. The activation function of hidden dense layers neurons is $tanh()$ and the output neuron is linear.

3.2 Shimmer Approximation with f_0 and k Variable

The value of k inversely affects the area under the energy curve of the spectrogram. Therefore, information about k value can be obtained through the energy average of the spectrogram. The model shown in previous section preserves the necessary information to estimate the energy average. Tests were performed with audio data for f_0 in $[200, 1000]$ Hz range, k in $[0, 0.4]$ range and $f_{\mathrm{mod}} = 8$ Hz. Results were satisfactory again. The model approximates shimmer with an MSE $< 10^{-4}$.

3.3 Shimmer Approximation with f_0, k and f_{mod} Variable

For f_0 in the range $[200, 1000]$ Hz, k in the range $[0, 0.4]$ and f_{mod} in the range $[5, 10]$ Hz it was necessary to create a more complex model than the previous one. Shimmer depends on the modulation frequency, so a new transformation is necessary. The first one was the transformation from time domain to frequency domain (spectrogram). The new (second) transformation is performed in a convolution layer at the initial part of the model (Fig. 4).

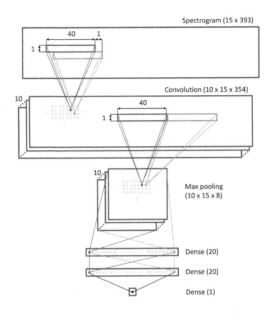

Fig. 4. Shimmer approximation model on signals with f_0 in the range $[200, 1000]$ Hz, k in the range $[0, 0.4]$ and f_{mod} in the range $[5, 10]$ Hz. The shape of convolutional layer windows is 1×40, strides 1×1. Convolutional layer has 10 sub-layers. The shape of *max pooling* layer windows is 1×40, strides 1×40. The network finishes with three dense layers of 20, 20 and 1 neurons.

Convolutional Layer. Each convolution layer neuron is connected to spectrogram through a *height* $= 1$ and *width* $= 40$ window. Convolution is performed on a single frequency (*height* $= 1$) in order to the f_0 detail level needed in the dense layers is not lost. 40-element width is the minimum required to hold a cycle of $min(f_{\mathrm{mod}})$. The number of elements of the spectrogram per modulation cycle (C) for a spectrogram of width W_s and an audio length L is:

$$C = \frac{W_s}{L \times min(f_{\mathrm{mod}})} = \frac{393 \text{ elements}}{2 \text{ sec} \times 5 \text{ Hz}} = 39.3 \text{ elements/cycle}$$

The window displacement in both directions is 1 step. This implies that on the frequency dimension there is no overlap, and in time dimension there are 39 overlapping elements between the windows of adjacent neurons. Finally, according to these definitions, the shape of each convolution filter or sub-layer is 15×354. The convolution layer consists of 10 sub-layers. This amount is a compromise between performance and the detail level of f_{mod} on the information sent to dense layers. Neurons of this layer have linear activation function. Weights are initialized with orthogonal random values. An attempt was made to initialize them with wavelet families for sinusoidal waves between 5 Hz y 10 Hz, but no improvement was achieved on the prediction accuracy.

***Max pooling* layer.** The neurons in the *max pooling* layer have a 1×40 window size on the convolutional layer. Again, $height = 1$ allows allows f_0 information be able to be transmitted to dense layers with no losing details. The 40-element width extends the visual field of this layer neurons to 2 cycles of $\min(f_{mod})$ on the spectrogram. In this way, the output value is invariant to the modulation signal translations. There is no overlap between the windows, so the size of each of the 10 sub-layers is 15×8 neurons.

The outputs of *max pooling* layer are connected to three layers with dense connections equal to those of the previous model.

For this model, 20 training tests were performed. The size of training dataset was 2500 elements. In all cases, results were compared with a test dataset (500 elements) during training and a validation dataset (500 elements) at the end. The best result, with 150 training cycles, obtained a MSE $= 5.8 \times 10^{-5}$ on the test dataset. In Fig. 5 expected and calculated shimmer values are displayed in ascending order for the 500 elements of test dataset.

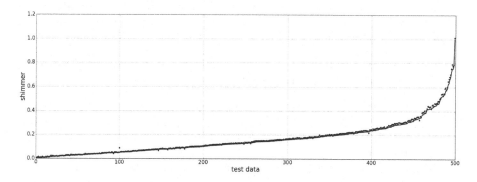

Fig. 5. Normalized shimmer. Expected (line) vs. calculated (dots) for elements in testing dataset (in ascending order of shimmer value).

4   Conclusion

It was verified that, for simple audio signal modulated in amplitude by a sinusoidal wave, with variable parameters of fundamental frequency, modulating frequency and modulation sensitivity, it is possible to obtain a neural model able to approximate the value of shimmer.

Under the conditions established in this work, it is possible to calculate shimmer without knowing f_0. Moreover, it can be affirmed that if the first layers of a deep neural network respects the structure of the second presented model, this neural network is able to use the value of shimmer, internally calculated, to perform classifications and other approximations.

5 Future Works

It is planned to extend the analysis, first by expanding the ranges of f_0 y f_{mod}, then adding harmonics and noise to the synthesized signals. Finally, it is planned to analyze the behavior of deep learning models for shimmer calculation on natural voices.

References

1. Jafari, M., Till, J.A., Law-Till, C.B.: Interactive effects of local smoothing window size and fundamental frequency on shimmer calculation. J. Voice **7**(3), 235–241 (1993)
2. Nieto, R.G., Marín-Hurtado, J.I., Capacho-Valbuena, L.M., Suarez, A.A., Bolaños, E.A.B.: Pattern recognition of hypernasality in voice of patients with cleft and lip palate. In: 2014 XIX Symposium on Image, Signal Processing and Artificial Vision (STSIVA), pp. 1–5. IEEE (2014)
3. Holi, M.S., et al.: A hybrid model for neurological disordered voice classification using time and frequency domain features. Artif. Intell. Res. **5**(1), 87 (2015)
4. Freitas, S.V., Pestana, P.M., Almeida, V., Ferreira, A.: Integrating voice evaluation: correlation between acoustic and audio-perceptual measures. J. Voice **29**(3), 390–e1 (2015)
5. Little, M.A., Costello, D.A., Harries, M.L.: Objective dysphonia quantification in vocal fold paralysis: comparing nonlinear with classical measures. J. Voice **25**(1), 21–31 (2011)
6. Lopes, L.W., Simões, L.B., da Silva, J.D., da Silva Evangelista, D., da Nóbrega E Ugulino, A.C., Silva, P.O.C., Vieira, V.J.D.: Accuracy of acoustic analysis measurements in the evaluation of patients with different laryngeal diagnoses. J. Voice **31**(3), 382–e15 (2017)
7. Hillenbrand, J.: Perception of aperiodicities in synthetically generated voices. J. Acoust. Soc. Am. **83**(6), 2361–2371 (1988)
8. Li, X., Tao, J., Johnson, M.T., Soltis, J., Savage, A., Leong, K.M., Newman, J.D.: Stress and emotion classification using jitter and shimmer features. In: IEEE International Conference on Acoustics, Speech and Signal Processing, ICASSP 2007, vol. 4, p. IV-1081. IEEE (2007)
9. Kotti, M., Stylianou, Y.: Effective emotion recognition in movie audio tracks. In: 2017 IEEE International Conference on Acoustics, Speech and Signal Processing (ICASSP), pp. 5120–5124. IEEE (2017)
10. Jacob, A.: Speech emotion recognition based on minimal voice quality features. In: 2016 International Conference on Communication and Signal Processing (ICCSP), pp. 0886–0890. IEEE (2016)
11. Sondhi, S., Vijay, R., Khan, M., Salhan, A.K.: Voice analysis for detection of deception. In: 2016 11th International Conference on Knowledge, Information and Creativity Support Systems (KICSS), pp. 1–6. IEEE (2016)

12. Palo, H.K., Mohanty, M.N., Chandra, M.: Sad state analysis of speech signals using different clustering algorithm. In: 2016 2nd International Conference on Next Generation Computing Technologies (NGCT), pp. 714–718. IEEE (2016)

13. Schuller, B., Steidl, S., Batliner, A.: The interspeech 2009 emotion challenge. In: Tenth Annual Conference of the International Speech Communication Association (2009)

14. Kim, H.J., Bae, K., Yoon, H.S.: Age and gender classification for a home-robot service. In: The 16th IEEE International Symposium on Robot and Human interactive Communication, RO-MAN 2007, pp. 122–126. IEEE (2007)

15. Teixeira, J.P., Fernandes, P.O.: Jitter, shimmer and hnr classification within gender, tones and vowels in healthy voices. Procedia Technol. **16**, 1228–1237 (2014)

16. Tsanas, A., Little, M.A., Fox, C., Ramig, L.O.: Objective automatic assessment of rehabilitative speech treatment in parkinson's disease. IEEE Trans. Neural Syst. Rehabil. Eng. **22**(1), 181–190 (2014)

17. Gómez-Coello, A., Valadez-Jiménez, V.M., Cisneros, B., Carrillo-Mora, P., Parra-Cárdenas, M., Hernández-Hernández, O., Magaña, J.J.: Voice alterations in patients with spinocerebellar ataxia type 7 (sca7): Clinical-genetic correlations. J. Voice **31**(1), 123-e1 (2017)

18. Kotti, M., Paternò, F.: Speaker-independent emotion recognition exploiting a psychologically-inspired binary cascade classification schema. Int. J. Speech Technol. **15**(2), 131–150 (2012)

19. Yamasaki, R., Montagnoli, A., Murano, E.Z., Gebrim, E., Hachiya, A., da Silva, J.V.L., Behlau, M., Tsuji, D.: Perturbation measurements on the degree of naturalness of synthesized vowels. J. Voice **31**(3), 389–e1 (2017)

20. Hinton, G., Deng, L., Yu, D., Dahl, G.E., Mohamed, A.R., Jaitly, N., Senior, A., Vanhoucke, V., Nguyen, P., Sainath, T.N., et al.: Deep neural networks for acoustic modeling in speech recognition: the shared views of four research groups. IEEE Sig. Process. Mag. **29**(6), 82–97 (2012)

21. Mitra, V., Sivaraman, G., Nam, H., Espy-Wilson, C., Saltzman, E., Tiede, M.: Hybrid convolutional neural networks for articulatory and acoustic information based speech recognition. Speech Commun. **89**, 103–112 (2017)

22. Collobert, R., Puhrsch, C., Synnaeve, G.: Wav2letter: an end-to-end convnet-based speech recognition system. arXiv preprint arXiv:1609.03193 (2016)

23. Amodei, D., Ananthanarayanan, S., Anubhai, R., Bai, J., Battenberg, E., Case, C., Casper, J., Catanzaro, B., Cheng, Q., Chen, G., et al.: Deep speech 2: end-to-end speech recognition in English and Mandarin. In: International Conference on Machine Learning, pp. 173–182 (2016)

24. Palaz, D., Collobert, R., et al.: Analysis of CNN-based speech recognition system using raw speech as input. Technical report, Idiap (2015)

25. Sainath, T.N., Kingsbury, B., Mohamed, A.R., Ramabhadran, B.: Learning filter banks within a deep neural network framework. In: 2013 IEEE Workshop on Automatic Speech Recognition and Understanding (ASRU), pp. 297–302. IEEE (2013)

26. Farrús, M.: Jitter and shimmer measurements for speaker recognition. In: 8th Annual Conference of the International Speech Communication Association, ISCA; 2007, pp. 778–781, International Speech Communication Association (ISCA) (2007)

27. Gu, Y., Li, X., Chen, S., Zhang, J., Marsic, I.: Speech intention classification with multimodal deep learning. In: Mouhoub, M., Langlais, P. (eds.) AI 2017. LNCS (LNAI), vol. 10233, pp. 260–271. Springer, Cham (2017). https://doi.org/10.1007/978-3-319-57351-9_30

28. Chang, J., Scherer, S.: Learning representations of emotional speech with deep convolutional generative adversarial networks. arXiv preprint arXiv:1705.02394 (2017)

29. Ghosh, S., Laksana, E., Morency, L.P., Scherer, S.: Representation learning for speech emotion recognition. In: INTERSPEECH, pp. 3603–3607 (2016)

30. Mao, Q., Dong, M., Huang, Z., Zhan, Y.: Learning salient features for speech emotion recognition using convolutional neural networks. IEEE Trans. Multimed. **16**(8), 2203–2213 (2014)

31. Ma, X., Yang, H., Chen, Q., Huang, D., Wang, Y.: DepAudioNet: an efficient deep model for audio based depression classification. In: Proceedings of the 6th International Workshop on Audio/Visual Emotion Challenge, pp. 35–42. ACM (2016)

32. Abumallouh, A., Qawaqneh, Z., Barkana, B.D.: Deep neural network combined posteriors for speakers' age and gender classification. In: Annual Connecticut Conference on Industrial Electronics, Technology & Automation (CT-IETA), pp. 1–5. IEEE (2016)

33. Qawaqneh, Z., Mallouh, A.A., Barkana, B.D.: Deep neural network framework and transformed mfccs for speaker's age and gender classification. Knowl. -Based Syst. **115**, 5–14 (2017)

34. Liu, Y., Wang, X., Hang, Y., He, L., Yin, H., Liu, C.: Hypemasality detection in cleft palate speech based on natural computation. In: 2016 12th International Conference on Natural Computation, Fuzzy Systems and Knowledge Discovery (ICNC-FSKD), pp. 523–528. IEEE (2016)

35. Cummins, N., Epps, J., Ambikairajah, E.: Spectro-temporal analysis of speech affected by depression and psychomotor retardation. In: 2013 IEEE International Conference on, Acoustics, Speech and Signal Processing (ICASSP), pp. 7542–7546. IEEE (2013)

36. Teixeira, J.P., Gonçalves, A.: Algorithm for jitter and shimmer measurement in pathologic voices. Procedia Comput. Sci. **100**, 271–279 (2016)

37. Shahnaz, C., Zhu, W.P., Ahmad, M.O.: A new technique for the estimation of jitter and shimmer of voiced speech signal. In: Canadian Conference on Electrical and Computer Engineering, CCECE 2006, pp. 2112–2115. IEEE (2006)

38. Dong, B.: Characterizing resonant component in speech: a different view of tracking fundamental frequency. Mech. Syst. Sig. Process. **88**, 318–333 (2017)

39. Liu, B., Tao, J., Zhang, D., Zheng, Y.: A novel pitch extraction based on jointly trained deep BLSTM recurrent neural networks with bottleneck features. In: 2017 IEEE International Conference on Acoustics, Speech and Signal Processing (ICASSP), pp. 336–340. IEEE (2017)

40. Schlotthauer, G., Torres, M.E., Rufiner, H.L.: A new algorithm for instantaneous F0 speech extraction based on ensemble empirical mode decomposition. In: 2009 17th European Signal Processing Conference, pp. 2347–2351. IEEE (2009)

41. Buder, E.H.: Acoustic analysis of voice quality: a tabulation of algorithms 1902–1990. In: Voice Quality Measurement, pp. 119–244 (2000)

42. Klingholz, F., Martin, F.: Quantitative spectral evaluation of shimmer and jitter. J. Speech Hear. Res. **28**(2), 169–174 (1985)

43. Schnupp, J., Nelken, I., King, A.: Auditory Neuroscience: Making Sense of Sound. MIT Press, Cambridge (2011)

Optimization for an Uncertainty Reduction Method Applied to Forest Fires Spread Prediction

María Laura Tardivo[1,2,3(✉)], Paola Caymes-Scutari[1,2],
Miguel Méndez-Garabetti[1,2], and Germán Bianchini[1]

[1] Laboratorio de Investigación en Cómputo Paralelo/Distribuido (LICPaD),
Dpto. de Ingeniaría en Sistemas de Información, UTN-FRM, Mendoza, Argentina
[2] Consejo Nacional de Investigaciones Científicas y Técnicas (CONICET),
Buenos Aires, Argentina
[3] Departamento de Computación, UNRC, Córdoba, Argentina
lauratardivo@dc.exa.unrc.edu.ar

Abstract. Forest fires prediction represents a great computational and mathematical challenge. The complexity lies both in the definition of mathematical models for describing the physical phenomenon and in the impossibility of measuring in real time all the parameters that determine the fire behaviour. ESSIM (Evolutionary Statistical System with Island Model) is an uncertainty reduction method that uses Statistic, High Performance Computing and Evolutionary Strategies in order to guide the search towards better solutions. ESSIM has been implemented with two different search strategies: the method ESSIM-EA uses Evolutionary Algorithms as optimization engine, whilst ESSIM-DE uses the Differential Evolution algorithm. ESSIM-EA has shown to obtain good quality of predictions, while ESSIM-DE obtains better response times. This article presents an alternative to improve the quality of solutions reached by ESSIM-DE, based on the analysis of the relationship between the evolutionary strategy convergence speed and the population distribution at the beginning of each prediction step.

Keywords: Forest fires · Prediction · Island model
Evolutionary Algorithms · Differential Evolution · Parallelism

1 Introduction

The prediction of natural phenomena, such as forest fires, is considered a very important task that implies a high degree of complexity and precision. Generally, simulation tools implement models that attempt to explain and predict the spread of fire on the ground. These models usually require certain input parameters to represent the various dynamic factors that determine the behaviour of the fire. However, it is not possible to have accurate values for all these factors before the fire ignition or during the fire spread. This lack of precision, also

© Springer International Publishing AG, part of Springer Nature 2018
A. E. De Giusti (Ed.): CACIC 2017, CCIS 790, pp. 13–23, 2018.
https://doi.org/10.1007/978-3-319-75214-3_2

called uncertainty, negatively affects the quality of the prediction. Therefore, the challenge lies in the development of computational methods that can improve the knowledge of the input parameters values, so as to reduce the uncertainty, and hence, to obtain more realistic predictions.

The Evolutionary Statistical System with Islands Model, ESSIM, [6] is an uncertainty reduction method that has been applied to forest fires prediction and is classified within the Data Driven Methods with Multiple Overlapping Solutions (DDM-MOS) [1]. ESSIM uses Evolutionary Strategies to guide the search process towards good quality solutions, a Statistical component to analyse the fire trend, and a parallel evaluation to obtain short term solutions. Its first computational design included Evolutionary Algorithms as search strategy, and the method was renamed ESSIM-EA. Subsequently, the Differential Evolution metaheuristic was used, determining the ESSIM-DE method. ESSIM-EA has proven to obtain good quality of predictions, meanwhile ESSIM-DE significantly reduces response times.

Both methods have been studied in recent years with the aim of improving their performance. Two static tuning studies were carried out for the evolutionary parameters of ESSIM-EA in [2,3]. Also, the parameters related to islands model of ESSIM-DE and the evolutionary parameters of ESSIM-DE, have been statically calibrated in [4] and [5], respectively. In these two last studies, some improvements were found for certain prediction steps, but they have been non significant. This paper presents a proposal to improve the quality obtained by ESSIM-DE based on the analysis of the population distribution at the beginning of each prediction step. The objective is to determine the relationship between the convergence speed of the metaheuristic that guides the search process, with respect to the predictions quality obtained in the different time steps of the fire's progress. This study represents the starting point for obtaining a general behaviour pattern that allows us to determine the distribution the population must have at the beginning of each prediction step.

The work is organized as follows. Section 2 describes the ESSIM method and the search metaheuristics used by ESSIM-EA and ESSIM-DE. Section 3 presents the proposal to improve the quality of predictions obtained by ESSIM-DE, called ESSIM-DE(r). Section 4 presents the experimentation carried out to validate the proposal. Finally, Sect. 5 presents the conclusion and future work.

2   ESSIM General Description

ESSIM is a method for uncertainty reduction designed with parallel evaluation through a double-hierarchy *master/worker* communication mechanism. Figure 1 presents the general scheme of ESSIM. The higher hierarchy level includes a process called *monitor*, which is in charge of sending initialization information, collecting the processed data in the final stage of the simulation and determining the output values. In the lower hierarchy level, the ESSIM processes are organized on islands. Each island is composed by a *master* process responsible for initializing a population of individuals, which represent different values combinations for the environmental conditions under which the fire occurs.

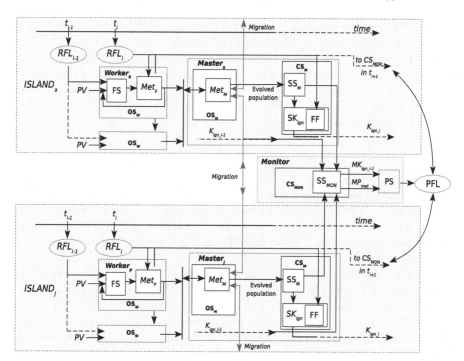

Fig. 1. General ESSIM diagram. **FS**: Fire Simulator, **Met**$_M$: Metaheuristic in *Master*; **Met**$_F$: Metaheuristic (fitness evaluation); **OS**$_W$: Optimization Stage in *Worker*; **OS**$_M$: Optimization Stage in *Master*; **SS**$_{MON}$: Statistical Stage in *Monitor*; **SS**$_M$: Statistical Stage in *Master*; **SK**$_{ign}$: Search for K$_{ign}$; **K**$_{ign\ t}$: key ignition value for instant t; **FF**: Fitness Function; **CS**$_M$: Calibration Stage in *Master*; **CS**$_M ON$: Calibration Stage in *Monitor*; **PS**: Prediction Stage; **PFL**: Predicted Fire Line; **RFLx**: Real Fire Line on instant x; **PV**: Parameter Vector (population individual); **MK**$_{ign}$: Monitor K$_{ign}$ value; **MP**$_{mat}$: Monitor Probability Matrix.

The *master* process distributes each individual among certain *worker* processes, which are assigned the task of performing the fire behaviour simulation for each received individual, task carried out in the Optimization Stage (**OS**$_W$). Also, the *workers* must evaluate the quality of the simulation, by means of a fitness function. To that end, the **OS**$_W$ stage has two internal sub-stages called Fire Simulation (**FS**) and the fitness function evaluation associated with the metaheuristic used by ESSIM as search engine (**Met**$_F$). **FS** must be fed with the real fire line at the time instant t_{i-1} (RFL_{i-1}) together with the individual depicting an input parameters vector (**VP**). In order to represent the different fire lines, the terrain is divided in cells and a neighbourhood relationship defines whether each cell will be burned, and also what time the fire will reach those cells. The output of **FS** consists of a map of the terrain in which each cell is labelled with its ignition time.

When **FS** ends the simulation, each obtained map is introduced in the Met_F stage, in order to compare the simulated map with the t_i instant real map (RFL_i) and thus to determine the fitness value for each individual. In ESSIM, the fitness function is given by the expression (1), where A represents the set of cells in the real map without the subset of burned cells before starting the simulations, and B represents the set of cells in the simulated map without the subset of burned cells before starting the simulation.

$$fitness = \frac{|A \cap B|}{|A \cup B|} \tag{1}$$

Subsequently, the fitness values together with the simulated map for each individual are sent to the *master* process, which is also in charge of performing the migration of certain selected individuals to another island. The amount of individuals selected is a parameter of ESSIM and they replace the worst members of the target island.

Once the population evolves through different generations or reaches a certain aptitude, it is introduced in the Calibration Stage ($\textbf{CS}_M$). In this stage the evolved population feeds a sub-stage called Statistical Stage ($\textbf{SS}_M$). The output of $\textbf{SS}_M$ is a probability matrix that considers the contribution of all the individuals and is used for a dual purpose. On the one hand, it is used to search the Key Ignition Value in the sub-stage SK_{ign} (Search K_{ign}). The K_{ign} value represents the wildfire behaviour pattern in a specified time interval, and it is used to make the prediction in the next time instant (t_{i+1}). The evaluation of the probability matrix is carried out in the Fitness Function stage (**FF**). On the other hand, the j outputs of the $\textbf{SS}_M$ together with the j K_{ign} values calculated by the j islands are sent to $\textbf{CS}_{MON}$. In this stage the *monitor* process selects the best K_{ign} value from all the islands (MK_{ign}). This value together with the probability matrix from the corresponding island (MP_{mat}) is used to make the prediction for the next instant of time (t_{i+1}) in the Prediction Stage (**PS**). For further details on other prediction methods types, on the searching K_{ign} value process and on ESSIM, see [5] or [7].

As previously mentioned in Sect. 1, it is possible to instantiate ESSIM with different search strategies in the evolutionary stages. The main characteristics of two strategies used with ESSIM are summarized below.

ESSIM-EA: Evolutionary Algorithms: Evolutionary Algorithms (EAs) are considered efficient search methods to solve optimization problems, inspired by the process of natural selection [8]. The search space is organized as a set of individuals that make up a population, each one representing a possible solution. The population evolves iteratively, through generations, imitating the principles of biological evolution and the survival of the fittest. To achieve this purpose, the process consists in selecting from the population a sample of parents, which are subjected to different operators to generate a set of offspring. Subsequently, they are introduced to the population replacing individuals with the worst features.

ESSIM-DE: Differential Evolution: The Differential Evolution algorithm (DE) is a population-based stochastic optimizer that uses vector differences to modify each individual in the population. In contrast to EA, the mutation, crossover and selection operators are applied in each generation to each individuals from the population. The mutation operator applies vector differences between each *current individual* and certain randomly selected individuals. Subsequently, each mutated individual is submitted together with the current individual to the crossing operator, generating a new vector, called *trial vector*. Finally, in the selection stage, the best candidate is determined between the *current individual* and the *trial vector*. The one with the best fitness function value will survive for the next generation.

3   ESSIM-DE(r): Optimization for ESSIM-DE

ESSIM-DE has shown to obtain a decreasing tendency in terms of average fitness values. In [7] it was observed that ESSIM-DE begins with a good performance, but as the fire progress, the fitness averages values show a downward trend for the successive steps. In such experiments the population is initialized with random values following a uniform distribution. This process is done only once, at the beginning of the execution. Then, the population evolves by means of the Differential Evolution operators: in DE all individuals participate in the mutation and crossover processes, so in each generation each population member is mutated and crossed with other individuals from the current generation. This approach differs from the way in which the Evolutionary Algorithms apply the operators, metaheuristic used by ESSIM-EA, in which the number of individuals participating in the evolutionary process is determined by a parameter defined by the user. In our experimentation, the usage of a value lower than 50% the total individuals is a configuration for which ESSIM-EA has obtained a good performance, regarding the predictions quality. This characteristic constitutes a marked difference between both metaheuristics. Therefore, this difference would possibly produce a negative impact on the results quality obtained by ESSIM-DE.

Taking into account the way in which each metaheuristic applies the evolutionary operators, it was proposed to analyse the distribution of the population fitness in the different prediction steps. The associated hypothesis is that ESSIM-DE can have a premature convergence: the whole population evolves in an accelerated way during the first time steps, thus it converges to a limited solution space which prevents from obtaining better individuals in the successive steps of the fire evolution. Therefore, it would be possible to alter this distribution by restarting the population at the beginning of each prediction step. In this way, Differential Evolution could explore a new solutions space, independent from the previous ones. Consequently, ESSIM-DE(r) was designed with a population diversification operator applied at the beginning of each prediction step, which **re-initializes the population** with random values within the range of each variable, following a uniform distribution.

Table 1. Real fire cases description: dimensions, slope, initial time, end time and time step for each case.

Case	Width (m)	Length(m)	Slope (degr.)	Ini. T. (min)	Incr. (min)	End T. (min)
A	95	123	21	2	2	12
B	60	90	6	2	2	10
C	75	126	19	3	1	9

With the aim of verifying the hypothesis, it was proposed to compare the distribution of the fitness reached by both ESSIM-DE and ESSIM-EA. To do this, both methods were subjected to experimentation using different cases of controlled burns carried out in Serra de Louçã, (Gestosa, Portugal) [9]. The size of each map was defined according to the available area, the characteristics of the land and the requirements of the project. For each case, discrete time intervals have been defined representing the spread of the fire front. Table 1 describes the characteristics of the three cases used in this work. It is important to note that ESSIM-EA and ESSIM-DE use a calibration step. Then, in order to feed the prediction chain, both methods cannot make predictions in the first instant of time.

The fitness of each population member was registered, with a population size of 200 individuals, and its distribution is analysed by means of boxplots. In order to facilitate the understanding of results, we selected the outputs obtained in an execution of case study C, consisting of six simulation steps, and the finalization condition was established to reach 15 evolutionary generations in each step.

Figure 2 shows three graphs corresponding to the second, fourth and sixth simulation step obtained with ESSIM-EA. To simplify the analysis, each chart includes three boxplots that represent the distribution of the population every five iterations.

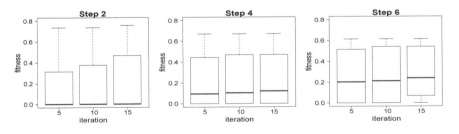

Fig. 2. Population fitness distribution obtained by ESSIM-EA for case C.

As can be seen from Fig. 2, in the second step the population starts with fitness values closer to zero (the median is close to zero). As the population evolves through different generations, the distribution changes slightly towards higher values. It can be seen that in iteration 15 of the sixth simulation step the median reaches a value close to 0.2 and the distribution boxplot reaches a maximum value of 0.6 (higher whisker).

Figure 3 shows the fitness of the population corresponding to the second, fourth and sixth simulation steps for ESSIM-DE. Unlike the previous case, it can be clearly seen that at the end of the second simulation step the population reaches fitness values closer to 0.8. It is also observed in the second simulation step that after five iterations the population has low distribution, which causes the method to reach its maximum exploration capacity, therefore in the successive steps Differential Evolution can not provide improvements. In this example, as well as in the rest of the considered cases, it is observed that ESSIM-DE converges faster than ESSIM-EA. This behaviour causes an accelerated tendency of the solutions towards local optima in the initial time instants of the fire spread. Therefore, in the last steps the metaheuristics can not bring improvements, which leads to a fitness declining tendency.

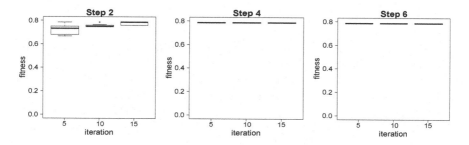

Fig. 3. Population fitness distribution obtained by ESSIM-DE for case C.

Ideally, it is intended that the developed methods obtain both short-term and reliable solutions, but the response speed and the high probability of convergence are often contradictory objectives [10]. This is the case of ESSIM-DE, since it obtains short-term solutions, with good quality in the first prediction steps, but with a decreasing trend. With the aim of improving the quality of the prediction, the population diversification operator of ESSIM-DE(r) allows the incorporation of a new solution space at the beginning of each prediction step. In this way, the original processing scheme of Differential Evolution is not altered and the optimization of the individuals is carried out according to the prediction step being considered. This variant of the method was named ESSIM-DE(r), to distinguish the version that includes the operator of diversification with restarting of the populations, with respect to the original version.

4   Experimentation and Obtained Results

To validate the proposal, different experiments were carried out with ESSIM-EA, ESSIM-DE and the new approach ESSIM-DE(r), using the three controlled burns cases of Table 1. In each experiment, the results obtained with 30 different seeds were averaged. The island model was configured with 5 islands, 7 *workers* per island in all methods. The migration process involves 20% of the population

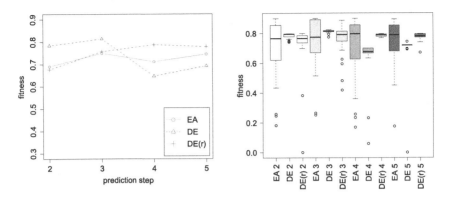

Fig. 4. Experiment I. *Left*: Average fitness values. *Right*: Distribution of the fitness prediction values.

individuals, and is carried out in each iteration. The finalization condition in the evolutionary process, per step, consists in reaching a fitness threshold of 0.7 for the best member of the population. This threshold was established taking into account a fitness value that represents an acceptable prediction quality. The size of each population was defined as 200 individuals. For ESSIM-DE and ESSIM-DE(r) the same configuration of evolutionary parameters was used: crossover probability 0.3, mutation factor 0.9, binomial crossover.

Figures 4, 5 and 6 show the obtained results. The left graphs of each figure correspond to the averages fitness values obtained for each prediction step and method. In each graph, the x axis represents the different prediction steps, and the y axis represents the average fitness values obtained from evaluating the predicted map with respect to the real map of the fire's progress. To simplify the notation, ESSIM-EA is symbolized by "EA", ESSIM-DE by "DE", and the ESSIM-DE(r) is symbolized "DE(r)". The left graphs of each figure represent the distribution of the 30 results obtained with different seed, grouped by colors (gray scale) according to the prediction step. The cases A, B and C of Table 1 were used in the experiments I, II and III, respectively.

Experiment I: It can be seen from the left graph of Fig. 4, that ESSIM-DE obtains the best fitness values for the first two prediction steps. However, the fitness values decline as the fire progresses. For its part, ESSIM-DE(r) obtains better results than ESSIM-EA in prediction steps 3, 4 and 5 with average fitness values close to 0.8. A low distribution of the fitness results obtained by ESSIM-DE(r) is also observed from the right graph of Fig. 4. This property is desirable for methods that operate with metaheuristics, since it is an indicator of the robustness of the method in effectively solving different instances of the problem [8]. According to both characteristics, we can conclude in this experiment that ESSIM-DE(r) is the method with the best performance.

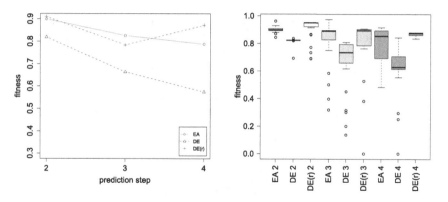

Fig. 5. Experiment II. *Left*: Average fitness values. *Right*: Distribution of the fitness prediction values.

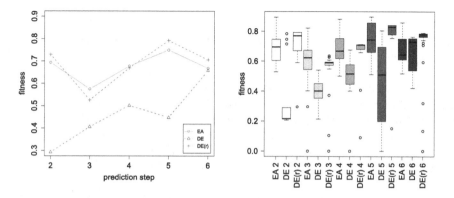

Fig. 6. Experiment III. *Left*: Average fitness values. *Right*: Distribution of the fitness prediction values.

Experiment II: The case used in experiment II consists of four simulation steps. It can be observed from the analysis of the left graph from Fig. 5, that ESSIM-DE and ESSIM-EA have fitness averages values decreasing tendency. However, this behaviour is not reflected in step 4 for ESSIM-DE(r), which obtains an average value close to 0.9 (remember that a fitness value of 1 is equivalent to a perfect prediction). Moreover, ESSIM-DE(r) obtains a very low distribution of the results in the fourth step (see right graph of Fig. 5), which indicates an excellent performance.

Experiment III: It can be observed from the left graph of Fig. 6, that ESSIM-DE(r) significantly improves the averages of fitness obtained with respect to ESSIM-DE, and obtains average values higher than those obtained by ESSIM-EA for prediction steps 2, 5 and 6. It is also possible to see from the boxplots in the right graph of Fig. 6, that ESSIM-DE(r) obtains a lower distribution of the results for these steps. Therefore, it is again corroborated that the proposal is effective, improving the performance of the original version of ESSIM-DE and surpassing the results obtained with ESSIM-EA for three prediction steps.

Table 2 shows the average execution times obtained for each experiment. In the experiments A and B, the proposal implemented with ESSIM-DE(r) to restart the population in each step causes the convergence to be slower, which leads to obtaining average execution times greater than ESSIM-DE. However, either of the two versions ESSIM-DE or ESSIM-DE(r) obtains better response time than ESSIM-EA, with a reduction of up to 80%.

Table 2. Average execution times

Experiment	ESSIM-EA	ESSIM-DE	ESSIM-DE(r)
I	01:01:15	**00:49:05**	00:54:20
II	00:50:10	**00:27:49**	00:32:48
III	02:11:38	00:41:20	**00:25:53**

From the analysis carried out, we can verify that there is a direct relationship between the convergence speed of the metaheuristics used as a search engine and the quality of the predictions obtained. The proposal to improve the quality of predictions has proven to be effective for the test cases considered: ESSIM-DE(r) has improved the quality of the solutions found, compared to the results obtained by both ESSIM-EA and the original version of ESSIM-DE, with low distribution of results. The execution times for ESSIM-DE(r) are similar and even lower than the original version of ESSIM-DE. All this indicates that the improvement proposal has been effective for the considered experiments.

5   Conclusions

This paper presents an alternative to improve the quality of the solutions obtained by the ESSIM-DE method, based on the analysis of the fitness population distribution at the beginning of each prediction step. It was corroborated that ESSIM-DE has a high convergence speed at the initial instants of the fire evolution. Therefore, in the last prediction steps DE can not provide improvements, which leads to a decreasing trend in the obtained fitness values. A variant was proposed to mitigate this effect without modifying the DE metaheuristic processing scheme. To achieve that purpose, it was decided to generate an initial population with uniform distribution at the beginning of each prediction step. This variant of the method was called ESSIM-DE(r), and it has been shown to improve the quality of the predictions, obtaining low distribution of the results for the cases considered.

This proposal considers the generation of a new search space at the beginning of each prediction step. However, in some cases it may be convenient that certain individuals from the population persist throughout the simulation, with the objective of maintaining some of the environmental conditions along the different prediction steps. In this sense, the proposal presented in this article does not allow to conserve such characteristics, since the entire population is regenerated in each step. For this reason, as future works we plan to analyse other alternatives to get out of stagnation without regenerating a completely different search space. The objective is to study and define a mathematical model that allows us to stablish the distribution that the population should follow at the beginning of each prediction step.

Acknowledgements. This work has been supported by UTN under the projects EIUTIME0003939TC and EIUTNME0003952, and by MEC-Spain under the project TIN2014-53234-C2-1-R. The first author would like to thank CONICET for the PhD Grant provided.

References

1. Bianchini, G., Denham, M., Cortés, A., Margalef, T., Luque, E.: Wildland fire growth prediction method based on multiple overlapping solution. J. Comput. Sci. **1**(4), 229–237 (2010)
2. Méndez Garabetti, M., Bianchini, G., Caymes Scutari, P., Tardivo, M.L.: Sistema Estadístico Evolutivo con Modelo de Islas: Calibración de parámetros evolutivos. In: International Symposium on Innovation and Technology, Lima, Perú, pp. 77–81 (2015)
3. Méndez Garabetti, M., Bianchini, G., Caymes Scutari, P., Tardivo, M.L.: ESS-IM applied to forest fire spread prediction: parameters tuning for a heterogeneous configuration. In: International Symposium SCCC 2016, Valparaiso, Chile, pp. 514–525 (2016)
4. Tardivo, M.L., Caymes-Scutari, P., Bianchini, G., Méndez-Garabetti, M.: Ajuste de Parámetros Evolutivos para el Método Paralelo de Reducción de Incertidumbre ESSIM-DE. XXII Congreso Argentino de Ciencias de la Computación, San Luis, Argentina, pp. 4–13 (2016)
5. Tardivo, M.L., Caymes-Scutari, P., Bianchini, G., Méndez-Garabetti, M.: Reducción de incertidumbre con Evolución Diferencial en la predicción de incendios forestales: sintonización y análisis de parámetros. Mec. Comput. **34**, 2903–2917 (2016)
6. Méndez Garabetti, M., Bianchini, G., Tardivo, M.L., Caymes Scutari, P.: Evolutionary-statistical system with Island model for forest fire spread prediction. In: VI Latin American Symposium on High Performance Computing, Mendoza, Argentina, pp. 61–64 (2013)
7. Tardivo, M.L., Caymes-Scutari, P., Bianchini, G., Méndez-Garabetti, M., Cortés, A.: Three evolutionary statistical parallel methods for uncertainty reduction in wildland fire prediction. In: International Conference on High Performance Computing & Simulation, Innsbruck, Austria, pp. 721–728 (2016)
8. Talbi, E.: Metaheuristics: From Design to Implementation. Wiley, New Jersey (2009)
9. Viegas D.X.: Project spread - forest fire spread prevention and mitigation. http://www.algosystems.gr/spread/
10. Price, K., Storn, R., Lampinen, J.: Differential Evolution - A Practical Approach to Global Optimization. Springer-Verlag New York, Inc., USA (2005). https://doi.org/10.1007/3-540-31306-0

Learning *When* to Classify for Early Text Classification

Juan Martín Loyola[1,2], Marcelo Luis Errecalde[1(✉)] (iD), Hugo Jair Escalante[3], and Manuel Montes y Gomez[3]

[1] Laboratorio de Investigación y Desarrollo en Inteligencia Computacional, San Luis, Argentina
merreca@unsl.edu.ar
[2] Instituto de Matemática Aplicada San Luis, San Luis, Argentina
[3] Instituto Nacional de Astrofísica, Óptica y Electrónica, Puebla, Mexico

Abstract. The problem of classification is a widely studied one in supervised learning. Nonetheless, there are scenarios that received little attention despite its applicability. One of such scenarios is *early text classification*, where one needs to know the category of a document as soon as possible. The importance of this variant of the classification problem is evident in tasks like sexual predator detection, where one wants to identify an offender as early as possible. This paper presents a framework for early text classification which highlights the two main pieces involved in this problem: classification with *partial information* and deciding the *moment* of classification. In this context, a novel approach that learns the second component (*when* to classify) and an adaptation of a temporal measurement for multi-class problems are introduced. Results with a classical text classification corpus in comparison against a model that reads the entire documents confirm the feasibility of our approach.

Keywords: Early text classification
Classification with partial information
Decision of the moment of classification

1 Introduction

Recent years have shown a tremendous growth in the machine learning field, solving very complex tasks with new algorithms, methods or architectures [5]. There are, however, settings of the classification problem that have received little attention despite its wide applicability. One of such scenarios is that of *early text classification* (ETC), which deals with the development of predictive models that can determine the class a document belongs to as soon as possible. Here a document is assumed to be processed sequentially, starting at the beginning and reading its containing parts one by one. In this context, it is desired to make predictions with as little information (as soon) as possible.

To date, only a few papers have approached this kind of scenarios [3,4,6]. Despite its low popularity, this topic has a major potential in practical applications. For instance, consider the problem of detecting sexual predators in chat

© Springer International Publishing AG, part of Springer Nature 2018
A. E. De Giusti (Ed.): CACIC 2017, CCIS 790, pp. 24–34, 2018.
https://doi.org/10.1007/978-3-319-75214-3_3

conversations. Here, the goal is to sequentially read a conversation and to determine as fast as possible whenever a sexual predator is involved; clearly, a detection using the whole conversation can only be used for forensics rather than for prevention. Other potential applications include the analysis of conversations that requires of a fast response (e.g., cyber-bullying prevention, detection of early traces of depression, suicidal speech identification) and classification processes where late classification implies some type of cost (e.g., a real-time system where one might need to classify a document without processing it completely to give the user a fast response, otherwise the user might leave the site).

It is important to note that the early text classification problem consists of two related and complementary tasks. On the one hand, the task of *classification with partial information* (CPI), which consists of obtaining an efficient predictive model when only partial information is available that has been read sequentially up to a certain point in time. The emphasis in this case is to determine which classification methods are more likely to achieve performance comparable to that obtained when classified using the entire document. On the other hand, we have the task of *decision of the moment of classification* (DMC), that is, in which point in time one can stop reading and classify with some degree of confidence that the prediction is going to be correct. Both tasks need to be consistently integrated into any system for the ETC problem. However, as we will see in the related work section, little efforts have been dedicated to comprehensive approaches that simultaneously address them.

This paper addresses that previous research gap by presenting a simple framework for ETC which explicitly models the CPI and DMC components. In our proposal, the CPI component is learned with standard machine learning algorithms as in other works in ETC. The novelty of our approach consists in also learning the DMC component given an initial dataset. Evaluations of the ETC systems were carried out with standard classification measures and also with others that take into account the time dimension. In this context, another contribution of our work is the adaptation of a previous temporal evaluation metric for multi-class classification. Experimental results of our approach in a classical text classification corpus show the feasibility of the proposal for the ETC task.

The remainder of this paper is organized as follows. Next section reviews related work on early text classification. Then, Sect. 3 describes the framework and shows some evaluation metrics that consider the time of classification. Section 4 reports experimental results that indicate the effectiveness of the proposal. Section 5 presents conclusions and discusses future work directions.

2   Related Work

As far as we know, the whole ETC problem was initially approached in [3]; although the focus was not on making predictions earlier but on improving the classification performance with a sequential reading approach. There, a Markov decision process (MDP) is proposed with two possible actions: *read* (the next sentence), or *classify*. A classifier is trained to learn good/bad state-action pairs on a high-dimensional space. A potential drawback of this approach would be the well-known scalability problems of MDPs.

In [4] an adaptation of Naïve Bayes is proposed to tackle the problem of classification with partial information. Although a similar performance to models that read the entire document is achieved, the DMC problem is not addressed. Our work starts from this limitation and tries to solve this issue.

Recently, in [6] the CPI and DMC aspects are both addressed by learning the CPI component and using a simple heuristic rule for DMC that consists in classifying a text as positive when exceeding a specific confidence threshold in the prediction of the classifier. The problem with that DMC approach is that is very dependent on the problem and put all the burden of selecting the appropriate thresholds on the ETC system's implementer.

Nevertheless, if we consider the problem of early classification in general (not restricting it to text), we can find different groups that have tackled the problem. For example, in [2] the problem of early classification of time series is formalized as a sequential decision problem involving two costs: quality and delay of the prediction. The method also provides the estimated time for classification, that is, how much of the remaining time series is needed to classify.

3   Early Text Classification Framework

Early text classification focus on the development of predictive models that determine the category of a document as soon as possible. It is assumed that the documents are read sequentially, starting at the beginning of the document and reading words in the order they appear. The objective is to predict the class of a document with as little information (as soon) as possible. In an abstract way, it is like the classic text categorization problem, that is, for a given document it is classified under the class that best fit what had been seen in the training phase. However, differences appear when we want to measure performance. While for classic text categorization problems we use measures like accuracy, precision, recall and the F_1 measure, for early text classification those are not enough. We need measurements that consider the *time* of (*delay* in) the prediction.

This need for temporal evaluation remarks two problems that are related and complementary to each other: classification with partial information and decision of the moment of classification. Our framework defines the way the initial corpus should be divided to train and test this task. The initial corpus is divided into a training and test sets, the first one to train the early text classifier and the second one to test it. We will denote the training set as Tr and the test set as Te. What follows describes the construction of the corpus and classifiers for the different parts of the problem.

3.1   Classification with Partial Information

The task of classification with partial information consists in obtaining an effective predictive model that predicts the class of a document when only partial information sequentially read up to a certain point of time is available. To achieve this, it is necessary to evaluate the performance of the model on partial documents. It should be noted, however, that when it comes to training the model, the entire document is used.

Given the training set Tr, we partition it in a training set for CPI, denoted TrP, and a test set for CPI, denoted TeP. Since we want to evaluate the performance on partial documents, we must modify the test set for CPI. To achieve this, it is necessary to define a window value $w \in \mathbb{N}$, which indicates the number of terms that are read in each time step. In this way, if $d_j = (t_1, \cdots, t_r)$ is the j-th document in TeP with r the number of terms in the document d_j and $t_1, \cdots, t_r$ the terms in the order they appear in it, then the documents $d_{j,1} = (t_1, \cdots, t_w)$, $d_{j,2} = (t_1, \cdots, t_{2w})$, $\cdots$ and $d_{j,\frac{r}{w}} = (t_1, \cdots, t_{\frac{r}{w}w})$ are part of the pumped test set TeP$'$. This process is repeated for all the document in TeP. For example, given the document "Do not look a gift horse in the mouth" from the test set TeP and $w = 3$, then "Do not look", "Do not look a gift horse" and "Do not look a gift horse in the mouth" will belong to TeP$'$.

Once the training and tests sets were constructed, a model was obtained with machine learning techniques. Nonetheless, the evaluation method was adapted to consider the performance of the model as the reading of the partial documents proceed. For this purpose, subsets of TeP$'$ with the same number of documents as the initial TeP test set were generated. Subset TeP$'_t$ is defined as all partial documents of TeP where the length (in number of terms) is less than or equal to $w \cdot t$. Also, if there exists $d_{j,l}$ and $d_{j,l+w}$ partial documents of d_j with l multiple of w and $l < l + w \leq w \cdot t$, only the largest partial document will belong to TeP$_t$, in this case $d_{j,l+w}$. Thus, the model performance is calculated for the different TeP$_t$ subsets by evaluating it as the terms of the windows are read.

3.2 Context Information

Trying to decide when to stop reading a document only using the class the CPI model returns is difficult. For this reason, we augment the data the DMC model gets with context information, that is, data from the body of the document that could be helpful for deciding the moment of classification. We propose to obtain these from three different sources:

- *Current document:* characteristics relative to the content of the current document. For example, number of: terms, different terms, most relevant terms for each class, stop words, etcetera.
- *Output from CPI:* features produced by the CPI model. This can be the class predicted, current window number and additional information from the model (this depends on the type of model picked for CPI). Regarding the latter, in the case of probabilistic classifiers we can have the probability assigned to each class.
- *Historic data:* related to the context information obtained in previous windows. That is, we apply an aggregation function δ (average, max, min, count, or other function) to some context information from previous window.

An example of historic information is the average probability given to all classes by the CPI model.

The features that in the end are provided to the DMC model depend on the problem under consideration and which are estimated to be more informative to this decision problem. The context information is calculated only for the test set TeP′ since the training and test sets for DMC are constructed from it.

3.3   Decision of the Moment of Classification

The task of decision of the moment of classification is to determine the point at which the reading of the document can be stopped with some certainty that the prediction of the classification made is correct. Given a feature vector, this model predicts if we should stop or keep reading. It is expected that when the model for DMC decides to stop reading, the class predicted by the model for CPI is the right one.

The initial corpus for DMC is constructed based in the context information, that is, the training and test sets are formed by the feature vectors generated based in the partial documents of TeP′. The problem here is that we do not have the labels indicating when to stop reading. They must be manually obtained or an automatic process should be devised to do it. Here we propose an automatic way to label the feature vector: if the category chosen by CPI is the correct one then the reading can be stopped; if, however, this is not correct we should keep reading. Finally, the corpus is divided into a training set TrM and a test set TeM. The construction and evaluation of the DMC model does not present any particularity, reason why any machine learning technique could be applied.

3.4   Architecture

Once the CPI and DMC models and the context information procedure have been defined, we can formalize the final architecture for our ETC framework. Figure 1 shows the role every model fulfills: CPI is responsible for predicting the category of the partial document, the context information procedure builds the feature vector and, finally, DMC is the one in charge of making the decision of the moment in which the reading of the document must be stopped.

A document classified with this architecture is processed in seven steps:

1. Read w contiguous terms;
2. Build the vector representation of the partial document for CPI;
3. Classify the partial document with CPI;
4. Build the feature vector for DMC;
5. Classify using DMC;
6. If DMC suggests keeping reading terms, return to point 1;
7. If DMC suggests stopping reading then return the category chosen by CPI for the partial document.

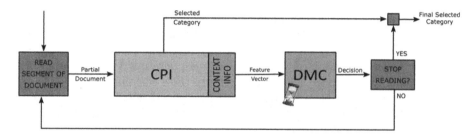

Fig. 1. Early text classification architecture.

3.5   Evaluation Metric

Since the ETC problem has not been addressed for many of the possible configurations, many aspects of it have not been yet defined. Among these is the evaluation of the model, since there is no measure to evaluate the temporary performance of it in a multi-class context. There exists, nonetheless, an evaluation metric for binary early classification [6] that considers the accuracy of the prediction and the delay taken by the system to make the decision. Here the delay is measured by counting the number of terms seen before giving the answer. Given a decision d made by the model at time k, the early risk detection error (ERDE) is defined as:

$$\text{ERDE}_o(d, k) = \begin{cases} c_{\text{fp}} & \text{if the decision } d \text{ is incorrectly positive} \\ c_{\text{fn}} & \text{if the decision } d \text{ is incorrectly negative} \\ lc_o(k) \cdot c_{\text{tp}} & \text{if the decision } d \text{ is correctly positive} \\ 0 & \text{if the decision } d \text{ is correctly negative} \end{cases} \quad (1)$$

The values given to c_{fp} and c_{fn} depends on the application domain and the implications of false positives and false negatives decisions. The factor $lc_o(k) \in [0, 1]$ encodes a cost associated to the delay in detecting true positives. In domains where late detection has severe consequences we should set c_{tp} to c_{fn}, that is, late detection is equivalent to not detecting the case at all. The function $lc_o(k)$ should be a monotonically increasing function of k. Losada and Crestani suggest:

$$lc_o(k) = 1 - \frac{1}{1 + e^{k-o}} \quad (2)$$

This function is parametrized by o, which controls the point where the cost grows more quickly. The overall error will be the mean of the ERDE values for all the documents.

Based on this metric, we propose a generalization for ETC when there are more than two classes. ERDE is redefined for each class i as:

$$\text{ERDE}_o(d, i, k) = \begin{cases} c_{\text{fp}}^i & \text{if the decision } d_i \text{ is incorrectly positive} \\ c_{\text{fn}}^i & \text{if the decision } d_i \text{ is incorrectly negative} \\ lc_o(k) \cdot c_{\text{tp}}^i & \text{if the decision } d_i \text{ is correctly positive} \\ 0 & \text{if the decision } d_i \text{ is correctly negative} \end{cases} \quad (3)$$

where d represents the decision made for all the categories, i the category on which the error is being calculated, d_i the decision on category i and k the time when the decision is made. Constants c_{fp}^i, c_{fn}^i and c_{tp}^i indicate the cost associated with the decision on the category being false positive, false negative or true positive, respectively. The values given to these constants depend on the particular addressed problem. Function $lc_o(k)$ is defined as before.

A limitation of Eq. (2) is that it does not consider the length of the document. It does not make sense to have one fixed point of penalization when documents have very dissimilar lengths. For instance, if the corpus contains papers and books, a fixed penalization point will harm one of them depending if the document is short or long. We proposed an alternative function to tackle this problem:

$$lc_o(k) = \frac{k}{o} \tag{4}$$

where o represents the length of the document measured in number of terms and k represents the number of terms read at the time of stopping the reading.

Then the early detection error (EDE) for a document is given by the sum of the ERDE for all categories. That is:

$$\text{EDE}_o(d, k) = \sum_{i=1}^{|\mathcal{C}|} \text{ERDE}_o(d, i, k) \tag{5}$$

Since only one category can be chosen by the model (single label problem) and the cost associated with true negatives is zero then the early detection error is reduced to:

$$\text{EDE}_o(d, k) = \begin{cases} lc_o(k) \cdot c_{\text{tp}}^i & \text{if the decision } d_i \text{ is correctly positive} \\ c_{\text{fn}}^j + c_{\text{fp}}^i & \text{if the decision } d_j \text{ is incorrectly negative} \\ & \text{and if the decision } d_i \text{ is incorrectly positive} \end{cases} \tag{6}$$

where the category i is chosen by the CPI and, in the case of misclassification, j is the correct category.

Overall early detection error is obtained by averaging on all documents.

4   Experiments and Results

To test the feasibility of our approach, we used in the experiments the well-known dataset R8 [1]. Based on the Reuters-21578 collection, R8 contains documents belonging to the eight classes with the highest number of training documents in that collection. These documents belong to only one class, thus allowing the corpus to be used for single-label text categorization. More detailed information of R8 is shown in Table 1.

For the experiments, the corpus was processed as follows: a bag-of-words representation of the documents was obtained using the TMG toolbox with a term-frequency weighting scheme [7]. Then, we split the corpus in training and

Table 1. Composition of the corpus R8.

Class	# train doc	# test doc	total # doc
Acq	1596	696	2292
Crude	253	121	374
Earn	2840	1083	3923
Grain	41	10	51
Interest	190	81	271
Money-fx	206	87	293
Ship	108	36	144
Trade	251	75	326
Total	5485	2189	7674

test set for the early text classification model in general and CPI. A window size $w = 3$ was chosen, that is, three terms were read between each run of the early text classification framework.

Based on results obtained in [4] we trained a Naïve Bayes classifier for the CPI model. The performance for the partial documents can be seen in Fig. 2. Clearly, we can accurately classify documents without reading all terms.

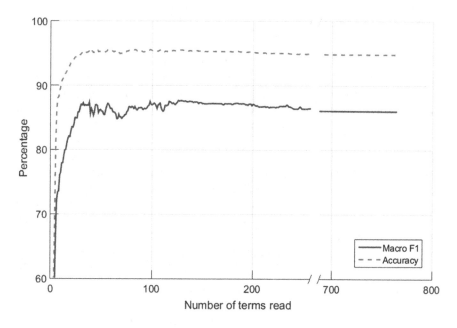

Fig. 2. Evaluation of the sets TeP_t.

Next, we needed to find out what features we could extract to decide *when* to classify a document. In the present work, the selected features were:

- Number of terms of the partial document.
- Number of distinct terms of the partial document.
- Number of relevant terms for each class. Here, we used the most frequent terms in each class.
- Class score given by the CPI model.
- Current window number.
- Historic data from previous windows. For each class we calculated the mean class score given by the CPI model in previous windows.

Finally, we used these features from the documents to build the training and test sets for the DMC model. We tested models trained with three different approaches provided by MatLab: *Naïve Bayes*, *k-ridge*, and an ensemble method (*GentleBoost*) which used neural networks as week classifiers. The performance of each classifier is shown in Table 2. From these results, we chose the GentleBoost classifier for the DMC model.

Table 2. Final estimation results for the precision, recall and F_1 measure.

Predictive DMC model	Precision estimation	Recall estimation	F_1 measure
Kridge	54.46%	57.52%	55.94
Naïve Bayes	56.19%	56.79%	56.48
Gentleboost	60.12%	78.87%	68.23

Once the CPI and DMC models were trained, our framework was tested and results are shown in Table 3. There, EDE_{10}^1 is the early detection error using the definition of $lc_o(k)$ that does not consider the length of the document with $o = 10$, and EDE^2 is the one that considers the length of the document. It can be noted that, for the F_1 measure (measure not considering time), a standard (full reading) model obtains a better result than the temporal one, although the result of our approach is still acceptable. However, when evaluating the temporal aspects, the advantages of the proposal presented in this work are evident: with respect to EDE_{10}^1, a reduction of 0.73 to 0.57 is achieved while for the EDE^2 error the reduction is of 1.05 to 0.73. It can also be observed that there is an average saving of 41.21 terms from the temporal versus the standard approach. Considering the average size of the documents in the R8 collection is 150 terms, this is a significant number of terms that are saved (28% of terms in average).

Table 3. Final results of the linear against the temporal model.

Type of model	F_1 measure	Average unread terms	EDE_{10}^1	EDE^2
Standard	85.97	0	0.73	1.05
Temporal (ETC architecture)	78.99	41.21	0.57	0.73

5   Conclusions

Early text classification has not been yet studied in depth, but numerous new applications in on-line detection and real-time systems give a new impetus to research works in this area. This trend has been evident in 2017 where the first conference directly related to ETC was organized and a new one is planned for 2018 (http://early.irlab.org/).

In this paper, we have formalized a simple framework that makes explicit two critical parts in ETC systems: (i) the classification with partial information, and (ii) the decision of the moment of classification. In this context, a novel approach that learns the second component is proposed and a new measure for evaluating multi-class ETC problems is defined.

While promising results were obtained with the R8 corpus reducing considerably the number of terms needed for classification, several directions for future improvements are easily identified. First of all, we can boost up the basic implementation used in the present work by augmenting the contextual information of the DMC model with other more informative features (for instance, using the words with the highest information gain as relevant words). Furthermore, different document representations and predictive models should be tested for CPI and DMC. Finally, we should test this framework in a more recent and competitive early classification corpus like the one presented by Losada and Crestiani [6] and also on other data sets where ETC approaches can be critical like the detection of sexual predators in chats or detection of suicidal discourse.

References

1. Cardoso-Cachopo, A.: Improving methods for single-label text categorization. Ph.D. thesis, Instituto Superior Tecnico, Universidade Tecnica de Lisboa (2007)
2. Dachraoui, A., Bondu, A., Cornuéjols, A.: Early classification of time series as a non myopic sequential decision making problem. In: Appice, A., Rodrigues, P.P., Santos Costa, V., Soares, C., Gama, J., Jorge, A. (eds.) ECML PKDD 2015. LNCS (LNAI), vol. 9284, pp. 433–447. Springer, Cham (2015). https://doi.org/10.1007/978-3-319-23528-8_27
3. Dulac-Arnold, G., Denoyer, L., Gallinari, P.: Text classification: a sequential reading approach. In: Clough, P., Foley, C., Gurrin, C., Jones, G.J.F., Kraaij, W., Lee, H., Mudoch, V. (eds.) ECIR 2011. LNCS, vol. 6611, pp. 411–423. Springer, Heidelberg (2011). https://doi.org/10.1007/978-3-642-20161-5_41
4. Escalante, H.J., Montes-y-Gómez, M., Pineda, L.V., Errecalde, M.L.: Early text classification: a naïve solution. In: Proceedings of the 7th Workshop on Computational Approaches to Subjectivity, Sentiment and Social Media Analysis, WASSA@NAACL-HLT 2016, San Diego, California, USA, pp. 91–99 (2016)
5. Krizhevsky, A., Sutskever, I., Hinton, G.E.: Imagenet classification with deep convolutional neural networks. In: Proceedings of the 25th International Conference on NIPS (NIPS 2012), pp. 1097–1105. Curran Associates Inc., USA (2002)

6. Losada, D.E., Crestani, F.: A test collection for research on depression and language use. In: Proceedings of Conference and Labs of the Evaluation Forum (CLEF 2016), Evora, Portugal, pp. 28–39 (2016)
7. Zeimpekis, D., Gallopoulos, E.: TMG: a MATLAB toolbox for generating term-document matrices from text collections. In: Kogan, J., Nicholas, C., Teboulle, M. (eds.) Grouping Multidimensional Data: Recent Advances in Clustering. Springer, Heidelberg (2006). https://doi.org/10.1007/3-540-28349-8_7

Distributed and Parallel Processing

Analysis of RAPL Energy Prediction Accuracy in a Matrix Multiplication Application on Shared Memory

Juan Manuel Paniego[1](✉), Silvana Gallo[1,3], Martín Pi Puig[1],
Franco Chichizola[1], Laura De Giusti[1], and Javier Balladini[2]

[1] Instituto de Investigación en Informática LIDI (III-LIDI),
Facultad de Informática, Universidad Nacional de La Plata, La Plata, Argentina
{jmpaniego,sgallo,mpipuig,francoch,
ldgiusti}@lidi.info.unlp.edu.ar
[2] Departamento de Ingeniería de Computadoras, Facultad de Informática,
Universidad Nacional del Comahue, Neuquén, Argentina
javier.balladini@fi.uncoma.edu.ar
[3] CONICET, Facultad de Informática, Universidad Nacional de La Plata,
La Plata, Argentina

Abstract. In recent years, energy consumption has emerged as one of the biggest issues in the development of HPC applications. The traditional approach of parallel and distributed computing has changed its perspective from looking for greater computational efficiency to an approach that balances performance with energy consumption. As a consequence, different metrics and measurement mechanisms have been implemented to achieve this balance. The objective of this article focuses on monitoring and analyzing energy consumption for a given application through physical measurements and a software interface based on hardware counters. A comparison of the energy values gathered by Intel RAPL versus physical measurements obtained through the processor power source is presented. These measurements are applied during the execution of a classic matrix multiplication application. Our results show that, for the application being considered, the average power required by the processor has an error of up to 22% versus the values predicted by RAPL.

Keywords: Energy consumption · Prediction · Power
Hardware counters · RAPL · Perf

1 Introduction

The goal of High Performance Computing (HPC) is to design and develop solutions to situations that require large computing capacities by using techniques and methods that allow using all available computing power to achieve maximum speedup and efficiency.

In recent years, due to existing limitations in energy resources, greater emphasis has been placed on researches related to the consequences of increasing processor temperature. The trend has been analyzing energy consumption on different applications

© Springer International Publishing AG, part of Springer Nature 2018
A. E. De Giusti (Ed.): CACIC 2017, CCIS 790, pp. 37–46, 2018.
https://doi.org/10.1007/978-3-319-75214-3_4

and developing consumption models to predict and plan for execution based on energy consumption metrics [2, 3].

Currently, power consumption efficiency is a very important metric that affects everything from mobile systems to large HPC centers. Daily energy consumption in the latter is very high and this metric increase over time. Therefore, monitoring power dissipation and energy consumption in every system has become a priority research area.

Many biggest clusters currently operating are formed by general-purpose machines that, above all, have a low monetary cost. By interconnecting dozens, hundreds or thousands of these devices, significant computational power is obtained, albeit with very high power consumption, which includes the energy required for cluster nodes to operate as well as the energy required to keep such nodes refrigerated, for example. For this reason, monitoring the energy used for each of the computers is a key to be able to reduce this variable.

This article focuses on monitoring and analyzing energy consumption for a matrix multiplication application through physical measurements and a software interface based on hardware counters.

The article is organized as follows: Sect. 2 presents an overview of related works in the energy consumption area. In Sect. 3, some basic concepts of energy consumption measurement are defined. After that, Sect. 4 details the methodology used to carry out the measurements. Then, in Sect. 5, the experimental work is described, whereas in Sect. 6, the results obtained are presented. Finally, Sect. 7 presents our conclusions and future work.

2 Related Work

Energy consumption in HPC has emerged as one of the major research areas in recent years due to the need of minimizing the environmental impact of the infrastructure required by computation centers, large servers, storage systems and refrigeration systems. To manage energy consumption, numerous applications and measurement instruments such as the ones used in this article have been designed.

When looking to determine a reference value corresponding to the consumption of an entire computation system, which is known as *coarse-grained measurements*, different instruments that intercept power sources and applications that extract the corresponding data are used. For example, external measurements with clamp probes and oscilloscopes [2, 3], or devices such as Watt's Up Pro combined with applications that take captured data and output information for the test scenario, such as PowerPack [11].

In other scenarios, power consumption information of a specific component (memory, disk, network, GPU) is needed. In those cases, *fine-grained measurements* are used. The implementation of the physical measurements included in this article for measuring CPU consumption was inspired in [9, 21] which, using Hall effect sensors, allows extracting the information from the corresponding device.

Other works have considered fine-grained measurements through sensors as invasive and highly complex, and have therefore studied estimation models based on hardware counters information. Such is the case of [4, 6, 7, 15, 17], where the power consumed by the entire system or its different components is estimated by means of fine-grained measurements. There are other models that are application-centered and whose objective is assessing application execution frequency [5, 18] or application scheduling [22]. More complex models have also been developed, such as models that include heterogeneity and consider GPU consumption [20, 24] and even models with a certain type of intelligence through *machine learning* [23].

Power estimation through fine grain models provided by processor manufacturers, such as *Running Average Power Limit* (RAPL) in the case of Intel [8, 14] and *Application Power Management* (APM) for AMD [1], have generated interest in the community in relation to whether the values obtained with them match actual physical measurements. For this reason, the reliability of counter registers and the consumption model have been questioned, and there are numerous works that attempt to validate the estimation by comparing the values obtained by the model with those obtained by the physical measurement methods mentioned above [9, 12, 13].

There are works that estimate coarse-grained power (or alternating current power of the entire system) from the fine-grained power model provided by processor manufacturers [4, 16].

3 Power Consumption Measurement

There are several approaches to measure the energy used during a certain period of time; however, only two of those are widely used.

On one hand, energy consumption can be monitored through certain *software measurement* interfaces that feed a refined power model with different system variables to obtain an estimated measurement of the current power consumption by the device. On Intel processors these variables are obtained through hardware counter records present in most processors designed in recent years, more specifically, since Sandy-Bridge micro-architecture [14].

On the other hand, power consumption control through external *physical measurement* uses different tools that are especially designed for that. There are publications where the power of the entire system is sampled through a clamp probe connected to a digital oscilloscope [2, 3]. In other cases, invasive techniques are used, where current sensors (Hall Effect) are attached to the power sources of the various devices in a computer [11].

3.1 Software Approach

For many years, microprocessor manufacturers installed hidden registers used for debugging hardware problems, but it wasn't until 1993 that their existence, and the possibilities they offer in relation to knowing very accurate data on processor status, became publicly known. Hardware counters are a set of special-purpose registers built in most modern micro-processors whose function is to store in a cumulative way certain events related to system hardware. In its latest designs, Intel has added specific events to measure power consumption.

Due to the potential offered by these counters, many tools have been developed that allow to specify events to be monitored, either for application profiling or to make adjustments during algorithm execution.

In the case of application profiling, *perf* emerges as a GNU/Linux application that displays a large number of events used in profiling and allows accessing them through the command line. Available events depend both on the architecture as well as on the Linux kernel being used. Due to the complexity involved in accessing counter values in real time, PAPI [19] turns up as an interface that allows accessing the various events and counter records from an algorithm's source code. Thus, it is possible to alter the application behavior based on the obtained power values.

As already mentioned, the design of consumption events led to research works focused on estimating power consumption for the different components in a computer system, obtaining power estimation models such as RAPL [8]. RAPL is a model that estimates energy using hardware counters and I/O models. RAPL uses measurement domains, which ensures fine-grained monitoring that may vary based on processor model.

The Package (PKG0) domain includes the power used by the entire socket. Then, PP0 encompasses the entire sub-system of cores and caches, while PP1 considers the consumption generated by circuitry that is external to the cores, such as onboard GPU. Lastly, the DRAM domain generates information about the energy used by the main memory. Since the PKG0 domain includes the PP0 and PP1 sub-domains, this is the domain that was selected to carry out energy measurements in this work.

3.2   Physical Approach

When physically monitoring power, there are two procedures that can be carried out: a coarse-grained procedure and a fine-grained one. The former consists in intercepting, using a suitable instrument, the variables required for calculating instant power: current and voltage. In a fine-grained procedure, the instant current that goes through the power inlet of the main devices in the system is monitored.

This article focuses on the second procedure. To this end, several devices are used. First, an Arduino UNO development board based on free hardware and equipped with an ATmega328P processor, 14 digital I/Os, 6 analog I/Os and a 16 MHz rate clock. Then, a couple of ACS712 sensors, which will be used to measure power through invasive Hall Effect. This type of sensors operate in a range between −5 and 5 Amps and have a resolution of 185 mV/A, powered at 5 V, as shown in Fig. 1a. On the other hand, the equipment whose energy consumption will be measured should have a power source with a 4-pin ATX 12V connection (see Fig. 1b), which is used mainly to power the CPU through the connector that can be seen in Fig. 1b.

4   Implementation

To carry out the measurements, two machines are required – a *study machine* which runs the target algorithm, and a *monitoring machine* that allows to capture physical measurements.

a) ACS712 Sensor   *b) ATX 12V*

Fig. 1. Devices required to carry out physical measurements.

Figure 2 shows a simple connection diagram. The mentioned sensors are serially connected to the ATX 12V power source, and the development board reads the values and send them to the monitoring machine. There, it runs a Python script responsible for receiving the data and save them to disk.

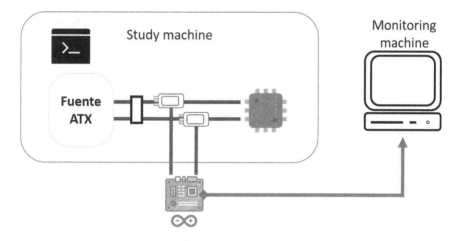

Fig. 2. Measurement diagram.

Finally, software-based measurements are carried out simultaneously with physical-based sampling using the *perf* tool. It should be noted that both procedures can be achieved at the same time because perf is a very light tool and, therefore, does not introduce a significant overhead. Synchronization between both machines is given through a TCP socket.

5   Experimentation

The specific measurements were performed on the machine labeled *study machine*, which consisted on a Gigabyte GA-H81M-H motherboard, an Intel Core I3-4170 processor (2 cores), an 8 GB DDR3 RAM memory and Ubuntu 14.04 operating system

(Kernel 3.16). The *monitoring machine* requires only one Python interpreter to obtain the values being sensored.

On the other hand, a basic matrix multiplication algorithm (1) was chosen as the case study because it represents a widely used problem which is part of solutions to larger-scale problems.

$$C_{i,j} = \sum_{k=1}^{p} A_{i,k} * B_{k,j} \tag{1}$$

There exists two different implementations, a serial and a multithreaded one using the OpenMP library. Both of them at an operation rate of 1.6 GHz.

6   Results

This section details the results corresponding to physical and software measurements. We include a brief graphical and descriptive analysis of the obtained data and then we discuss the results for the serial solution at different workloads. It should be noted that both physical and software measurements are done using an execution script that includes an idle-sleep segment (considered in the results) before and after the algorithm computation, as follows:

- *Sleep 2* s *(Idle State)*
- *Program execution*
- *Sleep 2* s *(Idle State)*

Figure 3 shows the power consumption of the serial version with a 2048 × 2048 matrix.

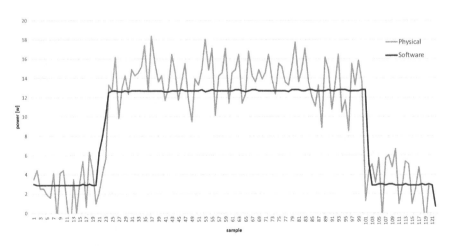

Fig. 3. Consumption profile, serial algorithm.

As it can be seen, the behavior of both approaches are similar. It should be noted that physical measurements appear to be "noisy" because we present instant data (i.e., not an average of sensored samples).

Below Table 1 lists average power values corresponding to both physical and software approximations when varying the workload for the serial algorithm.

Table 1. Active power (Watts) for the serial solution.

	1024	2048	4096	8192
Software measurement	12.35	12.70	13.07	12.90
Physical measurement	13.69	13.97	14.38	14.34

It is evident that the physical approach return higher values than software-based measurements. This deviation presents a linear behavior and shows a variation close to 10% (see Fig. 4).

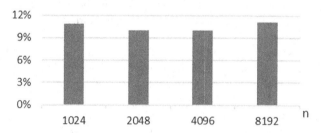

Fig. 4. Error ratio for the serial implementation.

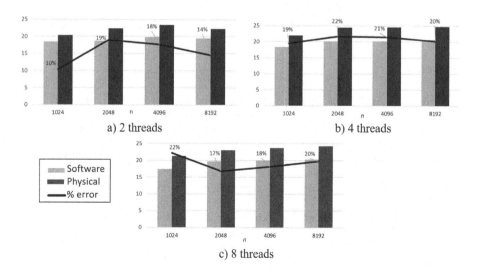

a) 2 threads

b) 4 threads

c) 8 threads

Fig. 5. Average power consumption for thread-based solutions (in Watts). The offset between software and physical measurements is also shown.

On the other hand, OpenMP solutions using 2, 4 and 8 threads yield the results that are shown in Fig. 5 (a, b and c, respectively).

As shown in the graph, it can be concluded that there is an increase in the offset between both measurements and it ranges between 10% and 22%.

7   Conclusions and Future Work

This work focused on monitoring and analyzing energy consumption for a matrix multiplication application through physical measurements and a software interface based on hardware counters.

A physical measurement environment was built, which consisted of an Arduino board with current sensors that allowed recording real measurements of the average power demanded by the processor. In addition, a data-capturing script was implemented in Python to store power data. On the other hand, *perf* was used to access the values returned by RAPL for the Intel processor being studied.

Based on the results, a linear deviation in average power values was observed between physical and software-based measurements, the former being higher in all the cases that were assessed. This difference between measurements is believed to also be affected by one or several hardware devices whose software-recorded consumption has not been analyzed. Additionally, a variable error between 10% and up to 22% was detected in matrix multiplication experiments, for different data sizes and threads number.

Finally, in the future we plan to work on the detection and analysis of the gap between software-based and physical measurements, as well as on the correlation between the internal methods versus an external AC measurement. After the external measurement validation, there is great interest in assessing power consumption in other system components, such as RAM memory and I/O, which have not been considered in this work.

References

1. AMD, AMD Family 15th Processor BIOS and Kernel Developer Guide (2011)
2. Balladini, J., Muresano, R., Suppi, R., Rexachs, D., Luque, E.: Methodology for predicting the energy consumption of SPMD application on virtualized environments. J. Comput. Sci. Technol. **13**(3), 130–136 (2013)
3. Balladini, J., Rucci, E., De Giusti, A., Naiouf, M., Suppi, R., Rexachs, D., Luque, E.: Power characterisation of shared-memory HPC systems. In: XVIII Argentine Congress of Computer Science Selected Papers. Computer Science & Technology Series, pp. 53–65 (2013)
4. Bircher, W., John, L.: Complete system power estimation using processor performance events. IEEE Trans. Comp. **61**(4), 563–577 (2012)
5. Lively, C., Wu, X., Taylor, V., Moore, S., Chang, H., Su, C., Cameron, K.: Power-aware predictive models of hybrid (MPI/OpenMP) scientific applications on multicore system. Comput. Sci. Res. Dev. **27**(4), 245–253 (2012)

6. Chen, X., Xu, C., Dick, R., Mao, Z.: Performance and power modeling in a multi-programmed multi-core environment. In: 2010 47th ACM/IEEE Design Automation Conference (DAC 2010), pp. 813–818 (2010)

7. Contreras, G., Martonosi, M.: Power prediction for Intel XScale processors using performance monitoring unit events. In: Proceedings of the 2005 International Symposium on Low Power Electronic and Design, ISLPED 2005, pp. 221–226 (2005)

8. David, H., Gorbatov, E.: RAPL: memory power estimation and capping. In: 2010 ACM/IEEE International Symposium on Low-Power Electronics and Design (ISLPED), pp. 189–194 (2010)

9. Desrochers, S., Paradis, C., Weaver, V.M.: A validation of DRAM RAPL power measurements. In: Second International Symposium on Memory Systems, pp. 445–470 (2016)

10. Diouri, M.E.M., Dolz, M.: Assessing power monitoring approaches for energy and power analysis of computers. Sustain. Comput. Inf. Syst. $4(2)$, 68–82 (2014)

11. Ge, R., Feng, X., Song, S., Chang, H.C., Li, D., Cameron, K.W.: PowerPack: energy profiling and analysis of high-performance systems and applications. IEEE Trans. Parallel Distrib. Syst. $21(5)$, 658–671 (2010)

12. Hackenberg, D., Ilsche, I., Schone, R., Molka, D., Schmidt, M., Nagel, W.E.: Power measurement techniques on standard compute nodes: a quantitative comparison. In: IEEE International Symposium on Performance Analysis of Systems and Software (ISPASS) (2013)

13. Hahnel, M., Dobel, B., Volp, M., Hartigl, H.: Measuring energy consumption for short code paths using RAPL. ACM SIGMETRICS Perform. Eval. Rev. 40, 13–17 (2012). Technische Universität Dresden

14. Intel Architecture Software Developer's Manual, volume 3: System Programming Guide (2009)

15. Isci, C., Martonosi, M.: Runtime power monitoring in high-end processors: methodology and empirical data. In: 36th IEEE/ACM International Symposium on Microarchitecture, p. 93 (2003)

16. Khan, K.N., Ou, Z., Hirki, M., Nurminen, J.K., Niemi, T.: How much power does your server consume? Estimating wall socket power using RAPL measurements. Comput. Sci. Res. Dev. 31, 207–214 (2016)

17. Lim, M., Porterfield, A., Fowler, R.: SoftPower: finegrain power estimations using performance counters. In: Proceedings of the 19th ACM International Symposium on High Performance Distributed Computing (HPDC 2010), pp. 308–311 (2010)

18. Lively, C., Taylor, V., Wu, X., Chang, H., Su, C., Cameron, K., Moore, S., Terpstra, D.: E-AMOM: an energy-aware modeling and optimization methodology for scientific applications on multicore systems. Comput. Sci. Res. Dev. $29(3$–$4)$, 197–210 (2014)

19. Mucci, P., Browne, S., Deane, C., Ho, G.: PAPI: a portable interface to hardware performance counters. In: Proceedings of the Department of Defense HPCMP Users Group Conference, pp. 7–10 (1999)

20. Nagasaka, H., Maruyama, N., Nukada, A., Endo, T., Matsuoka, S.: Statistical power modeling of GPU kernels using performance counters. In: International Green Computing Conference, pp. 115–122 (2010)

21. Picariello, F., Rapuano, S., Villano, U.: Evaluation of power consumption of workstation computers using benchmarking. In: Proceedings 12th IMEKO TC10 Workshop on Technical Diagnostics: New Perspective in Measurements, Tools and Techniques for Industrial Applications, University of Sannio, Italy, pp. 242–247 (2013)

22. Singh, K., Bhadhauria, M., McKee, S.A.: Real time power estimation and thread scheduling via performance counters. In: Workshop on Design, Architecture and Simulation of Chip Multi-Processors, vol. 37(2), pp. 46–55, May 2009

23. Song, S., Su, C., Rountree, B., Cameron, K.: A simplified and accurate model of power-performance efficiency on emergent GPU architectures. In: 2013 International Symposium on Parallel & Distributed Processing, IPDPS 2013, pp. 673–686 (2013)

24. Tsafack Chetsa, G.L., Lefevre, L., Pierson, J.M., Stolf, P., Da Costa, G.: Exploiting performance counters to predict and improve energy performance of HPC systems. Future Gener. Comput. Syst. **36**, 287–298 (2014)

Blocked All-Pairs Shortest Paths Algorithm on Intel Xeon Phi KNL Processor: A Case Study

Enzo Rucci[1]($\boxtimes$), Armando De Giusti[1], and Marcelo Naiouf[2]

[1] III-LIDI, CONICET, Facultad de Informática, Universidad Nacional de La Plata,
1900 La Plata, Buenos Aires, Argentina
{erucci,degiusti}@lidi.info.unlp.edu.ar
[2] III-LIDI, Facultad de Informática, Universidad Nacional de La Plata,
1900 La Plata, Buenos Aires, Argentina
mnaiouf@lidi.info.unlp.edu.ar

Abstract. Manycores are consolidating in HPC community as a way of improving performance while keeping power efficiency. Knights Landing is the recently released second generation of Intel Xeon Phi architecture. While optimizing applications on CPUs, GPUs and first Xeon Phi's has been largely studied in the last years, the new features in Knights Landing processors require the revision of programming and optimization techniques for these devices. In this work, we selected the Floyd-Warshall algorithm as a representative case study of graph and memory-bound applications. Starting from the default serial version, we show how data, thread and compiler level optimizations help the parallel implementation to reach 338 GFLOPS.

Keywords: Xeon Phi · Knights Landing · Floyd-Warshall

1 Introduction

The power consumption problem represents one of the major obstacles for Exascale systems design. As a consequence, the scientific community is searching for different ways to improve power efficiency of High Performance Computing (HPC) systems [8]. One recent trend to increase compute power and, at the same time, limit power consumption of these systems lies in adding accelerators, like NVIDIA/AMD graphic processing units (GPUs), or Intel Many Integrated Core (MIC) co-processors. These manycore devices are capable of achieving better FLOPS/Watt ratios than traditional CPUs. For example, the number of Top500 [2] systems using accelerator technology grew from 54 in June 2013 to 91 in June 2017. In the same period, the number of systems based on accelerators increased from 55 to 90 on the Green500 list [1].

Recently, Intel has presented the second generation of its MIC architecture (branded Xeon Phi), codenamed Knights Landing (KNL). Among the main differences of KNL regarding its predecessor Knights Corner (KNC), we can find the

A. E. De Giusti (Ed.): CACIC 2017, CCIS 790, pp. 47–57, 2018.
https://doi.org/10.1007/978-3-319-75214-3_5

incorporation of AVX-512 extensions, a remarkable number of vector units increment, a new on-package high-bandwidth memory (HBM) and the ability to operate as a standalone processor. Even though optimizing applications on CPUs, GPUs and KNC Xeon Phi's has been largely studied in the last years, accelerating applications on KNL processors is still a pending task due to its recent commercialization. In that sense, the new features in KNL processors require the revision of programming and optimization techniques for these devices.

In this work, we selected the Floyd-Warshall (FW) algorithm as a representative case study of graph and memory-bound applications. This algorithm finds the shortest paths between all pairs of vertices in a graph and occurs in domains of communication networking [14], traffic routing [12], bioinformatics [16], among others. FW is both computationally and spatially expensive since it requires $O(n^3)$ operations and $O(n^2)$ memory space, where n is the number of vertices in a graph. Starting from the default serial version, we show how data, thread and compiler level optimizations help the parallel implementation to reach 338 GFLOPS.

The rest of the present paper is organized as follows. Section 2 briefly introduces the Intel Xeon Phi KNL architecture while Sect. 3 presents the FW algorithm. Section 4 describes our implementation. In Sect. 5 we analyze performance results while Sect. 6 discusses related works. Finally, Sect. 7 outlines conclusions and future lines of work.

2 Intel Xeon Phi Knights Landing

KNL is the second generation of the Intel Xeon Phi family and the first capable of operating as a standalone processor. The KNL architecture is based on a set of *Tiles* (up to 36) interconnected by a 2D mesh. Each Tile includes 2 cores based on the out-of-order Intel's Atom micro-architecture (4 threads per core), 2 Vector Processing Units (VPUs) and a shared L2 cache of 1 MB. These VPUs not only implement the new 512-bit AVX-512 ISA but they are also compatible with prior vector ISA's such as SSE*x* and AVX*x*. AVX-512 provides 512-bit SIMD support, 32 logical registers, 8 new mask registers for vector predication, and gather and scatter instructions to support loading and storing sparse data. As each AVX-512 instruction can perform 8 double-precision (DP) operations (8 FLOPS) or 16 single-precision (SP) operations (16 FLOPS), the peak performance is over 1.5 TFLOPS in DP and 3 TFLOPS in SP, more than two times higher than that of the KNC. It is also more energy efficient than its predecessor [17].

Other significant feature of the KNL architecture is the inclusion of an in-package HBM called MCDRAM. This special memory offers 3 operating modes: *Cache*, *Flat* and *Hybrid*. In Cache mode, the MCDRAM is used like an L3 cache, caching data from the DDR4 level of memory. Even though application code remains unchanged, the MCDRAM can suffer lower performance rates. In Flat mode, the MCDRAM has a physical addressable space offering the highest bandwidth and lowest latency. However, software modifications may be required in order to use both the DDR and the MCDRAM in the same application.

Finally, in the *Hybrid mode*, HBM is divided in two parts: one part in *Cache mode* and one in *Flat mode* [5].

From a software perspective, KNL supports parallel programming models used traditionally on HPC systems such as OpenMP or MPI. This fact represents a strength of this platform since it simplifies code development and improves portability over other alternatives based on accelerator specific programming languages such as CUDA or OpenCL. However, to achieve high performance, programmers should attend to:

- the efficient exploitation of the memory hierarchy, especially when handling large datasets, and
- how to structure the computations to take advantage of the VPUs.

Automatic vectorization is obviously the easiest programming way to exploit VPUs. However, in most cases the compiler is unable to generate SIMD binary code since it can not detect free data dependences into loops. In that sense, SIMD instructions are supported in KNL processors through the use of guided compilation or hand-tuned codification with intrinsic instructions [17]. On one hand, in guided vectorization, the programmer indicates the compiler (through the insertion of tags) which loops are independent and their memory pattern access. In this way, the compiler is able to generate SIMD binary code preserving the program portability. On the other hand, intrinsic vectorization usually involves rewriting most of the corresponding algorithm. The programmer gains in control at the cost of losing portability. Moreover, this approach also suggests the inhibition of other compiler loop-level optimizations. Nevertheless, it is the only way to exploit parallelism in some applications with no regular access patterns or loop data dependencies which can be hidden by recomputing techniques [6].

3   Floyd-Warshall Algorithm

The FW algorithm uses a dynamic programming approach to compute the all-pairs shortest-paths problem on a directed graph [7,20]. This algorithm takes as input a $N \times N$ distance matrix D, where $D_{i,j}$ is initialized with the original distance from node i to node j. FW runs for N iterations and at k-th iteration it evaluates all the possible paths between each pair of vertices from i to j through the intermediate vertex k. As a result, FW produces an updated matrix D, where $D_{i,j}$ now contains the shortest distance between nodes i and j. Besides, an additional matrix P is generated when the reconstruction of the shortest path is required. $P_{i,j}$ contains the most recently added intermediate node between i and j. Figure 1 exhibits the naive FW algorithm.

4   Implementation

In this section, we address the optimizations performed on the Intel Xeon Phi KNL processor. First of all, we developed a serial implementation following the

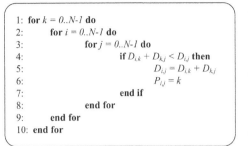

```
1: for k = 0..N-1 do
2:      for i = 0..N-1 do
3:          for j = 0..N-1 do
4:              if D_{i,k} + D_{k,j} < D_{i,j} then
5:                  D_{i,j} = D_{i,k} + D_{k,j}
6:                  P_{i,j} = k
7:              end if
8:          end for
9:      end for
10: end for
```

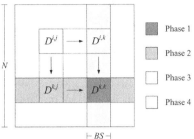

Fig. 1. Naive Floyd-Warshall algorithm

Fig. 2. Schematic representation of the blocked Floyd-Warshall algorithm

naive version described in Fig. 1, as this implementation will work as baseline. Next, we optimized the serial version considering data locality and data level parallelism. Finally, we introduced thread level parallelism exploiting the OpenMP programming model to obtain a multi-threaded implementation.

4.1 Data Locality

To improve data locality, the FW algorithm can be blocked [19]. Unfortunately, the three loops can not be interchanged in free manner due to the data dependencies from one iteration to the next in the k-loop (just i and j loops can be done in any order). However, under certain conditions, the k-loop can be put inside the i-loop and j-loop, making blocking possible. The distance matrix D is partitioned into blocks of size $BS \times BS$, so that there are $(N/BS)^2$ blocks. The computations involve $R = N/BS$ rounds and each round is divided into four phases based on the data dependency among the blocks:

1. Update the block k,k ($D^{k,k}$) because it is self-dependent.
2. Update the remaining blocks of the k-th row because each of these blocks depends on itself and the previously computed $D^{k,k}$.
3. Update the remaining blocks of the k-th column because each of these blocks depends on itself and the previously computed $D^{k,k}$.
4. Update the rest of the matrix blocks as each of them depends on the k-th block of its row and the k-th block of its column.

In this way, we satisfy all dependencies from this algorithm. Figure 2 shows a schematic representation of a round computation and the data dependences among the blocks while Fig. 3 presents the corresponding pseudo-code.

4.2 Data Level Parallelism

The innermost loop of FW_BLOCK code block from Fig. 3 is clearly the most computationally expensive part of the algorithm. In that sense, this loop is the

```
 1: function FW_BLOCK (D¹, D², D³, P, base)      13: for k = 0..R-1 do
 2:   for k = 0..BS-1 do                          14:   b = k × BS
 3:     for i = 0..BS-1 do                         15:   # Phase 1
 4:       for j = 0..BS-1 do                       16:   FW_BLOCK(D^{k,k}, D^{k,k}, D^{k,k}, P^{k,k}, b)
 5:         if D²_{i,k} + D³_{k,j} < D¹_{i,j} then  17:   # Phase 2
 6:           D¹_{i,j} = D²_{i,k} + D³_{k,j}        18:   for j = 0..R-1, j ≠ k do
 7:           P_{i,j} = base+k                      19:     FW_BLOCK(D^{k,j}, D^{k,k}, D^{k,j}, P^{k,j}, b)
 8:         end if                                  20:   end for
 9:       end for                                   21:   # Phase 3
10:     end for                                     22:   for i = 0..R-1, i ≠ k do
11:   end for                                       23:     FW_BLOCK(D^{i,k}, D^{i,k}, D^{k,k}, P^{i,k}, b)
12: end function                                    24:   end for
                                                    25:   # Phase 4
                                                    26:   for i, j = 0..R-1, i,j ≠ k do
                                                    27:     FW_BLOCK(D^{i,j}, D^{i,k}, D^{k,j}, P^{i,j}, b)
                                                    28:   end for
                                                    29: end for
```

Fig. 3. Blocked Floyd-Warshall algorithm.

best candidate for vectorization. The loop body is composed of an *if* statement that involves one addition, one comparison and (may be) two assign operations. Unfortunately, the compiler detects false dependencies in that loop and is not able to generate SIMD binary code. For that reason, we have explored two SIMD exploitation approaches: (1) guided vectorization through the usage of the OpenMP 4.0 *simd* directive and (2) intrinsic vectorization employing the AVX-512 extensions. The guided approach simply consists of inserting the *simd* directive to the innermost loop of FW_BLOCK code block (line 4). On the opposite sense, the intrinsic approach consists of rewriting the entire loop body. Figures 4 and 5 show the pseudo-code for FW_BLOCK implementation using guided and manual vectorization, respectively. In order to accelerate SIMD

```
 1: for k = 0..BS-1 do
 2:   for i = 0..BS-1 do
 3:     #pragma unroll
 4:     #pragma omp simd
 5:     for j = 0..BS-1 do
 6:       if (D²[i][k] + D³[k][j] < D¹[i][j]) then
 7:         D¹[i][j] = D²[i][k] + D³[k][j];
 8:         P[i,j] = base+k;
 9:       end if
10:     end for
11:   end for
12: end for
```

```
 1: for k = 0..BS-1 do
 2:   bk = _mm512_set1_epi32(base+k);
 3:   for i = 0..BS-1 do
 4:     dik = _mm512_set1_ps(D²[i][k]);
 5:     #pragma unroll
 6:     for j = 0..BS-1 by 16 do
 7:       dij = _mm512_load_ps (&D¹[i][j]);
 8:       dkj = _mm512_load_ps (&D³[k][j]);
 9:       sum = _mm512_add_ps (dik, dkj);
10:       mask = _mm512_cmp_ps_mask(sum, dij, CMP_LT_OS);
11:       _mm512_mask_store_ps(&D¹[i][j], mask, sum);
12:       _mm512_mask_store_epi32(&P[i][j], mask, bk);
13:     end for
14:   end for
15: end for
```

Fig. 4. Pseudo-code for FW_BLOCK implementation using guided vectorization

Fig. 5. Pseudo-code for FW_BLOCK implementation using intrinsic vectorization

computation with 512-bit vectors, we have carefully managed the memory allocations so that distance and path matrices are 64-byte aligned. In the guided approach, this also requires adding the *aligned* clause to the *simd* directive.

4.3   Loop Unrolling

Loop unrolling is another optimization technique that helped us to improve the code performance. Fully unrolling the innermost loop of FW_BLOCK code block was found to work well. Unrolling the *i*-loop of the same code block once was also found to work well.

4.4   Thread Level Parallelism

To exploit parallelism across multiple cores, we have implemented a multi-threaded version of FW algorithm based on OpenMP programming model. A *parallel* construct is inserted before the loop of line 13 in Fig. 3 to create a parallel block. To respect data dependencies among the block computations, the work-sharing constructs must be carefully inserted. At each round, phase 1 must be computed before the rest. So a *single* construct is inserted to enclose line 16. Next, phases 2 and 3 must be computed before phase 4. As these blocks are independent among them, a *for* directive is inserted before the loops of lines 18 and 22. Besides, a *nowait* clause is added to the phase 2 loop to alleviate the thread idling. Finally, another *for* construct is inserted before the loop of line 26 to distribute the remaining blocks among the threads.

5   Experimental Results

5.1   Experimental Design

All tests have been performed on an Intel server running CentOS 7.2 equipped with a Xeon Phi 7250 processor 68-core 1.40 GHz (4 hw thread per core and 16 GB MCDRAM memory) and 48 GB main memory. The processor was run in *Flat* memory mode and *Quadrant* cluster mode.

We have used Intel's ICC compiler (version 17.0.1.132) with the *-O3* optimization level. To generate explicit AVX2 and AVX-512 instructions, we employed the *-xAVX2* and *-xMIC-AVX512* flags, respectively. Also, we used the *numactl* utility to exploit MCDRAM memory (no source code modification is required). Besides, different workloads were tested: $N = \{4096, 8192, 16384, 32768, 65536\}$.

5.2   Performance Results

First, we evaluated the performance improvements of the different optimization techniques applied to the naive serial version, such as blocking (*blocked*), data level parallelism (*simd*, *simd (AVX2)* and *simd (AVX-512)*), aligned

Table 1. Execution time (in seconds) of the different optimization techniques applied to the naive serial version when $N = 4096$.

naive	blocked	simd	simd (AVX2)	simd (AVX-512)	aligned	unrolled
602.8	572.66	204.52	100.47	36.95	33.28	22.95

access (*aligned*) and loop unrolling (*unrolled*). Table 1 shows the execution time (in seconds) of the different serial versions when $N = 4096$. As it can be observed, blocking optimization reduces execution time by 5%. Regarding the block size, 256×256 was found to work best. In the most memory demanding case of each round (phase 4), four blocks are loaded into the cache (3 distance blocks and 1 path block). The four blocks requires $4 \times 256 \times 256 \times 4$ bytes $= 1024\,\mathrm{KB} = 1\,\mathrm{MB}$, which is exactly the L2 cache size.

As stated in Sect. 4.2, the compiler is not able to generate SIMD binary code by itself in the blocked version. Adding the corresponding *simd* constructs to the blocked version reduced the execution time from 572.66 to 204.52 s, which represents a speedup of 2.8×. However, AVX-512 instructions can perform 16 SP operations at the same time. After inspecting the code at assembly level, we realized that the compiler generates SSE*x* instructions by default. As SSE*x* can perform 4 SP operations at the same time, the 2.8× speedup has more sense since not all the code can be vectorized. Next, we re-compiled the code including the -*xAVX2* and -*xMIC-AVX512* flags to force the compiler to generate AVX2 and AVX-512 SIMD instructions, respectively. AVX2 extensions accelerated the blocked version by a factor of 5.8× while AVX-512 instructions achieved an speedup of 15.5×. So, it is clear that this application benefits from larger SIMD width. In relation to the other optimization techniques employed, we have found that the *simd (AVX-512)* implementation runs 1.11× faster when aligning memory accesses in AVX-512 computations (*aligned*). Additionally, applying the loop unrolling optimization to the *aligned* version led to higher performance, gaining a 1.45× speedup. In summary, we achieve a 26.3× speedup over the naive serial version through the combination of the different optimizations described.

Taking the optimized serial version, we developed a multi-threaded implementation as described in Sect. 4.4. Figure 6 shows the performance (in terms of GFLOPS) for the different affinity types used varying the number of threads when $N = 8192$. As expected, *compact* affinity produced the worst results since it favours using all threads on a core before using other cores. *Scatter* and *balanced* affinities presented similar performances improving the *none* counterpart. As the KNL processor used in this study has all its cores in the same package, *scatter* and *balanced* affinities distribute the threads in the same manner when one thread per core is assigned. Regarding the number of threads, using a single thread per core is enough to get maximal performance (except in *compact* affinity). This behavior is opposed to the KNC generation where two or more threads per core where required to achieve high performance. However, it should

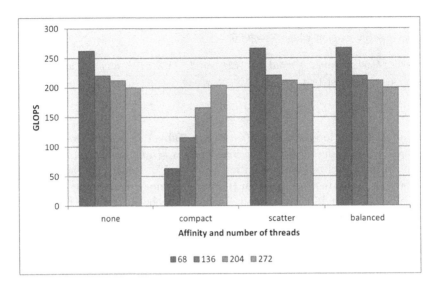

Fig. 6. Performance for the different affinity types used varying the number of threads when $N = 8192$.

not be a surprise since the KNL cores were designed to optimize single thread performance including out-of-order pipelines and two VPUs per core.

It is important to remark that, unlike the optimized serial version, the parallel implementation used a smaller block size since it delivered higher performance. A smaller block size allowed a finer-grain workload distribution and decreased thread idling, especially when the number of threads was larger than the number of blocks in phases 2 and 3. Another reason to decrease block size was that the L2 available space is now shared between the threads in a tile, contrary to the single threaded case. In particular, $BS = 64$ was found to work best.

Figure 7 illustrates performance evolution varying workload and MCDRAM exploitation for the different vectorization approaches. For small workloads ($N = 8192$), the performance improvement is little ($\sim 1.1\times$). However, MCDRAM memory presents remarkable speedups for greater workloads, even when the dataset largely exceeds the MCDRAM size ($N = 655536$). In particular, MCDRAM exploitation achieves an average speedup of $9.8\times$ and a maximum speedup of $15.5\times$. In this way, we can see how MCDRAM usage is an efficient strategy for bandwidth-sensitive applications.

In relation to the vectorization approach, we can appreciate that guided vectorization leads to slightly better performance than the intrinsic counterpart, running upto $1.03\times$ faster. The best performances are 330 and 338 GFLOPS for the intrinsic and guided versions, respectively. After analyzing the assembly code, we realized that this difference is caused by the prefetching instructions introduced by the compiler when guided vectorization is used. Unfortunately, the compiler disables automatic prefetching when code is manually vectorized.

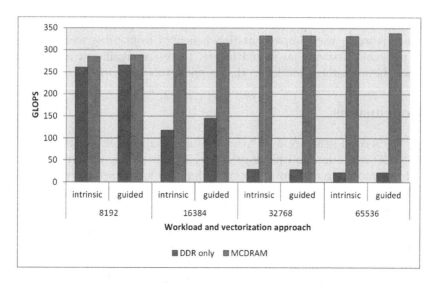

Fig. 7. Performance evolution varying workload and the MCDRAM exploitation.

6 Related Works

Despite its recent commercialization, there are some works that evaluate KNL processors. In that sense, we highlight [18] that presents a study of the performance differences observed when using the three MCDRAM configurations available in combination with the three possible memory access or cluster modes. Also, Barnes et al. [3] discussed the lessons learned from optimizing a number of different high-performance applications and kernels. Besides, Haidar et al. [9] proposed and evaluated several optimization techniques for different matrix factorizations methods on many-core systems.

Obtaining high-performance in graph algorithms is usually a difficult task since they tend to suffer from irregular dependencies and large space requirements. Regarding FW algorithm, there are many works proposed to solve the all-pairs shortest paths problem on different harwdare architectures. However, to the best of the authors knowledge, there are no related works with KNL processors. Han and Kang [10] demonstrated that exploiting SSE2 instructions led to 2.3 × −5.2× speedups over a blocked version. Bondhugula et al. [4] proposed a tiled parallel implementation using Field Programmable Gate Arrays. In the field of GPUs, we highlight the work of Katz and Kider [13], who proposed a shared memory cache efficient implementation to handle graph sizes that are inherently larger than the DRAM memory available on the device. Also, Matsumoto et al. [15] presented a blocked algorithm for hybrid CPU-GPU systems aimed to minimize host-device communication. Finally, Hou et al. [11] evaluated different optimization techniques for Xeon Phi KNC coprocessor. Just as this study, they found that blocking and vectorization are key aspects in this problem to achieve high performance. Also, guided vectorization led to better results than the manual approach, but with larger performance differences. Contrary to this work, their implementation benefited from using more than one thread per core. However, as stated before, there are significant architectural differences between these platforms that support this behavior.

7   Conclusions

KNL is the second generation of Xeon Phi family and features new technologies in SIMD execution and memory access. In this paper, we have evaluated a set of programming and optimization techniques for these processors taking the FW algorithm as a representative case study of graph and memory-bound applications. Among the main contributions of this research we can summarize:

- Blocking technique not only improved performance but also allowed us to apply a coarse-grain workload distribution in the parallel implementation.
- SIMD exploitation was crucial to achieve top performance. In particular, the serial version run $2.9\times$, $6\times$ and $15.5\times$ faster using the SSE, AVX2 and AVX-512 extensions, respectively.
- Aligning memory accesses and loop unrolling also showed significant speedups.
- A single thread per core was enough to get maximal performance. In addition, *scatter* and *balanced* affinities provided extra performance.
- Besides keeping portability, guided vectorization led to slightly better performance than the intrinsic counterpart, running upto $1.03\times$ faster.
- MCDRAM usage demonstrated to be an efficient strategy to tolerate high-bandwidth demands with practically null programmer intervention, even when the dataset largely exceeded the MCDRAM size. In particular, it produced an average speedup of $9.8\times$ and a maximum speedup of $15.5\times$.

As future work, we consider evaluating programming and optimization techniques in other cluster and memory modes as a way to extract more performance.

Acknowledgments. The authors thank the ArTeCS Group from Universidad Complutense de Madrid for letting use their Xeon Phi KNL system.

References

1. Green500 Supercomputer Ranking. https://www.green500.org/
2. Top500 Supercomputer Ranking. https://www.top500.org/
3. Barnes, T., et al.: Evaluating and optimizing the NERSC workload on knights landing. In: Proceedings of the 7th International Workshop on Performance Modeling, Benchmarking and Simulation of High Performance Computing Systems, PMBS 2016, Piscataway, NJ, USA, pp. 43–53. IEEE Press (2016)
4. Bondhugula, U., Devulapalli, A., Dinan, J., Fernando, J., Wyckoff, P., Stahlberg, E., Sadayappan, P.: Hardware/software integration for FPGA-based all-pairs shortest-paths. In: 2006 14th Annual IEEE Symposium on Field-Programmable Custom Computing Machines, pp. 152–164, April 2006

5. Codreanu, V., Rodrguez, J., Saastad, O.W.: Best Practice Guide - Knights Landing (2017). http://www.prace-ri.eu/IMG/pdf/Best-Practice-Guide-Knights-Landing. pdf
6. Culler, D.E., Gupta, A., Singh, J.P.: Parallel Computer Architecture: A Hardware/Software Approach, 1st edn. Morgan Kaufmann Publishers Inc., San Francisco (1997)
7. Floyd, R.W.: Algorithm 97: shortest path. Commun. ACM **5**(6), 345 (1962)
8. Giles, M.B., Reguly, I.: Trends in high-performance computing for engineering calculations. Philos. Trans. R. Soc. Lond. Math. Phys. Eng. Sci. **372**(2022), 1–14 (2014)
9. Haidar, A., Tomov, S., Arturov, K., Guney, M., Story, S., Dongarra, J.: LU, QR, and Cholesky factorizations: programming model, performance analysis and optimization techniques for the Intel Knights Landing Xeon Phi. In: 2016 IEEE High Performance Extreme Computing Conference (HPEC), pp. 1–7, September 2016
10. Han, S., Kang, S.: Optimizing all-pairs shortest-path algorithm using vector instructions (2005)
11. Hou, K., Wang, H., Feng, W.: Delivering parallel programmability to the masses via the Intel MIC ecosystem: a case study. In: 2014 43rd International Conference on Parallel Processing Workshops, pp. 273–282, September 2014
12. Jalali, S., Noroozi, M.: Determination of the optimal escape routes of underground mine networks in emergency cases. Saf. Sci. **47**(8), 1077–1082 (2009)
13. Katz, G.J., Kider Jr., J.T.: All-pairs shortest-paths for large graphs on the GPU. In: Proceedings of the 23rd ACM SIGGRAPH/EUROGRAPHICS Symposium on Graphics Hardware, GH 2008, pp. 47–55. Eurographics Association, Aire-la-Ville (2008)
14. Khan, P., Konar, G., Chakraborty, N.: Modification of Floyd-Warshall's algorithm for shortest path routing in wireless sensor networks. In: 2014 Annual IEEE India Conference (INDICON), pp. 1–6, December 2014
15. Matsumoto, K., Nakasato, N., Sedukhin, S.G.: Blocked all-pairs shortest paths algorithm for hybrid cpu-gpu system. In: 2011 IEEE International Conference on High Performance Computing and Communications, pp. 145–152, September 2011
16. Nakaya, A., Goto, S., Kanehisa, M.: Extraction of correlated gene clusters by multiple graph comparison. Genome Inform. **12**, 44–53 (2001)
17. Reinders, J., Jeffers, J., Sodani, A.: Intel Xeon Phi Processor High Performance Programming Knights Landing Edition. Morgan Kaufmann Publishers Inc., Boston (2016)
18. Rosales, C., Cazes, J., Milfeld, K., Gómez-Iglesias, A., Koesterke, L., Huang, L., Vienne, J.: A comparative study of application performance and scalability on the intel knights landing processor. In: Taufer, M., Mohr, B., Kunkel, J.M. (eds.) ISC High Performance 2016. LNCS, vol. 9945, pp. 307–318. Springer, Cham (2016). https://doi.org/10.1007/978-3-319-46079-6_22
19. Venkataraman, G., Sahni, S., Mukhopadhyaya, S.: A blocked all-pairs shortest-paths algorithm. In: Halldórsson, M.M. (ed.) SWAT 2000. LNCS, vol. 1851, pp. 419–432. Springer, Heidelberg (2000). https://doi.org/10.1007/3-540-44985-X_36
20. Warshall, S.: A theorem on boolean matrices. J. ACM **9**(1), 11–12 (1962)

Computer Technology Applied to Education

Numeric Line: A Códimo's Activity

Luciano Graziani, Gabriela Anahí Cayú, Matías Emanuel Sanhueza,
and Enrique Molinari[(✉)] [iD]

Universidad Nacional de Río Negro, Sede Atlántica,
Viedma, Río Negro, Argentina
{lgraziani,gcayu,msanhueza,emolinari}@unrn.edu.ar
https://www.unrn.edu.ar/

Abstract. Computational thinking is a fundamental skill for everyone, not just for computer scientists. Teaching computational thinking in primary and secondary school will not only help to inspire kids to continue their studies in Computer Science, but also will provide a set of valuable skills to use during their professional life in the Computer Science field or in any other field. In this work we present a Códimo's activity called Numeric Line. This activity was designed for students between 6 and 8 years old and with the goal of encourage, in a transparent way, one of the aspect of computational thinking: Algorithm design. The students play using a set of simple blocks (commands), trying to put a number in a numeric line, moving it across a maze. With this, the student reinforce their knowledge taught in classroom about natural and integer numbers, using computational thinking.

Keywords: Códimo · Education · Computational-thinking
Learning-objects · Programming-for-kids · Javascript

1 Introduction

Since 2014 the Universidad Nacional de Río Negro, has been promoting activities to bring programming to primary and secondary students. The goal was to try to inspire the students to continue their studies in computer science. In addition, Computational thinking is a fundamental skill for everyone, not just for computer scientists [9].

After two years of experience doing this, using tools like Alice, and seeing the difficulties in teachers and students we decided to build a tool to reinforce concepts taught in classroom, but using computational thinking. We called this tool Códimo.

In all Códimo's activities, the students reinforce concepts learnt in classroom, in any field like exact science, natural science, social science or any other, using concepts from computational thinking.

This work follows with Sect. 2, with the description of our proposal and a detailed explanation of the activity Numeric Line. The Sect. 3 describing technical details of how Códimo was built. The Sect. 4 with related work, the Sect. 5 with future work to finish with Sect. 6, the conclusions.

© Springer International Publishing AG, part of Springer Nature 2018
A. E. De Giusti (Ed.): CACIC 2017, CCIS 790, pp. 61–68, 2018.
https://doi.org/10.1007/978-3-319-75214-3_6

2 "Numeric Line": Coding to Learn

Numeric line is an activity for students from 6 to 8 years old (2nd grade and 3rd grade). It belongs to math area and can be used for students after their learn natural numbers, integers, the order relation and the numeric line.

The goal of the activity is to put a number in an empty position in the numeric line. It presents several levels of complexity. In the initial level the students will play with natural numbers of one digit. In the intermediate level with natural numbers of two digits and in the advanced level the students will play with integer numbers.

The activity presents a number in an initial position, a maze and a numeric line. The students must move the number and put it into the numeric line in a correct position. The only way to move the number is using blocks. Each block has a specific purpose like move the number in a direction or make the number to jump. To take the number from the initial position to an end position in the numeric line, the students must create a *program* joining the given blocks. Playing like this, the students reinforce math applying algorithm design, one of the aspects of computational thinking.

Using blocks to code has a fundamental pedagogic advantage over using classic syntactical constructions from a pseudo programming language. The blocks always form a syntactically correct *program*, which allows the students to don't have to deal with semicolons or non-closing brackets, and put the attention on the semantics, the effect that each block produce to the number. In this case, the effect is to move the number across the maze.

Figure 1 shows one of the exercises from the advanced level.

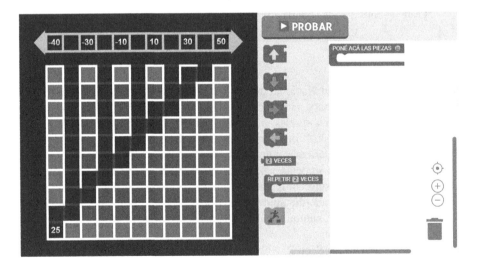

Fig. 1. Activity, advanced level

On the left of Fig. 1 you can see the maze and on top of it a numeric line. Each activity start with a number, in the case of the Fig. 1 the 25, and a numeric line with some empty positions. The number 25 must be put in an empty correct position in the numeric line. In the initial level the numeric line has only one empty position, but in the other levels there are more than one empty position, where one position is valid to put the number.

On the right of Fig. 1 you can see the blocks used by the students to move the number. Each block produce a defined effect on the number. We classify the blocks in the following way:

- Simple:
  - **Move up:** move the number up one position.
  - **Move to right:** move the number to the right one position.
  - **Move to left:** move the number to the left one position.
  - **Move down:** move the number down one position.
- Composed:
  - **N times:** repeat a single move in any direction n times.
  - **Repeat N times:** execute N times the set of simple blocks inside it.
- Designed for the activity:
  - **Jump:** once the number arrives to a valid position, the students must use this block to jump from the maze into the number line.

The blocks must be put inside the green container with a description "*Poné las piezas acá adentro*" (Put the pieces here).

With the *program* created the button "*Probar*" (Try it) can be pressed, there is when the program is interpreted moving the number across the maze. Once the execution finish, if the number ends up in a valid position, the activity propose to go to the next activity (in the same or in the next level) otherwise the activity can be repeat it. If the activity is repeated, the number to be moved change.

It is important for the authors to emphasize that "Numeric Line" is a math activity not a programming activity. Using the blocks we are stimulating one of the aspect of the computational thinking: algorithm design. But this is not the main goal of the activity which is to reinforce math (natural numbers, integers and the order in the numeric line). All the activities generated with Códimo are designed around this main goal because we think that will make teachers to use them during classroom without needing to deviate from their plan.

We say that the students will "code to learn", due to the main goal is to reinforce a specific topic given by their teachers instead of doing a programming activity where on the other hand, we would call "learn to code".

3 "Numeric Line": Technical Description

Códimo is a web application written in Javascript only. It works in the latest versions of the major browsers and, since its development is open source, in addition to see the code, is possible to collaborate by reporting errors, proposing ideas, or even making modifications. The repository can be found at: https://github.com/lgraziani2712/codimo.

3.1   Technologies Used

To be able to develop Códimo was necessary a wide set of tools, both for improve the Development Experience and for assure a good component design. Here below are listed the more meaningful tools and their purpose during development.

Application dependencies

- **Blockly:** "A library for building visual programming editors" [4]. It allows to implement a programming interface using blocks.
- **PixiJS:** "The [...] 2D WebGL renderer" [6]. Its role is to be the 2D Graphic Engine for the activities, that is to say, every animation for the "Numeric Line" activity are developed with this tool.
- **React:** "A Javascript library for building user interfaces" [3]. Is used for the construction of the web page, with the capability of creating dynamic routes without the need of developing a server. It allowed to integrate PixiJS and Blockly without much effort.

In the following figure can be appreciated how was designed the architecture of Códimo:

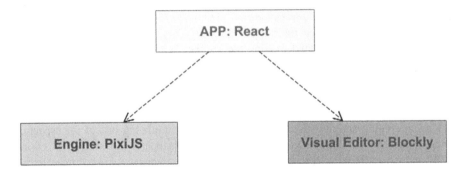

Fig. 2. Códimo architecture

As the Fig. 2 evidence, the architecture is integrated by three main components:

- **APP:** is responsible for manipulating the application URI's, as the load & unload of every dependency related to specific activities.
- **Engine:** is responsible for rendering the activity, parsing the sequence of instructions made by the student through the **Visual Editor**, and animating every single object according to the instructions that parse. Expose an interface used by the **APP**.
- **Visual Editor:** is responsible for listing every possible instruction for each activity, and offering a place for the student to create the solution using those instructions. Expose an interface used by the **APP**.

Each time the *APP* tries to load an activity, adds the *Engine* instance to the main renderer and request to generate the initial state of the activity. At the same time, adds the *Visual Editor*'s instance and request to create an editor with the necessary instructions for that specific activity.

The student always interacts with the *APP* and this delegates the tasks to the other two components.

Development Experience dependencies

- **Storybook:** "The UI Development Environment You'll ♥ to use" [8]. With this tool was possible to design and develop each visual component individually.
  To Códimo, a visual component not only refers to the text and buttons that go with the activities, but the *Engine* itself. Thus, was possible to design, for example, each animation of the number in an isolated manner.
- **Babel:** allows to transpile the latest versions of the Javascript language to code that can run in the latest versions of the major browsers. With this technology is possible to confirm that Códimo works at least with the latest two versions of Firefox, Chrome, Edge and Safari.
- **ESLint:** statically evaluates the Javascript code in search of syntax, structure and style errors.
- **FlowType:** "is a static type checker for Javascript" [2].
- **Jest:** is a testing framework for Javascript that innovates in certain aspects:
  - It analyses which files were modified since the last commit (when using a GIT repository) and executes by default only the tests related to those files.
  - When using the watcher option (useful while developing), is possible to filter tests from specific files, test names or by a regular expression.
  - **Snapshots:** it's a new way of testing data and raw components. It takes a variable and serialize its content into a file. Each time the test runs, it **diffs** the content of the file with the variable, and if there is a difference, the test fails and reports what was that difference. This is extremely useful when doing unit testing of HTML components since avoids validate each element specifically.
- **Webpack:** is a *module bundler*, a tool that allows to define which file types can be treated as modules. Webpack in particular can consider a wide range of file types (from images, json, css, videos) as a Javascript module, as long as it's configured to do that.
  Also offers a simple, and easy to configure, development server that watches for modifications and hot reload the changes by itself.
  The production version of Códimo, that asynchronous download the files requested by the selected activity and the specific exercise, is generated with Webpack.

Continuous Integration dependencies

- **CircleCI:** in Códimo is used for executing the battery of tests in an isolated environment, and reports if everything passes or not and which tests have failed. It runs every time anyone makes a commit, a Pull Request or a merge to the project.
- **Netlify:** adds a process of continuous deployment to the project. It runs every time anyone makes a commit, a Pull Request or a merge to the project. Also allows to see any version of the website at any time.

4 Related Work

There are various applications in the area that it intends to include Códimo. Some, like *CodeCombat* or *Pilas Engine*, are applications for play or create games or animations (respectively), in which is necessary to code to be able to make actions like moving a character to a specific place, picking an object, o to attack a creature. Another ones make the use of blocks, like *Alice*, *Scratch* or *Pilas Bloques* and others offers free access to educational resources in Computer Science and other disciplines like *Khan Academy*.

In addition to this applications, there is the *Hour of Code*, a global movement that offers a one-hour introductory activities to Computer Science, "designed to demystify "code", to show that anybody can learn the basics, and to broaden participation in the field of computer science" (The Hour of Code, 2017). The event takes place each year during Computer Science Education Week.

A really important element of this event is its repository of activities. Every person and organization can register an activity, among which are from Khan Academy, CodeCombat, Alice and Scratch.

The principal difference between the Hour of Code and Códimo, although subtle, it's significant: the first has as an objective "to show that anybody can learn the basics, and to broaden participation in the field of computer science", not the Computational Thinking per se. Of course, introducing into Programming also introduces into Computational Thinking, however isn't necessary the other way around. On the other hand, it would be highly possible to register an activity to the Hour of Code using Códimo since it was already used for the *Science and Technology Week*, in Argentina on September 2017.

Pilas Engine, on its part, is an Argentine application for develop video games and animations in 2D. Its main advantage is that each component and its methods are in Spanish, so it's possible to do things like this:

```
moneda = pilas.actores.Moneda()
```

However, it's not a Spanish pseudo language. The library *pilas* is written in Python, hence the code that anyone needs to write inevitable mixes English (when writing reserved words) with Spanish (when using the pilas engine library):

```
import pilasengine

class AceitunaEnemiga(pilasengine.actores.Aceituna)
def iniciar(self)
  self.imagen = "aceituna.png"
```

This adds an entry barrier for its use, since a K-12 student has low or zero knowledge of English (written and spoken), and since also doesn't know about programming, it will feel disoriented and it will lost interest quickly. Like CodeCombat, the fact that the student needs to explicitly write code makes this kind of applications unsuitable for introducing Computational Thinking.

Apart from that, exist more friendly applications for whom have their first contact with programming, like Alice: a platform for develop 3D video games and animations. Contains a battery of libraries with object models, characters and scenarios; allows to manipulate the light and camera; and to write a "script". This "script" is written using blocks visually similar to those of the puzzle, preventing to insert them in an unwanted manner. This way, by inserting the proposed blocks, and without explicitly knowing, the student generates an algorithm that it's translated into a game or an animation.

The main difference of Alice in comparison to CodeCombat is the use of blocks as a mechanism to write algorithms, which has a pedagogical fundament and advantage over the use of a programming language: a block always generates a syntactically well written algorithm, allowing students to focus only in understanding the semantic, in other words, the effect produced by the block over other elements. Also, by abstracting the use of the syntax, it allows a completely translation of every instruction.

However, as well as the other applications when compared to Códimo's activities, Alice lacks an essential element: it cannot be used outside the computer class. When Computational Thinking is discussed, is referenced the possibility to apply it in fields outside Computer Science, and it isn't possible to use Alice for that purpose.

As Alice, *Pilas Bloques* uses blocks as a mechanism for writing algorithms. Uses *Pilas Engine* as an engine, is web, and unlike Alice, who offers an empty scene as a canvas, Pilas Bloques presents a set of challenges.

Pilas Bloques is the more similar application to Códimo, since a challenge can represent a simple activity with a specific end: teach iteration, abstraction, modularization or conditionals. Anyway, it lacks of challenges that adapts activities from other disciplines.

5 Future Work

The authors will continue this job of introducing the computational thinking in the primary and secondary school with the following activities:

- Incorporate into the teaching process an evaluation. Applying FLOM [7] as the basis for activities design.
- Evolve Códimo to a framework, with clear extension points, in order to reduce the effort and time to create new activities. Any Javascript developer should be able to use Códimo to create activities.
- The computational thinking has several aspects, not only algorithm design, which was the one used in for activity. The abstraction, pattern recognition, the decomposition of a problem into multiple simple problems are others important aspects. It is our goal create more activities with this idea of "Code to learn" but applying also these other aspects of the computational thinking.

6 Conclusion

In this work we presented "Numeric Line", an activity implemented with Códimo. The goal of this activity is to introduce computational thinking in the primary school, in a way that result attractive for teachers and students. For the teachers because they don't need to deviate from their subjects and incorporating an activity with this characteristics gives them a new tool to motivate students to study. For the students, because they will acquire computation thinking skills while playing reinforcing concepts taught in classroom.

The main distinction from our proposal is the way in which we introduce computational skills. It is a transparent way. The goal is always to focus and work in the concepts related to the subjects from the curriculum, but to work in a different way with a new tool that encourage students to apply computational thinking.

References

1. Códimo. Donde el código, la imaginación y la motivación se encuentran (2017). https://codimo.netlify.com/. Accessed June 2017
2. Facebook. Flow is a static type checker for javascript (2017). https://flow.org/. Accessed June 2017
3. Facebook. React: A Javascript Library for Building User Interfaces (2017). https://facebook.github.io/react/. Accessed June 2017
4. Google. A library for building visual programming editors (2017). https://developers.google.com/blockly/. Accessed June 2017
5. Graziani, L., et al.: Códimo: Desarrollo del pensamiento computacional en las escuelas. In: II Jornadas Argentinas De Tecnología, Innovación y Creatividad 2016 - Workshop sobre Innovación en Centros Educativos y de Investigación (WICEI) (2016). http://jatic2016.ucaecemdp.edu.ar/trabajos/WICEI394TE-GrazianiJATIC2016.pdf. Accessed June 2017
6. PixiJS. The HTML5 Creation Engine (2017). http://www.pixijs.com/. Accessed June 2017
7. Sanchez, A.J., Perez-Lezama, C., Starostenko, O.: A formal specification for the collaborative development of learning objects. Procedia Soc. Behav. Sci. **182**, 726–731 (2015). http://www.sciencedirect.com/science/article/pii/S1877042815030955. Accessed June 2017
8. Storybook: The UI Development Environment You'll ♥ to use (2017). https://storybook.js.org/. Accessed June 2017
9. Wing, J.M.: Computational thinking. Commun. ACM **49**, 33–35 (2006). https://goo.gl/CHS4Yp. Accessed June 2017

AulasWeb Activity Selector: Using Virtual Characters as Companions to Educator Decisions

Alejandro Héctor González[1], Cristina Madoz[1], and Leandro Matías Romanut[2(✉)]

[1] School of Computer Science, Computer Science Research Institute LIDI (III-LIDI),
UNLP, La Plata, Argentina
{agonzalez,cmadoz}@lidi.info.unlp.edu.ar
[2] Department of Distance Education and Technologies, UNLP, La Plata, Argentina
leandro.romanut@presi.unlp.edu.ar

Abstract. This work originated as a research proposal for a graduate dissertation at the School of Computer Science of the UNLP. The product is currently being used in the AulasWeb virtual teaching and learning environment, which is based on Moodle. A virtual character is used in the activities and resources selector as a supplement to help educators include activities in virtual classrooms. The results obtained in experiences in real classes and the new modifications added to the character are also discussed.

Keywords: Virtual teaching and learning environments · Collaborative work
Virtual characters · b-learning

1 Introduction

Since 2004, the Department of Distance Education and Technologies (EADyT) of the Office of Academic Affairs of the National University of La Plata (UNLP) in Argentina has been organizing various training sessions aimed at educators in general, and university professors in particular who are interested in incorporating the concepts of distance education and use of digital technologies to their teaching practices. In different editions of these courses, it was observed that educators do not have significant experience in using virtual environments, and when they need to create and design classrooms, they find that there are a number of resources and activities they can use but they do not know exactly what the pedagogical objective of using them would be.

Different virtual teaching and learning environments were analyzed, such as Moodle (AulasWeb[1] and Qoodle[2]), Sakai[3], IDEAS[4], that are used at different universities, and their organization at the level of the system was reviewed, as well as the tools they offer for classroom creation and design. A more in-depth analysis of the collaborative tools offered by these environments was carried out, and the tools available in each of them

---

[1] https://aulasweb.ead.unlp.edu.ar/aulasweb/.
[2] https://acceso.uvq.edu.ar.
[3] https://sakaiproject.org/.
[4] https://ideas.info.unlp.edu.ar/login.

© Springer International Publishing AG, part of Springer Nature 2018
A. E. De Giusti (Ed.): CACIC 2017, CCIS 790, pp. 69–78, 2018.
https://doi.org/10.1007/978-3-319-75214-3_7

were also studied to determine if they are for individual or group use and the level of assistance each of them provides. This review of the assistance provided in each case for the tools offered, and taking these as starting point, resulted in a proposal to create the AulasWeb environment, used in EADyT, and a set of instructions that include potential pedagogical situations where collaborative work activities can be used. These instructions were created based on surveys distributed among experts in the use and coordination of virtual classrooms and on an analysis of the use collaborative work tools in virtual classrooms within AulasWeb. These instructions are accompanied by a virtual character that acts as a guide in the creation and design of virtual classrooms.

2   Theoretical Framework

Educational processes have incorporated an assortment of digital technologies that allow thinking and re-thinking teaching proposals. Among these, we can mentioned the so-called "virtual teaching and learning environments", for example, Moodle, Sakai, others with proprietary software such as WebCT or Blackboard; and so forth.

Virtual environment functionalities have evolved throughout the years and, since the arrival of Web 2.0, the possibilities for implementing online collaborative educational proposals have increased.

The addition of Information and Communication Technologies (ICTs) in education resulted in a number of changes and modifications in the way the educational processes in general are represented and carried out.

From a constructivistic standpoint, as Barriga puts it, "the classroom", rather than referring to a set of physical resources, is an interactive system in which a number of communicational transactions take place. This system creates a particular work environment for learning, determined by a set of organization and participation rules. This environment is called "learning environment" [1].

2.1   Educational Methodologies

Educational methodologies are related to the environment in which the teaching and learning processes occur. They define the use of media and educational resources, and they determine the actions that are carried out by the agents in the process – students, trainers, coordinators [2].

Bates explains that the educational methodology can change based on the amount of e-learning involved in the process. In on-site education, students share the same physical space at the same time, and learning occurs in a synchronous manner in the same place. This type of education is the one that has evolved the most given the history of education itself.

"E-learning is a convenient term to cover a wide range of uses of technology in teaching and learning. This includes both administrative and academic uses of information and communication technologies that support learning" [3].

As the use of e-learning increases in the different educational methodologies, two new terms are coined: b-learning and distributed learning.

González defines b-learning (hybrid or combined learning) as a methodology that combines on-site teaching with distance teaching, so that both learning experiences are essential to successfully achieve the learning goals [4, 5].

By fully involving e-learning, distance learning is referenced, since it involves different types of communication.

Some authors define distance education as follows:

"Distance teaching is a two-way (multi-way) technological communication system, which can be a mass communication system, based on the systematic and joint action of didactic resources and the support of an organization and tutoring, which, physically away from the students, help them achieve independent (cooperative) learning" [6].

"Distance education is planned learning that normally occurs at a place other than where teaching is carried out, and it therefore requires special course design, instruction and communication techniques, be it through electronic media or other type of technology, as well as special organization" [7].

Similarly, Mena, Diez and Rodríguez describe distance education as an educational methodology that, acting most of the time as intermediary in the pedagogical relationship between educators and learners using different media and strategies, allows establishing a particular type of institutional presence beyond the traditional geographical and populational coverage, which helps overcome time- and space-related issues [8].

Based on these definitions, distance education can nowadays be conceived as an educational process that establishes a pedagogical relationship between educators and students through different resources and strategies, the process being mediated by technologies. Teaching and learning environments support communication and exchange.

2.2 Collaborative Learning

Collaborative learning is a process in which students typically are in charge of designing the interaction structure and keeping control over the various decisions that affect their learning.

"Collaborative learning is acquiring skills and attitudes as a result of group interaction" [9].

Gros (2000) adds that, in a collaborative process, the parts commit to learning something together. What is to be learned can only be achieved if group work is done collaboratively. The decision as to how to perform the task, what procedures to adopt, how to split the work, the tasks that need to be carried out is made by the group. Communications and negotiation are key in this process [10].

2.3 Collaborative Writing

Storch explains that the possibilities offered by group or pair work in relation to writing were limited either to the process of brainstorming or to the final review process (peer review). She highlights that some research works have shown that the peer review process was beneficial for participants in relation to their ability to consider other positions and for the development of both writing and analytical and critical abilities. However, the author also argues that the tendency to drive and study collaborative writing just as a review process among peers is deficient because it focuses on the product and disregards the writing process [11].

In the collaborative writing process, students should participate throughout the production process and share the responsibility for the structure, contents, and language aspects of a text. The advantages of co-authorship, rather than peer review, revolve around aspects such as the following:

- Reflexive thinking is favored (especially if participants use mechanisms to defend or better explain their ideas);
- Participants can go beyond spelling or grammar and tackle questions pertaining to discourse; and,
- It may positively affect the knowledge that participants acquire about the language.

3   Virtual Teaching and Learning Environments

A Learning Management System (LMS) is an online software application that allows managing, distributing, monitoring, assessing and supporting various activities that were previously designed and programmed as part of a fully virtual training process (e-learning) or a partially on-site training process (b-learning), explains Cañellas Mayor [12].

3.1   Analysis of Virtual Teaching and Learning Environments

Some of the teaching and learning virtual environments that are used to study collaborative work activities are developed by free software communities, such as Moodle and Sakai, and some other are spaces developed by educational entities: Qoodle (National University of Quilmes, Argentina), AulasWeb (Presidency, National University of La Plata), and IDEAS (School of Computer Science, National University of La Plata).

For each of the environments selected, the following was analyzed: their origin, their organization on the level of the system, available user roles, tools offered for creating and designing classrooms, availability of external tools in addition to those included natively.

Then, the collaborative tools provided by each environment were analyzed.

For example, the Database activity is typical of Moodle, but it is not present in Sakai or IDEAS. The forum is an activity that is provided by all environments, but with varying features. In Moodle, there are different types: General Use, Questions and Answers, Each Individual Proposes a Topic, Blog, and Simple Discussion. In Sakai, there are no types, contributions can be moderated before they become visible, a topic is needed to start the forum or it will not be visible. Wiki activity is available in Moodle and Sakai – the former allows creating Wikis either collaboratively or individually, and it supports several formats (HTML, Creole, NWiki), while the latter does not have any remarkable feature. This resource is not available in IDEAS.

3.2   Collaborative Work and Virtual Teaching and Learning Environments

When the concept of collaborative learning is used in a virtual environment, the concept remains the same, but the conditions, and therefore the possibilities for using it, change drastically. A virtual environment offers tools that allow educators proposing and designing innovative activities to promote collaboration, communication and the production of knowledge, which increases the opportunities to learn and work as a team that are limited in on-site activities [13].

Barriga and Morales picked a selection of digital tools that allow collaborative learning in virtual environments [14]:

- Chat
- Blog
- Wiki
- Forum
- Breakout rooms
- Message board
- Online conferences
- Shared board
- E-mail

4   Development Context and Rationale

The graduate dissertation is part of the research project "*Technologies for Distributed Software Systems. Quality in Systems and Processes. ICT-mediated Educational Scenarios*", of the Computer Science Research Institute LIDI (III-LIDI) of the National University of La Plata, Argentina. It is considered for carrying out the training experience for educators held at the Department of Distance Education and Technologies of the UNLP. For a while now, there has been a lack of activities oriented to collaborative work in the proposals for courses using the tools provided by the AulasWeb environment (owned by the Department of Distance Education and Technologies and based on Moodle).

To analyze collaborative work tools available in virtual teaching and learning environments in more detail, an anonymous survey was conducted. This survey included open questions to collect as much information as possible. These surveys were distributed among educators and coordinators of virtual classrooms of the National University of La Plata, and they were aimed at obtaining information about their work with environments from the perspective of not only usability, but also as educators (interacting with students and materials) and accompanying different educational proposals of various educational levels (pre-graduate, graduate, post-graduate, extension). These surveys (54 in total) show that not everyone uses collaborative work tools and, in general, the tools that are most commonly used are forums and tasks.

Educator surveys helped design and develop brief instructions that identify some pedagogical and didactic situations where collaborative work tools can be used.

To analyze the answers provided by survey responders, the presence of collaborative tools in courses of the AulasWeb environment was reviewed. From the surveys completed by educators and classroom coordinators and the analysis made of collaborative activity use in courses, it can be assumed that educators face various issues when using collaborative work tools.

- Some of the collaborative work activities have a certain degree of complexity as regards configuration, which causes educators to avoid using them.
- Typically, educators do not try to make course activities more dynamic by including collaborative tasks. In general, they work with texts (file-type resources in AulasWeb), and the classroom becomes a "static" place where students download the document and work on the activity. This occurs for no real reason, both in extension classrooms and as in distance proposals.
- Educators are willing to work with collaborative activities, but they do not redesign or reformulate their educational practices, i.e., they do not tailor them to use such collaborative activities.

5   Tool Developed

With the purpose of developing a flexible tool that can be easily incorporated to any Moodle environment, we decided to change the code to allow the addition of a virtual character that collaborates in the selection of Moodle activities and resources.

Moodle's activity selector was used as starting point. On this selector's interface, the educator can see a list with all the activities and resources available in Moodle for addition to the classrooms. When one of these activities or resources is selected, a description of the tool is shown on the interface. From this selector, three functionalities branch out:

- Organizing the activities selector in three sections:
  - **Collaborative Work Activities** (Database, Chat, Forum, Glossary, Workshop, Task, Wiki, and other external tools such as VPL and BigBlueButton).
  - **Other Activities** (Query, Questionnaire, External Tool, Lesson, SCORM Package).
  - **Resources** (File, Folder, Label, Book, Page, URL).
- For each collaborative work activity, offering pedagogical help in relation to the educational situations in which the resource could be used.
- Offering an assistant that allows playing an audio file of the contents of the Help and seeing a practical example showing how to use the activity selected.

To continue our work on this tool, pedagogical instructions were added for each activity (Query, Questionnaire, External Tool, Lesson, SCORM Package) and resource (File, Folder, Label, Book, Page, URL) in the AulasWeb environment, which is based on Moodle. The virtual assistant was also included, with its already-developed functionalities: instruction playback and showing an example of the selected activity/ resource.

5.1   Virtual Character

A virtual character was created using the Pocoyize[5] application available at the "Pocoyó" website, which allows creating caricature avatars and download them free of charge (Fig. 1).

Fig. 1.   Manu, our technology tutor

The addition of a character is an attempt to generating a strategy that can guide educators in understanding collaborative work activities.

In this case, we decided to work with a character that fills the role of a technology tutor that accompanies students while they learn and helps them understand and use the technologies involved in the virtual classroom.

Characters are created based on a set of "personal features", in addition to a scenario, a history and one or more objectives. According to Rib Davis, the ingredients needed to build a character are those that result from an individual and that make each person different from the rest. Even though Rib describes how to create characters for theater, cinema and literature, the elements used for creating these can be adapted to the creation of virtual characters [15, 16].

In order to create a character, three aspects have to be considered:

1. How is the character when it is born (due to genetics and its environment)?
2. How does the character change and evolve through learning and experience?
3. How is the character now?

6   First Experience

The modified version of the activities selector that we developed was installed and used in the server where the AulasWeb environment (based on Moodle) of the Department of Distance Education and Technologies of the UNLP resides.

The Assistant was pilot-tested in the course "Introduction to the Use of Moodle-Supported Virtual Environments of the UNLP (AulasWeb – Cavila – External Courses)". The objective of the course is to help educators become familiar with basic concepts that will allow them implementing their courses and get closer to the basic edition of the virtual classroom tools offered by Moodle. The course was a b-learning course, it had a duration of 5 weeks with two 150-minute, on-site meetings that were organized as workshops using the tools available in Moodle. The course was carried out

---

[5] http://www.pocoyo.com/pocoyizador.

in 2015. The participants were 18 educators from the various academic units of the UNLP.

The course proposes the creation and design of a virtual classroom using as reference the educational proposal of the subject to which course participants belong. Students had to read help documentation and guidelines designed for the collaborative work activities, as well as use the Assistant to watch some use examples for the tools.

A survey was carried out, designed as an online form created with Google Drive, aimed at establishing the acceptance level of the prototype in the AulasWeb environment and receiving feedback, suggestions and ideas for improvement that can potentially be added to our development. Two of the questions in that survey stand out:

The first question, *Did you use the available instruction documents as help to design educational practices that involve collaborative work activities?* was answered affirmatively by all participants. This indicates that they used the help offered by the tool to plan and understand the use of the tool from a more pedagogical perspective rather than focusing just on the technological aspects.

The second question, *What is your opinion in relation to available instructions?*, follow-up question for the first question, showed several opinions, which were processed and grouped as percentages, including the verbatim comments of the educators:

- Fifty per cent said: *"They are useful and clear."*
- Twenty-five per cent said: *"They are very helpful, especially when you start working with the platform for the first time."*
- Twelve per cent said: *The information in the instructions is very good; it gives a general idea about each tool and examples to use it."*
- Thirteen per cent said: *"They are a good support tool for those of us who are not entirely familiar with the system."*

7   Conclusions

Different Virtual Teaching and Learning Environments were reviewed. The different LMSs used, both at the National University of La Plata and other universities, such as Sakai and Qoodle, were also analyzed. The comparative review of tools in general and collaborative work tools in particular allowed creating appropriate sets of instructions for the character, taking into account the strengths and weaknesses of use instructions for each of the tools.

A tool that helps create, design, use and include collaborative activities in the educational proposals that educators implement for their courses was developed.

The first experience with the tool shows good results, both in relation to understanding collaborative work activities from a pedagogical perspective, as well as from a technological point of view. Educators were in favor of having contextual help available, and they liked that this help included pedagogical indications.

The examples provided by the Assistant are considered to be useful and clear, which matches the assumption we had in relation to the type of information offered by Moodle's help manual. They allow understanding and interpreting the help text and using the examples for designing educational proposals.

The inclusion of a virtual assistant with a script involves going through a creative process that allows using various elements linked to multimedia, ranging from introducing the character, its background story and personality, to the procedures used for assisting in the use of collaborative activities. The addition of the audio channel was well received by educators, and it is a first attempt at improving accessibility for differently-abled individuals.

A technological and pedagogical contribution was made to the Department of Distance Education and Technologies of the UNLP by adding the Assistant to the LMSs that are currently used: AulasWeb, CAVILA - UNLP and External Courses, all of them based on Moodle.

8 Future Work

The following improvements are planned for future implementation on the tool that was developed:

- Distributing new surveys to assess impact on the teaching community and receiving feedback for improving the help and didactic suggestions available for each tool.
- Adding new features to customize the assistant in relation to image based on educator preferences: changing its clothes, skin color, hair color and style, eyes, mouth, body, voice.
- Adding new functions to Manu the Assistant:
  - Providing a FAQs space with automated answers.
  - Suggesting a list of external tools that can be included (embedded) within the AulasWeb environment. This list would consist of a brief description, a tutorial on use, and the link to the application web page. For instance, building online presentations (Prezi), designing interactive videos (Moovly), creating collages (Fotor - BeFunky), organizing time lines (Capzles), elaborating computer graphics (RAW), building label clouds (Tagxedo - Word it Out), developing collaborative walls (Padlet), building interactive images (Thinglink), etc.

References

1. Barriga, F.D.: Educación y nuevas tecnologías de la información y la comunicación: Hacia un paradigma educativo innovador (2008)
2. Jiménez, D.: Nuevos paradigmas educativos y modalidades educativas (2010). http://es.slideshare.net/auri_desi/modalidades-educativas-5551315
3. Bates, A.T.: Technology, E-Learning and Distance Education. Routledge, London (2005)
4. González, A.H.: Educación a Distancia y Tecnologías Digitales en la Enseñanza Universitaria (2015). https://prezi.com/v-vkyghu8zsc/2015-especializacion-en-docencia-universitaria-unlp/?utm_campaign=share&utm_medium=copy
5. González, C.: Cuadro comparativo: Blended learning, Distributed Learning, Online Learning (2012). http://es.calameo.com/read/001790350da562655eaed
6. García Aretio, L.: La Educación a Distancia. De la teoría a la práctica. Ariel editorial S.A. (2001)

7. Moore, M., Kearsley, G.: Distance Education: A Systems View. Wadsworth Publishing, Boston (1996)
8. Mena, M., Diez, L.M., Rodríguez, L.: El Diseño de proyectos de Educación a distancia. Colección Itinerarios. Ediciones La Crujía y Editorial Stella, Buenos Aires (2005)
9. Salinas, J.: El aprendizaje colaborativo con los nuevos canales de comunicación. In: Cabero, J. (ed.) Nuevas Tecnologías Aplicadas a la Educación, pp. 199–227. Síntesis, Madrid (2000)
10. Gros, B.: El Aprendizaje Colaborativo a través de la red: límites y posibilidades. In: Aula de Innovación Educativa, pp. 44–50 (2000). ISSN 1131-995X, N° 162 (2007)
11. Storch, N.: Collaborative writing: products, process, and students reflections. J. Second Lang. Writ. **14**, 153–173 (2005)
12. Cañellas Mayor, A.: LMS y LCMS: funcionalidades y beneficios (2014). http://www.centrocp.com/lms-y-lcms-funcionalidades-y-beneficios/
13. Harasim, L., Hiltz, S.R., Turoff, M., Teles, L.: Redes de aprendizaje. Guía para la enseñanza y el aprendizaje en red. Gedisa, Barcelona (2000)
14. Barriga, F.D., Morales, R.: Aprendizaje colaborativo en entornos virtuales: un modelo de diseño instruccional para la formación profesional continua. Rev. de Tecnol. y Comun. Educ., 4–25 (2009). México, ILCE, Año 22-23, No. 47-48
15. Rib, D.: Escribir guiones: desarrollo de personajes. Editorial Paidós, manuales de escritura, Barcelona, Spain (2004)
16. González, A.H.: TICs en el proceso de articulación entre la Escuela Media y la Universidad. Tesis de Maestría, Facultad de Informática, UNLP (2008)

Displaying the Collaborative Process as Meta-knowledge

Description of a Mirroring Strategy and Its Results

María Alejandra Zangara[1(✉)] and Cecilia Sanz[1,2]

[1] School of Computer Science, Computer Science Research Institute LIDI (III-LIDI), National University of La Plata, La Plata, Argentina
{azangara,csanz}@lidi.info.unlp.edu.ar
[2] Scientific Research Agency of the Province of Buenos Aires (CICPBA), Buenos Aires, Argentina

Abstract. There is consensus as regards the fact that group strategies and group building processes are a significant aspect of knowledge for those who work collaboratively. The decision as to which indicators educators select and display when accompanying collaborative groups is a strategic one. Likewise, the point in time when the group can access information about their collaboration – after the process is completed or during the process – is also important. In this article, we propose and discuss a collaborative work monitoring strategy that is implemented as a mirroring technique which has been tested in a post-graduate educational experience in 2016. Preliminary results would confirm the idea that the group benefits from knowing how the collaborative process is progressing and would also indicate that there is a greater awareness in each team member in relation to his/her own task and those of their peers.

Keywords: Collaborative work indicators · Collaborative work monitoring
Mirroring strategy · Meta-knowledge · Collaborative work

1 What, When and How to Display Collaboration

There is agreement as to the importance of group work and performance awareness by all participants in the group [1–4]. In [5], the authors describe three types of information that can be considered to be essential for collaborative learning:

- Public information about what group members effectively do, also mentioned in [6];
- Cognitive information about background knowledge and/or self-regulation abilities for learning in each member (also acknowledged in [7, 8]; and
- Social information about group dynamics, as perceived by collaborators [9].

In [10], there is an interesting analysis about the importance of the decisions and experiences of others for every individual in their everyday lives. This article mentions that the idea of computer systems supporting these activities was introduced as early as 1999, and that computer systems can be used to help these activities gain visibility and understand these relations. The concept of social translucence is thus introduced as a feature of computer systems that can facilitate communication, showing simple

© Springer International Publishing AG, part of Springer Nature 2018
A. E. De Giusti (Ed.): CACIC 2017, CCIS 790, pp. 79–89, 2018.
https://doi.org/10.1007/978-3-319-75214-3_8

quantitative aspects of user participation in a shared task. This approach is based on three features, also discussed in [10]. The first of these, visibility, refers to the idea that users can have access to social information that is presented as figures or charts. The second feature, awareness, considers the impact of the information of the activities being carried out by others on the activity carried out by each member and coexistence and collective work rules. Finally, the feature of responsibility refers to individual self-regulation processes that can occur as a result of user awareness about their own actions or the actions of the other members of the group. These pioneer ideas were continued by various authors to build work group performance visibility systems used for small groups, social groups and even networks.

As regards small groups, the work presented in [11], where [3, 12] are quoted, and where the concept of mirroring is further discussed, is relevant for our work. The authors define mirroring as "systems that reflect, or mirror, group interactions" (p. 119). These systems show interaction indicators that should be defined based on the type of work to be carried out and the composition of the group. There are other works, such as [13], that not only offer a description of the interaction events, but also present them based on predefined indicators and by comparison with expected standards. These indicators represent the status of the interaction, together with a set of expected or desirable values and parameters. There are different possible visualization types: bar charts, pie charts, map of forum topics (indicating task and topic dispersion) and even collective development of conceptual maps [4]. Based on the hypothesis of Dimitracopoulou [13], and in agreement with the publications mentioned above, this information could favor both group work itself as well as the work carried out by the coordinators that monitor and guide the group. Visualization structures, with appropriate representations, can help students with their meta-cognitive development, as well as help regulate the collaborative activity. Each tool that is used for the group task involves making decisions as regards the information or indicator that is shown, and how and when it is shown. The possibility of showing performance and progress information is closely linked to the situation of collaborative work, be it on-site or distance work, as well as with time management – synchronous or asynchronous. Once the group started its collaborative work, identifying specific points in time within the activity to show progress is a complex task. In the literature, indicators are most commonly displayed ex post facto, i.e., after the group work is completed. However, tools can and should define time windows (as Manuel Castells describes in [14]) for (abstract) breaks during work to see where it is going and how that relates to what was expected.

This article is organized as follows: Sect. 2, presents some background on collaboration monitoring tools, Sect. 3 describes the mirroring strategy proposed and its application, Sect. 4 discusses the results obtained, and Sect. 5 presents our conclusions.

2 Collaborative Work Visualization Tools

In this section, some tools used for monitoring collaborative work are classified and described to show how they support this activity, which indicators they show, and how visualization takes place. This background information has been used for the mirroring proposal described in the next section. Tools have been grouped in the following three categories:

- Mirroring Tools: this category includes tools that automatically mirror the activity of the members of the work group. These are graphical representations of the actions of each group member in each tool.
- Metacognitive Tools: this category includes the previous one (mirroring) and it also shows information about any deviations in the development of indicators from what was expected. Some examples could include marked heterogeneity in participation by group members, spread topics, etc.
- Guiding Systems: this category includes both previous ones and adds a space for educator guidance and intervention.

2.1 Big Five

These are visualization tools that match the Big Five groups theory. In [15], a set of visualization tools specific for collaborative work in computer environments is presented, all of them linked to the theoretical framework discussed by Bandura [16] as part of the social cognitive theory (SCT). This framework identifies the five abilities (big five) that define group work: 1. symbolization ability; 2. prefiguration and planning ability; 3. learning through observation; 4. self-regulation; 5. self-reflection. As an example of metacognitive tools, the Activity Radar can be mentioned, which is a circle that represents the participation range of each group member based on a standard refer-ence. This standard reference can be the average for the group in the past, a predefined standard or the activity of a group member. This standard is represented as the center point in the circle (see Fig. 1A).

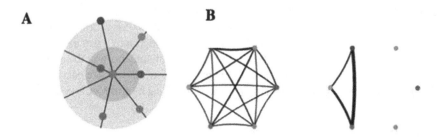

Fig. 1. A. Participation radar, according to Big Five. B. Interaction networks in two tools with different density and relations (taken from [15])

Another representation is based on Social Media Analysis (SMA). It quantifies the relations between players to create graphical networks that represent these relations as a whole. Networks have three basic components: players, boundaries, and relations. Players are represented by dots and relations are represented by lines joining them (Fig. 1B).

2.2   Drew. Dialogical Reasoning Educational Web Tool

According to [12], this is a web tool that shows a graphic representation of the topic map that is generated in an argumentative analysis system. It is developed as part of the SCALE Project of the European Community, which focuses on collaborative learning for argumentation using Internet in secondary schools. Its tools are designed to help students develop, refine and expand their argumentative knowledge in a given field. The educator has a specific role in the software that allows viewing what is going on and adding tasks and participants. For this reason, this tool is considered to belong to the Guiding Systems category.

2.3   iBee. Bulletin Board Enrollee Envisioner

Created and presented by [28], iBee is a software application that follows the bulletin board model and that works as a plug-in in a virtual teaching and learning environment. Its main features include: 1. Visualization in real time of the relation between key words and students; 2. Visualization of a conversation trajectory in a given period; 3. Visualization of student's most recent participation levels and key word use frequency; and 4. Message placement based on key words, represented through the flowers and bees metaphor, so that students can simply click to access them. iBee can be considered as a mirroring tool within the categories described above.

3   Implemented Mirroring Strategy

In this section, the mirroring visualization strategy that was designed and implemented to carry out a collaborative activity in a post-graduate course at the School of Computer Science of the UNLP is described. The course in question was "Distance Education," part of the Master in Information Technology Applied to Education. Cohort 2016 included 11 students. For this task, participants were divided into 2 groups: one with 5 members and another one with 6. The reduced number of students and the existence of only two work groups favored the development of this strategy, since each individual and group activity has to be thoroughly reviewed using each of the tools selected.

3.1   Description of the Mirroring Strategy

The eighth class in this course consists of a collaborative writing e-activity, where participants receive, as a first stage, an individual assignment (unknown to their classmates). In a second stage, they are asked to use their individual productions developed based on their individual assignments and collaboratively create a book. They have 6 weeks to work on this task, and it was during this period that the mirroring visualization strategy described below was carried out. The first activity consisted in telling the participants about the implementation of this strategy, describing the type of work that this would involve and emphasizing the use of the tools that had been made available to the groups to be able to carry out on-line monitoring tasks. Together with this initial information, a document detailing the map of indicators on which monitoring tasks would focus and a schedule for information presentation, based on the collaborative work stages considered in the assignment, was also distributed. The indicators selected to carry out the mirroring strategy can be divided into individual indicators and group indicators (see Table 1). Individual indicators consider, from a quantitative standpoint, the number of messages exchanged with other group members in each stage of the assignment and the number of messages in each of the tools being used. From a qualitative point of view, messages were classified based on their contents in: organization-oriented messages, group emotional/motivational management messages, and messages dealing with task-specific issues. The group indicators analyzed were linked to the concept of interdependence, and the creation of topic maps following [4] was also considered.

Table 1. Mirroring individual and group work indicators

Dimensions/ Indicator Categories	Indicators
DIMENSION: INDIVIDUAL CONTRIBUTION BY EACH MEMBER	

Contribution by each member to collaborative work	Quantitative analysis
	  • Number of messages exchanged with peers in each stage of the assignment.
	  • Number of messages in each tool
	Qualitative analysis
	  • Types of messages based on categories
	    - Organization
	    - Contents
	    - Emotion

DIMENSION: COLLABORATIVE WORK ITSELF	
Interdependence (Group Concept)	Topic conceptual map Topics and duration

To keep track of collaborative work process information, a GoogleSites site was used, since students were already familiar with it and mirroring information was easy to access.

When developing this type of strategies, defining how information is going to be viewed is of the utmost importance. In this case, the information presentation formats used were the following, depending on the indicators: bar chart showing message number and quality by type of message (contents, organization, emotions) for each member of the group, and a map of topics detailing duration, in weeks, for each topic. Each topic was identified with a color and, for each topic, the individuals that worked on it are identified (with their initials). On the other hand, a graph as the one shown in Fig. 2, showing the relation between topics and group members, was used. This graphic representation facilitates the analysis of participations and exchanges. For this proposal, graphs were built based on the following rules: (a) they have nodes: participants and topics; (b) the nodes corresponding to individuals are labeled with the initials of that individual, while topic nodes are labeled with the name of the topic; (c) all nodes are represented with color circles; (d) the lines linking each individual to a topic indicate that the former is related to the latter; (e) the size of the nodes increases as the number of incoming or outgoing lines increases, and (g) the thickness of the lines increases as the participation of an individual in a topic increases. Thus, the distance between the topic map and each group member can be seen, as well as the level of participation of each member.

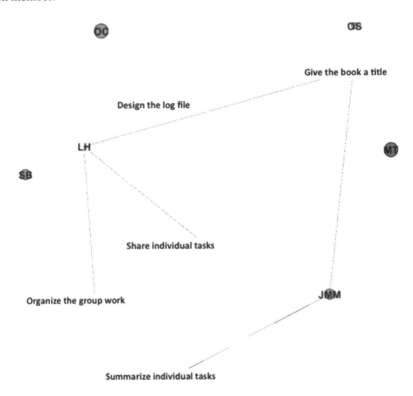

Fig. 2. Graph showing relations in mirroring information.

3.2 Impact of the Mirroring Strategy in Collaborative Work

In the week immediately following information publication weeks, a private individual inquiry instrument was responded by all group members to obtain feedback on their experience with collaborative work and the impact of the mirroring strategy. The instrument included 5 sections: 1. Personal data, 2. Individual work, 3. Use of tools, 4. Group work, and 5. Impact of the mirroring strategy. In this article, we focus on the feedback received in Sect. 5 of the instrument, which was aimed at obtaining the following information: information visualization frequency, information usefulness, attention to individual and/or group indicators, attention to the information of their own group versus that of the other group, information usefulness based on format, decisions that were changed based on the mirroring information obtained, and general opinion on how this strategy affected group work.

4   Results Obtained in the Mirroring Experience

In this section, the most significant results obtained through the inquiry described in the previous section, administered through an on-line survey, are discussed.

As regards the visualization frequency with which the information in GoogleDocs was referenced, the following questions were asked: How many times did you visit the information site for the collaborative process? Answer options established a frequency ranging from 1 to 5, 1 being Never and 5 being Daily. Figure 3 shows the results, which indicate that **30% of the students accessed the information daily, while 44% of them indicated a frequency between 3 and 4 on the scale**. They were also asked about their reasons to access the information. Below are some of the answers received: *"I was curious about the type of information that was being considered," "I was interested in knowing how information was presented and the data that were displayed about the participation of other group members,"* and *"I thought it was important to know if what happened as part of our collaborative work was present in the system."*

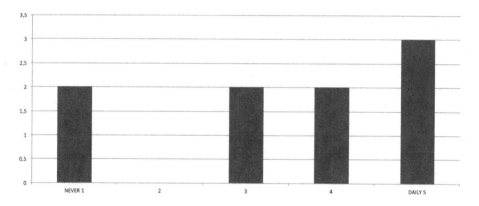

Fig. 3. Mirroring information site access frequency

The issue of **information type and format was of interest**, since the indicators that had been selected were at play and their potential to understand, communicate and even improve collaborative work. The corresponding question was: "What type of information did you find most useful?" Answer options listed all formats that had been used to present monitoring information: text, numerical values, data tables, bar charts, group work graphs, images, etc. The answers obtained are presented in Fig. 4.

More than one answer could be indicated in this item, since information types were no exclusive. Starting by the information that was selected by most participants (4 individuals), **activity presentation graphs, both individual and for the group should be mentioned**. In second place, participants selected **bar charts showing individual performance**: number of messages by category. Before adding these charts, the data tables used to generate them were presented. This information was also valued by students. Finally, the use of **text as integration, explanation and contextualization element was found valuable** as well. As regards as the reasons for selecting different visualization types, the following were given: *"Charts represent data in a clear and*

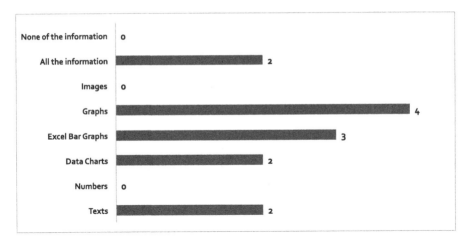

Fig. 4. Access to information by format

accurate manner," "Personally, I prefer to analyze charts rather than numbers," "I prefer graphs because I can see the connection between members and actions and types of messages." Data tables were also mentioned: *"I found the individual breakdown of participations and the data table and its subdivisions to be useful to me."* Both the text and the integration of different types of information in the site were valued as well: *"All reports were read carefully. Charts, tables and graphs were easier to interpret, but a textual description is always useful to have"* and *"Every element enriched process statistics in its own way and complemented the other elements."*

To point to the initial hypothesis, the following was asked: *What decisions were changed as a result of the information presented in the site? (options are divided in three aspects: emotion, contents, organization).* The answers obtained are presented in Fig. 5.

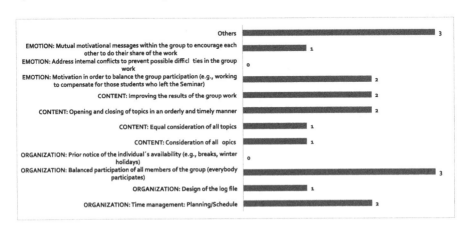

Fig. 5. Decisions made based on the mirroring strategy

To point to the initial hypothesis, the following was asked: **What decisions were changed as a result of the information presented in the site?** (options are divided in three aspects: emotion, contents, organization). The answers obtained are presented in Fig. 5.

Figure 5 shows that **organization decisions** were affected the most by knowledge obtained through the mirroring strategy. Within organization decisions, two key components can be identified: time management and balanced participation of all group members. As regards member participation, it could be tracked through the site using the individual information component. As regards **content decisions**, all of them were identified as having been affected by this strategy. **Emotion-related decisions** affected by information obtained through the mirroring strategy were motivation-related: knowing what each participant had done on the individual and group levels helped create messages aimed at achieving higher involvement and level of activity from everyone. As regards organization-related issues, students mentioned the following: *"I think the main goal was to organize member time management to finish as soon as possible with individual responsibilities. It allowed us to organize taking into account the time we had in order to be able to finish the task within the expected time. We also had to take into account the creation of a summary for the topic assigned to a member that dropped the course." "It was also useful to reinforce meta-knowledge about individual performance: Seeing the data made me realize that at points my contribution had been really low".*

5 Conclusions

The governing idea behind this work is the importance of information in a collaborative work process as a metacognitive component of performance, both individual and collective. Knowing how each individual and their peers work is seen as a valuable contribution, both to the process as well as to the result of group work. This knowledge of metacognitive nature is important both for group members as well as for the coordinator, whose job is to guide students and intervene if required. In this article, a mirroring strategy that was designed and implemented with a group of post-graduate students as metacognitive experimentation space was described. The results obtained support the idea presented in [13] as regards the visibility, awareness and responsibility that having this information about their own performance promotes among the members of a group. Among the findings of our experience, the following can be mentioned: (a) the number of organization-related messages changed; as soon as message type-related data were included in the mirroring site, the group started communicating in terms of task planning and organization; (b) most participants monitored the information shown on the site about their individual tasks, and each of them made sure that the site showed accurate information about what they had done. They even sent private messages explaining why they had not been able to carry out a specific task. From this visualization, it was observed that group members monitored what they did (and what they did not do) individually, and what their peers (from both groups) produced during the 6-week period assigned for this task. In this sense, we believe that the implemented strategy is relevant, since it confirms several of the hypotheses reviewed as background information. It also opens up new study paths, since it presents new findings about the types of visualization that affected the process the most. In the future, we will continue to carry out experiences to increase the number of participants and thus produce more conclusive results.

Acknowledgments. Special thanks to the REFORTICCA (Resources for Empowering ICT, Science, and Environment Educators) project, funded by the Scientific Research Agency of the Province of Buenos Aires (CICPBA), which will allow promoting this experience among other educators and students in the Province of Buenos Aires, Argentina.

References

1. Avouris, N., Komis, V., Margaritis, M., Fidas, C.: ModellingSpace: a tool for synchronous collaborative problem solving. In: Proceedings of International Conference on Educational Multimedia & Telecommunications, pp. 381–386 (2004)
2. Avouris, N., Margaritis, M., Komis, V.: Modelling interaction during small-group synchronous problem-solving activities: the Synergo approach. In: Proceedings of ITS 2004 Workshop on Designing Computational Models of Collaborative Learning Interaction, pp. 13–18 (2004)
3. Jermann, P., Soller, A., Muehlenbrock, M.: From mirroring to guiding: a review of the state of art technology for supporting collaborative learning. In: European Conference on Computer-Supported Collaborative Learning EuroCSCL 2001, pp. 324–331 (2001)
4. Martínez Maldonado, R.: Analysing, visualising and supporting collaborative learning using interactive tabletops. Doctoral dissertation, The University of Sydney, Australia (2014)
5. Bodemer, D., Dehler, J.: Group awareness in CSCL environments. Comput. Hum. Behav. **27**(3), 1043–1045 (2011)
6. Janssen, J., Erkens, G., Kirschner, P.A.: Group awareness tools: it's what you do with it that matters. Comput. Hum. Behav. **27**(3), 1046–1058 (2011)
7. Dehler, J., Bodemer, D., Buder, J., Hesse, F.W.: Guiding knowledge communication in CSCL via group knowledge awareness. Comput. Hum. Behav. **27**(3), 1068–1078 (2011)
8. Sangin, M., Molinari, G., Nüssli, M.A., Dillenbourg, P.: Facilitating peer knowledge modeling: effects of a knowledge awareness tool on collaborative learning outcomes and processes. Comput. Hum. Behav. **27**(3), 1059–1067 (2011)
9. Phielix, C., Prins, F.J., Kirschner, P.A.: Awareness of group performance in a CSCL-environment: effects of peer feedback and reflection. Comput. Hum. Behav. **26**(2), 151–161 (2010)
10. Erickson, T., Kellogg, W.: Social translucence: an approach to designing systems that support social processes. ACM Trans. Comput. Hum. Interact. (TOCHI) **7**(1), 59–83 (2000). Special issue on human-computer interaction in the new millennium, Part 1
11. Dimitracopoulou, A.: Designing collaborative learning systems: current trends & future research agenda. In: Proceedings of the 2005 Conference on Computer Support for Collaborative Learning: Learning 2005: The Next 10 Years!, pp. 115–124. International Society of the Learning Sciences (2005)
12. Serpaggi, X., Baker, M., Quignard, M., Lund, K., Séjourné, A., Corbel, A., Jaillon, P.: DREW: un outil internet pour créer des situations d'apprentissage coopérant. In: Desmoulins, C., Marquet, M., Bouhineau, D. (eds.) EIAH 2003 Environnements Informatiques Pour l'Apprentissage Humain, Actes de la Conférence EIAH, pp. 109–113, April 2003

13. Dimitrakopoulou, A., Petrou, A., Martínez, A., Marcos, J.M., Kollias, V., et al.: State of the art of interaction analysis for Metacognitive Support & Diagnosis (D31.1.1). EU Sixth Framework Programme priority 2, Information society technology. Network of Exc. (2006)
14. Campbell, S.W., Castells, M., Fernandez-Ardevol, M., Qiu, J.L., Sey, A.: Mobile communication and society: a global perspective. Int. J. Commun. **1**(1), 7 (2007)
15. Kay, J., Maisonneuve, N., Yacef, K., Reimann, P.: The big five and visualisations of team work activity. Intelligent Tutoring Systems, pp. 197–206. Springer, Heidelberg (2006)
16. Bandura, A.: Social Foundations of Thought and Action. Prentice Hall, Englewood Cliffs (1986)
17. Mochizuki, T., Kato, H., Yaegashi, K., Nagata, T., Nishimori, T., Hisamatsu, S.I., Suzuki, M.: Promotion of self-assessment for learners in online discussion using the visualization software. In: Proceedings of the 2005 Conference on Computer Support for Collaborative Learning: Learning 2005: The Next 10 Years!, pp. 440–449. International Society of the Learning Sciences, May 2005

Virtualization in Education: Portable Network Laboratory

Mercedes Barrionuevo[1(✉)], Cristian Gil[1], Matias Giribaldi[1], Christopher Suarez[1], and Carlos Taffernaberry[1,2]

[1] Universidad Nacional de San Luis, Ejército de los Andes, 950-5700
San Luis, Argentine Republic
{mdbarrio,ctaffer}@unsl.edu.ar
[2] Universidad Tecnológica Nacional, Facultad Regional Mendoza, Rodriguez 273,
M5502AJE Mendoza City, Argentine Republic

Abstract. The goal of virtualization is the complete reproduction of physical computer networks in software, being able to work with logical devices and logical network services. To help the traditional teaching methodology through experimentation, the students can use a virtual and portable laboratory whenever and wherever they want. PNL (Portable Network Laboratory) is a tool for the deployment of a virtualized environment of computer networks allowing to connect, configure and communicate client and server applications. Its objective is to allow the student a suitable environment to verify the proper operation of the network services they are studying. This paper presents the main considerations of the design and the implementation of PNL, as well as the results obtained.

Keywords: Virtualization · Network services · Free software
Computer networks · Education

1 Introduction

Nowadays, our society access to Internet through the use of World Wide Web protocol, emails, programs that allow information sharing, etc., without knowing how these applications and protocols actually interact each other. However, the study of data networks is important for students to know how network services are able to transmit and interpret messages sent and received through the network.

Configure and test the proper operation of the most common services used on the Internet is essential for every student of Information and Communication Technologies (ICT). Being able to do tests in a safe environment, and the capability to return to an initial and stable configuration, is a goal of every course dedicated to network services.

Allowing the applications to run on a virtual network just like a physical network is an achievement of network virtualization. Additionally, performing different sets of configuration tests and command execution or applications, allowing to save the current state and recover it after a while is one of the advantages of using virtualized environments.

In this paper is proposed the creation of a Portable Network Laboratory, an important tool for the development of practices in the "Services in Network Operating System"

© Springer International Publishing AG, part of Springer Nature 2018
A. E. De Giusti (Ed.): CACIC 2017, CCIS 790, pp. 90–98, 2018.
https://doi.org/10.1007/978-3-319-75214-3_9

course and all other matters of the Computer Networks University Technician (TUR) of the National University of San Luis that require its use, helping teachers and students in the teaching-learning process. PNL is the result of the authors of this document's final work.

The rest of this document is organized in the following way: the next section describes the theoretical concepts involved in the development of the prototype. Section 3 specifies basic aspects of the proposed tool design, describing the context where it will be used and the issues addressed. Section 4 shows trials and experimental tests. After that, is explained the criteria used in the selection of the prototype technology adopted. Finally, conclusions and future work are detailed.

2   Background

This section introduces different concepts used in the development of our work, highlighting the virtualization, types and implementations. Then, different technologies are described.

2.1   Virtualization

When a computer is used, the operating system (OS) is installed and executed directly over the hardware and it takes advantage of its potential in a complete way. However, there are some kind of program called virtualization software or virtual machine that emulates certain hardware, taking advantage of the real resources of the computer. On top of these softwares is possible to install an OS as it was on a real computer, calling it guest OS. The guest OS works, broadly speaking, like a main OS, so all his functions and characteristics are available, turning it into a perfect tool for making tests.

Virtualization refers to the process of physical devices replacement for virtual ones, availables by using a software. Servers, workstations, networks, and applications can be virtualized. In order to do that, the virtualization software manages the physical resources of that machine: memory, CPU, storage, and network bandwidth, among the most relevant aspect.

With the decrease of the amount of physical equipment, the virtualization brings benefits like reduction in maintenance costs and energy consumption. This originates a consolidation of the serves, optimizing the use of the physical space.

2.2   Virtualization Types

In Virtualization, there are several ways to achieve the same result through different levels of abstraction, being the most used [2, 3]:

- *Paravirtualization*: this mechanism adds a special set of instructions (called hypercalls), replacing the instructions of the set of instructions referred to the architecture of the real machine. In the ×86 architecture, for example, the hypervisor is executed just above the physical hardware (Ring 0) so the guests OS run at higher levels. The core of the guests OS needs to be modified in order to use the hypercalls. On the other hand, the advantage is a virtualization low overload.

- *OS level*: this technique virtualizes the physical server at the OS level. Here, the host OS is a modified kernel that allows the running of multiple isolated containers, also known as Virtual Private Servers (VPS) or virtualized servers. Each container is an instance that shares the kernel of the host OS. It has a low overload, and its implementations are widely used. The main inconvenient is that it does not allow to virtualize different OS types others than host OS.

- *Full Virtualization:* this technique is used for the emulation of a processor architecture over other architecture. It allows to run unmodified guests OS, emulating each instruction of the first one through the code translation on the second. The advantage of the full emulation of the processor is its portability multi-platform and OS. The disadvantage is the overload caused by the emulation on software of the complete set of instructions.

- *Hardware Assisted:* this type of virtualization implements a new Ring (Ring −1) with a higher privilege than the four Rings normal processor architecture. The CPU extensions for the virtualization support allow to run the guests OS without any modification, so they work in Ring 0, while the hypervisor runs in Ring −1. This allows to support the virtualization without using the full virtualization or paravirtualization. The advantage of this technique is the reduction of the overload caused by the software emulation.

Each of the types of virtualization named can be implemented using various techniques such as those listed below.

2.3 Virtualization Implementations

In order to implement virtualization environments there are different technologies. In this subsection a survey of some existing technologies is made:

- *KVM (Kernel based Virtual Machine)* [4]. It's a free software tool which allows the assisted virtualization by hardware, for Intel and AMD platforms. It's included by default from the kernel 2.6.20 of Linux, allowing fast implementations. Is supported by the community and has a huge amount of administration tools that can be used together.

- *Xen* [5]. Is a hypervisor for virtualization developed with free software. The virtualization is implemented with paravirtualization or assisted hardware. It has a spread support in the developer's community and a mature implementation, for over 10 years.

- *LXC (Linux Container)* [6]. Is an interface in user space for OS Level virtualization, and it is implemented with a powerful API (Application Program Interface) and simple tools, allowing the Linux users to create and manage containers in an easy way. The development of this interface was made using free software and the support is actually included in the majority of Linux distributions. Its development started in 2008 year.

- *Docker* [7]. Is a tool of free software that implement OS level virtualization, allowing to package environments and applications that later can be deployed over other OS with this technology. Docker accesses to the virtualization of Linux kernel by the libcontainer library, or indirectly through LXC. This project began in 2013.
- *Proxmox* [9]. Is an open code platform that does not virtualize by itself. It uses the KVM hypervisor to support hardware assisted virtualization and LXC to support OS level virtualization. It has a very complete administration web site, allowing to make all administration from a web browser. It is based on Debian distribution, available since 2009.
- *VirtualBox* [10]. Is a virtualization software that uses hardware assistance and full virtualization techniques. The software was offered under a privative software licence, but in 2007, after years of development, an Open Source Edition version came up, Virtualbox OSE under the GPL 2 licence.
- *Qemu* [11]. Is a tool that allows virtualization and hardware architecture emulation. When it is used to virtualize, Qemu uses a full virtualization technique, when is used as a hardware emulator, it can execute another architecture's programs. It can be used together with the hypervisor Xen o KMV. The first stable version of the software dates from 2006, so it's development is mature.

There are other virtualization softwares, but the previous ones only were considered in this paper for free licences reasons.

3   Design of a Portable Network Laboratory: PNL

The main objective of this work is to create an environment where a computer network can be built using a virtualization method. Below is detailed the context in which it will be used, the problems and motivations, the objectives pursued and the technologies used to create the PNL prototype.

3.1   Context

A network service is an application that provides information to different clients that do a request for it. Generally, network services are installed over the OS of one or more servers to share information and resources with client computers.

The present work has as main objective to be used in the "Network Operating Systems Services" course corresponding to the 3rd level of the Computer Networks University Technician (TUR). This course develop high practical skills in the students since it is mainly based on configuration, start-up and test of different services.

The network services used in this course are: Dynamic Host Configuration Protocol (DHCP), Email (SMTP), Domain Name System (DNS), Hypertext Transfer Protocol (HTTP), Proxy, Firewall, Virtual Private Network (VPN) and Server Message Block (SMB).

3.2 Problems and Motivation

Due the practical nature of the subject, in its first cohort during the 2009 year there were several drawbacks to carry out this practices efficiently in the Physical, Mathematics and Natural Sciences Faculty Laboratory of the San Luis National University. Some of these are detailed below:

- Limitation in amount of networks for carrying out the studies of routing on network layer. It was needed at least two physical networks or an active device capable to create different Vlan, but there was no availability.
- Limitation in multi-homed network interfaces. The machines that had the role of routers, needed at least two network interfaces, but there was no availability.
- Limitation in the number of computers, which didn't allow access the services from many clients simultaneously.
- Unavailability of free software to install some services in the proprietary OS installed in the computers.
- Lack of administration permissions in laboratory computer's OS to install and/or modify the services to be tested.
- Propagation of services tested to the complete faculty's network such as DHCP and DNS, delivering fake network address, gateways and resolutions to domain names to the whole campus.
- Finally, if the students tried to recreate these practices at their homes, they may find the same or greater limitations, because they usually had only one computer available.

With the aim of improving laboratory practices, particularly the teaching-learning process, the motivation for the PNL implementation appears.

3.3 Previous Work: ADIOS Distribution

As a short term alternative to solve some of the problems presented in point 3.2 a survey among various virtualization software and test scenarios was done.

Different simulation alternatives were evaluated, such as Cisco Packet Tracer [12], CLOONIX [13] or virtualization tools such as VNUML (Virtual Network User Mode Linux) [14] of the Madrid Polytechnic University, or ADIOS [15] of the Australian CQ University. Due his functionality and use of scarce hardware resources, ADIOS was selected. It is a distribution based on Fedora Release 8 live CD that uses User Mode Linux (UML) [16] to create virtual machines, has some services needed by the Course already installed, and a very flexible network topology [17], as can be seen in Fig. 1.

As the ADIOS distribution is free and open source, it was possible to make several modifications over the years, adapting it to the matter needs. Some of the changes were:

- De-assignment of pre-configured network addresses, and active interfaces in the VMs, in order to activate and configure the necessaries in each exercise.
- Installation of OpenLDAP service; telnet, elinks, mutt and thunderbird client applications.
- Problem resolution related IPv6 addresses assigned through EUI-64, due to poorly generated mac addresses.

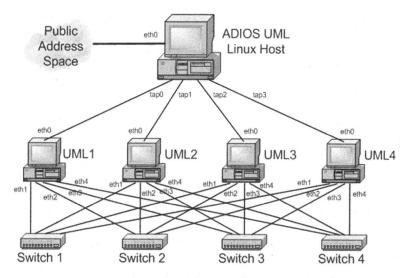

Fig. 1. Interconnection detail between ADIOS VM network cards.

- Scripts creation to store changed configuration files and a command history executed in each virtual machine.
- Accessibility modification, such as: font size in terminals and creation of a GUI to start or stop virtual machines.

At now, the distribution (with a size of 650 Mb) is fully functional to perform all the practices of the course, allowing it to be used from a liveCD. Therefore, without installing any software, students can perform the exercises proposed in faculty laboratory, or at their home. The only they need is a computer with a CD reader and at least 512 MB of RAM memory.

However, new problems arose due to the hardware update in the FCFMyN laboratories two years ago. The ADIOS kernel (2.6.24) does not recognize some new multi-core processors, so it does not work with them, getting a kernel panic while is booting.

In addition to this new limitation, the version of the services on which ADIOS was developed have ten years old. Many of them presents new features that are desirable to be teached in this course. An attempt was made to update ADIOS to newer version of the different services used, but due to dependency problems of other packages and the kernel itself, it was impossible to do so.

3.4 Proposed Goals

The specific objectives and scope of PNL are detailed below:

- Develope a free and open source tool.
- Deploy a virtualized computer network in an unique physical computer without installing additional software in his OS.
- Create a working set with at least 6 nodes and different OS on its.

- Interconnect in different way the created nodes, in order to satisfy different link layer topologies.
- Store all the configuration changes done to use them in the future.
- Create a bootable image to boot from a DVD or a USB.
- Resources optimization in order to be used in hardware limited computers.

3.5 Proposed Technologies for the Development

For the implementation of the different nodes, the use of virtualization technologies is proposed, which allows to abstract and isolate the different nodes from each other. Between they emphasize KVM, XEN, LXC, VirtualBox, Qemu, Uml.

The proposal of link layer connectivity between nodes is the use of virtual interfaces (vnics) and virtual switches, such as Open Vswitch. An alternative method to consider is the use of Vlans.

To deploy application services, the use of GPL software is proposed, which allows great flexibility in order to make different configuration types.

Storage in virtual machines is proposed through the use of Snapshot technologies, applied in each virtual machine (depending on the hypervisor to be used), or through the use of storage technologies such as LVM.

In order to get resources optimization in virtual machines, the use of a CLI (Character Line Interface) interface is proposed, such as the Bourne Shell.

4 Test Bed

In this section the tests that were made in each of the virtualizations are presented. In order to do that, two computers were used with the following hardware:

- Computer 1: AMD Athlon (tm) 64 × 2 dual core processor with 2 Gb of RAM memory, disk storage SAMSUNG HD080HJ of 8 Gb. Motherboard ASUS M2N-MX SE Plus.
- Computer 2: AMD Athlon (tm) 64 × 2 dual core processor with 2 Gb of RAM memory, disk storage of 160 Gb. Motherboard ASUS M2N-MX SE Plus.

On the other hand, the OS used were Ubuntu 12.04 LTS, Debian 8 and Debian 9.

4.1 Tasks in Each Virtualization Environment

- Study of LXC, VNX, CLOONIX and snapshots technologies.
- Virtualization of LAN and WAN networks, testing the connection between the different hosts.
- Interconnection between two, four and six virtual hosts.
- Quantification of the resources consumption of the virtual machines.
- Installation, verification and testing of the services used in the Course.
- Access and interaction to a graphical remote desk of a virtual machine using free software VNCserver tool.

Following the network scheme proposed by ADIOS, the Linux support was used for bridging and, according to the docker documentation about it [18, 19], it was possible to successfully set up an environment with the same characteristics.

4.2 Technologies Comparison

After the installation of all the tools needed for a correct operation of each one of the virtualizations techniques, a comparison was made between them. Table 1 shows the comparison made in detail.

Table 1. Comparison between virtualizations techniques.

Feature	KVM	Virtual Box	QEMU	LXC
Disk space	6 Gb per virtual machine	8 Gb per virtual machine	2 Gb per virtual machine	488 Mb per container
RAM memory space	300 Mb per virtual machine	512 Mb per virtual machine	512 Mb per virtual machine	14 Mb per container
Host interconnection	Yes	Yes	Yes	Yes

5 Technology Selection Criteria and Prototype Evaluation

As one of the objectives proposed was that the laboratory can be reproduced by the students in their homes, and due not all the computers have hardware support for virtualization, the techniques that uses hardware assistance were discarded and therefore KVM was not used.

Additionally, it was not necessary to emulate other processor architectures in the proposed laboratory, so the use of QEMU to virtualize did not add any improvement.

Finally, from the comparison made in Table 1, and with the feature "few hardware resources" in mind, was decided to make the prototype using the virtualization tool DOCKER.

The prototype developed is in evaluation process nowadays. Although it has had a preliminary evaluation by the Course Professors, the real and exhaustive evaluation will be carried out when the students will use it next year, in "Services in Network Operating System" Course. Then, it can be analyzed the weaknesses and strengths present in PNL.

However, it was possible to observe the correct construction of various network topologies, the correct communication between different hosts and the correct operation of all the services used in the Course. The prototype is available to be downloaded and used for free [20].

6 Conclusions and Future Work

PNL meet almost all of the proposed goals. The work showed in this paper is considered very important in the development the practices of "Services in Network Operating

System" course, being a fundamental tool in the process of teaching-learning. As a free software development, it is permitted to use it by another course, that needs some similar requirements.

On the other hand, we are analyzing the possibility to add Microsoft Windows as guest OS, in order to develop the practice of SMB and test it on different OS.

It is also desired that PNL can be executed from a removable media like a USB, to store the changes of configurations, because this objective not reached yet.

References

1. Chowdhury, N.M.K., Boutaba, R.: A survey of network virtualization. Comput. Netw. **54**(5), 862–876 (2010)
2. Rodríguez-Haro, F., Freitag, F., Navarro, L.: A summary of virtualization techniques. Procedia Technol. **3**, 267–272 (2012). ISSN 2212-0173
3. Pal, A.S., Pattnaik, B.P.K.: Classification of virtualization environment for cloud computing. Indian J. Sci. Technol. **6**(1), 3965–3971 (2013). ISSN 0974–6846
4. Kernel Virtual Machine. Web site. https://www.linux-kvm.org/
5. XEN Project. Web site. https://www.xenproject.org/
6. LXC. Linux Containers. Web site. https://linuxcontainers.org/
7. Docker Enterprise Edition. Web site. https://www.docker.com/
8. Introducing Execution Drivers and Libcontainer. http://blog.docker.io/2014/03/docker-0-9-introducing-execution-drivers-and-libcontainer/
9. Proxmox. https://www.proxmox.com/
10. Virtualbox. https://www.virtualbox.org/
11. Qemu Process Emulator. http://www.qemu.org/
12. Packet Tracer. http://www.packettracernetwork.com/
13. Cloonix Routing and Network Simulation. http://www.brianlinkletter.com/tag/cloonix/
14. VNUML. Virtual Network UML. https://www.dit.upm.es/vnumlwiki/index.php/Main_Page
15. Richter, N., et al., ADIOS. Web site. http://os.cqu.edu.au/adios
16. The User Mode Linux Home-page. Web site. http://user-mode-linux.sourceforge.net/
17. Giacchini, M., INFN-LNL, L., Richtes, I.N.: LivEPICS: EPICS Official Distribution Made in LNL. Adios y Networking
18. Marmol, V., Jnagal, R., Hockin, T.: Networking in Containers and Container Clusters. In: Proceedings of Netdev 0.1. February 2015
19. Docker Networking. https://docs.docker.com/engine/userguide/networking/
20. Mediafire. http://www.mediafire.com/file/52tx4ra8j1pk1ov/livecd.iso

Graphic Computation, Images
and Visualization

A Shadow Removal Approach for a Background Subtraction Algorithm

Rosana Barbuzza[1,3], Leonardo Dominguez[1,2], Alejandro Perez[1,3],
Leonardo Fernandez Esteberena[1,2], Aldo Rubiales[1,3],
and Juan P. D'amato[1,2(✉)]

[1] PLADEMA, Universidad Nacional del Centro de la Provincia de Buenos Aires,
Buenos Aires, Argentina
juan.damato@gmail.com
[2] National Council Scientific Technical Research,
CONICET, Buenos Aires, Argentina
[3] Comisión de Investigaciones Científicas,
CICPBA, Buenos Aires, Argentina

Abstract. This paper presents preliminary results of an algorithm for shadow detection and removal in video sequences. The proposal is that from the base of the background subtraction with the Visual Background Extraction (ViBE), which identifies areas of movement, to apply a post processing to separate pixels from the real object and those of the shadow. As the areas of shadows have similar characteristics to those of the objects in movement, the separation becomes a difficult task. Consequently, the algorithms used for this classification may produce several false positives. To solve this problem, we set to use information of the object involved such as the size and movement direction, to estimate the most likely position of the shadow. Furthermore, the analysis of similarity between the present frame and the background model are realized, by means of the traditional indicator of normalized cross correlation to detect shadows. The algorithm may be used to detect both people and vehicles in applications for safety of cities, traffic monitoring, sports analysis, among others. The results obtained in the detection of objects show that it is highly likely to separate the shadow in a high percentage of effectiveness and low computational cost; allowing improving steps of further processing, such as object recognition and tracking.

Keywords: Video processing · Object detection · Segmentation

1 Introduction

Video analysis systems have become a useful tool not only in industry but also in the research field. Digital video surveillance has proved fundamental for both forensics pericia and crime prevention. Particularly, security in Argentina is a critical issue which must be dealt with immediately; therefore, many monitoring centers and camera observers have arisen. Being this procedure not efficient

© Springer International Publishing AG, part of Springer Nature 2018
A. E. De Giusti (Ed.): CACIC 2017, CCIS 790, pp. 101–110, 2018.
https://doi.org/10.1007/978-3-319-75214-3_10

enough, it is highly important to count with techniques of video analysis that may help operators with their daily tasks. Consequently, this research group has submitted different research works mainly showing the architecture of an open distributed system, and also scalable [1].

The complexity of the presented algorithms lies in working in dynamic environments, as exterior cameras are, being under the threat of weather conditions. To diminish these hardships, moving windows as detailed in [2], are usually used, being their objective focusing on applying a logic operation to process only those movements detected within their range of vision.

These object tracking algorithms are eventually used in video-analysis platforms to detect and analyze certain situations of special interest. In this context, shadows considerably affect the perception of the detected objects, as shown in Fig. 1, since it drastically alters an aftermath classification by color or size; then, it has to be reduced someway.

Fig. 1. Images of different cases were the shadow changes the object size and form.

The present research work focuses on being able to detect and eliminate shadows from videos in grayscale, or color space transformed to grayscale (i.e. rgb2gray o HSV corresponding to component Value). This consideration is proper since many low-cost cameras do not usually provide images of sufficient quality, also affected by video stream compression. The novelty of the suggested method is that it uses information coming from the object and its orientation, to determine before hand the position of the shadow. Then, a traditional method is applied in the external region of the object which considers characteristics of texture and color in areas of shadows.

This research work is organized as follows: Sect. 2 describes states of the Arts; Sect. 3 the VIBE method for background subtraction and the introduced modifications. In Sects. 4 and 5, the proposal shadow detection method and the results are presented. Finally, Sect. 6 presents conclusions and future works.

2   State of the Art

The techniques of detection of events used in Video-Survillance systems are mainly based on quickly discriminating of movement from a fixed video camera. Research works as [3], describe the most common algorithms to detect and track objects. In [4], there is a special comparison between the different algorithms of basic detection, concluding that their combination may be absolutely useful to diminish false positive rates; while keeping the time and rate of true positives.

The background subtraction commonly used classify shadows as a part of the objects, what alters both size and shape of the objects, affecting consequently the efficacy of such algorithms [5]. Also, it hinders some other procedures which need the result of the detection of objects, such as classification or tracking of the trajectory and also, analysis of certain behavior: loitering, vandalism, traffic lawbreaking, among others. This problem also affects those techniques based on characteristics [6].

There is different research on the detection and separation of shadows. Some algorithms that worked with static images are computationally complex and are not applicable for video analysis in real time [7]. Other algorithms are specially designed for video in either greyscale or color, and also have a lower computational cost. To perform classification, most bases on the basic common characteristics of the area with shadows: areas darker than the background Of the scene, uniform and invariable color or texture, etc. Even though these characteristics allow creating candidates to determine the areas of shadows, they are not decisive; therefore, all of the methods fail in the classification because many times part of the objects also satisfy these conditions [8,9]. In specific, another group of algorithms include information about the geometry of the shadow or the illumination model, some of them only specialized in the shadows of people.

3   Background Subtraction in Video

The present research work makes use of the Visual Background extractor (ViBE), as suggested in [10], which behaves properly in different environments commonly used in video surveillance. Among the virtues in applying this method we may highlight the low computing time, the high detection rates and the strength in noise existence, highly necessary features in surveillance camera captures used at present. Likewise, the present proposal may be also applied to some other algorithms [3]. Figure 2 depicts background subtraction accomplished with ViBE for a particular frame of urban video surveillance. In the example, the original image

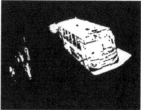

Fig. 2. Video image, left, and background subtraction with ViBE, right, for a video captured in a video surveillance camera.

is shown and to its left, the foreground components detected, people and vehicles. The shadow projection coming from the bus is part of the object, notably deforming its shape, and increasing its size to approximately a 50%.

ViBe is a pixel based modeling background algorithm, choosing at random way samples of the intensity of each pixel considering the previous frames from the incoming video. Figure 3 depicts the sequence of steps of the original ViBe algorithm and the modules included for a better classification. The module Detection, classifies scenes as background or foreground, calculating the distance between each pixel in a present image with regard to the samples stored in the background model.

Updating of the background model for each pixel is aleatory, being likely to replace one of the stored values for a new intensity value of the same pixel in the present frame (Fig. 3, module Update model). This updating mechanism allows preserving background pixels, while motion ones are partially discarded in time. It is essential that only those pixels processed and classified as background replace samples in the corresponding background model. Inserting wrongly classified pixels which belong to objects in motion, foreground, or that become uncertain in the classification may significantly alter the detection results. This instance is of utmost importance since it has allowed the introduction of improvements to the original ViBE method achieving a better rate detection, mainly to adapt the algorithm to scene movements or dynamic background, detected as false positives, or the refilling of those objects not fully detected, false negatives [11,12].

This paper adds the algorithm of morphologic operation such as opening, closing, holes refilling. In order to attain connected components, the larger objects are selected whereas the little and isolated ones are discarded (Contour and Refilling module). Once this process was carried out, the algorithm of cast shadow separation of the real object is applied (Shadow module).

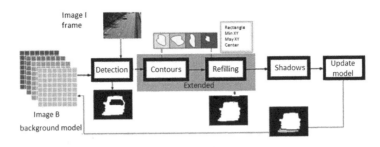

Fig. 3. ViBE algorithm and implementation of modules of improvement

The present module suggests correcting only those pixels classified as foreground which correspond to shadows. It should be noticed that it is not proper to classify shadows as background, since these samples should not modify or alter the background model, when updating the model, to avoid further errors when classifying.

4 Shadow Detection Proposal

To detect and eliminate shadows it is possible to apply the Normalized Cross Correlation NCC between the present image, I, and an image representative of the background, B, adjusting with properties typical of a shadow as shown in [13] and also, incorporating to the original NCC method, elemental knowledge of the objects to improve detection rate, both detailed below.

4.1 Identification of Potential Pixels with NCC

NCC indicator allows identifying similar images with different scales of intensity. To represent the background, B, an image obtained from those samples randomly selected by ViBE as representative of the background model was used, see Fig. 3.

For each pixel (i, j) classified as foreground by ViBe, neighbours in a square region R were considered centered in this pixel. The candidate pixels to be classified as shadows are those whose value of correlation is high, considering this region of neighbours:

$$C(i,j) = \sum_{n=-N}^{N} \sum_{m=-N}^{N} (I(i+n, j+m) * B(i+n, j+m)) \tag{1}$$

where $I(x, y)$ and $B(x, y)$ is the intensity value of the pixel in images I and B, respectively; and the size of R is $(2N + 1)^2$.

The correlation gets normalized as:

$$NCC(i,j) = \frac{C(i,j)}{\sqrt{mI(i,j)} * \sqrt{(mB(i,j))}} \tag{2}$$

where $mI(i, j)$ and $mB(i, j)$ are the second central moment within the same region R centered in the pixel (i,j), in image I y B, respectively.

The reference value to detect shadows with NCC (Eq. 2) is a high value defined within the [0.95–0.98] range [13], being used as a previous step to detect possible candidates.

Then, pixels are rectified using statistics in region R considering the analysis of the relationship between the values of intensity corresponding to images I and N for each pixel (i, j)

$$\alpha(i,j) = \frac{I(i,j)}{B(i,j)} \tag{3}$$

The areas of shadow have to be adjusted to a definite range of values, where α in Eq. 3 is usually defined in [0.4–1] range, because of the darkness of the shadow over the background model [13]. Furthermore, the standard deviation of the α relationship calculated in region R of neighbours must have a low value since the area of shadow is a homogeneous region. It is advisable to consider a standard deviation lower than 0.05 in region R bearing a size of 5×5 pixels, and N equal to 2. The problem of the original method [13] is that it generates false negatives whenever the value of the intensity of the object coincides with the values of the shadow.

Figure 4 depicts a frame of the video *Pedestrians* [14] and another frame of a video of urban surveillance (right). The first row in Fig. 4 highlights the result of the background subtraction with ViBE. It can also be observed in the case of the pedestrian that the shadow (false positives) is not connected to the body; and in the case of the vehicle, the shadow is projected in the lower part, deforming the object.

In the second row in Fig. 4, parameters recommended for NCC (Eq. 2) larger than 0.95 and for α within the range [0.4–1] were used. It can be observed that shadow detection may not always be right, as happens on the legs of the pedestrian, and also, on the glasses of the vehicle, generating false negatives. The method is not working properly, mainly in the scenes where there is light reflex, or when the background resembles the shadow. In these cases, different values of α and standard deviation were considered, depending on the noise in the video signal, and in cases where the shadow turns darker.

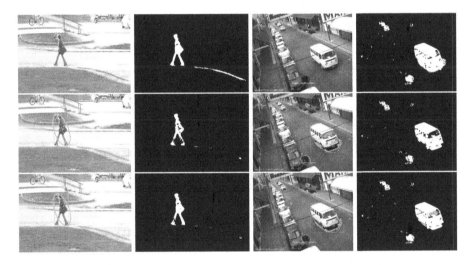

Fig. 4. Background subtraction and shadow detection. Original image or Object contour with detected shadow (left) and resulting mask (right). ViBE algorithm (top). Shadow detection algorithm with NCC (center) and Shadow detection with the proposed algorithm (below)

4.2   Shadow Elimination Based on Object Information

The purpose of this project was not to apply previous rules for NCC in potential areas of the true object, Firstly, shadow classification is performed at the level of a rectangular region or detected blob (components connected to the foreground mask detected by ViBE) and not of each isolated pixel as it happens in the original version of the method [13]. Therefore, the suggestion is to utilize the spacial information within this region in image I. When working with videos of people or vehicles from a video with a fixed camera, it was considered to include further knowledge of some of their properties such as orientation, shape or size.

If the case is to enclose people or vehicles within an ellipse using the mass center of the foreground mask, it is highly likely that the projection of the shadow exceeds the limits of the ellipse as it is the case of the vehicle in Fig. 4. Conversely, the projection of the shadow may remain separated in a different ellipse as it is the case of the pedestrian.

Directional distribution is calculated in each blob to find the ellipse that best adjusts to the distribution of pixels foreground. As a result of this method, an ellipse is defined through its major axis, the minor axis and the orientation of the major axis as regards the horizontal axis [15]. Furthermore, these values had to be adapted to cover all of the objects, both people and vehicles; and at the same time, not to exceed the limits of the blob. Heuristically, a factor of 1.8 became the right one for the major axis and the 1.6 for the minor axis.

As a first approach not to invade in the sequence the areas of the real object, it was considered that the height and width of the human body keep a certain proportion and that a person walks erected. Thus, the rule of decision to determine that there is a person in a blob is by the size of the area, the relationship between the major and minor diameter of the ellipse being greater or equal to 3, and finally, that the orientation of the major axis is kept close to 90°. Figure 4 above depicts the major diagonal of the ellipse being almost vertical for a person and almost horizontal for the major diagonal of the ellipse that encloses the shadow. To identify vehicles, orientation may vary; however, the size of the blob for this case is larger than that which contains people, bicycles or motorcycles.

Last row in Fig. 4 shows that the results of the proposed algorithms improve as regards the original algorithm of ViBE+ (Fig. 4, above) and also, of ViBE+ [13] (Fig. 4, center). The pedestrian has no shadow over their legs. Moreover, no shadows are considered on the windows of the vehicles, false negatives. Whenever a shadow is detected outside the ellipse, the algorithm follows over the neighbouring pixels maintaining its continuity even if it overpasses the pixels the borders of the ellipses.

5   Results

The proposed algorithm was tested with the real videos *Pedestrians* and *Highway* of data base [14,16], which were taken with static cameras used in videosurveillance. These videos have images groundtrue to calcule the rate of accuracy and compare results. Hence, the library of classic algorithms of background subtraction allows comparing with the recent methods and contributions in the area. As for the present study case, the obtained results are analyzed with some other traditional stochastic methods like VIBE+ and Gaussian Mixture Model (GMM) [3].

Each method was analyzed through two wellknown evaluation metrics Precision, Recall as:

$$Precision = \frac{TP}{(TP + FP)} \tag{4}$$

$$Recall = \frac{TP}{(TP + FN)} \tag{5}$$

where FN the number of false negatives, FP the number of false positives, TP the total number of positives and TN the total number of negatives. Getting in this case a better result metrics when approach to 1. Also, an indicator over errors on shadows as,

$$TShadow = \frac{nbErrorShadows}{FP} \tag{6}$$

where nbErrorShadows the total of false positives produced in the area of shadows according to the groundtrue, and FP the number of false positives.

Table 1 depicts the values of the equations detailed above for approximately 700 frames of *Pedestrians* video and, in Table 2 the values for 1300 frames of *Highway* video.

Table 1. Values of indicators for each method with video Pedestrians

Methods	Recall	Precision	Tshadow
GMM [17]	0.98	0.93	0.22
ViBE+ [10]	0.93	0.96	0.50
ViBE+NCC [13]	0.83	0.99	0.11
Proposed ViBE+NCC+Information	0.91	0.99	0.07

Table 2. Values of indicators for each method with video Highway

Methods	Recall	Precision	Tshadow
GMM [17]	0.89	0.91	0.81
ViBE+ [10]	0.84	0.92	0.95
ViBE+NCC [13]	0.58	0.94	0.47
Proposed ViBE+NCC+Information	0.85	0.94	0.55

It can be observed for both videos *Pedestrians* and *Highway*, that by using the method ViBE+ o GMM, the percentage TShadow is much higher, close to the double, than the proposed method. Method ViBE+NCC [13] increases the amount of false negatives getting the Recall metric to considerably diminish in regard to ViBE+ (for *Pedestrians* from 0.93 to 0.83 and for *Highway* from 0.84 to 0.58). Furthermore, both videos with the proposed method, it may be noticed that there is an increase in the Precision with regard to ViBE+, indicating a reduction in the amount of false positives. Finally, with the proposed method ViBE+NCC+information, the rate Recall and Precision is comparable to that of the methods ViBE+ and GMM; however, the percentage of those wrongly classified in the area of shadows with TShadows is notoriously smaller.

6 Conclusions

The present research work shows the preliminary results of the method of detection and separation of the shadow, based on contextual information, which are promising. The videos have been processed and visualized their classification in real time since the algorithm has computational low cost. It was also possible to diminish the error in the classification in regard to the application of traditional NCC, calculating the orientation and probable location of the object and determining either people or vehicle.

Future works will attempt to incorporate the automatic adaptation of the thresholds for α range, considering the variation of the intensity of the shadow when processing the video, as the algorithm has difficulty in finding areas of darker shadows. Another challenge aims to achieve that the parameters of the algorithm automatically adapt to different times of the day and, and comparing quantitatively with some other reference methods.

References

1. Dominguez, L., Perez, A., Rubiales, A., Damato, J., Barbuzza, R.: Herramientas para la detección y seguimiento de personas a partir de cámaras de seguridad. In: Proceedings del XXII Congreso Argentino de Ciencias de la Computación, pp. 251–260 (2016)
2. Kruegle, H.: CCTV Surveillance: Video Practices and Technology. Butterworth-Heinemann, Newton, MA, USA (2014)
3. Legua, C.: Seguimiento automático de objetos en sistemas con múltiples cámaras (2013)
4. Shaikh, S.H., Saeed, K., Chaki, N.: Moving Object Detection Using Background Subtraction, pp. 15–23. Springer, Cham (2014). https://doi.org/10.1007/978-3-319-07386-6
5. Azab, M., Shedeed, H., Hussein, A.: A new technique for background modeling and subtraction for motion detection in real-time videos. In: IEEE International Conference on Image Processing, pp. 3453–3456 (2010)
6. Hadi, R., Sulong, G., George, L.: Vehicle detection and tracking techniques: a concise review. Sig. Image Process. Int. J. **5**, 1–12 (2014)
7. Fredembach, C., Finlayson, G.: Simple shadow removal. In: Proceedings of the 18th International Conference on Pattern Recognition (ICPRA 2006), pp. 832–835 (2006)
8. Qin, R., Liao, S., Lei, Z., Li, S.Z.: Moving cast shadow removal based on local descriptors. In: 20th International Conference on Pattern Recognition, pp. 1377–1380 (2010)
9. Chen, F., Zhu, B., Jing, W., Yuan, L.: Removal shadow with background subtraction model vibe algorithm. In: 2013 2nd International Symposium on Instrumentation and Measurement, Sensor Network and Automation (IMSNA), pp. 264–269 (2013)
10. Barnich, O., Van Droogenbroeck, M.: Vibe: a universal background subtraction algorithm for video sequences. IEEE Trans. Image Process. **20**(6), 1709–1724 (2011)

11. Gervasoni, L., Damato, J., Barbuzza, R., Vénere, M.: Un método eficiente para la sustracción de fondo en videos usando gpu. Enief 2014, Revista Mecánica Computacional, pp. 1721–1731 (2014)
12. Barbuzza, R., Damato, J., Rubiales, A., Dominguez, L., Perez, A., Venere, M.: Un método para la sustracción de fondo en videos inestables. Enief 2014, Revista Mecánica Computacional, pp. 3409–3417 (2016)
13. Jacques, J.C.S., Jung, C.R., Musse, S.R.: Background subtraction and shadow detection in grayscale video sequences. In: XVIII Brazilian Symposium on Computer Graphics and Image Processing (SIBGRAPI 2005), pp. 189–196 (2005)
14. Goyette, N., Jodoin, P.M., Porikli, F., Konrad, J., Ishwar, P.: Changedetection. net: a new change detection benchmark dataset. In: Computer Vision and Pattern Recognition Workshops (CVPRW), pp. 1–8 (2012)
15. Lahoz Beltra, R., Ortega, J., Fernandez Montraveta, C.: Métodos estadísticos en biología del comportamiento. Editorial Complutense (1994)
16. Sobral, A., Vacavant, A.: A comprehensive review of background subtraction algorithms evaluated with synthetic and real videos. Comput. Vis. Image Underst. **122**, 4–21 (2014)
17. Zivkovic, Z.: Improved adaptive Gaussian mixture model for background subtraction. In: 2004 Proceedings of the 17th International Conference on Pattern Recognition (ICPR 2004), vol. 2, pp. 28–31 (2004)

A Tutorial on the Implementations of Linear Image Filters in CPU and GPU

Alvaro Pardo[✉]

Facultad de Ingeniería y Tecnologías,
Universidad Católica del Uruguay, Montevideo, Uruguay
apardo@ucu.edu.uy

Abstract. This article presents an overview of the implementation of linear image filters in CPU and GPU. The main goal is to present a self contained discussion of different implementations and their background using tools from digital signal processing. First, using signal processing tools, we discuss different algorithms and estimate their computational cost. Then, we discuss the implementation of these filters in CPU and GPU. It is very common to find in the literature that GPUs can easily reduce computational times in many algorithms (straightforward implementations). In this work we show that GPU implementations not always reduce the computational time but also not all algorithms are suited for GPUs. We believe this is a review that can help researchers and students working in this area. Although the experimental results are not meant to show which is the best implementation (in terms of running time), the main results can be extrapolated to CPUs and GPUs of different capabilities.

Keywords: Linear image filtering · GPU · CUDA

1 Introduction to Linear Filtering

Image filtering is one of the most studied problems in the image processing community. Image smoothing, sharpening, feature detection and edge detection are some of the applications of image filtering. In the literature we can find two broad categories of image filters: linear and non linear. More recently, non local methods attracted the attention of researchers in the area. In fact, several of the state of the art algorithms are both non local and non linear (see [4] for more details). In this tutorial we will focus on the analysis and implementation, both in CPU and GPU, of linear filtering methods. The approach will be strongly connected to the theory of linear systems and digital signal processing. We refer the interested reader to [1,9] for further details on these areas. First we recall that a filter, or system, that takes an input image to produce and output one, is said to be linear if for all linear combinations of inputs produce a linear combination of outputs with the same weighting coefficients. Before analyzing linear image

© Springer International Publishing AG, part of Springer Nature 2018
A. E. De Giusti (Ed.): CACIC 2017, CCIS 790, pp. 111–121, 2018.
https://doi.org/10.1007/978-3-319-75214-3_11

filter using tools from linear systems we will describe linear image filters in their most basic form using sliding windows (convolution masks).

We start with a simple linear averaging filter in which each pixel $x = (i, j)$ of the output image is computed as the average of all pixels in a 3×3 window centered at x in the input image. Processing the whole image can be expressed with a sliding window algorithm. Given the pixel x the average filter can be implemented moving a 3×3 window with weights $1/9$ across the input image. Mathematically this can be formulated as:

$$g(i, j) = \sum_{i'=-1}^{1} \sum_{j'=-1}^{1} w(i', j') f(i + i', j + j') \tag{1}$$

where $f(.,.)$ and $g(.,.)$ are the input and output images and $w(.,.)$ is the window containing the filter weights. In the previous example of linear averaging $w(m, n) = 1/9$ for all (m, n). Changing the values of $w(m, n)$ different filters can be obtained. Inspecting Eq. (1) we can see that is very similar to a two dimensional convolution. Recalling the theory of linear systems we know that the output of a linear and invariant system can be obtained convolving the input f with the impulse response of the system h: $g = f * h$[1]. The impulse response of an image filter can be obtained as the output of the filter when the input image is a discrete impulse. If $\mathcal{N}$ is a neighborhood of the same size of the sliding window centered at pixel (i, j) and $h(.,.)$ is the impulse response of the filter, Eq. (1) can be rewritten as a discrete convolution:

$$g(i, j) = \sum_{(m,n) \in \mathcal{N}} h(i - m, j - n) f(m, n). \tag{2}$$

The main difference between Eqs. (1) and (2) is the range of indexes (i, j) and (m, n). Both formulations convey useful information; the first one is more suited for interpretation while the second one enables us to connect linear image filtering with convolution and the frequency response of the filter.

The Eq. (2) can be reformulated interchanging the role of h and f; instead of moving h across f we move f and leave h fixed. To do that we center h around the origin and extend it filling it with zeros outside the original window range and extend the input image outside the original range $[0, M - 1] \times [0, N - 1]$. In this way the Eq. (2) turns into: $g(i, j) = \sum_{(m,n)} h(m, n) f(i - m, j - n)$. In the next section we will use this formulation to obtain the frequency response of linear image filters.

1.1   Z Transform and Frequency Response

The Z transform is a very useful tool in the context of linear and invariant systems, signal processing and discrete control theory [1]. To justify the Z transform we will first deduce it starting from the convolution product. If we consider an

---

[1] The filter impulse response h is sometimes referred as filter kernel.

input image $f(i, j) = z_x^i z_y^j$ with z_x and z_y arbitrary complex numbers, the output signal is: $z_x^i z_y^j \sum_m \sum_n h(m, n) z_x^{-m} z_y^{-n}$. This simple result shows that $z_x^i z_y^j$ are eigenfunctions of linear and invariant filters with corresponding eigenvalues $H(z_x, z_y) = \sum_m \sum_n h(m, n) z_x^{-m} z_y^{-n}$. This expression is known as the Z transform of $h(m, n)$ or transfer function of the filter. One of the most important properties of the Z transform states that the convolution of two signals is the product of their respective Z transforms, see [1] for details. Hence, if f and g are the input and output signals related by $g = f * h$, their relationship in the Z space is: $G(z_x, z_y) = H(z_x, z_y) \cdot F(z_x, z_y)$. If we evaluate the Z transform in the unit sphere we obtain the Fourier transform. The Fourier transform of h is $H(\theta_x, \theta_y) = \sum_{(m,n)} h(m, n) exp(-j(\theta_x m + \theta_y n))$, the frequency response of the filter. In the following section we will use the Z transform to study image filters and propose alternative formulations for some of them. The interested reader can obtain more information about the Z transform in [1].

2 Implementation of Linear Image Filters

In this section we discuss the implementation of linear image filters using the tools presented in previous sections. We will describe the implementation details and address the computational complexity of each approach. One of the goals of the following analysis is to determine the best implementations given the filter characteristics (window size, symmetry, etc.,). First we show how to implement the filters in their traditional sequential form used for CPU algorithms. Later on, we study the parallel versions of the same algorithms suited to GPU architectures.

2.1   Convolution

The implementation of Eqs. (1) and (2) is straightforward. Basically, the idea is to visit every pixel in the image and apply the corresponding equations. Typically, the sliding window approach, Eq. (1), is the first option since is very easy to understand and code. The trickiest part of the implementation is the management of the border conditions. That is, how to process pixels close to the image borders where part of the filter window falls out of the image.

Convolution Computational Cost. To conclude the description of this method we will estimate the number of operations needed to implement it. To simplify the estimation we will assume that the image size is $N \times N$ and the window filter size is $(2W + 1) \times (2W + 1)$. It can be easily seen that each pixel demands $(2W + 1)^2$ operations and therefore the total number of operations is of order $N^2(2W + 1)^2$. To avoid confusions we distinguish computational cost from computational time.

2.2   Separable Convolution

A filter is said to be separable if its kernel can be broken into two one-dimensional vectors that multiplied give the original filter response: $w(i,j) = u(i)v(j)$. The convolution of an image with a separable kernel can be implemented with two one-dimensional convolutions. First, each row in the image is convolved with v, then the result is processed across columns convolving it with u. The mathematical justification can be easily obtained substituting $w(i,j) = u(i)v(j)$ into (2):
$g(i,j) = \sum_m u(m) \left(\sum_n v(n)f(i-m, j-n) \right).$

Separable Convolution Computational Cost. Convolution with separable kernels requires $N(N(2W+1)) + N(N(2W+1)) = 2N^2(2W+1)$ operations. The reduction in the number of operations is $(2W+1)/2$ compared to the traditional two-dimensional convolution. Therefore, the larger the kernel the better speed-up can be obtained with this approach.

2.3   Special Case: Box Filtering

The box filter is an average filter with uniform weights; the output at pixel $x = (i,j)$ is the average of all pixels in the filtering window:

$$g(i,j) = \sum_{i'=-W}^{W} \sum_{j'=-W}^{W} \frac{1}{(2W+1)^2} f(i+i', j+j')$$

The beauty of this filter is that it can be implemented using integral images to reduce the number of operations. The integral image of an image f at pixel (i,j), denoted as $S_f(i,j)$, is the sum of all elements in the rectangular region with upper-left and lower-right vertices $(0,0)$ and (i,j): $Sf(i,j) = \sum_{i' \leq i, j' \leq j} f(i,j)$ Given the pixel (i,j), the output of the box filter can be obtained using the integral image as follows: sum the pixels in the square region defined by the points $(i-W, j-W)$ and $(i+W, j+W)$ and divide it by the number of pixels in the window (recall that the filter window is $[-W, W] \times [-W, W]$. This can be easily implemented with integral images [3]:

$$g(i,j) = \frac{1}{(2W+1)^2} [S_f(i+W, j+W) - S_f(i+W, j-W) \qquad (3)$$
$$- S_f(i-W, j+W) + S_f(i-W, j-W)].$$

The computation of the box filter implies two steps: the computation of the integral image and, after that, the computation of the output using Eq. (3). This formulation is especially useful when we need to filter the image at different scales, i.e. with different filter sizes, because the first step can be reutilized and regardless the filter size, the second step has always the same cost in terms of operations. In order to estimate the cost, in terms of operations, we have to estimate the cost of computing the integral image and the actual filter, from Eq. (3).

It can be easily seen that the computation of the integral image requires N^2 operations. On the other hand, the filtering requires only four operations per pixel so the total number of operations to apply the filter is $4N^2$. Therefore, the total number of operations for the case of the box filter using integral images is $5N^2$. As said before, this does not depend on the filter size. This is why integral images are very attractive to filter the same image at different scales (the work of Viola and Jones popularized this idea [10]).

Moving Average Filter. Moving Average Filters are in fact an implementation of the Box Filter. Using the two-dimensional Z transform it can be shown that the relationship between the Z transforms of input and output images is:

$$G(z_x, z_y) = \frac{F(z_x, z_y)}{(2W+1)^2} \sum_{i=-W}^{W} \sum_{j=-W}^{W} z_x^i z_y^j$$

$$= \frac{F(z_x, z_y)}{(2W+1)^2} \frac{z_x^{W+1} - z_x^{-W}}{1 - z_x} \frac{z_y^{W+1} - z_y^{-W}}{1 - z_y}.$$

Taking the inverse Z transform the previous equation gives:

$$g(i+1, j+1) = g(i+1, j) + g(i, j+1) - g(i, j) + \frac{1}{(2W+1)^2} [f(i-W, j-W)$$
$$- f(i+W+1, j-W) - f(i-W, j+W+1)$$
$$+ f(i+W+1, j+W+1)].$$

The computation cost to process an $N \times N$ image in this case is $7N^2$, similar cost as the separable convolution.

3   Introduction to GPU Programming Using CUDA

In this section we review the main concepts behind GPUs and the parallel implementation of algorithms using this technology. In particular we will use CUDA. For a more detailed presentation we refer to [8].

GPUs are highly parallel processors with many cores and the ability to run multiple threads that provide high performance computing. The architecture of the GPUs, traditionally optimized for graphic applications, has some limitations; less cache and flow control limitations. GPUs provide advantages in applications where the same computations can be applied in parallel to may data elements. However, memory transfers from main memory to device memory (GPU) have to be considered. A GPU implementation pays off if its computation cost it s higher that memory access cost. To process data with an algorithm implemented in the GPU the data must be transferred from main memory to the device, process it in the device and transfer back to main memory. Therefore, the computation cost must be higher enough to pay the overhead introduced by memory transfers. CUDA (Compute Unified Device Architecture) is a programming language by nVidia that allows programming the GPUs abstracting the code from the actual hardware details (OpenCL is another option). Provides the user a high level interface so that he can take advantage of the capabilities of GPUs without having to directly handle the hardware. The CUDA programming model allows the user to use GPU capabilities from a simple interface similar to C language (C language extension). CUDA proposes three abstractions: a hierarchy of thread groups, shared memory and synchronization [6]. These abstractions provide an easy way to understand and handle parallelization. These abstractions are designed so the actual implementation does not need to know the details of the hardware (number for cores, etc.) (see Fig. 1). The idea is to divide the problem in blocks of threads. Then each block of threads works cooperatively to solve the problem. In this way scalability is easily achieved, see Fig. 1. To understand image filtering implementations on GPUs, and to make this article self-contained, we first review the basics using a simple examples of vectors and matrices addition (This section is based on [6]).

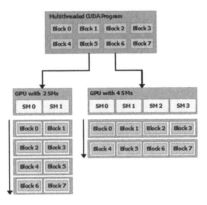

Fig. 1. From [6]: *A multithreaded program is partitioned into blocks of threads that execute independently from each other, so that a GPU with more multiprocessors will automatically execute the program in less time than a GPU with fewer multiprocessors.*

CUDA Kernels. A kernel is a function that runs N times in parallel on N different threads. In the following code a kernel is used to sum in parallel to vectors of dimension N using N threads (see Fig. 2).

```
// Kernel definition
__global__ void VecAdd(float* A, float* B, float* C){
    int i = threadIdx.x;
    C[i] = A[i] + B[i];
}
// Kernel invocation with N threads
VecAdd<<<1, N>>>(A, B, C);
```

Fig. 2. Kernel to sum two vectors.

CUDA threads are three dimensional vectors which enable processing blocks up to dimensions three. The following code in Fig. 3 shows how to add two matrices.

```
__global__ void MatAdd(float A[N][N],
                       float B[N][N], float C[N][N]){
    int i = threadIdx.x;
    int j = threadIdx.y;
    C[i][j] = A[i][j] + B[i][j];
}
// Kernel with one block of NxNx1 threads
int numBlocks = 1;
dim3 threadsPerBlock(N, N);
MatAdd<<<numBlocks, threadsPerBlock>>>(A, B, C);
```

Fig. 3. Kernel to sum two matrices.

Since the number of threads is bounded (in actual GPUs by 1024) and all threads of a block reside in the same core, when dealing with large vectors or matrices, the problem must be organized into several blocks. CUDA blocks can be organized into one, two or three dimensional grids. In this way, the problem can be organized into a number of blocks per grid and threads per block. This allows for flexibility to organize the omputations. The code in Fig. 4 shows how to add two matrices organizing the computation into blocks of size 16×16. The matrices are divided with a tiling of 16×16. Since there is no guarantee that N is multiple of 16, inside the kernel we must verify that the pixel (i, j) resided inside the matrices. The choice of blocks of size 16×16 can be modified to take advantage of the GPU capabilities.

```
__global__ void MatAdd(float A[N][N],
                       float B[N][N], float C[N][N]){
    int i = blockIdx.x * blockDim.x + threadIdx.x;
    int j = blockIdx.y * blockDim.y + threadIdx.y;
    if (i < N && j < N)
        C[i][j] = A[i][j] + B[i][j];
}
// Kernel invocation
dim3 threadsPerBlock(16, 16);
dim3 numBlocks(N / threadsPerBlock.x, N / threadsPerBlock.y);
MatAdd<<<numBlocks, threadsPerBlock>>>(A, B, C);
```

Fig. 4. Kernel to add two matrices using CUDA blocks.

4   Image Filtering in GPUs

This section discussed the GPU implementation using CUDA of the image filters presented above. We will use the basic notions of GPU programming with CUDA introduced in previous section.

4.1   Convolution

The code in Fig. 5 is a direct implementation of 3×3 linear image filter. The code is very similar to the one in C used for the CPU. The main difference is that in this case the pixel indices i and j are obtained from the grid and block organization of the computation on the device. This implementation follows the same philosophy of the code seen before to add two matrices. The code snippet in Fig. 6 shows how to organize the memory allocation and kernel invocation.

```
__global__ void filter(float *f, float* g, int rows, int cols){
  int i = blockIdx.x * blockDim.x + threadIdx.x;
  int j = blockIdx.y * blockDim.y + threadIdx.y;
  ...

  if ( i>=w && j>=w && i<cols-w && j<cols-w ){
    float h[3][3] = {...};
    float sum = 0;
    for (int ii=-w; ii<=w; ii++){
      for (int jj=-w; jj<=w; jj++){
        float fij = f[ (i+ii)*rows + (j+jj) ];
        sum += h[ii+w][jj+w] * fij;
      }
    }
  // store output. sumh is the sum of all weights h[][]
  g[i*cols + j] = sum/sumh;
}
```

Fig. 5. Kernel for direct implementation for liner image filtering.

The first two columns of Table 1 show the results of executing the CPU and GPU version of the sliding window (convolution) method. For small images, the overhead time of memory transfers is higher than the computation cost and therefore the GPU implementation does not give any speed up. For larger images the GPU is an alternative to speed up linear image filtering (the speed ups factors are shown in parenthesis). Although the breakpoint of when GPU outperforms CPU can depend on the hardware (CPU & GPU), the main result holds valid; for small images and filters of low computational demands (small windows) GPUs are not faster than CPUs due to the memory transfer overheads.

```
// HOST memory
float *f = new float[arraySize];
float *g = new float[arraySize];
// DEVICE memory (GPU)
cudaMalloc((void**)&df, size * sizeof(float));
cudaMalloc((void**)&dg, size * sizeof(float));
// Copy image f from DEVICE to HOST
cudaMemcpy2D(df, pitch, f, size*sizeof(float)*fils,
            cudaMemcpyHostToDevice);
// Kernel invocation
dim3 block(16, 16);
dim3 grid(fils/16, cols/16);
filter <<<grid,block>>>(df, dg, fils, cols);
// Copy result from DEVICE to HOST
cudaMemcpy(g, dg, size*sizeof(float), cudaMemcpyDeviceToHost);
```

Fig. 6. Kernel to add two matrices using CUDA blocks.

CUDA Texture Memory. Texture memory is a read-only memory that can be used to improve performance. Optimizing memory access in the GPU provides benefits in terms of computational time [8]. Texture memory is one of the most basic improvements that can be added to the code of the image filter. The only modification in the kernel code is the access to pixel data f[i][j] using float fij = tex2D(texf, i + ii, j + jj) where texf is a texture connected to array f. In Table 1 we can see that the use of texture memory reduces the running time. Once again, we observe that the differences appear for large images.

4.2 Separable Convolution

The GPU implementation of a separable filter needs two kernels; one to filter by rows and the other by columns. Separable convolution can provide speedups around 3 times[2]. According to [7] the use of texture memory and other memory optimizations an additional speedup of factor 2 can be obtained (see [7] for details).

5   Results and Discussion

CPU versus GPU. The first result is that when dealing with small images GPU does not provide advantages over CPU (see columns 1 and 2 from Table 1). The actual size of the image where one implementation outperforms the other depends on hardware features. However, the observation holds valid and, as we said before, is due to memory transfers from host to device and backwards. Furthermore, on the CPU side there is still room for improvements using, for

---

[2] In https://blog.kevinlin.info/nvidia-cuda-gpu-computing-and-computer-vision/ there is a detailed analysis of the separable implementation.

example, parallelization with multicores. Therefore, the GPU implementation paysoff for large images on when additional operations will be performed in the GPU with the same data. That is, when other processes will be applied to the same image. In this case, the data transfer cost is shared among several process and makes GPU more attractive. Since in many areas we are seeing an increasing use of high definition images (HDTV, Ultra HDTV), we can expect to have to process large images and therefore GPUs are obviously a good alternative. This is the case of mobile platforms which include a GPU to handle image and video data.

Algorithms. Now we discuss the impact of the algorithms that reduce the computation cost. First we reviewed separable convolution which is a case of interest since many traditional image filters are separable (Gaussian filters, Sobel filters for edge detection, etc.). From the data in Table 1 we can observe and speedup of $\times 1.5$ for a filter of size 3×3. This factor agrees with the estimation in Sect. 2.2. In this case $W = 1$ so the theoretical computation cost reduction is $3/2$. As we mentioned in Sect. 4.2 GPU implementation of separable convolution gives an additional speed up (see [7]). To illustrate the benefits of applying the correct algorithms to decrease the computational cost and improve running times, we discussed Box Filters in Sect. 2.3. Box filters are a special case of linear image filters with many real applications due to their reduced computational cost [9]. The last column of Table 1 shows the obtained running times for a CPU implementation. We must be careful when directly comparing this implementation with the others since this is a special filter (with uniform weights). If we assume that all algorithms implement the same box filter, using a uniform kernel, we can see that the implementation of the box filter (MAF) outperforms all other algorithms. Hence, if the application allows a box image filter then the MAF is a simple and computational efficient algorithm (there is no need for a GPU implementation). Finally, if we need a multiscale version of the box filter, the use of integral images is a good solution. In [2,5] the authors compare GPU and CPU implementation of integral images.

Table 1. Running times in mseg for a 3×3 filter. GeForce GT 430 (96 cores, 1400 Mhz). Intel i7-2600 3.4 GHz, 16 GB RAM, Windows 7 64 bits. (1) Standard CPU. (2) Direct GPU. (3) Direct GPU using texture memory. (4) CPU separable convolution. (5) CPU implementation of MAF.

N	CPU texture (1)	GPU texture (2)	GPU texture (3)	CPU sep. (4)	MAF (5)
512	10	65 ($\times 0.15$)	65 ($\times 0.15$)	7 ($\times 1.42$)	1
1024	42	76 ($\times 0.55$)	75 ($\times 0.55$)	25 ($\times 1.68$)	4
2048	165	105 ($\times 1.58$)	91 ($\times 1.83$)	105 ($\times 1.58$)	17
4096	660	202 ($\times 3.27$)	162 ($\times 4.07$)	440 ($\times 1.50$)	66

6   Conclusions

In this paper we presented an overview of linear image filtering, its basic results based on the theory of linear and invariant systems, and different algorithms to implement the filter. We reviewed different algorithms to reduce the computational cost and discussed their CPU and GPU implementations. We discussed pros and cons of algorithms and their implementations. Based on the results presented in Table 1 we can see that image size must be considered to select the most suited implementation. This paper was intended to understand the basics behind linear image filtering using CPU and GPUs. In real applications, libraries such as NPP (nVidia Performance Primitives) or ArrayFire to name two, must be considered.

References

1. Oppenheim, A.V., Schafer, R.W., John, R.B.: Discrete-Time Signal Processing. Prentice Hall, Englewood Cliffs (1989)
2. Bilgic, B., Horn, B.K.P., Masaki, I.: Efficient integral image computation on the GPU. In: Intelligent Vehicles Symposium (IV), pp. 528–533. IEEE (2010)
3. Krig, S.: Computer Vision Metrics. Textbook Edition. Springer, Cham (2016)
4. Milanfar, P.: A tour of modern image filtering: new insights and methods, both practical and theoretical. IEEE Sig. Process. Mag. **30**(1), 106–128 (2013)
5. Nehab, D., Maximo, A., Lima, R.S., Hoppe, H.: GPU-efficient recursive filtering and summed-area tables. ACM Trans. Graph. (TOG) **30**(6), 176 (2011)
6. nVidia: Cuda c programming guide (2017)
7. Podlozhnyuk, V.: Image convolution with CUDA. NVIDIA Corporation white paper, June 2097(3) (2007)
8. Sanders, J., Kandrot, E.: CUDA by Example: An Introduction to General-Purpose GPU Programming, Portable Documents. Addison-Wesley Professional, Upper Saddle River (2010)
9. Smith, S.W., et al.: The Scientist and Engineer's Guide to Digital Signal Processing. California Technical Pub, San Diego (1997)
10. Viola, P., Jones, M.: Rapid object detection using a boosted cascade of simple features. In: Proceedings of the 2001 IEEE Computer Society Conference on Computer Vision and Pattern Recognition, CVPR 2001, vol. 1, pp. I-511–I-518. IEEE (2001)

Natural User Interfaces:
A Physical Activity Trainer

Nicolás Jofré[(✉)], Graciela Rodríguez, Yoselie Alvarado,
Jacqueline Fernández, and Roberto Guerrero

Laboratorio de Computación Gráfica (LCG), Universidad Nacional de San Luis,
Ejército de los Andes 950, San Luis, Argentina
{npasinetti,gbrodriguez,ymalvarado,jmfer,rag}@unsl.edu.ar

Abstract. Despite the known health benefits of regular participation
in physical activity people still refuse this practise. Nowadays, Virtual
Reality (VR) is a very powerful and compelling computer tool by which
humans can interface and interact with computer-generated environments. In this paper, we propose a virtual training system which can be
customized for the physical activity level of the user. System provides real
time visual action guide and a performance's feedback of users through
a Natural User Interface (NUI). We conduct a brief pilot study to evaluate our virtual trainers in which participants' performance doing physical activities is evaluated via our NUI. Initial results indicate that virtual
training through a NUI is motivating and entertaining for any kind of
user, in particular for individuals with low level of physical activity.

Keywords: Virtual Reality (VR)
Embodied Conversational Agent (ECA)
Natural User Interface (NUI) · Virtual physical activities · Kinect

1 Introduction

Virtual Reality technology has become a very popular technology integrating the
newest research achievements in the fields of computer graphics, sensor technology, ergonomics and Human-Computer Interaction (HCI) theory. As a research
tool, Virtual Reality provides numerous opportunities of what can be done and
seen in a virtual world that is not possible in real world [1,2].

In HCI area, Embodied Conversational Characters have emerged as an specific type of multimodal interface, where the system is represented as a person
conveying information to human users via multiple modalities such as voice
and hand gestures, where the internal representation is modality-independent,
both propositional and non-propositional. Embodied Conversational Character
answers questions and performs tasks through interaction in natural language-
style dialogues with users contrasting the traditional view of computers [3].

A. E. De Giusti (Ed.): CACIC 2017, CCIS 790, pp. 122–131, 2018.
https://doi.org/10.1007/978-3-319-75214-3_12

Virtual human research has progressed rapidly over the last 18 years. The first implemented work of this type appeared in 2008 and many works of Embodied Conversational Characters have recently emerged due to interfaces have great potential as smart assistants, travel agents or investment advisors, among others [4–8].

Verbal and non-verbal behavior of virtual characters has become more and more sophisticated as a result of advances in behavior planning and rendering [9]. VR uses these characters for user-environment interaction, where system must collect gestural, positional, sound and biometric user information through use of sophisticated devices [10]. These devices have incremented their simplicity and user-friendliness over time, improving interaction and giving rise to Natural User Interfaces [11]. These interfaces are used to solve problems in many areas such as medicine, robotics, non-verbal communication, among others.

In last years sedentary lifestyle has become an increasing problem for people's health. It is reported to be indeed the cause of several serious illnesses like obesity, diabetes, hypertension and so on. There are many reasons why people do not perform any physical activity: motivational lack, time constraints, difficulties to start, gym membership fees, equipment costs, among others. Physical activity is defined as any bodily movement produced by skeletal muscles that results in energy expenditure.

In order to provide a more natural interaction between humans and machines, HCI works have brought about the wide focus on body motion recognition. This involves the recognition of physical movement of the head, hands, arms, face or body with the aim of conveying kinesic information [12].

In this context, there are some commercial applications like *Nintendo* or *Xbox Games* which provide different entertainment activities [13,14]. These applications track user's body movements, such as knees, arms, legs, waist, hip, among others. However, the aim is not focused on obtaining a healthier lifestyle and training is not personalized.

There exist many physical activities research works in HCI [15–19]. From previous studies, the existing work technologies for this purpose are smart phone applications, sensor devices and image processing, with a few solutions implementing virtual characters [20–22]. Those last-mentioned share in common a low-cost virtual training computer application for users who need to undertake regular physical exercise or cognitive tasks at home, with identified specific shortcomings in user's interface, interaction's place and evaluating methods.

In this work we present a training system based on an Embodied Conversational Agent as a real-time simulation approach to train and guide people's physical activities through a NUI.

This paper is arranged as: a design guidelines of our system is introduced in Sect. 2. Our system is described in Sect. 3. The system architecture is explained and illustrated in Sect. 4. The evaluation and results are shown in Sect. 5. We conclude our paper and propose some future works in Sect. 6.

2   Design Guidelines

In 2005, researchers from different Universities of the United States provided a state of the art of pervasive computing in sport technologies, with the aim to encourage new research in this emerging area and to describe how technology can be applied to sports [23]. They identified three areas of application - *athletic performance, entertainment* and *support for referees* - pointing out some research lines for each, such as studying which sensors are more appropriate to monitor the performance of different kinds of athletes and studying the use of games and special equipment to encourage users to exercise harder.

As was stated in Sect. 1, our work's proposal is the study result of several works related to virtual trainers [20–22,24]. From this, two relevant concepts have been identified: *standard physical activities* (considered by a lot of works) and *learning methods* (used by many similar systems).

2.1   Standard Physical Activities

Levels of participation in physical activity remain low across many age groups, and some strategies to increase activity levels throughout the population are needed. Particularly, is possible to perform a generic levels classification on two groups:

1. Average-to-High Level: people with active jobs or that occasionally play sports and people considering physical activity as regular.
2. Low Level: people with office's work or with relaxing daily life activities.

It is necessary and important to identify and use strategies for making physical activities that are both effective and cost-effective. In general, physical activities can be distinguished in **flexibility exercises** (stretch, do yoga), **muscle fitness exercises** (wall climb, use exercise bands), **vigorous sports and recreation** (play sports, hike, play active games), **vigorous aerobics** (ride a bike, jog, jump rope), **moderate physical activity** (walk, play games, do yard work).

At the same time, these activities can be associated to levels of participation in physical activity of people as follows:

– Average-to-High Level: flexibility exercises, muscle fitness exercises, vigorous sports and recreation, and vigorous aerobics.
– Low Level: flexibility exercises and moderate physical activity.

2.2   Learning Method

Virtual-reality-enhanced interactive learning environments are increasingly common. VR brings together a mixture of virtual and real-life scenarios for a wide range of potential possibilities in teaching and learning.

In this context, *Game Based Learning* (GBL) is a learning method leveraging the power of computer games to captivate and engage end users for a specific purpose, such as to develop new knowledge and skills [25]. From past reviewed studies, the minimum components required in all online games for learning are: *back story and story line, game mechanics, rules, immersive graphical environment, interactivity, challenge/competition* and *risks* [26]. Additionally, many educators use this method in combination with the following metaphors for an educational game [27]:

- Acquisition: to transfer information from who owns it (the teacher) to a passive receiver (the student).
- Imitation: focuses on imitation of model behaviors through observing the reactions of others to the facts.
- Experimentation: it is applied in the learning of specific activities, complex or dangerous tasks, since it promotes active and contextualized learning processes, mainly related to practical activities and physical abilities to a great extent.
- Participation: the transmitted content by the teacher is taken as a learning stimulus, which occurs naturally and difficult to predict.
- Discovery: learning by discovery can be an individual or social activity; the crucial point is that it creates new contents through the active student's participation.

3   System Description

The basic idea was to simulate an environment where the user can train in a green space accompanied by a virtual trainer.

For user-system interaction, a sport field scenario was modeled and rendered. Scenario was set up with ambient sound, inanimated objects (benches, lights, trees) and animated objects (people). Particularly, people on stage are avatars. The user can navigate through the park, paddle court and other places allowing social interaction. The trainer is a female animated character called **Sara**. This was developed to provide a visual action guide in real time and an actions assessment after physical users' exercises.

As was mentioned in Sect. 2.2, a computer educational game requires certain components and can use several metaphors. While our system allows physical training, it is also an intention to add entertainment to interaction. Additionally, as it has seen in Sect. 2.1, it is possible to perform a generic level classification and to associate certain activities for each level. Thus, some components and metaphors will be indicated along this section.

According to the referred levels, this work established the following particular activities:

- Average-to-High Level: single-leg squats, mountain climbers, tuck jumps and burpees.
- Low Level: squats, lying hip raises, side lunges and frog jumps.

At the interaction's beginning, *Sara*'s face representation welcomes the user and explains him about system's operation (*Acquisition*). The user have to choose one participation level and consequently, the associated level's activities from a *Graphic User Interface* (GUI). The act of choosing a level and an activity implies to enter voice data through a microphone. It is assumed that the user will choose a level according to his/her daily life activities.

After selection, system will show *Sara* in full body to start teaching user selected activity's actions. User's actions are captured and compared to standard *Sara*'s actions (see Fig. 1) while giving, in real time, a fitness score representing how well user performs actions (*Challenge*), besides providing an activity completeness percentage. *Sara* will then provide interpreted feedback based on obtained fitness score and how user can improve his/her actions (*Imitation* and *Experimentation*).

Considering that each physical exercise is related to a bodily movements set which have limbs' degrees associated (information provided by real trainer stored in a database), system provides a fitness score (percentage of mistakes 0%–100%) comparing input movements degrees with stored movements degrees.

Fig. 1. System operation.

The system was developed to work on a computing platform for immersive collaborative 3D virtual world visualization (*Immersive Graphical CAVE-like environment*). This platform allows the user to play an appropriate role (through a character) during system's explanation, physical activity and feedback according with conversational aspects of virtual trainer (which results in a *Verbal Natural User Interface*).

User's actions are captured by a motion sensing input device [28]. The motion device is able to detect the shape of a human body by using an RGB camera and depth sensor (*Skeleton Tracking*). User and bodily sensor must be located inside CAVE-like environment for an enhanced interaction (*interactivity*) and a better recognition of user movements during physical activity (resulting in a *Gestural Natural User Interface*).

4   System Architecture

The implemented training system is an integrated system consisting of three subsystems working in an independent parallel way: a *CAVE-like Subsystem*, a *Conversational Character Subsystem* and a *Motion-NUI Subsystem*. The system comprises the hardware and software necessary to gather the information obtained during the interaction between the user and the training system: via a motion sensing device, sound system, microphone, screen/projection surfaces and projectors, among others.

In the *CAVE-like Subsystem* (immersive environment), the user's movements are captured by the *Motion-NUI Subsystem* which sets in motion the avatar animation according with the user movements and notifies to *Conversational Character Subsystem* a percentage of mistakes done by body area. According to the obtained percentage the character advises users how well they are doing the exercises. Figure 2 shows an overview of training system.

CAVE-like SubSystem will provide the necessary structure for attributes definition, rendering and collaborative multi-visualizations, as well as the needed interactive resources. *Cake-like multi-VRmedia Subsystem* is an approach on a computing platform for immersive collaborative visualization of 3D and dynamic system proposed by [29].

Conversational Character SubSystem is composed by a Conversational Character gifted with human figure animation and verbal communication skills, like natural language processing (by *Automatic Speech Recognition mechanism* (ASR)) and speech recognition and synthesis (by *Text-To-Speech mechanism* (TTS)). This subsystem, named *CAVE-VOX* was presented and evaluated in [7,30] and it was based on previous work [31]. This particular Conversational Character has a collection of responses relevant to a physical activities topic.

Motion-NUI SubSystem is a NUI based on gestures that corresponds with bodily movements. This subsystem obtains, processes and replies information about user's movements. User data is collected thought a motion device, which uses a depth sensor and obtains a 3D input based on user location and posture. The 3D input is utilized for two aspects: user movements analysis and animation data matching. User movements analysis calculates the difference between 3D input and data stored from a predefined data base, and animation data matching calculates the correspondence between 3D input (user body) and user's virtual

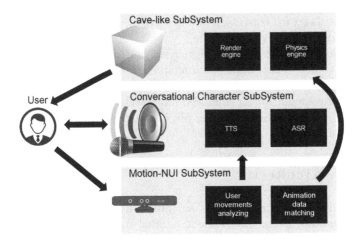

Fig. 2. System architecture.

avatar (virtual body). After animation data matching an avatar animation is set up for reply the user movements.

5 System Evaluation

A pilot test was applied to a twenty-two participants group between 16 and 60 years old. At first, the system functions were explained and demonstrated to the users undertaking the testing. Every user was then required to explore every function and try it out by him/herself.

As was mentioned in Sect. 3, participants must be classified in some level. From the total participants, 8 chose the Average-to-High Level and 14 the Low Level.

During the test, each participant is required twice to execute some corresponding level's activity. Each activity consisted of three sets of exercises: a set of 15 repetitions (first set), a set of 30 repetitions (second set) and a set of 40 repetitions (third set).

Each execution was evaluated in different days (at least two days in between) due to it is not recommended anyone exercise more than once in two days [32]. According with each execution an average percentage of completeness by set were recorded (See Tables 1 and 2).

For Low Level, the percentage of completeness increased significantly as increasing the execution allowing to achieve an incremental learning. For Average-to-High Level, the percentage of completeness gradually increased with each execution, however, the difference among third set and the others was not overwhelming.

Table 1. Completeness' averages for Low Level

Attempt	First set	Second set	Third set
1	82%	73%	66%
2	96%	86%	89%

Table 2. Completeness' averages for Average-to-High Level

Attempt	First set	Second set	Third set
1	95%	87%	71%
2	97%	96%	94%

6   Conclusions and Future Works

This paper involved the development and evaluation of a training system based in an ECA. We described the design and learning aspects, along with the standard physical activities considered for the implemented system. We introduced the general and most important issues of the training system like, *CAVE-like*, *Conversational Character*, and *Motion-NUI SubSystem*.

The obtained results show that people doing regular physical exercises had no difficulties with virtual exercising but they had an appreciable period of adjustment during first execution. On the other hand, people in Low Level had considerable difficulties and a major period of adjustment on all testing. As regards period of adjustment, we considered that it is necessary to make usability tests and include interviews with children.

Future works will be oriented to:

– improve user's experience, adding new challenges related to physical activities,
– develop additional evaluations of the existing virtual training system,
– extend the pilot test.

References

1. Sherman, W., Craig, A.: Understanding Virtual Reality: Interface, Application, and Design. Elsevier, San Francisco (2002)
2. Blascovich, J., Bailenson, J.: Infinite Reality: Avatars, Eternal Life, New Worlds, and the Dawn of the Virtual Revolution. William Morrow & Co., New York (2011)
3. Mancini, M., Pelachaud, C.: Generating distinctive behavior for embodied conversational agents. J. Multimodal User Interfaces **3**(4), 249–261 (2009)
4. Cassell, J., Bickmore, T., Campbell, L., Vilhjálmsson, H., Yan, H.: Human conversation as a system framework: designing embodied conversational agents. In: Embodied conversational agents, pp. 29–63. MIT Press, Cambridge (2000)
5. Mancini, M.: Multimodal Distinctive Behavior for Expressive Embodied Conversational Agents. Universal Publishers (2008)

6. Chen, Q., Torroni, P., Villata, S., Hsu, J., Omicini, A. (eds.): PRIMA 2015. LNCS (LNAI), vol. 9387. Springer, Cham (2015). https://doi.org/10.1007/978-3-319-25524-8

7. Jofré, N., Rodriguez, G., Alvarado, Y., Fernández, J., Guerrero, R.: Virtual humans conversational character for a cave-like environment. In: XX Congreso Argentino de Ciencias de la Computación, vol. 20, pp. 937–946 (2014)

8. Pérez, J., Cerezo, E., Serón, F.: E-VOX: a socially enhanced semantic ECA. In: Proceedings of the International Workshop on Social Learning and Multimodal Interaction for Designing Artificial Agents, DAA 2016, New York, pp. 2:1–2:6. ACM (2016)

9. Kopp, S., Wachsmuth, I.: Model-based animation of co-verbal gesture. In: Proceedings of Computer Animation, pp. 252–257. IEEE (2002)

10. Burdea, G., Coiffet, P.: Virtual reality technology. Int. J. e-Collab. **2**(1), 61–64 (2006)

11. Blake, J.: Nat. User Interfaces in.NET. Manning Pubs Co Series. Manning Publications Company, Greenwich (2012)

12. Koenemann, J., Burget, F., Bennewitz, M.: Real-time imitation of human whole-body motions by humanoids. In: 2014 IEEE International Conference on Robotics and Automation (ICRA), pp. 2806–2812, May 2014

13. Sheff, D.: Game Over: How Nintendo Conquered the World. Vintage, New York (2011)

14. Andrews, J., Baker, N.: Xbox 360 system architecture. IEEE Micro **26**(2), 25–37 (2006)

15. Miller, K., Adair, B., Pearce, A., Said, C., Ozanne, E., Morris, M.: Effectiveness and feasibility of virtual reality and gaming system use at home by older adults for enabling physical activity to improve health-related domains: a systematic review. Age Ageing **43**(2), 188–195 (2013)

16. Mellecker, R., McManus, A.: Active video games and physical activity recommendations: a comparison of the gamercize stepper, XBOX Kinect and XaviX J-Mat. J. Sci. Med. Sport **17**(3), 288–292 (2014)

17. Nathan, D., Huynh, D., Rubenson, J., Rosenberg, M.: Estimating physical activity energy expenditure with the kinect sensor in an exergaming environment. PLoS ONE **10**(5), e0127113 (2015)

18. Campos, C., del Castillo, H.: The benefits of active video games for educational and physical activity approaches: a systematic review. J. New Approaches Educ. Res. **5**(2), 115 (2016)

19. Jofré, N., Rodríguez, G., Alvarado, Y., Fernández, J., Guerrero, R.: El uso de la realidad virtual inmersiva en terapias motricess. In: XIX Workshop de Investigadores en Ciencias de la Computación (2017)

20. Li, B., Maxwell, M., Leightley, D., Lindsay, A., Johnson, W., Ruck, A.: Development of exergame-based virtual trainer for physical therapy using kinect. In: Schouten, B., Fedtke, S., Schijven, M., Vosmeer, M., Gekker, A. (eds.) Games for Health 2014, pp. 79–88. Springer, Wiesbaden (2014). https://doi.org/10.1007/978-3-658-07141-7_11

21. Pedraza-Hueso, M., Martín-Calzón, S., Díaz-Pernas, F., Martínez-Zarzuela, M.: Rehabilitation using kinect-based games and virtual reality. Procedia Comput. Sci. **75**, 161–168 (2015)

22. Shaw, L., Tourrel, R., Wunsche, B., Lutteroth, C., Marks, S., Buckley, J.: Design of a virtual trainer for exergaming. In: Proceedings of the Australasian Computer Science Week Multiconference, p. 63. ACM (2016)

23. Chi, E., Borriello, G., Hunt, G., Davies, N.: Guest editors' introduction: pervasive computing in sports technologies. IEEE Pervasive Comput. **4**(3), 22–25 (2005)
24. Cózar-Gutiérrez, R., Sáez-López, J.: Game-based learning and gamification in initial teacher training in the social sciences: an experiment with MinecraftEdu. Int. J. Educ. Technol. High. Educ. **13**(1), 2 (2016)
25. Tan, P., Ling, S., Ting, C.: Adaptive digital game-based learning framework. In: Proceedings of the 2nd International Conference on Digital Interactive Media in Entertainment and Arts, pp. 142–146. ACM (2007)
26. Derryberry, A.: Serious games: online games for learning (2013)
27. Simons, P., Ruijters, M.: Varieties of work related learning. Int. J. Educ. Res. **47**(4), 241–251 (2008)
28. Zhang, Z.: Microsoft kinect sensor and its effect. IEEE Multimed. **19**(2), 4–10 (2012)
29. Alvarado, Y., Moyano, N., Quiroga, D., Fernández, J., Guerrero, R.: A virtual reality computing platform for real time 3D visualization. In: Augmented Virtual Realities for Social Developments. Experiences Between Europe and Latin America, pp. 214–231. Universidad de Belgrano (2014)
30. Alvarado, Y., Claudia, G., Gil Costa, V., Guerrero, R.: ARENA simulation model of a conversational character's speech system. In: Computer Science & Technology Series XXII Argentine Congress of Computer Science-Selected Papers, pp. 119–129. Universidad de La Plata (2017)
31. Serón, F., Bobed, C., Latorre, P.: The Vox system. In: Augmented Virtual Realities for Social Developments. Experiences Between Europe and Latin America, pp. 130–159. Universidad de Belgrano (2014)
32. World Health Organization: Recomendaciones mundiales sobre actividad física para la salud (2010)

Software Engineering

Proposal for the Formation of Experimental Pair Programmers

Mauricio Dávila[1(✉)], Marisa Panizzi[1], and Darío Rodríguez[2,3]

[1] Master's Degree Program in Information Systems, Universidad Tecnológica Nacional, Facultad Regional Buenos Aires, Castro Barros 91, C1178AAA C.A.B.A, Argentina
davilamr.80@gmail.com, marisapanizzi@outlook.com
[2] Engineering Group for Virtual Workstations and Information Systems Research Group, Department of Technological Productive Development, Universidad Nacional de Lanús, 29 de Septiembre 3901, B1826GLC Lanús, Buenos Aires, Argentina
dariorodriguez1977@gmail.com
[3] Commission for Scientific Research - CIC, Calle 526 e/10 y 11, B1906APP La Plata, Buenos Aires, Argentina

Abstract. This work proposes a protocol aimed to form homogeneous experimental pairs of programmers to ensure that two individuals with the same characteristics are undistinguishable in terms of their abilities as programmers. This protocol enables the measurement and evaluation of the characteristics of programming languages independently of the programmers' skills or the lack of them. A test case is presented so that it validates the protocol. To this end, the protocol will be applied to a group of C language programmers to show that the members of the experimental pairs formed do not show significant differences, in terms of quality and time, in the coding of a specification.

Keywords: Experimentation in software engineering · Protocol
Experimental pair programmers · Programming

1 Introduction

At present, there is a great diversity of programming languages and this often makes it difficult to select the language that better adapts to the needs of a given development. The selection of a programming language to find a solution entails multiple factors of analysis, many of which are subject to the generated source code and the time employed to generate it.

Using the systematic reviews method [1], a documentary research has been conducted on studies which discuss the metrics that can be established on the generated code with a given programming language [2–5]. When metrics are used to determine whether a language is the best choice compared to another one, it must not be overlooked that such metrics only focus on the resulting code and do not take into consideration the characteristics of the programmer who built the code. This may result in the sub classification or over classification of a language as a result of the skills or the lack of them of the programmers using it. This poses a problem when it comes to designing an

© Springer International Publishing AG, part of Springer Nature 2018
A. E. De Giusti (Ed.): CACIC 2017, CCIS 790, pp. 135–144, 2018.
https://doi.org/10.1007/978-3-319-75214-3_13

experiment to determine the language to be used, since the group of programmers who use language A may have a higher level of knowledge than the group of programmers who use language B or vice versa, which would impact on the results of the experiment. One possible solution to this problem would be to have a group of programmers who can solve the same task in the languages that are being evaluated.

Beyond the difficulty in gathering this group of individuals with the necessary knowledge in each language to be evaluated, this solution poses some additional difficulties which arise when designing experiments.

Both Juristo and Moreno [6] and Wohlin et al. [7] argue that the experiments performed in the field of software engineering are strongly influenced by the characteristics of the individuals, like in other sciences, generally known as social sciences. Juristo and Moreno [6] enumerate some issues related to social factors and the specific characteristics of the software development that must be taken into consideration when designing experiments.

- Learning effect: If an individual should solve the same issue applying different programming languages, it is highly probable that they will learn more and more about the issue and that the final result will be better than the first one, simply due to the fact that the individual knows more about the issue rather than due to the fact that the programming language is better.
- Boredom effect: the individuals get bored or tired of the experiment and put less effort and interest as time passes by.
- Enthusiasm effect: It may happen that the individuals who use an old programming language are not motivated to do a good job while those who use a new programming language are.
- Experience effect: when performing an experiment that involves programmers, it is to be expected that there will be different levels of both knowledge and skill about the programming language used.
- Unconscious formalization: it happens when the same individual uses two or more programming languages with different levels of definition or formality.
- Setting effect: the emotional state of participating individuals is closely related to their performance.

A set of actions to consider so as to control the abovementioned effects is described below:

- Learning effect: do not use the same group of individuals to work on a development using more than one programming language.
- Boredom effect: motivate the individuals who perform the experiment in the same way regardless of the group they belong to.
- Enthusiasm effect: do not inform the individuals about the hypotheses or objectives of the experiment.
- Experience effect: to control this effect, experimental pair programmers who are undistinguishable in terms of their knowledge and skills regarding the programming language will be formed.

- Unconscious formalization: aspects regarding the level of knowledge of each individual should be considered when it comes to the programming language employed when forming the experimental pair.
- Setting effect: it must be taken into consideration that all the steps of the experiment should be carried out under the same conditions.

In the field of software engineering, it is common to face a need to perform experiments with a reduced group of people who apply different treatments on the objects of study. Taking into account that comparing experimental units within homogeneous pairs not only increases the accuracy of the analysis but also allows us to control most of the undesired effects [6] when performing an experiment, this work is based on the hypothesis that it is possible to form homogeneous experimental pairs of programmers and that, therefore, two subjects with the same characteristics are undistinguishable in terms of their abilities as programmers. This hypothesis leads to the following research questions: is it possible to form undistinguishable experimental pairs in terms of abilities and skills as programmers? If so, do they require the same amount of time to solve the same task with the same programming language?

In Sect. 2, a protocol for the formation of experimental pairs programmers is proposed. In Sect. 3, the validation of the protocol is performed through a pilot test; and in Sect. 4, conclusions and future lines of research are presented.

2 Proposal for the Formation of Experimental Pair Programmers

When it comes to deciding how to form homogeneous pairs of programmers, the authors adhere to Campbell [8], who argues that many factors may indirectly affect the performance of an individual, but only three are direct determinants of performance: *knowledge, skill* and *motivation*. For this reason, a protocol will be designed with the aim to form experimental pairs of programmers who are homogeneous in terms of both level of knowledge and skills, and it will be assumed that the participants to be characterized do not show significant differences regarding motivation.

The first step consists in identifying the methods used to categorize programmers in other experimental research studies (Sect. 2.1). Then, the guidelines considered for the design of the categorization instruments used in the experiment are described (Sect. 2.2). Lastly, (Sect. 2.3) presents a mechanism to form homogeneous experimental pairs of programmers based on the characterization made.

2.1 Programmers' Experience

Like in most human activities, individual performance in software development varies considerably from one person to another and mechanisms should be articulated so that such variations do not affect the results of the study. Feigenspan et al. [9] conducted a documentary work which analyzed 161 publications and found nine ways used by researchers to determine a programmer's experience. These authors define experience as the amount of knowledge acquired regarding the development of programs.

- Years: in forty-seven works, the number of years a programmer had been programming in general or in a company or in a certain language was used to determine their experience in the programming field.
- Education: In nineteen of the articles reviewed, participants' education was used to indicate their experience, which included information about the level of education obtained (pre-university, undergraduate, graduate, etc.) or the grades obtained in their course of studies.
- Self-estimation: In twelve works, participants were asked to estimate their own experience.
- Specific survey: In nine works, the authors applied a survey to evaluate programming experience.
- Size: the size of the programs written by the participants was used as an indicator in six articles.
- Exam: In three works, an exam on programming was administered to evaluate the experience of the participants.
- Supervisor: In two works, in which professional programmers acted as participants, a supervisor was in charge of estimating their experience.
- Not specified: authors often argue that programming experience was estimated but they did not specify how. That was the case in thirty-nine works.
- Not controlled: programming experience was not mentioned at all in forty-five works, which compromises the validity of the corresponding experiments.

2.2 Characterization of Programmers

It is necessary to develop a characterization method that is not based on the perception that each individual has on their own skill as a programmer since less competent people tend to overestimate their skills because they do not have enough knowledge to recognize their own limitations and it is also common for more prepared people to tend to underestimate their achievements and competences [12]. This characterization is aimed at establishing a set of the programmer's abilities in order to find programming pairs that may be considered homogeneous. The purpose of the characterization is to ensure that two individuals with the same characteristics are undistinguishable in terms of their abilities as programmers. To this purpose, it was decided that a broad set of skills of the programmer would be analyzed. The authors agree on the idea that the elaboration of a characterization based only on few criteria may result in serious errors. Some characteristics of the programmers are not related to the programming language and others are dependent upon it. For this reason, guidelines to develop two characterization instruments will be set, one disregarding the programming language (in Spanish, CILP) and another taking into account the programming language (in Spanish, CDLP). There exists a large number of measures to capture attributes of software processes and products which have traditionally been performed by relying on the experts' proficiency, and this situation has frequently led to a certain degree of inaccuracy in the definitions, properties and assumptions of the measurements, making the use of measurements difficult, their interpretation dangerous and the results of many validation studies contradictory [10]. For the development of characterization tools, the general procedure for the design of a measurement instrument proposed by Sampiere [11] and the method for the definition of valid measurements proposed by Genero et al. [10] were taken into account, adapting such procedures to the needs of this work.

Due to issues related to the synthesis demanded by this publication, it is not possible to detail each of the steps followed to define either the instruments or the content of each of their dimensions.

Table 1 presents the content domains of the variable (dimensions), the indicators for each dimension and the nomenclature proposed for the dimensions of the instrument that will be used for the independent characterization of the programming language.

Table 1. Variable, dimensions, nomenclature for each dimension and their indicators.

Variable to be measured	Dimension	Nomenclature	Indicator
Characteristics which are independent of the programming language	*Education level*	***CILP1***	It refers to the education level attained by the participant, whether formally or informally
	Experience	***CILP2***	It refers to the years of experience as a programmer and to the number of languages the participant declares to know
	Comprehension of a specification	***CILP3***	Ability of the programmer to understand a simple specification and the time spent on it
	Comprehension of a pseudocode	***CILP4***	Ability of the programmer to interpret the operation of pseudocode blocks and the time spent on it
	Algorithmic ability	***CILP5***	Ability of the programmer to develop a solution with pseudocode and the time spent on developing such solution

Table 2 shows the content domains of the variable (dimensions), the indicators for each dimension and the nomenclature proposed for the dimensions of the instrument that will be used to measure the dependent characterization of the programming language.

Table 2. Variable, dimensions, nomenclature for each dimension and their indicators.

Variable to be measured	Dimension	Nomenclature	Indicator
Characteristics which are dependent on the programming language	*Language chosen*	**CDLP1**	It refers to the programming language that the participant declares to handle more fluently and to the years of experience using it
	Theoretical knowledge	**CDLP2**	It refers to the level of knowledge that the participant has on theoretical aspects of the programming language
	Comprehension of the source code	**CDLP3**	Ability of the programmer to interpret the operation of pseudocode blocks and the time spent on it

Regarding the decision on the type and format of the instrument and the context of its administration, the mixed procedure for data collection will be used, consisting of two questionnaires (CILP and CDLP) and an interview.

In order to minimize characterization errors, once the participant has answered the questionnaire, an individual interview will be conducted in which the interviewer will ask some questions so that the participant can justify their answers. If the participant provides a correct justification, the interviewer will consider it valid.

The context of administration will be a room with one computer for each programmer since the first phase, the one related to the questionnaire, is self-administered. Therefore, this can be done individually or simultaneously with a group of people. Then, the interview is conducted individually.

2.3   Mechanism to Form Experimental Pairs

It is important to design a mechanism to ensure that the experimental pairs are formed by homogeneous subjects, which means that, according to their characterization, they should be undistinguishable or have negligible differences.

Criterion for the use of variables. Multiple variables emerge from the characterization procedure, some of them related to characteristics which are independent of the programming language and others related to characteristics dependent on the programmer's performance in a certain programming language.

Normalization. The normalization process consists in converting the values of the independent variables so that they are expressed in the range [0–10], regardless of their original scale. This step will ensure that none of the variables included in the distance calculation is weighted more heavily than the others.

Penalty for time spent. Each of the variables measured is accompanied by the time spent by the participant to complete the exercises related to such variable. In order to form experimental pairs which are undistinguishable not only in terms of knowledge but also in terms of time required to solve a task, a score penalty will be applied according to the time spent on the it. The score obtained will be reduced by 10% every 5 min.

Distance calculation. In a scenario where multiple variables need to be evaluated, all of them quantitative and whose values belong to the interval [0, 10] after the normalization process, the criterion used to determine the distance between two subjects must be defined. Since an n-dimensional space is being considered, the Euclidean distance calculation will be applied (Fig. 1).

$$d(p,q) = \sqrt{(p_1 - q_1)^2 + (p_2 - q_2)^2 + \cdots + (p_i - q_i)^2 + \cdots + (p_n - q_n)^2}.$$

Fig. 1. Euclidean distance [14]

The calculation of the distance between participants will be performed, where the value of the module of the difference between variables of the same type does not exceed a threshold. This restriction will make it possible to establish the maximum distance tolerated, which shall not entail a significant difference in a single variable.

Algorithm for the selection of experimental pairs. The algorithm follows a sequential process in which it makes a decision at each step. It must select the minimum distance among the options available and then in the next step the algorithm has an identical problem, but with fewer options than in the previous step, and applies the same selection function to make the following decision [13].

3 Case for the Validation of the Protocol

A series of actions were taken to demonstrate the level of initial reliability and validity of the measurement instruments. The characteristics included in the formation of experimental pairs are: Comprehension of a Specification (CILP3), Comprehension of a Pseudocode (CILP4), Algorithmic Ability (CILP5), Theoretical Knowledge (CDLP2) and Comprehension of the Source Code (CDLP3).

To perform the initial pilot test, we recruited people of legal age who declared to know C programming language, and formed a group of 14 programmers. After each participant was characterized, they were asked to solve a task of medium complexity. Then, the protocol for the formation of experimental pairs of programmers was applied in order to determine whether the members of each experimental pair showed any significant differences in solving the task. If the experimental pairs formed by applying the protocol do not present significant differences when solving the same task using the same language, both the instruments and the protocol for the formation of experimental pairs can be deemed to have reached a stable version.

The results obtained from the characterization process are shown in Table 3. Table 4 presents the corresponding distance matrix. The intersections painted in black represent the subjects who should be ruled out since they have shown a distance over fifty percent in at least one of their dimensions. The experimental pairs obtained after applying the algorithm are highlighted in gray. Finally, the time differences between the programmers in each experimental pair are presented Table 5.

Table 3. Normalized results of the characterization.

Subject	CDLP2	CDLP3	CILP3	CILP4	CILP5
1	2.40	0.00	10.00	0.00	1.64
2	8.10	6.75	9.00	5.00	6.36
3	6.40	4.00	7.50	5.00	2.73
4	9.00	9.00	4.50	5.00	6.36
5	6.30	2.25	6.75	7.00	2.18
6	7.20	6.00	4.50	9.00	0.67
7	8.10	0.00	7.50	4.50	1.48
8	5.60	2.25	10.00	4.50	4.43
9	8.00	4.50	6.75	9.00	2.96
10	6.30	4.50	4.50	4.50	7.64
11	7.20	2.50	6.75	5.00	1.86
12	9.00	6.75	9.00	9.00	5.45
13	5.60	0.00	7.50	5.00	7.00
14	6.40	0.00	9.00	4.50	3.87

Table 4. Distance matrix

ID	2	4	5	7	9	11	12	14
2	-	5.11	7.07		6.14	6.65	4.20	
4	5.11	-			7.34		6.49	
5	7.07		-	3.95	3.54	2.23	6.88	4.38
7			3.95	-	6.58	2.83		9.20
9	6.14	7.34	3.54	6.58	-	4.67	4.17	7.00
11	6.65		2.23	2.83	4.67	-	7.44	4.03
12	4.20	6.49	6.88		4.17	7.44	-	
14			4.38	9.20	7.00	4.03		-

Table 5. Differences in time spent by each member of the experimental pair

Subjects		Difference	
		Time	%
2	4	6	7.06%
5	11	3	2.48%
7	14	5	4.76%
9	12	5	4.35%

With regard to the time spent to perform the characterization, the average time for the characterization that was independent of the programming language was 28 min; for the characterization dependent on the programming language, the average was 19 min; and for the interview, an average of 6 min was used for each participant. In Table 5, it can be observed that there are no significant differences between the members of the experimental pairs of programmers in relation to the time spent on solving the same task.

4 Conclusions and Future Work

With the aim of proposing a protocol for the formation of experimental pairs of programmers, a document analysis was conducted on the benefits brought by this type of experiment to the software engineering sector. Two instruments were designed to characterize programmers. Using the data obtained from these characterization instruments, a procedure for the formation of experimental pairs was defined.

Finally, a validation case was implemented to verify whether the members of the experimental pairs obtained showed any differences in solving the same programming task.

It can be concluded that in terms of the formation of experimental pairs of programmers, the protocol worked satisfactorily and it is thus considered to have an acceptable level of reliability, validity and objectivity since it was consistent in the results provided.

The future lines of work identified are the need to: (1) apply the protocol to other programming languages and (2) use the protocol to form experimental pairs of subjects using different programming languages in order to determine whether a given programming language affects computing productivity.

References

1. Argimón, J.: Métodos de Investigación Clínica y Epidemiológica. Elsevier, Barcelona (2004). ISBN 8174-709-2
2. Halstead, M.: Elements of Software Science. Elsevier Science Inc., New York (1977)
3. McCabe, T.J.: A complexity measure. IEEE Trans. Softw. Eng. **4**, 308–320 (1976)
4. Riaz, M., Mendes, E., Tempero, E.: A systematic review of software maintainability prediction and metrics. In: Proceedings of the 2009 3rd International Symposium on Empirical Software Engineering and Measurement, pp. 367–377. IEEE Computer Society (2009)
5. Rilling, J., Klemola, T.: Identifying comprehension bottlenecks using program slicing and cognitive complexity metrics. In: 10th IEEE Working Conference on Reverse Engineering, pp. 115–125. IEEE, Oregon (2003)
6. Juristo, N., Moreno, A.M.: Basics of Software Engineering Experimentation. Springer, London (2013)
7. Wohlin, C., Runeson, P., Höst, M., Ohlsson, M.C., Regnell, B., Wesslén, A.: Experimentation in Software Engineering. Springer, Heidelberg (2012). https://doi.org/10.1007/978-3-642-29044-2
8. Campbell, J.P., McCloy, R.A., Oppler, S.H., Sager, C.E.: A theory of performance. In: Schmitt, N., Bormann, W.C., et al. (eds.) Personnel Selection in Organizations, pp. 35–70. Jossey-Bass, San Francisco (1993)

9. Feigenspan, J., Kästner, C., Liebig, J., Apel, S., Hanenberg, S.: Measuring programming experience. In: IEEE 20th International Conference on Program Comprehension (ICPC), pp. 73–82. IEEE (2012)
10. Genero, M., Cruz-Lemus, J.A., Piattini, M.: Métodos de Investigación en Ingeniería del Software. RaMa (2014)
11. Sampieri, R.H., Collado, C.F., Lucio, P.B.: Metodología de la investigación. McGraw-Hill, Mexico (2010)
12. Kruger, J., Dunning, D.: Unskilled and unaware of it: how difficulties in recognizing one's own incompetence lead to inflated self-assessments. J. Pers. Soc. Psychol. **77**(6), 1121 (1999)
13. Soriano, M.A.: Algoritmos Voraces. Facultat d'Informàtica, U.P.C. (2007). http://www.cs.upc.edu/~mabad/ADA/curso0708/GREEDY.pdf. Accessed 3 Jan 2017
14. Elena, D., Deza, M.M.: Encyclopedia of Distances, p. 94. Springer, Heidelberg (2009). https://doi.org/10.1007/978-3-642-00234-2

Reusing a Geographic Software Product Line Platform: A Case Study in the Paleontological Sub-domain

Fiorella Pesce[1], Sofia Caballero[1], Agustina Buccella[1,2(✉)],
and Alejandra Cechich[1]

[1] GIISCO Research Group, Departamento de Ingeniería de Sistemas, Facultad de
Informática, Universidad Nacional del Comahue, Neuquen, Argentina
{fiorella.pesce,sofia.caballero,agustina.buccella,
alejandra.cechich}@fi.uncoma.edu.ar
[2] CONICET, Buenos Aires, Argentina

Abstract. Developing Software Product Lines (SPLs) is a paradigm oriented to reusing software within particular domains. Key aspects within this paradigm are the inherent particularities of these domains and the techniques applied to systematize the ways to maximize reuse. In this article, we describe a process for creating SPLs by reusing through domain hierarchies, starting from the geographical domain and going deeper into the paleontological sub-domain. In particular, our process is based on standardizations and previous techniques already applied to another geographical sub-domain, which is marine ecology. Here we show how these techniques are applied in the paleontological sub-domain, improving the systematic reuse of software artifacts.

Keywords: Software Product Lines · Domain reuse
Geographic domain · Paleontology

1 Introduction

Software Product Line Engineering (SPLE) [6,13,18] proposes a software development process whose main objective is to maximize the reuse of artifacts to obtain faster-developed and high-quality software applications. Considering that the SPL development focuses on domain-oriented reuse, the success of the development depends on the identification, use and administration of the artifacts inside those domains; and therefore, the application of specific techniques for systematizing reuse becomes crucial.

The geographical domain [11] is broad in the sense it includes general aspects applicable to all products within this domain. Here, the creation of an SPL can be impracticable (the amount of variability that would have to be defined within each service will become unmanageable). So, it is logical to think about the division into different sub-domains, where each one has certain characteristics of the geographical domain, such as zooming in a map, obtaining coordinates, etc.; and certain

© Springer International Publishing AG, part of Springer Nature 2018
A. E. De Giusti (Ed.): CACIC 2017, CCIS 790, pp. 145–154, 2018.
https://doi.org/10.1007/978-3-319-75214-3_14

special characteristics such as knowing the depth of the ocean in certain areas. In this way, we build components designed to be part of a hierarchy of domains; that is, a set of general services is defined at the level of the geographical generic domain, and it is applicable to any SPL implemented within the included sub-domains.

In the literature, SPLE is a very active research area where there are many proposals for techniques or methods that improve the activities involved in SPL development. This can be seen in the number of literary or systematic reviews that exist today focused on techniques for modeling, implementation, validation, and so on [4,5,12,16]. Similar approaches to our proposal addressing a hierarchy of domains can be those related to the development of software ecosystems or multiple software product lines [7,15]. In general, these works focus on the problem of having developed components for different domains that must then work together to be integrated within the same development. In our case, these problems are minimized since the components are designed to be part of a hierarchy within the geographical domain sharing already defined standardizations.

A first approximation to our approach has been presented in [9,10] where we have built an SPL within the marine ecology sub-domain, but taking common services from higher-level domains such as the oceanographic and the geographical. In these works, we have defined a methodology for the creation of SPLs that designs and implements a series of *software artifacts* necessary to communicate and model the domain based on standardizations and proper techniques. In this article we show the development process for the creation of SPLs, based on the previously presented methodology [9,10], but focusing on reusing artifacts now created and adapted to the paleontological sub-domain. In particular, we focus on three of the software artifacts created as part of the domain engineering.

This article is organized as follows. In the next section we briefly describe our SPL development process oriented to the geographic domain and its sub-domains. In Sect. 3 we show a case study where we apply this process to the paleontological sub-domain. Here, we model the information relevant to excavations to find paleontological pieces. Then, we performed a preliminary validation where we analyzed improvements due to reuse. Finally, we address conclusions and future work.

2   Development Process for Building Domain-Oriented SPLs

Figure 1 shows the four steps of our process for the domain engineering during SPL development. Recall that this engineering is responsible for identifying, capturing and organizing all the source information collected. As a result, it generates a software platform with a set of reusable and configurable artifacts that provide a common environment [18].

In our development methodology, domain engineering is divided into two types of analyses: *domain* and *organizational*. The former involves the analysis and design of the information within a specific domain but focusing on a general

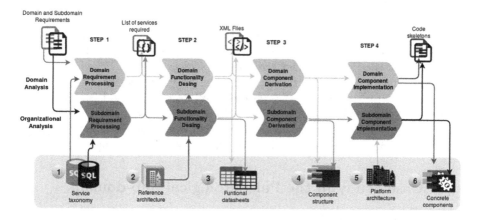

Fig. 1. Development process as part of the domain engineering, along with created and used software artifacts

view. Then, the organizational analysis uses the previous information to adapt it to the context of the SPL under development. In our application case, during the domain analysis the general geographical domain must be analyzed, obtaining common services that could be relevant to a set of sub-domains. Then, during the organizational analysis, the activities are focused on the specific sub-domain, in our case, on the paleontological sub-domain.

In Fig. 1 we can see the six software artifacts that must be developed or used in the four steps of the domain engineering. In general, each artifact is built during the domain analysis (artifacts in gray color) and refined and completed in the organizational analysis (artifacts in black). The first artifact, which is one of the inputs of step 1, is the *service taxonomy* built as a hierarchical structure. It shows the categories that allow classifying the different services. In previous works, we have built this taxonomy for the geographical domain considering the Architecture Services standard (defined in the OpenGIS Service Architecture)[1], and the ISO/DIS 19119 std.[2] as a basis for defining services and their categories [10].

The second artifact is a *reference architecture* used as input of step 2 – *functionality design*. This architecture must specify a preliminary structure for the interaction of the services defined in the taxonomy. As we can see, there is only one instance of it in gray because it is reused from the one specified in the ISO 19119 std. In addition, in this step we must create the *functional datasheets* that specify each of the functionalities of the geographical domain (in gray) and the particular sub-domain (in black). They are designed through the interaction of the necessary taxonomy services. Also, each functional datasheet is represented by a set of XML files that allow to automatically analyzing these models in search of inconsistencies or incompatibilities when specifying the variability [8,20]. Then, in step 3, the *domain component derivation* should be performed to

---

[1] The OpenGIS Abstract Specification: Service Architecture, 2002.
[2] Geographic information. Services International Standard 19119, ISO/IEC, 2005.

create reusable components based on the information defined in the functional datasheets [1, 19]. As part of this step and the following one (*component implementation*) we have defined, in previous works, initial mechanisms that assist in the creation of the fourth artifact (*component structure*) [2].

Finally, the refined artifacts determine the structure of the software that implement the fifth artifact – the *platform architecture*. It models the way in which each refined functional datasheet (based on the taxonomy refinement) is implemented as software components. This platform is then used in the configuration of the products to create the architecture of a specific application.

3   A Case Study in the Paleontological Sub-domain

First of all, it is necessary to introduce some particular aspects of this domain. In Fig. 2, we show part of the conceptual model where we focus on the classes that help us to understand the defined functionalities. To build the model, in addition to the elicited information of the expert users of the paleontological sub-domain, we have extracted information from the ISO standards 19109 and 19107 for geographical data, the ISO standards 21127:2014[3], LIDO[4], and CIDOC[5]. These three latest standards are specific to the paleontological sub-domain since they define and classify services and protocols required for the management of collections inside museums and the representation of paleontological pieces.

Figure 2 shows in gay color those classes that have been defined by the expert users and in black color those extracted from the three latest standards. According to the ISO 21127 std., any action that is carried out on a physical object is represented as an activity. In particular, the activity of *prospecting* is the one that reveals areas in which the *extracting* can be carried out by a group of professionals. In the case of finding some *specimen*, the activity of setting up a *jacket* (through the activity of *jacketing*) initiates. A jacket can contain *biological objects – specimen* or *piece*. These are subjected to mechanical and/or chemical procedures to correctly remove the object found. In addition, the geographical information, such as areas and points, has been represented using the MADS (Modeling of Application Data with Spatio-temporal features) [17] approach.

Then, based on this conceptual model and the functional requirements of the sub-domain, we built the *paleontological service taxonomy*. It was defined following the basis described in [10] through the realization of an iterative process that involved all the stakeholders – expert users, software engineers and developers, and used the geographical taxonomy defined by the ISO 19119 std. Also here, we used the specific rules of the sub-domain (already mentioned previously) and the reference architecture of ISO 19119 already applied for the SPL in the marine ecology sub-domain [9].

---

[3] Information and documentation – A reference ontology for the interchange of cultural heritage information.

[4] LIDO – Lightweight Information Describing Objects Version 1.0 – http://network. icom.museum/cidoc/working-groups/lido/what-is-lido/.

[5] CIDOC Conceptual Reference Model Version 6.0 – http://www.ccc-crm.org.

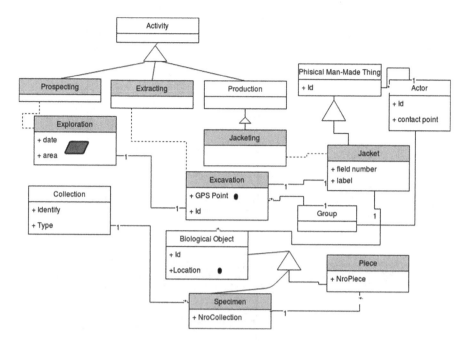

Fig. 2. Part of the data model for the paleontological sub-domain

The reference architecture is a three-layer architecture in which the services of the taxonomy [10] are defined and classified. The first is the *human interaction* layer grouping together the services used to manage the user interface, graphics, and visualization aspects. The second is the *processing* layer, responsible for coordinating the functionalities required by the sub-domain. At the same time, it coordinates the services of the upper layer of human interaction and the lower layer, called *model administration*, which is responsible for handling data and storage.

The taxonomy, which is defined based on the layers of the architecture, has a set of main categories in which the corresponding services should be included. In Fig. 3 we can see some services of the category *human interaction* (HI) already defined previously [10]. These services belong to the geographical domain (in gray and italic), and to the marine ecology sub-domain (in black and italic). Also, the services of the paleontological sub-domain (in black and bold) are defined. We can observe some of them that deal with different ways of information visualization. In this case, we see the attributes of explorations and excavations that can be displayed as tables or by means of labels directly on a map.

In this way, as a result for each category, the complete taxonomy for the paleontological sub-domain is obtained with reused and inherited services from the geographical domain.

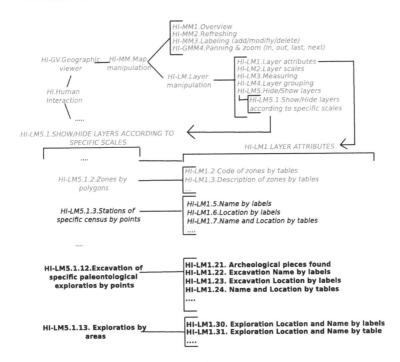

Fig. 3. Some services of the HI category defined by the domain hierarchy

The next step is the creation of the functional datasheets (third artifact) with the functionalities of the sub-domain based on the services of the paleontological taxonomy and the reference architecture. The elaboration of these datasheets follows the same guidelines defined in previous works [1, 14] and uses our supporting tool called *Datasheet Modeler* [14]. It allows developers to create the datasheets by using variability [1] and taxonomy services, and translating to XML files. Figure 4 shows the functionality *Load excavations*, which allows registering a new excavation of an exploration already existing in the system. As we can see, an interaction is carried out between the services of the taxonomy already defined in order to carry out the functionality. The variability represented in this case defines that the data load must contemplate that it can be done in places without internet connections or GPS devices. Therefore, excavation data (such as geographical coordinates and found objects) must be allowed by manually entering information. At the same time, if it is required by any product, the options of loading data that come from spreadsheets files and/or through the devices that contain GPS, are also contemplated.

Then, the XML files of each of these datasheets are created automatically as outputs of the tool. These files allow us to process datasheets automatically, for instance for posterior validation [19, 20]; and create a preliminary structure of reusable components (artifact 4) [2, 3], which will be later part of the architecture

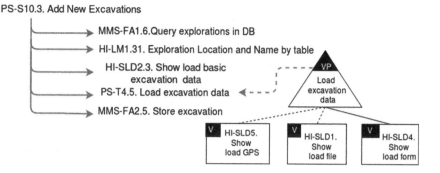

Fig. 4. Functionality representation of *Load excavations* in a functional datasheet

of the platform (artifact 5). These components (artifact 6) must be implemented in the last step.

4 A Preliminary Evaluation of Reuse

In this section we performed an evaluation for analyzing the degree of reuse achieved in two of the artifacts created and described in the previous section.

Firstly, we have analyzed the reuse of the service taxonomy considering the number of services that we have defined for the paleontological sub-domain. For this evaluation we have analyzed three types of services:

- *Completely Reusable Services (CRS)* are those services of the geographical domain or some sub-domain, which are used without modification by the functionalities of the paleontological SPL. Examples of these services are those that are black and red in Fig. 3 and that are related to this sub-domain.
- *Reusable Services for Specialization (RSS)* are new services generated from services already defined for other domains. Examples of these services are the blue ones in Fig. 3.
- *Unreusable Services (URS)* are services created completely new without relationship with the services of the previously developed taxonomy.

Based on these types of services, and from a total of 120 services defined as useful, we identified a 25% as CRS, 58.3% as RSS and 16.6% as URS. Figure 5(a) shows these percentages graphically.

Then, for analyzing the functionalities, we simulated the creation of a product in which we chose a set of ten functionalities (defined in the functional datasheets) as part of the SPL platform, and we have randomly instantiated them in order to generate a new product. To illustrate this process, in Fig. 6 we show the *Load Excavations* datasheet, in which we have instantiated the variability for loading information by using forms or by means of GPS devices. In this way, the resulting product will offer both options for loading an excavation.

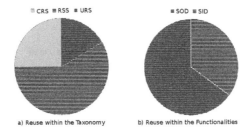

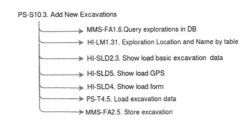

Fig. 5. Analysis of the reuse achieved in the taxonomy and instantiated datasheets

Fig. 6. *Load Excavations* functionality instantiated for a particular product

A similar process was carried out for each of the ten functionalities used for the creation of the product. For analyzing the reuse, we have analyzed the number of *Services of Other Domains (SOD)* used in the functionalities and the number of *Services Included in the Domain (SID)* of the taxonomy. The SODs are those that we have classified as the sum of the CRSs and RSSs, and the SIDs are the URSs. From this analysis, the results show, in Fig. 5(b), a percentage of approximately 65% of SOD and 35% of SID. This result is reasonable considering that many functionalities use RSS services (specialized for the sub-domain).

5   Conclusion and Future Work

In this work, we have shown a process for SPL development oriented to the reuse of software artifacts within a hierarchy of domains. Based on previous work, we have generated artifacts in a new sub-domain – the paleontological – illustrating a possible reuse of our platform. At the same time, we have performed a preliminary analysis of the reuse achieved in the construction of some of these artifacts showing promising results.

As future work, we will extend the process for building the artifacts that are involved in the application engineering of the SPL.

References

1. Buccella, A., Pol'la, M., Cechich, A., Arias, M.: A variability representation approach based on domain service taxonomies and their dependencies. In: International Conference of the Chilean Computer Science Society (SCCC), Talca (2014)

2. Arias, M., Buccella, A., Cechich, A.: Smooth transition from abstract to concrete SPL components: a client-server implementation for the geographic domain. In: Proceedings of the IEEE ARGENCON 2016. GRSS: IEEE GRSS, Buenos Aires (2016)
3. Arias, M., Buccella, A., Cechich, A.: Un marco de trabajo para la gestión de requerimientos de software en líneas de productos de software. In: XLIII Conferencia Latinoamericana en Informática. SLISW - Simposio Latinoamericano de Ingeniería de Software, CLEI 2017 (2017, to appear)
4. Bashroush, R., Garba, M., Rabiser, R., Groher, I., Botterweck, G.: Case tool support for variability management in software product lines. ACM Comput. Surv. **50**(1), 14:1–14:45 (2017). http://doi.acm.org/10.1145/3034827
5. Benavides, D., Segura, S., Ruiz-Cortés, A.: Automated analysis of feature models 20 years later: a literature review. Inf. Syst. **35**, 615–636 (2010)
6. Bosch, J.: Design and Use of Software Architectures: Adopting and Evolving a Product-Line Approach. ACM Press/Addison-Wesley Publishing Co., New York (2000)
7. Bosch, J.: From software product lines to software ecosystems. In: Proceedings of the 13th International Software Product Line Conference, SPLC 2009, pp. 111–119. Carnegie Mellon University, Pittsburgh (2009)
8. Braun, G., Pol'La, M., Cecchi, L., Buccella, A., Fillottrani, P., Cechich, A.: A DL semantics for reasoning over OVM-based variability models. In: 30th International Workshop on Description Logics (DL 2017), France (2017, to appear)
9. Buccella, A., Cechich, A., Arias, M., Pol'la, M., Doldan, S., Morsan, E.: Towards systematic software reuse of GIS: Insights from a case study. Comput. Geosci. **54**, 9–20 (2013). http://www.sciencedirect.com/science/article/pii/S0098300412003913
10. Buccella, A., Cechich, A., Pol'la, M., Arias, M., Doldan, S., Morsan, E.: Marine ecology service reuse through taxonomy-oriented SPL development. Comput. Geosci. **73**, 108–121 (2014). http://www.sciencedirect.com/science/article/pii/S0098300414002155
11. Burrough, P., McDonnell, R.: Principles of Geographical Information Systems. Oxford University Press, Oxford (1998)
12. Capilla, R., Sánchez, A., Dueñas, J.C.: An analysis of variability modeling and management tools for product line development. In: Proceedings of the Software and Services Variability Management Workshop: Concepts, Techniques, and Tools, pp. 32–47 (2007)
13. Clements, P.C., Northrop, L.: Software Product Lines: Practices and Patterns. Addison-Wesley Longman Publishing Co., Inc., Boston (2001)
14. Mancuso, M., Buccella, A., Cechich, A., Arias, M., Pol'la, M.: Datasheet modeler: Una herramienta de soporte para el desarrollo de funcionalidades en líneas de productos de software. In: Proceedings of the XXI Argentine Congress of Computer Science, CACIC 2015, Junin (2015)
15. Manikas, K., Hansen, K.M.: Software ecosystems - a systematic literature review. J. Syst. Softw. **86**(5), 1294–1306 (2013)
16. Munir, Q., Shahid, M.: Software product line: survey of tools. Master's thesis, Linkopings University, Linkopings (2010)
17. Parent, C., Spaccapietra, S., Zimányi, E.: Spatio-temporal conceptual models: data structures + space + time. In: Proceedings of the 7th ACM International Symposium on Advances in Geographic Information Systems, GIS 1999, pp. 26–33. ACM Press, New York (1999)

18. Pohl, K., Böckle, G., van der Linden, F.J.: Software Product Line Engineering: Foundations, Principles and Techniques. Springer, Heidelberg (2005). https://doi.org/10.1007/3-540-28901-1
19. Pol'la, M., Arias, M., Buccella, A., Cechich, A.: Un sistema de anotaciones para la especificación de componentes de una línea de productos de software. Revista Tecnología y Ciencia de la Universidad Tecnológica Nacional **6**(1), 116–122 (2015)
20. Pol'la, M., Buccella, A., Arias, A., Cechich, A.: Sevatax: service taxonomy selection & validation process for SPL development. In: XXXIV International Conference of the Chilean Society of Computer Science (SCCC 2015). IEEE Computer Society Press, Santiago (2015)

Performance Evaluation of a 3D Engine for Mobile Devices

Federico Cristina[1,2], Sebastián Dapoto[1,2(✉)], Pablo Thomas[1,2], and Patricia Pesado[1,2]

[1] Instituto de Investigación en Informática LIDI, Universidad Nacional de La Plata,
La Plata, Argentina
{fcristina,sdapoto,pthomas,ppesado}@lidi.info.unlp.edu.ar
[2] Centro Asociado Comisión de Investigaciones Científicas de la
Provincia de Buenos Aires, La Plata, Argentina

Abstract. Currently there are several frameworks for the development of 3D mobile applications, but all of them have a common issue: performance is a critical aspect to consider, even more relevant than in desktop computers, which generally have a greater computing power. The profiling or performance analysis tools that these frameworks have can help, to some extent, to determine the possible existence of bottlenecks in the execution of applications. However, this type of tool has certain limitations such as covering only a spectrum of the possible causes of the problem or limiting the analysis to certain scenarios in particular. This article proposes an evaluation and impact measurement of the key features related with performance on 3D mobile applications.

Keywords: Unity engine · Mobile devices · 3D applications · Performance

1 Introduction

Nowadays, mobile devices are increasingly sophisticated and their technological evolution allows them to execute complex applications with rigorous hardware requirements.

However, when these applications are visual and include three-dimensional graphics, it is possible to notice some degradation in the flow of execution. This loss in execution efficiency is due to the characteristics of the device in which the application is executed, but also to the characteristics of the development tool and/or its implementation.

The number of frameworks for the development of interactive 3D mobile applications is constantly increasing. Each of these frameworks have different characteristics that make them suitable for different types and magnitudes of project.

By choosing a particular framework it is possible to base itself on various criteria such as: the existing community, the supported coding languages, the ease of use, the quality of the resulting 3D graphics, among others. However, one of the main points of interest is to obtain a good performance in terms of visualization and fluency.

In mobile devices, the limited processing capacity (for example, compared with that of desktops) is more relevant. For this reason, it is important to know the capabilities and limitations of the framework to be used in terms of visualization performance.

© Springer International Publishing AG, part of Springer Nature 2018
A. E. De Giusti (Ed.): CACIC 2017, CCIS 790, pp. 155–163, 2018.
https://doi.org/10.1007/978-3-319-75214-3_15

In order to achieve this objective, this paper proposes an evaluation that allows isolating, analyzing and dimensioning the incidence of the main characteristics related to the visual performance of 3D mobile applications.

This evaluation provides support to the software engineer of 3D mobile applications, enabling the identification of factors that slow down the visual performance of these applications, and allowing them to adjust the critical points until achieving the desired fluidity.

The rest of the paper is organized as follows: Sect. 2 describes the motivation of the proposed analysis; Sect. 3 presents the evaluation in detail; Sect. 4 shows the experimentation carried out and, finally, in Sect. 5 the conclusions and the future work are exposed.

2   Motivation

The gestation of the performance analysis proposed by this work begins during the development process of two mobile applications: R-Info3D [1] and InfoUNLP3D [2]. The first application is a 3D learning environment of basic algorithmia, while the second one is a virtual 3D scenario of the Facultad de Informática - Universidad Nacional de La Plata. Both projects resulted in immersive applications, which by their nature present a high computational cost, mainly in terms of visualization [3].

Both in the implementation process and in its subsequent execution in different mobile devices, limitations were found regarding the obtained performance. We proceeded to recognize the critical points that affected visual fluidity and determined certain thresholds that should not be overcome. This analysis led to modify the applications to achieve better performance in different types of mobile devices.

Prior to the beginning of the development of the aforementioned tools, an analysis of the main free-use engines for the development of 3D mobile applications was made. The considered engines were: Unity [4], one of the most popular and simple to use; Unreal Engine [5], which compared to other engines is somewhat more complex to use and with higher hardware requirements; CryEngine [6], thought mainly for first person 3D developments, its installation and use are not trivial processes.

R-Info3D and InfoUNLP3D were developed with the Unity framework. Given that there is no optimal framework in all possible aspects, the choice of Unity over the rest of the 3D mobile development frameworks analyzed was based on a series of factors, among which stand out:

- Tutorials: there are a lot of tutorials and examples that guide the new user in the learning process of the use of the framework. These tutorials are categorized according to the type of development, they are audiovisual and are provided with all the necessary elements needed (objects, audios, images, scripts, etc.).
- Documentation: the user manual [7] is comprehensive, easy to understand and properly subdivided into different categories. It contains a lookup engine that facilitates the search of a particular topic or functionality.
- Software/hardware requirements: the system requirements are considerably lower compared to other similar frameworks. This, accompanied by a simple and fast

installation, encourages the user/developer to start quickly with the use of the framework.

- Available components: it has a repository (Asset Store) where it is possible to find a wide variety of components that can accelerate the development of applications. It contains a component lookup engine that allows complex searches through different types of filters.
- Ease of learning/use: the framework is versatile and allows working in two different languages: C# and Javascript. This, added to the documentation, the tutorials, the repository and the existing community, generates an ideal scenario to quickly learn to use the framework and solve any problem that may arise in the process.
- Community: the great popularity of Unity is a major factor when choosing it. It is the most used 3D framework and its community is composed of more than two million users [8]. It contains a forum subdivided into categories where it is possible to raise the situations or problems that may arise during the application development process.

There are different proposals for performance analysis of 3D engines for mobile applications. One of these proposals [9] evaluates the performance of the applications taking into account the consumption of CPU and/or GPU that they generate. Other works [10, 11] base their evaluation on an analysis of the main features and functionalities of the frameworks, resulting in a comparative table or list.

None of these works adopt the approach proposed in the present paper, that is to give some kind of guidance for the development of 3D mobile applications based on the final achieved visualization performance.

3   Proposed Evaluation

The main objective of the proposed evaluation is to isolate each of the main characteristics covered by a 3D application; especially those that have a direct impact on the performance, response time and flow of execution of the applications generated with the engine [12].

Characteristics such as the number of polygons, lights and shadows, the use of textures and/or transparencies, the visualization of particle systems and the calculation of the physics of objects that make up the scene are examples of the main items to be evaluated.

Although the incidence of these characteristics on performance varies according to the software and hardware on which the application is executed, the tests carried out show that there is a common pattern of performance degradation in relation to the increase in visual requirements.

Based on the previously mentioned set of characteristics, a series of independent tests is defined to evaluate the performance. These tests are listed below:

1. Basic Mesh Rendering: simple objects without texture in motion are presented on screen in a scene without lighting or shadows. Objects must rotate continuously at constant speed. The number of objects on the screen will grow according to the time

elapsed. The number of frames per second (FPS) is accounted throughout the simulation according to the number of objects.

2. Complex Mesh Rendering: it consists in visualizing a complex object in movement, which must contain a high number of polygons. The rendering distance (clipping plane) increases as the test progresses. The FPS is accounted throughout the simulation depending on the rendering distance.

3. Lights & Shadows: a simulation similar to the basic mesh rendering is performed, but in this case the scene contains lighting and objects with projection and reception of shadows. The FPS is accounted according to the number of objects.

4. Textures: a simulation similar to the basic mesh rendering is performed, but in this case the objects have complex textures, such as transparencies, reflections, etc. The FPS is accounted according to the number of objects.

5. Particle Systems: a scene is created where new instances of a particle system are progressively presented (for example smoke, sparks, explosion, etc.). The FPS is accounted for according to the number of particle systems.

6. Physics: a simulation similar to the basic mesh rendering is performed, but in this case the objects are subject to physics rules, such as gravity. The FPS is accounted throughout the simulation according to the number of objects.

The use of this set of tests simplifies considerably the task of determining the critical points in the developed applications, thus enabling a better calibration of the analyzed characteristics.

In particular for this work, cubes were used as simple objects, while for the rendering test of a complex object, the building model of the Facultad de Informática was chosen. The model used in the InfoUNLP3D application, contains more than 500,000 polygons and a large number of windows. Due to the latter, for the textures tests, "glass transparency" was applied to the elements. As for the particle system, one similar to that used by the robot in R-Info3D when executing a repositioning instruction (Pos) was generated.

4   Experimentation

The experiments consisted in performing the test set previously detailed over a set of mobile devices with different characteristics. The devices used in the tests were three smartphones and two tablets: Samsung Galaxy S2 (smartphone), Samsung Galaxy J5 (smartphone), LG L5 II (smartphone), Asus MemoPad FHD10 (tablet) y Acer B1-730 (tablet). These devices present considerable differences performance-wise, and have different hardware architectures, such as ARM and x86.

Figures 1 and 2 show the average values of the results obtained from the tests executed over all the devices, considering two different quality rendering configurations that Unity provides: *Fastest* (the lowest) and *Fantastic* (the highest) [13].

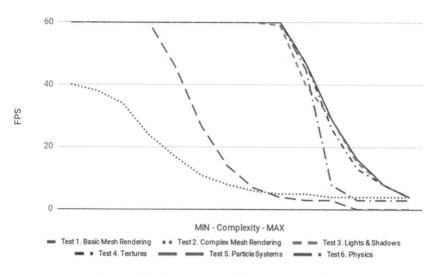

Fig. 1. FPS. Evolution of each test, *Fastest* quality.

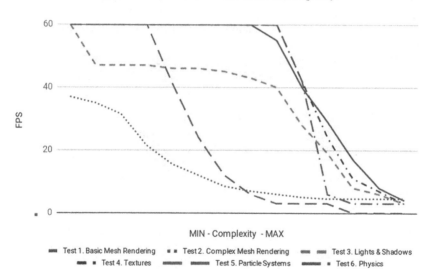

Fig. 2. FPS. Evolution of each test, *Fantastic* quality.

In all cases and depending on the type of test, the information is normalized according to the possible range of minimum and maximum values for each test. In tests 1, 3, 4, 5 and 6 the number of objects on screen starts at 1 and gradually increments throughout the simulation until reaching a high value, such as 10000 objects. For the test 2, the evolution in this case is the rendering distance, that can vary from a minimum of 200 up to a maximum of 2000 distance units. Additionally, the ideal frame rate considered is 60 FPS.

The results of the tests offer an interesting set of conclusions, which allow the possibility for the correspondent optimization of the application. The following observations results from applying the proposed evaluation specifically for the current case of study.

- Basic mesh rendering using both *Fastest* or *Fantastic* quality does not present performance differences. Both curves show almost the same evolution throughout the simulation.
- Light affects the performance under *Fantastic* quality, but not under *Fastest* quality, configuration which seems to completely ignore lights calculations. Lights/shadows rendering is one of the key factors in respect to visual performance, as it will be later explained in this paper.
- The amount of polygons (+500 k) under the complex mesh simulation is excessively high for the set of mobile devices used in the tests in order to achieve a fluent visualization. Both *Fastest* and *Fantastic* quality settings suffered the same degradation.
- Textures application does not seem to considerably affect general performance, at least with the selected texture (which includes transparency), applied through a standard shader, and with a moderate texture size.
- Being 2D, particle systems are not considerably affected by quality change; but a high number of systems prohibits the correct execution of the simulation, given the large amount of individual calculations required for each of the particles of each system.
- Both Collision detection and Physics have a relatively minor impact over performance, when a reasonable number of objects are displayed in the scene (for instance, less than 2000 cubes).

Figure 3 shows the FPS coefficient between *Fastest* and *Fantastic* quality configurations. A value of 1 implies that the test behaves the same under both configurations; whereas a value greater than 1 implies a factor of degradation under *Fantastic* relative

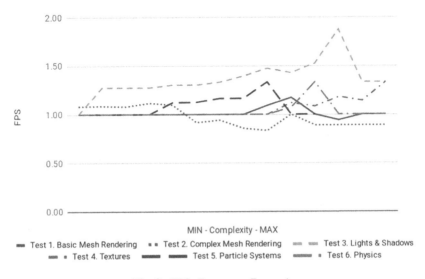

Fig. 3. FPS. *Fastest* vs. *Fantastic*.

to *Fantastic*, and a value less than 1 implies the opposite. Thanks to test 3 is possible to clearly appreciate the performance degradation under *Fantastic* configuration, with an average of 50% less fluent than *Fastest* configuration (which obviously relegates graphical quality in this matter).

Additionally, as previously explained, the complexity of the object to be renderized (test 2) equally impacts on both *Fastest* and *Fantastic* configurations, and after certain threshold there is practically no distinction between each configuration.

Thanks to this analysis, it was possible to achieve an acceptable balance between graphical quality and visualization fluency in each of the developed applications in Unity. Figure 4 presents a scene of InfoUNLP3D application with the highest possible level of detail, considering characteristics such as textures, lights and shades; but with a extremely poor FPS performance. Figure 5 shows the same scene once modified in order to achieve máximum fluidity, although relegating in excess the characteristics previously mentioned. Figure 6 presents the achieved results thanks to the selected optimal calibration, based on the results of the tests. In this calibration both image quality and visualization fluidity is considered. For instance, the use of spot lights is omitted in order to avoid shadow processing, given that the objective of the application is not to present a photorealistic rendering, but to serve as a reference guide for students.

Fig. 4. InfoUNLP3D. Maximum level of detail.

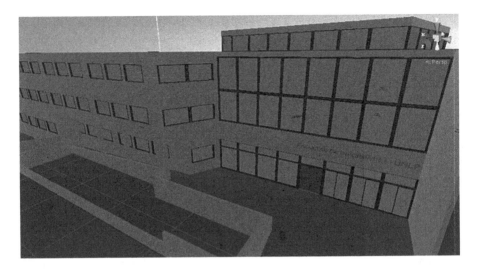

Fig. 5. InfoUNLP3D. Minimum level of detail.

Fig. 6. InfoUNLP3D. Selected optimal calibration.

Under this context, a new feature was added to the Info UNLP 3D application that allows the user to configure the rendering distance (and therefore the number of polygons on the scene). By avoiding rendering the most distant elements in the scene, fluidity is gained without losing functionality, which is based on navigate the building gathering information about the nearby rooms. This new option allows the use of the application on devices with lower processing power.

5   Conclusions and Future Work

The present paper proposes a set of heuristics that allows to establish the key factors that degrade visualization fluidity of 3D mobile applications.

Thanks to the proposed evaluation method it is possible to identify these factors in order to redesign an application and considerably reduce performance problems.

As a proof of concept and to test its effectiveness, the evaluation method was applied over Unity engine. Simulation tests were carried on, gathering as a result the required information in order to execute the correspondent optimizations on the applications developed with the mentioned engine.

As starting point, a 3D mobile application developer has a set of guidelines to consider in order to aid visual performance optimization.

As a future work, the same evaluation method will be applied over other 3D mobile application engines such as Unreal Engine or CryEngine, and ideally will be perform a comprehensive performance comparison between these frameworks for each of the evaluated characteristics.

References

1. Cristina, F., Dapoto, S., Thomas, P., Pesado, P.: 3D mobile prototype for basic algorithms learning. In: Computer Science & Technology Series - XXI Argentine Congress of Computer Science, Selected Papers, pp. 239–247 (2016). ISBN: 978-987-4127-00-6
2. Cristina, F., Dapoto, S., Thomas, P., Pesado, P.: InfoUNLP3D: an interactive experience for freshman students. In: Computer Science & Technology Series - XXII Argentine Congress of Computer Science, Selected Papers, pp. 249–256 (2017). ISBN: 978-987-4127-28-0
3. Linowes, J.: Unity Virtual Reality Projects (2015). ISBN-13: 978-1783988556
4. Unity. https://unity3d.com
5. Unreal Engine. https://www.unrealengine.com/
6. CryEngine. https://www.cryengine.com/
7. Unity online manual. http://docs.unity3d.com/Manual/index.html
8. Unity Blogs: The Unity Community. https://blogs.unity3d.com/2014/03/11/we-got-karma/
9. Messaoudi, F., Simon, G., Ksentini, A.: Dissecting games engines: the case of Unity3D. In: International Workshop on Network and Systems Support for Games (NetGames) (2015). Electronic ISSN: 2156-8146
10. Pattrasitidecha, A.: Comparison and evaluation of 3D mobile game engines. Chalmers University of Technology. University of Gothenburg (2014)
11. Petridis, P., Dunwell, I., Panzoli, D., Arnab, S., Protopsaltis, A., Hendrix, M., de Freitas, S.: Game engines selection framework for high-fidelity serious applications. Int. J. Interact. Worlds (2012). Article ID 418638, https://doi.org/10.5171/2012.418638
12. Optimizing Graphics Performance. https://docs.unity3d.com/Manual/OptimizingGraphics Performance.html
13. Unity Manual: Quality Settings. https://docs.unity3d.com/Manual/class-QualitySettings.html

Assistant for the Evaluation of Software Product Quality Characteristics Proposed by ISO/IEC 25010 Based on GQM-Defined Metrics

Julieta Calabrese, Rocío Muñoz, Ariel Pasini[✉], Silvia Esponda,
Marcos Boracchia, and Patricia Pesado

School of Computer Science, Computer Science Research Institute LIDI
(III-LIDI), National University of La Plata, 50 y 120, La Plata,
Buenos Aires, Argentina
{jcalabrese, rmunoz, apasini, sesponda,
marcosb, ppesado}@lidi.info.unlp.edu.ar

Abstract. An assistant to evaluate the characteristics, proposed by ISO/IEC 25010, of a software product using GQM (Goal, Question, Metric) is presented. A set of questions was defined whose combined answers allow obtaining a logical metric applicable to the characteristics proposed by ISO/IEC 25010. For this work, the characteristic of Security was used as case study, the corresponding metrics were defined, and the results obtained when applying them to three case studies are presented.

Keywords: Quality · Software product · GQM · ISO/IEC 25000

1 Introduction

The number of software developing companies has increased significantly together with the increase in the demand for products from the sector. For this type of companies, software quality has a key role, in particular as a differentiating element for competitiveness and corporate image, and because the monetary losses these companies can suffer as a consequence of software quality issues are significant. In this context, the activities related to software quality and its evaluation are becoming ever so important [1].

An organization can be interested in evaluating its product as a differentiator from its competitors by ensuring delivery times and lower failure rate in the product after its implementation to production; through establishing agreements in the service sector by defining quality parameters that the product must meet before delivery; by detecting software product flaws and remove them before delivery; by evaluating and controlling

Computer Science Research Institute LIDI (III-LIDI) - Partner Center of the Scientific Research Agency of the Province of Buenos Aires (CICPBA).

the performance of the software product developed, ensuring that it will be capable of yielding the results taking into account given time and resource restrictions; by ensuring that the software product developed complies with the necessary levels for security characteristics (*Confidentiality*, *Integrity*, *Authenticity*, *Non-Repudiation*, etc.); and so forth.

In this sense, the ISO 25000 family, known as SQuaRE (Software Product Quality Requirements and Evaluation) is born as a response to these needs. Its objective is creating a common framework to assess the quality of the software product. It is a replacement of the previous ISO/IEC 9126 and ISO/IEC 14598, Quality models and metric generation [2–4].

In this article, we propose a software product evaluation assistant based on the metrics defined in ISO/IEC 25010 using the GQM approach [5].

Section 2 briefly describes the ISO/IEC 25000 family and the approach proposed in GQM. Then, Sect. 3 describes the model used to evaluate the characteristics proposed by ISO/IEC 25010 using the GQM approach, in particular, the characteristic of *Security*. After that, three case studies are presented, where the evaluation model is applied and the results obtained are discussed. Finally, conclusions are presented.

2 Quality Models and Metric Generation

2.1 The ISO/IEC 25000 Family

Quality management is required in organizations due to the significance it has on various fronts: on the product level, establishing the quality achieved and the characteristics present in the products; on the level of the organization, establishing a procedural framework that allows improvement; as well as on the level of the processes.

To organize and unify all standards related to software product quality, ISO/IEC published in 2005 the document ISO/IEC 25000:2005 - SQuaRE (Software Product Quality Requirements and Evaluation), also known as the ISO 25000 family. Within ISO/IEC 25000, ISO/IEC 25010 - *System and software quality models* and ISO/IEC 25040 - *Evaluation process*, described below, stand out.

ISO/IEC 25010 - System and Software Quality Models
It replaces ISO/IEC 9126-1:2001. It adds new internal and external characteristics, grouping them under the name of software product quality. The main change made is the addition of the *Compatibility* characteristic, which is related to the possibility of exchanging information between systems, and the *Security* characteristic, which is related to the concepts of confidentiality and access to information [6].

Each of these software product quality characteristics is subdivided into sub-characteristics that define them in more detail, as shown in Fig. 1.

ISO/IEC 25040 - Evaluation Process
It replaces ISO/IEC 14598-1:1999. The new version defines 13 processes in five stages:

(1) Establishing evaluation requirements: a. Establishing the purpose of the evaluation. b. Obtaining product quality requirements. c. Identifying the parts of the product that should be evaluated. d. Defining the strictness of the evaluation.

Fig. 1. Software product quality characteristics

(2) Specifying the evaluation: a. Selecting the evaluation modules. b. Defining decision criteria for metrics. c. Defining decision criteria for the evaluation.

(3) Designing the evaluation: a. Planning evaluation activities.

(4) Performing the evaluation: a. Carrying out the measurements. b. Applying decision criteria for metrics. c. Applying decision criteria for the evaluation.

(5) Finishing the evaluation: a. Reviewing the results of the evaluation. b. Creating the report for the evaluation. c. Reviewing the quality of the evaluation and obtaining feedback. d. Treating evaluation data [7].

2.2   GQM (Goal, Question, Metric)

GQM (Goal, Question, Metric) is a method that uses a metric to measure certain goal in a given way. The measurement model has three levels:

- Conceptual Level (Goal): a goal is defined for an object, which can be a product, a process or a resource, in relation to several quality models, from several points of view and relative to a specific environment.
- Operational Level (Question): a set of questions is refined based on the goal and aimed at checking if the goal is met. These questions are intended to characterize the object being measured (product, process or resource) in relation to a given quality issue and establishing its quality from that point of view.
- Quantitative Level (Metric): a set of metrics, which can be objective or subjective, is linked to every question, so that each question can be answered quantitatively.

A GQM model is developed by identifying a set of quality and/or productivity goals, at a corporate, division or project level. From those goals and based on models of the object being measured, questions are created to define those goals as thoroughly as possible. The next step is specifying the measures that should be taken to answer the questions and follow up in relation to how the products and processes meet those goals. Once the measures are specified, information compilation procedures should be developed, including validation and analysis procedures [5].

3   Quality Characteristics Evaluation Model

The model developed here consists in defining a set of questions based on the GQM approach that will then show, through logical connectors, to which extent the goals proposed are met.

As case study, we considered the characteristic **Security**, which includes the following sub-characteristics: *Confidentiality*, *Integrity*, *Non-Repudiation*, *Responsibility* and *Authenticity*.

CONFIDENTIALITY: It evaluates the ability to protect against non-authorized access to data and information, be this accidental or deliberate.

INTEGRITY: It evaluates the ability of the system or computer to prevent non-authorized accesses or modifications to computer data or programs.

NON-REPUDIATION: It evaluates the ability to prove the actions or events that have taken place, so that such actions or events cannot be repudiated later on.

RESPONSIBILITY: It evaluates the ability to unequivocally track the actions carried out by an entity.

AUTHENTICITY: It evaluates the ability to prove the identity of an individual or a resource.

3.1   Questionnaire

Based on the characteristics described above, 33 true/false questions were defined (Table 1).

Table 1. Questionnaire for the *Security* characteristic

ID	Question
Q1	Is it a requirement for the password to be at least 8 characters long?
Q2	Is it a requirement for the password to include both upper- and lower-case characters?
Q3	Is it a requirement for the password to include both numbers and letters?
Q4	Is it a requirement for the password to include special characters?
Q5	Does the system use secure connection through HTTPS?
Q6	Are database data encrypted?
Q7	Does the system allow access to functionalities to which no permissions have been granted?
Q8	Does the system allow access to the database by any individual?
Q9	Does the system allow access to application server code by any individual?
Q10	Is the physical server accessible to any individual?
Q11	Is the remote server accessible to any individual?

(continued)

Table 1. (*continued*)

ID	Question
Q12	Does the system redirect to non-secure sites?
Q13	Does the system request registration confirmation via e-mail when a new user registers?
Q14	Does the system allow any individual to modify the database?
Q15	Does the system allow any individual to modify the application server code?
Q16	Does the system allow SQL injections?
Q17	Does the system keep a history of actions performed?
Q18	Does the system have data encryption algorithms?
Q19	Does the system have a cryptographic method, such as digital signature?
Q20	Does the system request confirmation when an action is performed?
Q21	Is the system protected with SSL certificates?
Q22	Does the system issue a warning when accessing from an unknown location?
Q23	Does the system send an e-mail report of the operations done?
Q24	Does the system keep a record of date and time of logins to the system?
Q25	Does the system record the type of browser and operating system used to enter the site?
Q26	Does the system record the IP address from which the site is accessed?
Q27	Does the system check identity through a digital certificate?
Q28	Does the system have two-step verification?
Q29	Is a second-level key required to enter the system?
Q30	Does the system check identity through biometric data?
Q31	Does the system check identity through a code card?
Q32	Does the system check identity through credentials?
Q33	Does the system check identity through a digital signature?

3.2 Evaluation Criteria (EC) Description

To achieve our objective, the answers to the questions were combined through logic, establishing a score for each EC (Table 2).

Table 2. Evaluation Criteria (EC) description

ID	Name	Description	Equation	Points
C-1	Secure connections	A connection is considered to be secure if it uses HTTPS and there is no redirecting to non-secure sites	Q5 & $\sim$Q12 = T	1
C-2	Access control	No unauthorized access to functionalities, the database, application code, and physical or remote servers should be allowed	if Q7 | Q8 | Q9 | Q10 | Q11 = F	1

(*continued*)

Table 2. (*continued*)

ID	Name	Description	Equation	Points
C-3	Data encryption	Database data should be encrypted	Q6 = T	1
C-4	Low-level password	A password is considered to be low level if it is less than 8 characters long, does not include upper and lower case, does not include letters and numbers and does not include special characters	Q1 | Q2 | Q3 | Q4 = F	0
	Mid-level password	A password is considered to be mid-level if it is at least 8 characters long or it includes upper and lower case or letters and numbers or special characters	Q1 | Q2 | Q3 | Q4 = T	0.5
	High-level password	A password is considered to be high level if it is at least 8 characters long and it includes upper and lower case, letters and numbers and special characters	Q1 & Q2 & Q3 & Q4 = T	1
I-5	Access prevention	Unauthorized access to functionalities, the database and application code should be prevented; SQL injections should not be allowed	Q7 | Q8 | Q9 | Q16 = F	1
I-6	Modification prevention	Unauthorized database data modification and application code should be prevented	Q14 | Q15 = F	1
I-7	Data confirmation	Registration should be confirmed via e-mail	Q13 = T	1
NR-8	Operations carried out	A history of actions should be available, or they should be sent by e-mail	Q17 | Q23 = T	1
NR-9	Encryption method	There should be a data encryption algorithm or a cryptographic method, such as digital signature, or protection through SSL certificates	Q18 | Q19 | Q21 = T	1
NR-10	Action confirmation	A confirmation should be requested when performing a given action	Q20 = T	1
NR-11	Location registration	A notification should be issued if the system was accessed from an unknown location	Q22 = T	1
R-12	Action and data records	A history of actions should be available, or a record showing system access date and time or the IP address from which the system was accesses and the type of browser and operating system used	Q17 | Q24 | Q25 | Q26 = T	1
R-13	Location control	A notification should be issued if the system is accessed from an unknown location	Q22 = T	1

(*continued*)

Table 2. (*continued*)

ID	Name	Description	Equation	Points
A-14	Identity verification	The system should check identity through any of the following methods: biometric data, code card, credentials, digital signature or digital certificate	Q27 | Q30 | Q31 | Q32 | Q33 = T	1
A-15	Additional verification	Two-step verification should be used, or a second level key should be required to enter the system, or a registration confirmation via e-mail should be used	Q28 | Q29 | Q13 = T	1

3.3 Metrics for Each Sub-characteristic

EC were combined to define the metrics that meet the goals of each sub-characteristic. For each of them, a name, a purpose, an application method, input values and equation used were defined.

Confidentiality

Metric: *Confidentiality*

Purpose: *How efficient is the system when protecting against non-authorized access to data and information, be this accidental or deliberate?*

Application method: *Answering EC questions corresponding to the sub-characteristic "Confidentiality" and calculating the score obtained by adding the score for each EC that meets the expected goal. "Total score" is the maximum score that can be obtained.*

Inputs: *A = Score obtained. B = Total score.*

Equation: $X = A/B$

Observations: The EC to be used are: C-1, C-2, C-3 and C-4.

Integrity

Metric: *Integrity*

Purpose: How capable is the system to prevent non-authorized accesses or modifications to computer data or programs?

Application method: *Answering EC questions corresponding to the sub-characteristic "Integrity" and calculating the score obtained by adding the score for each EC that meets the expected goal. "Total score" is the maximum score that can be obtained.*

Inputs: *A = Score obtained. B = Total score.*

Equation: $X = A/B$

Observations: The EC to be used are: I-5, I-6 and I-7.

Non-Repudiation

Metric: *Non-Repudiation*

Purpose: *How capable is the system to prove the actions or events that have taken place, so that such actions or events cannot be repudiated later on?*

Application method: *Answering EC questions corresponding to the sub-characteristic "Non-Repudiation" and calculating the score obtained by adding the score for each EC that meets the expected goal. "Total score" is the maximum score that can be obtained.*

Inputs: *A = Score obtained. B = Total score.*

Equation: $X = A/B$

Observations: *The EC to be used are: NR-8, NR-9, NR-10 and NR-11.*

Responsibility

Metric: *Responsibility*

Purpose: *How capable is the system to unequivocally track the actions carried out by an entity?*

Application method: *Answering EC questions corresponding to the sub-characteristic "Responsibility" and calculating the score obtained by adding the score for each EC that meets the expected goal. "Total score" is the maximum score that can be obtained.*

Inputs: *A = Score obtained. B = Total score.*

Equation: $X = A/B$

Observations: *The EC to be used are: R-12 and R-13.*

Authenticity

Metric: *Authenticity*

Purpose: *How capable is the system to prove the identity of an individual or a resource?*

Application method: *Answering EC questions corresponding to the sub-characteristic "Authenticity" and calculating the score obtained by adding the score for each EC that meets the expected goal. "Total score" is the maximum score that can be obtained.*

Inputs: *A = Score obtained. B = Total score.*

Equation: $X = A/B$

Observations: *The EC to be used are: A14 and A15.*

The equations used for each sub-characteristic are listed in Table 3.

Table 3. Equations for each sub-characteristic.

Metric	Equation
Confidentiality	$(C1 + C2 + C3 + C4)/4$
Integrity	$(I5 + I6 + I7)/3$
Non-Repudiation	$(NR8 + NR9 + NR10 + NR11)/4$
Responsibility	$(R12 + R13)/2$
Authenticity	$(A14 + A15)/2$

4 Case Studies

The evaluation process was carried out, following the structure presented in ISO/IEC 25040, for three web applications to evaluate their *Security* characteristic.

Case (a) It has been in production for approximately 18 months, it has more than 3,200 users, and an average of 500 daily logins.

Case (b) It has been in production for approximately 30 months, it has more than 160 users, and an average of 75 daily logins.

Case (c) It is in a testing stage, it has ten users with a minimal login frequency by the users that are testing the application.

4.1 Establishing Evaluation Requirements

The purpose of the evaluation is to measure the security of three web systems by analyzing different aspects of such systems. The characteristic of "*Security*," as defined in ISO/IEC 25010, was selected.

Two of the systems to be evaluated are in their final version and are currently being used by different users. The remaining system is running in a test version and is being used by different people responsible for carrying out tests.

4.2 Specifying the Evaluation

The metrics used for each sub-characteristic are those defined in Sect. 3. Acceptance criteria for these sub-characteristics are:

Not acceptable: $0 <= X < 40$
Minimally acceptable: $40 <= X < 60$
Target range: $60 <= X < 90$
Exceeds requirements: $90 <= X <= 100$

The result shall be considered as acceptable if all sub-characteristics are rated as Minimally acceptable, Target range or Exceeds requirements.

4.3 Designing the Evaluation

To carry out the evaluation, three developers from the web systems to be analyzed (one developer from each system) were asked to use T/F to answer the questions listed in Sect. 3.1. They were asked to use an Excel spreadsheet that was provided to them, which was set so that values A and B corresponding to each metric were automatically calculated.

4.4 Carrying Out the Evaluation

The evaluation was carried out as planned and the following results were obtained:

Case (a) *Confidentiality* 88%, *Integrity* 67%, *Non-Repudiation* 50%, *Responsibility* 50% and *Authenticity* 0%

Case (b) *Confidentiality* 75%, *Integrity* 100%, *Non-Repudiation* 75%, *Responsibility* 50% and *Authenticity* 50%

Case (c) *Confidentiality* 0%, *Integrity* 33%, *Non-Repudiation* 50%, *Responsibility* 0% and *Authenticity* 0%

4.5   Completing the Evaluation

Case study (a) has the sub-characteristics *Confidentiality* and *Integrity* within the acceptable range, *Non-Repudiation* and *Responsibility* are minimally acceptable, and *Authenticity* is unacceptable.

Case study (b) exceeds expectation in relation to *Integrity*, has acceptable *Confidentiality* and *Non-Repudiation* characteristics, and *Responsibility* and *Authenticity* that are minimally acceptable.

Case study (c) is minimally acceptable as regards *Non-Repudiation*, and unacceptable for *Responsibility*, *Authenticity*, *Integrity* and *Confidentiality*.

Figure 2 shows a comparison of the sub-characteristics evaluated in each of the cases.

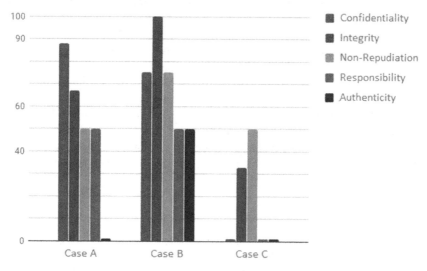

Fig. 2. Sub-characteristics in each case study

Characteristic Analysis – *Security*

Case study (a) does not meet evaluation requirements since its *Authenticity* sub-characteristic is in an unacceptable range: the system does not check identity through any valid method and it does not have a two-step verification process, a second-level key or registration confirmation via e-mail.

Case study (b) is considered to meet evaluation requirements because all of its sub-characteristics are within an acceptance range.

Case study (c) does not meet evaluation requirements because only its *Non-Repudiation* sub-characteristic is in an acceptable range. In this case, the *Authenticity* sub-characteristic is unacceptable for the same reasons as in case study (a). As regards *Responsibility*, it is considered to be unacceptable because the system does not keep a history of actions or an access record, nor does it issue a notification when it is accessed from an unknown location. In relation to *Confidentiality*, the system does not have secure connections or access control, and there is no encryption of database data or criteria set for creating secure passwords. Finally, as regards *Integrity*, even if the system uses a procedure to prevent non-authorized modifications to the database and system code, this is not enough to achieve an acceptance level because it does not have any procedures to prevent unauthorized access to functionalities and there are no data confirmations sent via e-mail.

5   Conclusions

The ISO/IEC 25010 standard offers a quality model to evaluate a set of characteristics applicable to a software product. We presented an evaluation model applicable to characteristics and sub-characteristics that is based on the GQM approach, which starts from a specific goal and then creates questions related to that goal. The answers to these questions are then combined to obtain the metric in question. Questions were created for the sub-characteristics of the **Security** characteristic, and a set of rules was generated to evaluate the answers to those questions. Then, these answers were combined to produce the metrics corresponding to each sub-characteristic and, therefore, for the characteristic as a whole.

Three web systems were evaluated, and only one successfully passed the test. The evaluation of the other systems was useful to detect shortcomings in them.

In the future, we plan to expand the model by creating questions and evaluation criteria for the other characteristics included in the ISO/IEC 25010 standard.

References

1. Esponda, S., Pesado, P.: Ambiente para la ayuda a la mejora de procesos en las PyMEs. Master Dissertation, School of Computer Science – National University of La Plata (2013)
2. ISO: ISO/IEC 25000:2014 Systems and software engineering – Systems and software Quality Requirements and Evaluation (SQuaRE) – Guide to SQuaREtle (2014)
3. IRAM and ISO: IRAM-NM-ISO IEC 9126-1 Information Technology. Software Engineering. Product Quality. Part 1 - Quality Model (2009)
4. IRAM;ISO: IRAM-ISO-IEC 14598-1 Information Technology. Software Engineering. Software Product Evaluation. Part 1: General Overview (2006)
5. Basili, V.R., Caldiera, G., Rombach, H.D.: The goal question metric approach. Encycl. Softw. Eng. 2(1994), 528–532 (1994)

6. ISO: ISO/IEC 25010:2011 Systems and Software Engineering – Systems and Software Quality Requirements and Evaluation (SQuaRE) – System and software quality models (2011)
7. ISO: ISO/IEC 25040:2011 Systems and Software Engineering – Systems and Software Quality Requirements and Evaluation (SQuaRE) – Evaluation Process (2011)

Databases and Data Mining

Recommender System Based on Latent Topics

María Emilia Charnelli[1,3]([✉]) [iD], Laura Lanzarini[2][iD], and Javier Díaz[1]

[1] LINTI - Research Laboratory in New Information Technologies,
National University of La Plata, La Plata, Argentina
mcharnelli@linti.unlp.edu.ar, jdiaz@unlp.edu.ar
[2] III LIDI - Computer Science Research Institute LIDI Computer Science School,
National University of La Plata, La Plata, Argentina
laural@lidi.info.unlp.edu.ar
[3] CONICET - National Scientific and Technical Research Council,
Buenos Aires, Argentina

Abstract. Collaborative filtering is one of the most used techniques in recommender systems. The goal of this paper is to propose a new method that uses latent topics to model the items to be recommended. In this way, the ability to establish a similarity between these elements is incorporated, improving the performance of the recommendation made. The performance of the proposed method has been measured in two very different contexts, yielding satisfactory results. Finally, the conclusions and some future lines of work are included.

Keywords: Recommender systems · Collaborative filtering
Latent topic modeling

1 Introduction

Recommender systems analyze patterns of interest to users such as articles or products, to provide personalized recommendations that satisfy their preferences [1]. Suggestions intervene in various decision-making processes, such as which items to buy, which movies to watch, or which books to read. The term item is used to indicate what the system recommends to users [2]. For this purpose, it is necessary to model the items that are to be recommended. Generating of a model from the textual and unstructured information of a set of items represents a great challenge. The analysis of latent topics has emerged as one of the most efficient methods for classifying, grouping and retrieving textual data. Discovering topics in short texts is crucial for a wide range of tasks that analyze topics, such as characterizing content, modeling user interest profiles, and detecting latent or emerging topics. The BTM biterm topic model [3] allows to efficiently extract the topics that characterize a set of short texts. BTM can obtain the underlying topics in a set of documents and a global distribution of each topic within each of them, through the analysis of the generation of biterms.

The most common approach for a recommender system is the collaborative filtering technique based on neighborhood models. Its original form is based on

© Springer International Publishing AG, part of Springer Nature 2018
A. E. De Giusti (Ed.): CACIC 2017, CCIS 790, pp. 179–187, 2018.
https://doi.org/10.1007/978-3-319-75214-3_17

the similarities between users [4]. These user-user methods estimate unknown scores based on registered scores of like-minded users. Subsequently, the analogous approach became popular but now taking into account the similarities between items [5,6]. In these methods, a score is calculated using assessments made by the same user on similar items. Better scalability and improved accuracy make the item approach more favorable in many cases [7,8]. In addition, item-item methods are more likely to explain the reasoning behind the predictions. This is because the users are familiar with the elements previously preferred by them, but do not know the supposedly similar users. Most item-item approaches use a measure of similarity between the ratings they have.

This paper proposes a method based on the item-item approach that uses a model of latent topics to model the items that need to be recommended and establishes a similarity between these elements that improve the performance of the recommendation. The evaluation of the proposed method is done through a set of educational materials from the Merlot [9] digital repository and a movie dataset from MovieLens [10]. This article is organized as follows: the second section describes the extraction and modeling of latent topics, the third section describes the proposed method, the fourth section shows the experimental results. Finally, the fifth section presents the conclusions and future lines of work.

2   Extraction of Latent Topics

For the extraction of the topics in the descriptions of the items, BTM (Biterm Topic Model) was used, which is an unsupervised learning technique that discovers the topics that characterize a set of brief documents.

Let a set of N_D documents be called corpus where W is a set of all the words of the corpus, a topic is defined as a probability distribution over W. Therefore, a topic can be characterized by its T most likely words. Given a K number of topics, the objective of BTM is to obtain the K distributions on each of the words. A "biterm" denotes a pair of words without order that co-occur in a short document. In this case, two different words in a document construct a biterm.

Given a corpus with N_D documents and a W unique-word vocabulary, it is assumed to contain N_B biterms $\boldsymbol{B} = \{b_i\}_{i=1}^{N_B}$ with $b_i = (w_{i,1} \in W, w_{i,2} \in W)$, and K topics expressed over W. Let $z \in [1, K]$ be a variable to indicate a topic. The probability $P(z)$ that a document in the corpus is of a topic z, defined as a multinomial K-dimensional distribution $\boldsymbol{\theta} = \{\theta_k\}_{k=1}^{K}$ with $\theta_k = P(z = k)$ and $\sum_{k=1}^{K} \theta_k = 1$. The distribution of words by topic $P(w|z)$ can be represented as a matrix $\Phi \in R^{K \times W}$ where the kth row ϕ_k is a multinomial distribution W-dimensional with input $\phi_{k,w} = P(w|z = k)$ and $\sum_{w=1}^{W} \phi_{k,w} = 1$. Given the parameters α and β, the main assumption of the model is that each of the documents of the corpus were generated in the following way:

1. A topic distribution $\boldsymbol{\theta} \sim Dirichlet(\alpha)$ is chosen for all the corpus
2. For each topic $k \in [1, K]$
   - A word distribution is extracted for the topic $\phi_k \sim Dirichlet(\beta)$
3. For each biterm $b_i \in \boldsymbol{B}$
   - A topic assignment is extracted $z_i \sim Multimonial(\boldsymbol{\theta})$
   - Two words are extracted $w_{i,1}, w_{i,2} \sim Multimonial(\phi_{z_i})$

Taking into account the generation mechanism assumed by BTM, the likelihood can be obtained for the entire corpus given the parameters α and β from the probability of each of the biterms:

$$P(\boldsymbol{B}|\alpha,\beta) = \prod_{i=1}^{N_B} \int \int \sum_{k=1}^{K} P(w_{i,1}, w_{i,2}, z_i = k|\boldsymbol{\theta},\boldsymbol{\Phi})d\boldsymbol{\theta}d\boldsymbol{\Phi} \tag{1}$$

$$= \prod_{i=1}^{N_B} \int \int \sum_{k=1}^{K} \theta_k \phi_{k,w_{i,1}} \phi_{k,w_{i,2}} d\boldsymbol{\theta}d\boldsymbol{\Phi} \tag{2}$$

Obtaining exactly the parameters $\boldsymbol{\theta}$ and $\boldsymbol{\Phi}$ that maximize the likelihood of (2) is an intractable problem. Following the proposal in [11], the parameters $\boldsymbol{\theta}$ and $\boldsymbol{\Phi}$ can be approximated using Gibbs sampling [12].

To infer the topics of a document, that is, to evaluate $P(z|d)$ for the document d, the proportion of topics of a document is derived through the topics of the biterms. If d contains N_d biterms, $\{b_i^{(d)}\}_{i=1}^{N_d}$,

$$P(z|d) = \sum_{i=1}^{N_d} P(z|b_i^{(d)})P(b_i^{(d)}|d) \tag{3}$$

2.1 Evaluation Criterion

To evaluate the quality of the topics obtained, the coherence metric proposed by Mimno et al. [13] is used. Given a topic z and its T most probable words $V^{(z)} = (v_1^{(z)}, ..., v_T^{(z)})$ where $v_i^{(z)} \in W$ for $i = 1...T$, the coherence score is defined as:

$$C(z; V^{(z)}) = \sum_{t=2}^{T} \sum_{l=1}^{t} \log \frac{D(v_t^{(z)}, v_l^{(z)}) + 1}{D(v_l^{(z)})}$$

where $D(v)$ is the frequency of the word v in all documents, $D(v,v')$ is the number of documents where the words v and v' co-occur. The coherence metric is based on the idea that words that belong to the same concept will tend to co-occur within the same documents. This is empirically demonstrable because the coherence score is highly correlated with the human criterion.

To evaluate the overall quality of a set of topics, the average of the coherence metric is calculated for each of the topics obtained $\frac{1}{k}\sum_k C(z_k; V^{(z_k)})$. These results allow us to determine the number of topics that best represent the entire corpus.

3   Method Proposed

Let K be the number of topics that represent a set of items, each of them is modeled according to the probability distribution shown in (3).

Given a list of m users $U = u_1, u_2, .., u_m$ and a list of n items $I = i_1, i_2, ..., i_n$, each user has a list of items I_u, with a score associated to each item r_{ui}. Each item is assigned a score of 1 to 5.

In order to evaluate the similarity between two items from the probability distributions obtained with BTM, the proposed method uses the divergence of Kullback and Leibler [14]. Given two probability distributions P and Q, the divergence function is defined as:

$$D_{KL}(P,Q) = \sum_i P(i) \log \frac{P(i)}{Q(i)}$$

From this divergence, it is possible to define the similarity between two items p and q as follows:

$$sim(p,q) = \exp(-D_{KL}(p,q))$$

To estimate the rating of a new item m given a user u, the following method is proposed to predict $\hat{r}_{um}$:

1. The probability distributions are obtained for each of the items that the user evaluated I_u, as shown in the Sect. 2.
2. The probability distribution of the material m is obtained.
3. The similarity sim of m is calculated with each I_{u_j}.
4. The similarities are ordered, and the first t are chosen, where t is a parameter that defines the size of the neighborhood to be considered.
5. From the most similar t, the prediction is calculated:

$$\hat{r}_{um} = \mu_m + \frac{\sum_{j=1}^{t} sim(m,j)(r_{uj} - \mu_j)}{\sum_{j=1}^{t} sim(m,j)}$$

where r_{uj} is the score of item j given by user u, and μ_j and μ_m are the average scores of j and m respectively.

4   Experimental Results

Two databases were used in this work, one of educational materials and the other one of films. The first one provides information on users and Computer Science educational materials in the Merlot [9] digital repository. The data involves more than 984 materials and more than 260 users who uploaded, evaluated or commented on each of the publications. Also, public information about publications and users was available. The data extracted from each of the publications was: title, type of material, date of creation, date of update, user who made it, reviewer review from 1 to 5, user review from 1 to 5, comments, and the unstructured textual description. The second dataset is about movie ratings in MovieLens [10]. This dataset contains 100,000 scores from 1 to 5 by 943 users for 1682 movies, where each user rated at least 20 movies; of the films the title and the date are known; and in addition, the arguments of each of them were collected.

When it comes to operating with textual information, it is necessary to resort to Text Mining techniques in order to represent each description in a vector of terms. This was carried out through a process consisting of several stages. In a first stage, the contents were unified in a single language. Then a stopwords filter was applied, which is responsible for filtering the words that match any indicated stopword. English language stopwords were filtered; words relating to the context. URLs and non-text characters were also deleted. Then, each word in the text was reduced to its root by applying the Snowball [15] stemming algorithm. The importance of this process is that it eliminates syntactic variations related to gender, number and verbal time. Once the roots of each of the words are obtained, the frequency of appearance of each of them in the publications was calculated and the words that appear more than once were chosen.

From the structured textual information, the modeling of latent topics was obtained through BTM for the set of educational materials and films. To evaluate these models, for each number of topics between 2 and 30, the coherence obtained was averaged, randomly sampling the test and training set in 1000 iterations. Figure 1 shows the average of the coherence of the model with respect to the quantity of topics extracted in the material dataset. The number of topics in which there is a break in the growth of the function of average coherence is of interest. In this case, the optimal value is between 5 and 7 latent topics.

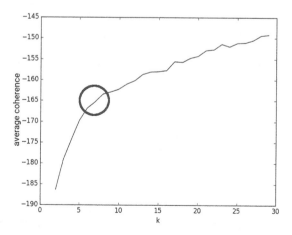

Fig. 1. Materials dataset. Average coherence for different Ks

Table 1 shows the topics obtained with $K = 7$ for the materials dataset. For each of the topics, the six most important words are shown, i.e., those that are more likely to belong to that topic.

Table 1. Materials dataset. Model of topics obtained with BTM

Topic	Most important words in the topic				
1	programming	software	data	algorithms	design
2	information	technology	computing	internet	systems
3	programming	java	language	tutorial	software
4	resources	design	systems	development	security
5	design	information	programming	interaction	human
6	binary	fractions	codes	numbers	tutorial
7	numbers	stars	interactivate	graph	simulation

The evaluation methodology for the proposed method applies 10-fold cross-validation. This evaluation process was repeated 50 times to obtain a significant sample on which the results are averaged. This process was applied to the proposed method, identified as KNN Topic Model, and the KNN collaborative filtering methods, KNN Mean [7] based on the item-item and user-user approach, SlopeOne [16] and on the method based on latent factor models (SVD) [17].

The proposed method and KNN methods receive as a parameter the number of neighbors to consider. The size of the neighborhood has a significant impact on

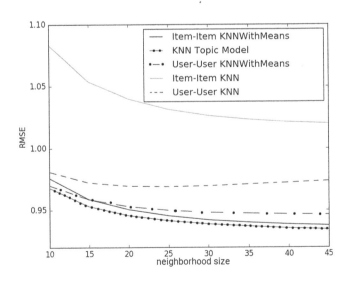

Fig. 2. Movies dataset. Influence of the neighborhood size

the quality of the prediction [4]. Figure 2 shows the RMSE (Root Mean Squared Error) for different numbers of neighbors in the different algorithms. The error decreases as the number of neighbors grows. The error for the proposed KNN Topic Model method is always below for different neighborhood values. In addition, it is observed that after 40 neighbors the RMSE decreases slowly for each of the algorithms.

The results of the 50 executions of the cross validation for each algorithm using the material dataset are shown in the Table 2 and the results when using the movie dataset are shown in the Table 3. The number of neighbors $t = 40$ was established for all neighborhood-based models. The items of the material dataset were represented as a multinomial 7-dimensional distribution and the items of the movie dataset as a 10-dimensional multinomial distribution. To evaluate the predictions of the proposed method against the results of the other algorithms, the precision metrics calculated were RMSE (Root Mean Squared Error), MAE (Mean Absolute Error) and FCP (Fraction of Concordant Pairs), which measures the proportion of pairs of well-classified items [18]. Unlike RMSE and MAE, the value of FCP is better the higher it is, since it measures a proportion.

Table 2. Educational Materials dataset. Results obtained

	KNN Model Topic	KNN item-item	KNN Mean item-item	KNN user-user	KNN Mean user-user	SlopeOne	SVD
Mean RMSE	**0.6047**	0.6848	0.8412	0.7757	0.6339	0.6575	0.6420
Mean MAE	0.4403	0.4566	0.5544	0.5126	0.4333	0.4336	**0.3443**
Mean FCP	**0.6517**	0.2075	0.4820	0.1400	0.3333	0.4133	0.4329

Table 3. Movies dataset. Results obtained

	KNN Model Topic	KNN item-item	KNN Mean item-item	KNN user-user	KNN Mean user-user	SlopeOne	SVD
Mean RMSE	**0.9340**	1.0203	0.9385	0.9732	0.9466	0.9426	0.9402
Mean MAE	**0.7359**	0.8044	0.7375	0.7680	0.7462	0.7409	0.7396
Mean FCP	0.6879	0.5990	0.6867	0.6948	**0.6946**	0.6865	0.6889

It is observed that the proposed method is competitive against two sets of different datasets. For the dataset of educational materials, the KNN Topic Model method obtains a lower RMSE error and a higher FCP ratio. However, the MAE metric is lower for SVD. It is emphasized that with the little information of the materials that are available, through the use of topic modeling it is possible to improve the FCP. In the movie dataset, more information about the interests of the users is available, so that the proposed method, although having a competitive result, does not exceed the FCP value with respect to the user-user KNN Mean approach.

5   Conclusions and Future Lines of Work

In the present paper we managed to model a set of items detecting latent topics in their descriptions. This allowed us to know which are the topics that describe the items and how they relate to each other. The methodology used in the proposed method and the validation metrics applied present preliminary results that are satisfactory and competitive compared to traditional methods. As future work, the application of the proposed method in other databases with associated textual information is foreseen. It is also interesting to incorporate information about the opinions and tastes of the user from other contexts. The results of this work are an addition to the work previously presented in [19], where a modeling of users was proposed through the information obtained with BTM when identifying the topics of interest of the students of the Computer Science School of the UNLP through their publications made in Facebook groups. In turn, this work is related to a larger project, whose objective is to create a recommender system for digital educational materials.

References

1. Adomavicius, G., Tuzhilin, A.: Toward the next generation of recommender systems: a survey of the state-of-the-art and possible extensions. IEEE Trans. Knowl. Data Eng. **17**(6), 734–749 (2005)
2. Ricci, F., Rokach, L., Shapira, B.: Introduction to recommender systems handbook. In: Ricci, F., Rokach, L., Shapira, B., Kantor, P. (eds.) Recommender Systems Handbook, pp. 1–35. Springer, Boston (2011). https://doi.org/10.1007/978-0-387-85820-3_1
3. Cheng, X., Yan, X., Lan, Y., Guo, J.: BTM: Topic modeling over short texts. IEEE Trans. Knowl. Data Eng. **26**(12), 2928–2941 (2014)
4. Herlocker, J.L., Konstan, J.A., Borchers, A., Riedl, J.: An algorithmic framework for performing collaborative filtering. In: Proceedings of the 22nd Annual International ACM SIGIR Conference on Research and Development in Information Retrieval, pp. 230–237. ACM (1999)
5. Linden, G., Smith, B., York, J.: Amazon.com recommendations: item-to-item collaborative filtering. IEEE Internet Comput. **7**(1), 76–80 (2003)
6. Sarwar, B., Karypis, G., Konstan, J., Riedl, J.: Item-based collaborative filtering recommendation algorithms. In: Proceedings of the 10th International Conference on World Wide Web, pp. 285–295. ACM (2001)
7. Bell, R.M., Koren, Y.: Scalable collaborative filtering with jointly derived neighborhood interpolation weights. In: 2007 Seventh IEEE International Conference on Data Mining, ICDM 2007, pp. 43–52. IEEE (2007)
8. Takács, G., Pilászy, I., Németh, B., Tikk, D.: Major components of the gravity recommendation system. ACM SIGKDD Expl. Newslett. **9**(2), 80–83 (2007)

9. California State University: Merlot - multimedia educational resource for learning and online teaching (2017). https://merlot.org. Accessed 30 June 2017
10. GroupLens Research: Movielens datasets (2017). https://grouplens.org/datasets/movielens/. Accessed 30 June 2017
11. Griffiths, T.L., Steyvers, M.: Finding scientific topics. Proc. Nat. Acad. Sci. **101**(Suppl 1), 5228–5235 (2004)
12. Geman, S., Geman, D.: Stochastic relaxation, gibbs distributions, and the bayesian restoration of images. IEEE Trans. Pattern Anal. Mach. Intell. **6**, 721–741 (1984)
13. Mimno, D., Wallach, H.M., Talley, E., Leenders, M., McCallum, A.: Optimizing semantic coherence in topic models. In: Proceedings of the Conference on Empirical Methods in Natural Language Processing, pp. 262–272. Association for Computational Linguistics (2011)
14. Kullback, S., Leibler, R.A.: On information and sufficiency. Ann. Math. Stat. **22**(1), 79–86 (1951)
15. Gupta, V., Lehal, G.S.: A survey of common stemming techniques and existing stemmers for Indian languages. J. Emerg. Technol. Web Intell. **5**(2), 157–161 (2013)
16. Lemire, D., Maclachlan, A.: Slope one predictors for online rating-based collaborative filtering. In: Proceedings of the 2005 SIAM International Conference on Data Mining, pp. 471–475. SIAM (2005)
17. Mnih, A., Salakhutdinov, R.R.: Probabilistic matrix factorization. In: Advances in Neural Information Processing Systems, pp. 1257–1264 (2008)
18. Koren, Y., Sill, J.: Collaborative filtering on ordinal user feedback. In: IJCAI, pp. 3022–3026 (2013)
19. Charnelli, M.E., Lanzarini, L., Diaz, J.: Modeling students through analysis of social networks topics. In: XXII Congreso Argentino de Ciencias de la Computacion CACIC 2016, pp. 363–371 (2016)

Automatic Characteristics Extraction for Sentiment Analysis Tasks

Juan M. Rodríguez[1,2(✉)] (iD), Hernán D. Merlino[2], and Ramón García-Martínez[2]

[1] PhD Program in Computer Sciences, National University of La Plata (UNLP),
La Plata, Bs. As., Argentina
jmrodriguez1982@gmail.com
[2] Systems Information Research Group, Department of Productive and Technological
Development, National University of Lanús, Lanús, Bs. As., Argentina
hmerlino@gmail.com

Abstract. The following article proposes the use of Open Information Extraction Methods (OIE), in particular ClausIE, to automatically obtain characteristics from movie reviews. Within automatic summary generation and sentiment analysis frameworks, this approach is compared with other two in which manual steps are used to obtain the characteristics of a service or product. The obtained result shows that ClausIE can be used for the extraction of characteristics in a semi-automatic way. It requires a minimum manual intervention that is explained in the results section.

Keywords: Sentiment analysis · Characteristics extraction
Knowledge extraction · Semantic relations extraction
Open information extraction · Natural language processing

1 Introduction

The task of mining film reviews in order to obtain an automatically summary consists mainly in three tasks. The first task is to obtain the pair: characteristic-opinion analyzing one by one the constituent sentences of the review. The second task is to identify the polarity (positive or negative) of each opinion. And the final task consist in building a structured list based on the characteristics and opinions found, calculating the polarity of each characteristic as the average polarity of all opinions in which each characteristic was found [1]. The present work focuses mainly on improving the first of the mentioned tasks, which is, the identification of characteristics and words that express opinions, but mainly in the identification of characteristics.

Characteristics, also called aspects, are individual elements of a larger entity, each of which can be evaluated independently. For instance, a restaurant has the following characteristics: *food*, *atmosphere*, *service* and *price*. Even, if you know that you are talking about a particular restaurant which offers a particular dish such as: "fish tacos with French fries" this dish can be a characteristic.

The main difference between sentiment analysis on reviews and the automatic summary of reviews with sentiment analysis is that in the first case only the global polarity of given text (the review) is calculated, while in the second case the main characteristics are extracted from the text and then the polarity of each characteristic is calculated individually.

Aspects play an important role in sentiment analysis because although it's very valuable to have the general idea of an opinion, the review of aspects (individual characteristics) plays a fundamental role in the decision making process. A classic example is the review of a product, where often a single aspect is decisive for a user to decide to buy it (typically the price and/or the quality).

The focus of this work is the extraction of characteristics. We sought an automatic solution based on the use of a method of Open Information Extraction. In particular, a solution based on ClausIE method [2] was proposed.

1.1 Introduction to Open Information Extraction (OIE)

Knowledge extraction is any technique which allows that an automated process analyze unstructured information sources, such as texts written in natural language and extract the embedded knowledge in order to represent it in a structured way, able to be manipulated in an automatic reasoning processes, for instance: a production rule or a subgraph in a semantic network. The information obtained as output of this type of process is called: *piece of knowledge* [3, 4].

In 2007 Michele Banko introduces a new concept in the field of knowledge extraction, which is called: Open Information Extraction (OIE). It is a paradigm of knowledge extraction where a computer system makes a single pass on the total unstructured information sources in natural language format (called corpus of documents) given as input and extracts a large set of relational tuples without requiring any kind of human participation. In the same work Banko presents a method called TEXT RUNNER, which is the first method that works within this new paradigm [5]. Since this work was published other methods of knowledge extraction were proposed under the paradigm that Banko called Open Information Extraction or just OIE.

Semantic relation extraction methods that work in accordance with the OIE paradigm return a tuple for each semantic relation discovered. The tuple has the form (Entity 1, Relation, Entity 2), where entities are usually well-identified objects, persons, places, companies, dates, etc., and the relationship is the semantic relationship between the two entities, often factual information, such as "Who did what to whom". To illustrate this, consider the following sentence:

Albert Einstein, who was born in Ulm, has won the Nobel Prize.

Extracting the relationships in the sentences and expressing them as a tuple in the form (Entity 1, Relation, Entity 2) should return the following:

- (Albert Einstein, has won, the Nobel Prize)
- (Albert Einstein, was born in, Ulm)

1.2   The Selected Method: ClausIE

A documentary investigation was carried out in [6] over a few semantic relation extraction methods, which work in accordance with the Open Information Extraction paradigm and it was found that ClausIE was, according to its authors [2] the method that achieved a better precision. This assertion was tested in [7] where a partial publication was made of a comparative evaluation between ClausIE and other similar information extraction methods: ReVerb [8] and OLLIE [9]. A final version of the results is in the process of being published. But these results would be favorable to ClausIE, which is why this method was selected for this work.

2   Related Works

Blair-Goldensohn and other used in [10] a hybrid method to extract the characteristics of the reviews, consisting in two methods: a dynamic method and a static extraction method. They searched for nouns or compound nouns, constituted by two or three words that appeared in some phrases that indicated a sentiment load (polarity) or phrases that matched with certain syntactic patterns that were possible indicators of an opinion. They found that the patterns were more accurate than the occurrence of nouns in phrases loaded with sentiments. The most productive pattern they had was looking for sequences of nouns that had an adjective immediately before, so they found, for instance, phrases like "…great fish tacos…", in restaurant reviews. They included "fish tacos" as a characteristic, because this was a very common dish (a characteristic dish) for the restaurants evaluated in the reviews.

For the second approach, the static method for characteristics extraction, they took 1500 random sentences of hotels and restaurants reviews and they manually labeled them indicating the "coarse-grained" characteristics they found there. They called these characteristics "coarse-grained" because they are very general. They are the characteristics that can be found in any hotel or restaurant. These were not as specific as: "fish taco" (which is a "fine-grained" characteristic). The characteristics were the following: *food*, *decor*, *service*, and *value* for restaurants and *rooms*, *location*, *dining*, *service*, and *value* for hotels. They also included a category *other*, to label sentences that did not include any of the previous characteristics. Then they trained a classifier with the set of labeled cases. Finally they used the already trained classifier to detect aspects in any other sentences.

In [1] was carried out an experiment similar to the proposed in this article. An automatic summary of IMDB films reviews was made, focused on finding opinions about the characteristics of a given film. The authors defined a film characteristic as an element (*staging*, *music*, etc.) or as people (*director*, *actor*, etc.) mentioned in an opinion. The authors manually defined a list of main characteristics (called characteristics of type element) that are relevant in a film and for the characteristics associated with people they used the full cast list as it is published in IMDB for a given film.

The element-type characteristics selected manually were the following six:

- OA: general
- ST: script

- CH: character design
- VP: visual effects
- MS: sound and music effects
- SE: special effects

Each feature was associated with multiple keywords, for instance the characteristic *script* was associated to the different keywords: *story, plot, script, storyline, dialogue, screenplay, ending, line, scene* and *tale*. To obtain these keywords, they worked with a dataset of 1100 IMDB film reviews manually labeled. Then the keywords associated with a characteristic were obtained just filtering the most frequent words.

3   Current Problems

Authors in [10] found a fundamental problem with the first approach, the dynamic method; the problem is that the found aspects are only fine-grained. It is not trivial to deduce that *fish soup* and *lobster soup* are part of a larger aspect that could be: *soups, entrances* or just *food*.

About the second approach, the classifier achieved a fairly high *precision*. It obtained 86.9% for *service* and 90.3% for *price* in the case of restaurants. For hotels it achieved 83.9% of *precision* for *service* and 83.3% for *price*. The *recall* was little lower, it was between 54.5% and 69.7% for the mentioned cases. However, this method has the disadvantage of needing a set of cases manually labeled.

The main problem associated with the work carried out in [1] is the need to know the set of relevant characteristics before generate the manual labeling.

4   Proposed Solution

In order to elaborate experimental tests, a dataset of 2000 film reviews extracted from the IMDB site was used and hand-labeled in two sets: a group of 1000 positive reviews and another of 1000 negative reviews. The data set was originally created by Pang and Lee [11] to train a text classifier to perform tasks of sentiment analysis. Since then the dataset has been available on the web and has been used in other publications.

4.1   Obtaining Characteristics

The semantic relation extraction method under OIE paradigm: ClausIE, was executed over the dataset. ClausIE returns for each semantic relation a tuple of the form: (Entity 1, Relation, Entity 2) where "Entity" is any syntactic element that refers to something concrete: a person, a place, a brand, etc. (although it can also be a date or another type of abstract entity), ClausIE uses an entity name detection algorithm for it (NER). It was surmised that the characteristics of a movie should be able to be detected as entities. And in a fairly large corpus, these would be repeated with a higher frequency than other possible entities. At least the characteristics called fine-grained [10].

The obtained semantic extractions were ordered by the number of times an initial "Entity" was repeated. Then the results were filtered to show only those that start with the article "the", in this way we avoid listing pronouns and other frequently used words. The list obtained is shown in Table 1.

Table 1. Repetitions of the first entity starting with "the"

Entity 1	Repetitions
The film	3538
The movie	1637
The story	683
The plot	501
The audience	396
The script	387
The characters	320
The director	258
The two	234
The filmmakers	197
The acting	192
The actors	184
The camera	147
The world	143
The dialogue	140
The cast	128
The man	123
The ending	114
The music	112
The scenes	101
The result	100
The performances	99
The special effects	99

The list shown in Table 1 corresponds well with a list of characteristics (or keywords that indicate characteristics according to the nomenclature in [1]). However, the generation of this list required two manual steps, so its generation was not completely automatic. These steps were the following:

- An arbitrary cut at 99 repetitions, we didn't take more elements than those that appear up to 99 times.
- Manual elimination of some entities that do not correspond to films characteristics: *the two, the camera, the world, the man* (marked in bold).

Comparing the generated word list, with the list of keywords characteristic that presented in [1], it is observed that there are 12 common words out of 38. However, in the list of Table 1 there are 8 high-frequency words that were not used in the work of Zhuang and others [1]. Finally, it should be noted that with the 12 common words found, the coarse-grained characteristics defined in [1] are all covered, although some groups have only one word. This is shown in Table 2.

Table 2. Coarse-grained characteristics and their associated keywords in [1].

Characteristics	Keywords
OA	**Film, movie**
ST	**Story, plot, script**, storyline, **dialogue**, screenplay, **ending**, line, **scene**, tale
CH	**Character**, characterization, role
VP	**Scene**, fight-scene, action-scene, action-sequence, set, battle-scene, picture, scenery, setting, visual-effects, color, background, image
MS	**Music**, score, song, sound, soundtrack, theme
SE	**Special-effects**, effect, CGI, SFX

The 12 keywords in common are shown in bold. The other keywords found would belong to the coarse-grained characteristics OA and CH, according to the following list:

- **CH:** acting, actors, cast, performances
- **OA:** director, audience, filmmakers, results

4.2 Sentiment Analysis of Each Characteristic

For the following analysis, the list in Table 1 was taken as a list of characteristics (without counting the filtered words) because the goal of this article is obtaining features automatically. For each characteristic, a sentiment analysis task was performed using Senti-Wordnet 3.0 which is a sentiment lexicon [12].

We proceeded as follows: all the semantic extractions were recovered for a given review, then each extraction was joined in a single sentence concatenated "Entity 01" with "Relationship" with "Entity 02". And if any characteristic in the list appeared in the resulting sentence then it was evaluated using the SentIWordNet 3.0 lexicon. At last, according to the result of the polarity obtained, positive or negative, this characteristic was marked with a 1 (positive) or a −1 (negative) in a final result table.

Finally, for each of the reviews with at least one characteristic, the values of the polarities of each characteristic were sum together in order to obtain a global result or polarity for the review. This last step was carried out in order to compare the analysis of the characteristics, which together should be identical to the global analysis, against the labeled polarity of the review. If the polarities don't match, maybe the characteristics weren't representative of the film or maybe the calculation of the polarity of each characteristic was wrong.

5   Results and Conclusions

The overall *precision* for sentiment analysis (more specifically the obtaining of the polarity), using SentiWordNet 3.0 over the 2000 films reviews is 0.662; There are 1324 reviews ranked correctly. This is the floor on which the characteristics analysis is based, a low floor, especially when comparing the obtained results against supervised classification methods such as those used by Pang and Lee [11].

Only in 1187 reviews was found at least one characteristic to analyze, which is equivalent to 59% of them.

The sum of the positive and negative polarities of each of the characteristics, to obtain the global polarity of the review, gave a *precision* of 0.619, that is, 735 correctly classified of 1187 (the ones that had at least one characteristic). Although it is a low number, it is close to the overall accuracy of SentiWordNet 3.0. On that same segment of reviews, the 1187 that have at least one characteristic, SentiWordNet 3.0 obtained, working directly over the full text of the review, a *precision* of 0.666, which is a total of 790 correctly classified.

However, the average *precision* obtained was greater than that calculated in [1], where the average *precision* of different pairs of characteristics-opinions for different films was calculated and the obtained value was: 0.483. Nevertheless, since the set of used reviews is different (the one used by the authors is not available) and the way of analyzing the polarity is different, the precisions are not directly comparable. It is cited only as a reference.

Finally, the main positive result is the extraction almost automatically (with minimal manual intervention) of the characteristics of a product or service (in this case, films). The characteristics may not be exhaustive, when compared with those used in the work of Zhuang and others [1] but they are representative and undoubtedly used more frequently in the analyzed dataset. The sentiment analysis over individual characteristics does not improve the overall performance of the used method (in this case the sentiment lexicon SentiWordNet) but remains consistent with the *precision* of the method.

6   Future Research Lines

The revision and comparison of this approach with other extraction methods of automatic characteristics such as SABER [13] is a future work.

References

1. Zhuang, L., Jing, F., Zhu, X.Y.: Movie review mining and summarization. In: Proceedings of the 15th ACM International Conference on Information and Knowledge Management, pp. 43–50. ACM, November 2006
2. Del Corro, L., Gemulla, R.: ClausIE: sclause-based open information extraction. In Proceedings of the 22nd International Conference on World Wide Web, pp. 355–366. International World Wide Web Conferences Steering Committee, May 2013

3. García-Martínez, R., Britos, P.V.: Ingeniería de Sistemas Expertos. Nueva Librería, Buenos Aires (2004). ISBN 987-1104-15

4. Gómez, A., Juristo, N., Montes, C., Pazos, J.: Ingeniería del Conocimiento. Editorial Centro de Estudios Ramón Areces (1997). ISBN 84-8004-269-9

5. Banko, M., Cafarella, M.J., Soderland, S., Broadhead, M., Etzioni, O.: Open information extraction for the web. In: IJCAI, vol. 7, pp. 2670–2676, January 2007

6. Rodríguez, J.M., Merlino, H., García-Martínez, R.: Revisión sistemática comparativa de evolución de métodos de extracción de conocimiento para la web. In: XXI Congreso Argentino de Ciencias de la Computación (CACIC 2015), Buenos Aires, Argentina (2015)

7. Rodríguez, J.M., Merlino, H.D., Pesado, P., García-Martínez, R.: Performance evaluation of knowledge extraction methods. In: Fujita, H., Ali, M., Selamat, A., Sasaki, J., Kurematsu, M. (eds.) IEA/AIE 2016. LNCS (LNAI), vol. 9799, pp. 16–22. Springer, Cham (2016). https://doi.org/10.1007/978-3-319-42007-3_2

8. Fader, A., Soderland, S., Etzioni, O.: Identifying relations for open information extraction. In: Proceedings of the Conference on Empirical Methods in Natural Language Processing, pp. 1535–1545. Association for Computational Linguistics, July 2011

9. Schmitz, M., Bart, R., Soderland, S., Etzioni, O.: Open language learning for information extraction. In: Proceedings of the 2012 Joint Conference on Empirical Methods in Natural Language Processing and Computational Natural Language Learning, pp. 523–534. Association for Computational Linguistics, July 2012

10. Blair-Goldensohn, S., Hannan, K., McDonald, R., Neylon, T., Reis, G.A., Reynar, J.: Building a sentiment summarizer for local service reviews. In: WWW Workshop on NLP in the Information Explosion Era, vol. 14, pp. 339–348, April 2008

11. Pang, B., Lee, L., Vaithyanathan, S.: Thumbs up?: sentiment classification using machine learning techniques. In: Proceedings of the ACL 2002 Conference on Empirical Methods in Natural Language Processing, vol. 10, pp. 79–86. Association for Computational Linguistics, July 2002

12. Baccianella, S., Esuli, A., Sebastiani, F.: SentiWordNet 3.0: an enhanced lexical resource for sentiment analysis and opinion mining. In: LREC, vol. 10, pp. 2200–2204, May 2010

13. Caputo, A., Basile, P., de Gemmis, M., Lops, P., Semeraro, G., Rossiello, G.: SABRE: a sentiment aspect-based retrieval engine. In: Lai, C., Giuliani, A., Semeraro, G. (eds.) Information Filtering and Retrieval. SCI, vol. 668, pp. 63–78. Springer, Cham (2017). https://doi.org/10.1007/978-3-319-46135-9_4

Hardware Architectures, Networks and Operating Systems

Modular Petri Net Processor
for Embedded Systems

Orlando Micolini$^{(\boxtimes)}$, Emiliano N. Daniele, and Luis O. Ventre

Laboratorio de Arquitectura de Computadoras (LAC) FCEFyN, Universidad
Nacional de Córdoba, Córdoba, Argentina
{orlando.micolini,luis.ventre}@unc.edu.ar,
endaniele@gmail.com

Abstract. Reactive and concurrent embedded systems execute restricted
algorithms depending on the requirements. It is possible to implement one of
these hardware-software systems by using a Petri Net Processor. If logic and
policy are decoupled from the system actions, then we can improve maintainability and system validation. To achieve this, the Petri Processor is integrated
with other traditional processors, forming a heterogeneous multi-core processor,
which allows to verify the system using Petri Net mathematical formalisms. In
this article, a Modular Petri Processor Architecture is exposed, as well as the
inclusion of programmable queues that enhance maintainability, module
re-usage and semantic extension.

Keywords: Petri Processor · Petri Net · FPGA · IP core
Heterogeneous multi-core processor

1 Introduction

Heterogeneous multi-core processors include specific capabilities that are not available
in homogeneous multi-core processors. Reactive and concurrent embedded systems
need to comply with specific non-functional requirements [1]. These systems interact
with their environment, from which they receive input events and to where they
generate output reactions. The environment is the one imposing the rate at which the
system needs to generate the reactions. During this interaction, the system should react
as quickly as possible to satisfy the timing restrictions. This response time depends not
only on the algorithm used, but also on the platform capabilities, which make them
essential for estimating the overall response time of the final system [2].

The system proposed in this article is a heterogeneous system, with a Petri Processor (PP) and a General-Purpose Processor (GPP). The PP receives events, process
them to calculate the next system state, while the GPP calculates and executes actions,
thus decoupling logic from the actions of the system [3].

The proposed architecture implements an innovative way to relate hardware and
system logic by using a synchronization monitor. Because of this, the software prescind
from taking care of the critical sections of the code, and the synchronization functions,
since the PP is the one performing those tasks. Furthermore, there is a univocal

© Springer International Publishing AG, part of Springer Nature 2018
A. E. De Giusti (Ed.): CACIC 2017, CCIS 790, pp. 199–208, 2018.
https://doi.org/10.1007/978-3-319-75214-3_19

relationship between the program that the PP executes and the Petri Net model used, which guarantees the same properties that the model verifies.

The requirements for Concurrent and Reactive Embedded Systems [4] are: precision, reliability and structural flexibility. To reach those requirements, the PP is programmed using the model directly, resolving the execution of the events, and the state of the system. The PP, then, processes and orders events based on the restrictions of the system.

Applications of this processor are not only tied to reactive embedded systems, since it can be used to solve parallel systems. Many problems have been solved by using Petri Nets [5, 6].

The architecture of previously implemented PP was monolithic [3, 4]. In the current article we propose and develop a modular PP that preserves the same advantages of the previous PP, while adding new features to it. Certain situations were taken into consideration, like the use of naming conventions when implementing internal circuitry as well as external interfaces, which helped to standardize the components.

1.1   Objectives

General Objective
Modularize each PP function to optimize system maintainability and add programmable event queues.

The first implementation is aimed at generating reusable and standardized hardware components. This allows to add, remove or replace components in an easy way, so the PP can be adjusted to fit small embedded systems by only instantiating the necessary modules for a given application.

The ability to program the event queues allows the PP to execute different non-autonomous Petri nets, which increases the semantic capabilities of the system.

2   Petri Nets

2.1   Ordinary Petri Nets (PN)

An Ordinary Petri Net (PN) [7] is a quintuple defined by PN = (P, T, I−, I+, M_0) where:

- $P = \{p_1, p_2, \ldots, p_n\}$ is a finite non-empty set of places.
- $T = \{t_1, t_2, \ldots, t_m\}$ is a finite non-empty set of transitions.
- Given that P and T form a bipartite graph, the following is true: $P \cap T = \{\emptyset\}, P \cup T \neq \{\emptyset\}$
- Γ, Γ^+ are the incidence relationships between the places inputs and outputs, which relate Places and Transitions (Γ) or relate Transitions and Places (Γ^+). The Incidence Matrix is defined as: $I = \Gamma^+ - \Gamma$
- $M_0 = [m_0(p_1), m_0(p_2) \ldots, m_0(p_n)]$ is the initial marking vector of the PN, which represents the number of Tokens that each Place contains.

Taking the Incidence Matrix definition into account, a PN is then defined as a quadruple: PN = (P, T, I, M_0).

2.2   Synchronized Petri Nets or Non-autonomous Petri Nets

This type of PN introduce events modelling to the equation and they are an enhancement of the Ordinary PN [3, 8].

Non-autonomous PNs are used for modelling systems where the external discrete events synchronize the firing of the transitions. These events are tied to the transitions. In Fig. 1 the transition is synchronized with the event E^3, and the firing is produced when the following requirements are met:

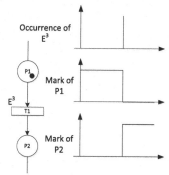

- The transition is enabled
- The associated event occurs

Changes outside of the system trigger the external events (this includes changes in time) while internal events are changes within the system itself. Synchronized Petri Nets can be then defined as a triple:

Fig. 1. Transition associated to an event.

PNsync = (PN, E, sync) where:

PN is a marked PN, E is a set of external events and *sync* is the function that relates Transitions T with $E \cup \{e\}$, where $\{e\}$ is the null event. All firings are atomic and instantaneous.

2.3   Perennial and Non-perennial Events

There are three types of events that can be associated with a Non-autonomous PN: perennial events, non-perennial events and automatic or null events [3].

Perennial events are those that, when they are triggered, they stay requesting a firing until the firing and synchronization conditions are met (the result will be the firing of the associated transition). These events are kept in the input queue until the associated Transition is fired.

Non-perennial events will fire a Transition, only if the transition was enabled before the event arrives; if the transition is not enabled, the event is discarded. In the PP implementation, there is a period of tolerance of two clock cycles for the Transitions to be enabled until the event is discarded.

Null or **Automatic** events {e} are associated with the automatic Transitions. These special types of Transitions are described in the next section.

2.4   Automatic Transitions

There is a type of internal event that is always generated and available, named $\{e\}$. In a Synchronized PN, one or more transitions can be associated with the Automatic

Event {e}. This means that those Transitions can be fired automatically as soon as they are enabled, since the automatic event is "always happening".

2.5 Conflicts Among Transitions

We can find conflicts among transitions in a synchronized PN when:

- Two or more transitions are enabled
- Their associated events occur simultaneously
- If one of the enabled transitions is fired, then some of the other transitions become disabled

Mathematically, the conflicts are defined as:

$$|\{t_s\}| > 1 \wedge |\{E^s\}| > 1 \, y \, t_i, t_j \in \{t_s\}$$

Where:

- $\{t_s\}$ is a set of enabled transitions
- $\{E^s\}$ is a set of events associated to the transitions $\{t_s\}$
- $t_i \, y \, t_j$ are transitions in conflict. They share at least an entry point with another place. If one of the transitions is fired, the other transition will be disabled. All these conflicts can be solved by a priority policy [6].

2.6 Relationship Between Events and the Incidence Matrix

If the semantics of a transition fire in a non-autonomous PN are analyzed, we find that the Incidence Matrix is the conjunctive evaluation of the columns (transitions) and the rows (places). This means that, if we have an Incidence Matrix of $m \times n$ dimension, n combinations of m logic variables are evaluated, so if we consider that every transition has an event associated, then we could write an expression like the following:

$$s_i = \left(\bigwedge_{h=0}^{m-1} (M(p_h) \geq i_{hi}) \, and \, E^i \right),$$

Where i_{hi} are the elements of the Matrix I and $M(p_h)$ is the marking value of the place h. The result s_i holds the elements of the vector of enabled transitions.

The PP executes this equation and is the foundation of its direct programmability since we can consider the Matrix and the Events, the equivalent of the program. This architecture executes an extended non-autonomous PN, and taking its semantic capability into account, gives us a Touring Machine [9, 10].

3 Architecture of the PP

The PP developed and presented in this article, reveals changes in the architecture implemented in [11]. The big difference resides in the programmable queues, the modularization of the hardware and the specific optimizations of each module.

The main building blocks of the PP are: the core, the queues, the priority module and the interfaces to connect to external devices.

3.1 Core

The main responsibility of the core module is to keep the internal state of the PN that the processor executes. Figure 2 displays the overall architecture of the processor, where the modules that form the core are marked with (*).

The core is composed of the following components: the Incidence Matrix, the Marking Vector and the Fire Requests Vector.

The responsibilities of each component are:

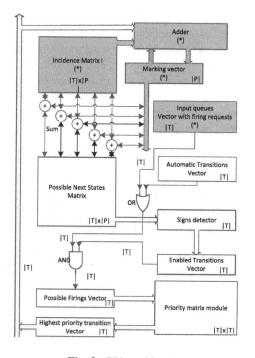

Fig. 2. PP's architecture

- **Incidence Matrix I**: stores the Incidence Matrix of the PN. Its dimension is equal to $|T| \times |P|$. All values stored are integers.
- **Marking Vector**: Stores the vector M of the PN, that is, the state of the PN. All stored values are positive integers.
- **Input queues**: their interfaces expose a vector to the PP, where each position represents the connection with each transition. Each position of the vector can be equal to 1 if there are events in the correspondent queue, or equal to 0 if there are no events queued.
- **Automatic Transitions Vector:** each position of this vector represents each transition. If a transition is configured as automatic, then its correspondent position in this vector will be equal to 1.
- **Possible Next States Matrix**: corresponds to the sum of each column of the Matrix I with the Marking Vector. Each i-th column of this matrix has the state that would be reached if the i-th transition were triggered.
- **Signs detector**: it is a vector where each position corresponds to a column of the Possible Next States Matrix. If any of the values in a column is negative, then the position in its vector will be equal to 1, meaning that the firing of this column would reach an unreachable marking (negative values mean that we would try to fire a disabled transition).
- **Enabled Transitions Vector**: it is the negated output of the signs vector.

- **Possible Firings Vector**: stores the possible firings of the PN, which is calculated from the Enabled Transitions Vector and the Requested Firings Vector (Input queues *or* Automatic transitions).

3.2 Processor Operation

As well as the previous PP [3], this new version of the PP also executes a PN in two clock cycles. Single server semantics has been adopted for this implementation.

Cycle 1 – Calculations. In this cycle, the PP calculates the transition that will be fired. To achieve this, the marking vector is added to every column in the incidence matrix, so we can obtain the signs of the possible next state that would be reached with every possible firing. This is stored in a new matrix where the column i holds the signs of the next markings.

The output of the Possible Next States Signs Matrix is the input of the Sign detector module. This module performs an '*or*' operation with all values stored in each column. If any of those values are negative, it means that the next state will not be reachable (the correspondent transition is not enabled).

The enabled transitions vector stores a value of 1 in those positions where the columns of the Possible Next States Matrix did not have negative values.

To calculate the transitions that can be fired, the information of two other vectors is needed: The requested firing vector (the output of the input queues) and the automatic transitions vector. The first one represents which transitions were requested to be fired by sending specific instructions to the processor (external event). The second one represents those transitions that do not require explicit firing events, because they are associated with the null event $\{e\}$.

Finally, to determine which transition the processor will fire, the Possible Firings Vector is inputted to the Priority Module. The output of this module is the id of the enabled and requested transition with the highest priority. The vector will hold a single value of 1 in the position that corresponds to the selected transition. This transition will be fired in the next cycle.

Cycle 2 – Update. In this cycle the firing is performed and the marking vector is updated. To achieve this, the selected transition vector works as a column selector. The adder (which can be found at the top of Fig. 2) carries on the sum of the marking vector with the selected column of the Matrix I. The result of the sum is stored back into the marking vector.

Besides, if applicable, the queues are updated; the correspondent output queue counter is incremented and the correspondent input queue counter is decremented.

3.3 Queues

Both the input and output queues of the PP have been redesigned to make them configurable.

There is one instance of an input queue and one instance of an output queue for every transition that the PP has. Each of those instances contains a saturated counter (only positive integers). Each counter is equipped with a max detector (for the overflow signal) and a zero detector (this is used for marking the queue as empty).

Input queue

The input queue stores the firing requests for the configured PN transitions. In Fig. 3(a), the external interfaces are shown. There are three modes of operation.

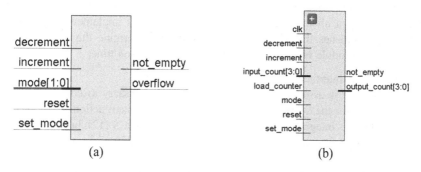

Fig. 3. (a) Input queue, (b) Output queue

Mode 1 – Normal Mode (Perennial event, default mode): The binary counter is incremented whenever a new firing request is issued (this is achieved via a specific instruction to the PP), and it is decremented on each fire performed on cycle 2. Since this is counting perennial events, the counter will keep its count until the increment or decrement signals of the module modifies it. In this case, the events queued are kept until the associated transition is fired. This is the only mode previous PP queues had.

Mode 2 – Automatic transition: In this operation mode the signal **not_empty** is kept high, see Fig. 3(a). This can be interpreted as a transition that is always requested to be fired, that is, an automatic transition.

Mode 3 – Non-perennial event: All events that are counted are non-perennial. After a certain amount of time (two clock cycles of the PP), the counter will be reset, and thus the associated transition could not be fired after that time.

Output queue

As seen on Fig. 3(b), output queues store the amount of firings performed. If a transition is fired, the output queue associated with it will increment its counter. When the queue is read (with a specific instruction) the counter will be decremented. The output queues have two different operation modes.

Mode 1 – Reporting mode: In this mode, the internal counter is incremented when the associated transition is fired and decremented when the counter is read (to check if a transition was fired). If the interruptions are enabled in the GPP, an interruption will be generated when the counter is different than zero.

Mode 2 – Non reporting mode: In this mode, the internal counter is not used and the signal **not_empty** is always equal to zero.

Priorities and conflicts among transitions

The PP cannot detect a conflicting state, so it treats transitions as if they were all in conflict. The Possible firing vector of the PP represents all those transitions.

The PP fires only one transition per execution cycle (single server model). This solves the conflicts issue and makes the system deterministic; the priority module makes the decision about which transition to fire. This is implemented as a binary matrix that establishes the necessary relationships to determine the highest priority transition. This module is also configurable during execution time.

Microblaze MCS Interface

Given that the PP is associated with a GPP [3], it is necessary to connect both processors in order for the system to perform the required system actions. The GPP that was chosen for this integration is the softcore Microblaze MCS [12], because of its low impact on the system resources and because it is well supported by the development tools from Xilinx.

The software architecture is very simple and it is made of one main program and two drivers. The first driver exposes a communication interface that we use for connecting to the PP (**pp_driver**) and the second one (**external_comm**) initializes and controls the UART module to send instructions and info through a serial connection.

4 Results

Several application cases were executed to evaluate the PP performance. It has been used successfully for controlling production lines, like the ones presented by Naiqi Wu y MengChu Zhou in [13]. The comparisons have been conducted by taking into consideration the results obtained in [3], which were very similar.

4.1 FPGA Resources

To determine the amount of resources used and to compare them with other implementations, a PP was instantiated multiple times, varying the number of elements of the vectors and matrices. Multiple synthesis of the core were performed as well, and data lengths of 4 and 8 bits were used.

Figure 4 shows the amount of FPGA resources used for each synthesized configuration. Registers are related to the number of flip-flops consumed, while LUTs, are directly related to the hardware architecture of the FPGA Atlys, which was the platform we used for implementing the PP.

In Fig. 4 an exponential use of resources is shown a long as we increase the number of elements in the vectors and matrices.

A very important discovery was that 4 bit configurations use approximately the same amount of registers than 8 bit configurations, even when an 8 bit configuration has fewer elements in the vectors and matrices (and in some cases, the number of registers decrease). For example, configuration $32 \times 32 \times 4$ consumes fewer resources than configuration $24 \times 24 \times 8$.

This means that we can process bigger PNs, if we can restrict the data length for a given application.

Due to the optimization of the IP Core, the resources impact of using Microblaze, is considered constant (12.72% of all LUTs available and 21.09% of registers). These resources are the same for all the PP architectures.

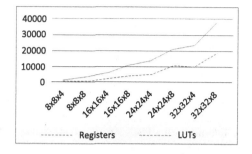

Fig. 4. Graph of resource consumption

4.2 Frequency Analysis

To perform a frequency analysis, we followed the same approach as explained in the previous section. This shows the maximum frequency that each implementation could reach. The data length has a negligible effect in the max frequency reached. For example, if we compare configurations 8 × 8 × 4 and 8 × 8 × 8, the difference in frequency is just 2 MHz (80.073 MHz and 78.422 MHz respectively). However, if we increase the number of elements of the matrices and vectors, that is, if we increase the size of the PN, then the frequency is significantly lower. For example, between configurations 8 × 8 × 8 and 16 × 16 × 8 there is approximately a 23 MHz difference (78.422 MHz and 55.32 MHz respectively). The boundaries of frequency are mostly due to the model of FPGA used.

5 Conclusions

In the current project, the PP was extended, modularized so it is an enhanced version of the one presented in [3]. An interconnected system was achieved, in replace of the monolithic version of previous implementations. The module design and the inclusion of programmable queues did not impact negatively on the resources required.

The programmability of the queues, which now support different modes of operation and types of events, is a huge step forward. Besides, the maintainability of the PP has been simplified, so it is easier to add new features in the future, like the possibility of executing Hierarchical PNs, temporal PNs, etc. The control stage of the processor is the only module that needs to be modified for that.

The results obtained from the optimizations implemented in the hardware level show that the PP is suitable for Embedded Systems that require up to 32 conditions (transitions), 32 logic variables (places) and 32 simultaneous events.

The addition of a serial communication module allowed to have a testable, programmable and configurable PP. All these can be now performed from any PC terminal.

The modular implementation of the PP implies a step forward for maintainability, scalability and the future auto-configuration of the PP. Furthermore, the programmable queues have increased its semantic capability.

References

1. Munir, A., Gordon-Ross, A., Ranka, S.: Modeling and Optimization of Parallel and Distributed Embedded Systems. Wiley Press, New York (2016)
2. Gamatié, A.: Designing Embedded Systems with the Signal Programming Language: Synchronous, Reactive Specification. Springer, New York (2009). https://doi.org/10.1007/978-1-4419-0941-1
3. Micolini, O.: Arquitectura asimétrica multicore con procesador de Petri, Facultad de Informática: La Plata, Argentina, Ph.D. thesis (2015)
4. Bainomugisha, E., et al.: A survey on reactive programming. ACM Comput. Surv. (CSUR) **45**(4), 52 (2013)
5. Moutinho, F., Gomes, L.: Distributed Embedded Controller Development with Petri Nets: Application to Globally-Asynchronous Locally-Synchronous Systems, vol. 150, pp. 43–67. Springer, Heidelberg (2015). https://doi.org/10.1007/978-3-319-20822-0
6. Haustermann, M.: Applications of Petri Nets (2017). https://www.informatik.uni-hamburg.de/TGI/PetriNets/applications/
7. Diaz, M.: Petri Nets Fundamental Models, Verification and Applications. Wiley Inc., Hoboken (2009)
8. David, R., Alla, H.: Discrete, Continuous, and Hybrid Petri Nets. Springer, Heidelberg (2010)
9. Hopcroft, J., Motwani, R., Ullman, J.: Introduction to Automata Theory, Languages, and Computation. Prentice Hall, London (2006)
10. Popova-Zeugmann, L.: Time and Petri Nets. Springer, Heidelberg (2013)
11. Micolini, O., et al.: Procesador de Petri para la Sincronización de Sistemas Multi-Core Homogéneos. In: CASE Congreso Argentino de Sistemas Embebidos (2012)
12. Xilinx, I.: Microblaze processor reference guide. Reference manual 23 (2011)
13. Wu, N., Zhou, M.C.: System Modeling and Control with Resource-Oriented Petri Nets. CRC Press, Boca Raton (2010)

A Novel Performance Metric for Virtual Network Embedding Combining Aspects of Blocking Probability and Embedding Cost

Enrique Dávalos$^{(\boxtimes)}$ and Benjamín Barán

Facultad Politécnica, Universidad Nacional de Asunción,
Campus Universitario UNA, San Lorenzo, Paraguay
edavalos@pol.una.py
http://www.pol.una.py

Abstract. Network Virtualization offers a solution for Future Internet and it is a key enabler for cloud computing applications. *Virtual Network Embedding* (VNE) problem deals with resource allocation of a physical infrastructure to Virtual Network Requests (VNRs). Several performance metrics are employed in order to evaluate the efficiency of specific VNE approaches. These existing metrics, mostly related to Infrastructure Provider profit, are computed at the end of the VNE process, after embedding many VNRs. This work proposes a novel performance metric, VNE-NP (*VNE Normalized Profit*) which combines aspects of the two metrics most used in the literature: *Blocking Probability* and *Embedding Cost*.

Keywords: Network Virtualization · Performance metrics
Virtual Network Embedding

1 Introduction

Network architecture is critical for cloud computing applications, which require distributed datacenters interconnected through high data transfer and low delay networks [1]. Besides, a high level of virtualization in datacenters resources and networking devices are required for the provisioning of cloud services, which explains the increasing importance of technologies related to Network Virtualization [2].

The problem of optimally assigning resources of a physical network to *Virtual Network Requests* (VNRs) is usually named *Virtual Network Embedding* (VNE) problem and it is the main resource allocation challenge in Network Virtualization [3].

Several performance metrics have already been used to compute how optimal or efficient a specific VNE approach is. Surveys as [3,4] present these metrics, which are computed at the end of a VNE process (a large amount of VNR mappings), and are related to Quality of Services (QoS) or profit issues.

In this work, we present an overview of the performance metrics that are used to evaluate profit-related aspects. Next, a new performance metric is proposed

© Springer International Publishing AG, part of Springer Nature 2018
A. E. De Giusti (Ed.): CACIC 2017, CCIS 790, pp. 209–218, 2018.
https://doi.org/10.1007/978-3-319-75214-3_20

for the first time, named *VNE Normalized Profit* (VNE-NP), considering both aspects of efficiency in finding a possible mapping of a specific VNR as well as physical network resources utilization.

The rest of this work is organized as follows: Sect. 2 presents a VNE formulation and main performance metrics, while the performance metrics related to economical profit are discussed in Sect. 3. Section 4 proposes the novel VNE-NP metric and a VNE example shows its viability. Section 5 concludes this work.

2   Virtual Network Embedding (VNE) Problem

2.1   Physical Network

When considering a VNE problem, a physical network is modeled as an undirected graph $G^P = (N^P, L^P)$ where N^P is the set of physical nodes and L^P is the set of bi-directional physical links.

Each physical node $n^P \in N^P$ can be considered as connected to a datacenter whose available computing capacity is represented by a single parameter c^n, usually called *computing resource capacity*.

At the same time, the physical links $l^P \in L^P$ interconnect physical nodes. Each physical link is characterized by its available bandwidth indication, i.e. its capacity to support data traffic.

2.2   Virtual Network Requests

Each virtual network request (VNR) is also usually modeled as an undirected graph $G^V = (N^V, L^V)$ where N^V is the set of virtual nodes and L^V is the set of virtual links. The requirements of each virtual node and each virtual link are typically related with the same parameters that characterize physical nodes and links respectively, i.e. each virtual node requires a specific number of computing resource units, while each virtual link requires a specific bandwidth.

2.3   VNE Problem Formulation

A given VNE algorithm should process one VNR at a time, trying to efficiently allocate virtual nodes into physical nodes and virtual links into paths formed by physical links. Therefore, a VNR allocation process can be divided in two mapping functions:

1. *Virtual Node Mapping* (VNM), which assigns each virtual node n^V to a physical node n^P:

$$VNM := f(n^V \rightarrow n^P) \tag{1}$$

2. *Virtual Link Mapping* (VLM), which assigns to each requirement of virtual link l^V a path of consecutive physical links:

$$VLM := f(l^V \rightarrow p^P) \tag{2}$$

$p^{\mathrm{P}} \in P^{\mathrm{P}}$ where P^{P} is the set of all possible paths (or lightpaths in the case of a physical optical network) between a pair of physical nodes which host the corresponding pair of virtual nodes interconnected by l^{V}.

A feasible solution must comply with specified restrictions, mostly related to the availability of physical resources to host virtual nodes or links, and the nature of the physical network.

Each VNR allocation may be chosen to optimize a single objective function, or multiple objective functions, in order to choose the most convenient solution among all feasible alternatives. In this sense, each VNR allocation can be considered as an optimization problem, with a discrete and finite number of solutions that satisfy specific restrictions.

If the VNE process succedded in finding a feasible (and ideally optimal) solution, then the VNR is *embedded* and the physical resources required are assigned to it. Otherwise, the VNR is *blocked*. There is not partial VNR allocation.

2.4   VNE Global Performance Metrics

The individual result in the allocation or blocking of a single VNR does not define the real efficiency of the whole VNE process. The VNE process comprises multiple VNR allocations and it is evaluated by global, long-term *Performance Metrics*, which can only be computed at the end of a whole VNE process, typically given by a period of working (or simulation) under a required load environment.

VNE performance metrics can be classified into those related to: (i) resources spending or economical profit, (ii) Quality of Service issues, and (iii) others metrics [3]. The main performance metrics, utilized in almost all VNE approaches, are those related to resource spending or economical profit. Therefore, they will be explained in detail in next section.

3   Resources Spending or Economical Profit Metrics

These type of metrics try to measure how efficient is the VNE method in the utilization of physical resources or to accept the maximum number of VNRs. In this context, the most referenciated/used performance metrics are:

- *Accepted Ratio* [5];
- *Embedding Cost* [6];
- *Embedding Revenue* [7]; and
- *Revenue/Cost Relation* [8].

3.1   Accepted Ratio

Accepted Ratio performance metric [5] measures the relation between the number of accepted (not blocked) VNRs (VNR_{Acc}) over the total number of VNRs considered in the process (VNR_{Tot}):

$$Accepted\ Ratio = \frac{\sum VNR_{\mathrm{Acc}}}{\sum VNR_{\mathrm{Tot}}} \tag{3}$$

The values of *Accepted Ratio* is in the range $[0,1]$ and higher values of this metric indicate better performance of a specific approach. For online problems, this metric is usually considered as its complement and called *"Blocking Rate"* or *"Blocking Probability"*:

$$Blocking\,Rate = \frac{\sum VNR_{\text{Block}}}{\sum VNR_{\text{Tot}}} \tag{4}$$

where $\sum VNR_{Block}$ is the number of blocked VNRs, and therefore:

$$Blocking\,Rate = 1 - Accepted\,Ratio \tag{5}$$

Accepted Ratio represents the efficiency in finding a solution for allocating a VNR. However, an approach specially designed to declive this metric, can accept all VNRs with fewer amount of required resources and with simpler topologies, while blocking more complex VNRs.

3.2   Embedding Cost

Embedding Cost [6] or *Physical Resource utilization* performance metric computes total cost of embedding, in terms of physical resources that were needed to embed accepted requests.

The embedding cost of an individual VNR_i ($Cost_i^{\text{VNR}}$) can be considered as proportional to physical resources needed to perform virtual node and virtual link mappings:

$$Cost_i^{\text{VNR}} = (\gamma \sum_{N^{\text{P}}} c_{n,i}^{\text{P}} + \delta \sum_{L^{\text{P}}} B_{l,i}^{\text{P}}).HT_i \tag{6}$$

where $c_{n,i}^{\text{P}}$ represents physical node resources assigned to virtual nodes of VNR_i; $B_{l,i}^{\text{P}}$ are physical link resources (bandwidth) assigned to virtual links of VNR_i; while γ and δ are coefficients that relate real costs per time unit of node resources and bandwidth resources of physical paths. At the same time, HT_i is the Holding Time (lifetime) of a single request VNR_i. If the problem is a static VNE, HT_i can be considered as equal to 1, or it may not be considered at all.

The *Embedding Cost* performance metric can be defined as the sum of all the embedding costs corresponding to accepted (not blocked) VNRs:

$$Embedding\,Cost = \sum_{\text{Acc}} Cost_i^{\text{VNR}} \tag{7}$$

The values of this metric are not normalized and the VNE strategy must try to *minimize* its value, looking for an efficient utilization of physical resources. However, this metric does not consider neither the number of blocked VNRs, nor the number of total resources successfully embedded, so it is also a partial view of VNE efficiency.

3.3   Embedding Revenue

Embedding Revenue considers that the revenue of a VNR is proportional to the number of total node and link resources requested by virtual networks [7,9].

The potential revenue of a single VNR_i, or $Revenue_i^{\text{VNR}}$ (which can be effective, once embedded) can be defined as:

$$Revenue_i^{\text{VNR}} = (\alpha \sum_{N^{\text{V}}} c_{n,i}^{\text{V}} + \beta \sum_{L^{\text{V}}} B_{l,i}^{\text{V}}).HT_i \tag{8}$$

where α and β are coefficients related to real revenue per time unit, of each unit of computing capacity resources $c_{n,i}^{\text{V}}$ required by a virtual node and amount of spectrum/wavelength $B_{l,i}^{\text{V}}$ required by virtual links (network resources) of VNR_i.

The *Embedding Revenue* performance metric can be defined as the sum of all potential revenues corresponding to all accepted VNRs:

$$Embedding\,Revenue = \sum_{\text{Acc}} Revenue_i^{\text{VNR}} \tag{9}$$

The *Embedding Revenue* is a metric that must be *maximized*, looking for better profit of the *Infrastructure Provider* or *InP* and, as the previous metric, their values are not normalized.

3.4   Revenue/Cost Relation

Revenue/Cost Relation performance metric indicates the ratio between *Embedding Revenue* and *Embedding Cost* [8,10]:

$$Rev/CostRelation = \frac{Embedding\,Revenue}{Embedding\,Cost} \tag{10}$$

This VNE performance metric does not express global efficiency of a VNE approach, because it is focused, as *Embedding Cost* and *Embedding Revenue* metrics, only in accepted VNRs. A VNE strategy rejecting a lot of VNRs may be very efficient in physical resources utilization, and therefore with a good *Revenue/Cost Relation*, but with a high blocking probability.

Revenue/Cost Relation performance metric must be *maximized*, for a good profit of the *InP*. Furthermore, if the values of parameters α, β, γ, and δ are taken equal to one, this metric can be considered as normalized, with its values varying between 0 (in the worst case) and 1 (for a perfect VNE process with all virtual links mapped to single physical links) [8].

4   A Novel Profit-Related Performance Metric: VNE-NP

As we have seen, the diversity in the topology of each VNR and the resources that requires, makes that none of the above mentioned performance metrics is able to reflect all the different aspects of the problem, failing in adequately comparing the efficiency of two or more different approaches.

The *Accepted Ratio* metric evaluates only how many VNRs were accepted, without taking into account neither the potential lost revenue when large VNRs were blocked nor the efficiency in the utilization of physical resources in the VNE process. In terms of *InP* profit, there can be a considerable difference in blocking a relative large VNR, than blocking a small one that only requires a small number of resources.

The *Embedding Cost* metric only evaluates how efficiently is the VNE approach in physical resources utilization, with no consideration about the number of blocked VNRs and their potential lost revenue.

On the other hand, the rest of the considered metrics: *Embedding Revenue* and *Revenue/Cost Relation* do consider the revenue generation of accepted requests but gives a partial evaluation since only consider the cost of accepted VNRs.

To mitigate this situation with the already published metrics, a novel profit-related performance metric is proposed in this work, named *Virtual Network Embedding Normalized Profit* (VNE-NP). First, *Potential Revenue* is defined as the Total Revenue of *both* accepted and blocked VNRs (not only accepted VNRs as in *Embedding Revenue*):

$$Potential\,Revenue = \sum_{Tot} Revenue_i^{VNR} \tag{11}$$

The VNE-NP metric is defined by:

$$VNE - NP = \frac{Embed.Revenue - Embed.Cost}{Potential\,Revenue} \tag{12}$$

It is important to notice that while *Embedding Revenue*, *Embedding Cost* and *Revenue/Cost Relation* are computed over only the accepted (not blocked) VNRs as can be seen in (7), (9) and (10), the *Potential Revenue* (11) considers both accepted and blocked VNRs.

The VNE-NP performance metric expresses *Net Profit* of a single successfully embedded VNR as the difference between its Revenue and Cost, which are normalized by the total *Potential Revenue* of all VNRs in the process (blocked and accepted VNRs).

An additional benefit of VNE-NP is its normalization over potential total revenue, which permits a better comparison among different instances of the problem.

This way, VNE-NP takes into account all important aspects of profit for a VNE process, including:

1. the ability of finding a feasible solution for any VNR and therefore to accept the larger possible potential source of profit (*Potential Revenue*);
2. the efficiency of a VNE algorithm in physical resources utilization in the embedding process; and
3. the ability in generating more revenue, accepting more complex requests.

Table 1. A comparison among the five VNE performance metrics studied

Performance Metric	Min/ Max	Normalized	Affected by blocked VNRs	Affected by utilization of physical res.	Affected by getting more revenue
Accepted Ratio	Max	Yes	Yes	No	No
Embedding Cost	Min	No	No	Yes	No
Embedding Revenue	Max	No	Yes	No	Yes
Rev./Cost Relation	Max	Yes	No	Yes	Yes
VNE-NP	Max	Yes	Yes	Yes	Yes

The above advantages are shown in Table 1, which compares the five metrics in these three above mentioned aspects.

In what follows, an example is presented to show the difference of using VNE-NP with respect to other known metrics and how it can represent a better figure of merit for *InP* profit for different situations.

4.1   An Example of VNE-NP Application

In Fig. 1(a) it can be seen a physical network with five nodes (n_1^P to n_5^P) and six links (l_1^P to l_6^P). Each physical node has three available CPU units and each physical link has two bandwidth units (indicated in parenthesis). Figure 1(a) also shows three VNRs (VNR 1, VNR 2 and VNR 3) which must be embedded in the physical network using a VNE approach. Each virtual link requires one bandwidth unit, and each virtual node requires one CPU unit, which are not indicated in the figure for simplicity.

We also consider three different VNE algorithms (VNE algorithms A, B and C) which offers three different embedding solutions showed at Figs. 1(b), (c) and (d) respectively.

As we can see in Fig. 1(b), VNE Algorithm A only was able to embed VNRs 1 and 2 while VNR 3 could not be allocated, because there were not enough physical link resources. On the other hand, in Fig. 1(c), Algorithm B succedded in embedding VNRs 2 and 3, but it could not embed VNR 1. However, Algorithm C was successfull in embedding the three VNRs, as it is showed in Fig. 1(d).

Notice that the three VNRs require different numbers of virtual nodes and virtual links and the total demand of resources are different, and that is why they represent different amount of profit for the *InP*.

Let us calculate and compare the values of the five performance metrics related to InP profit already defined: *Accepted Ratio, Embedding Cost, Embedding Revenue, Revenue/Cost Relation* and *VNE-NP*.

Taking $\alpha = \beta = 2$ (The revenue of embedding a virtual node or link gives to the InP an equivalent revenue of two physical units), and $\gamma = \delta = 1$ (CPU units cost the same as Bandwidth units), Table 2 shows the values of the five different performance metrics for the three VNE algorithms.

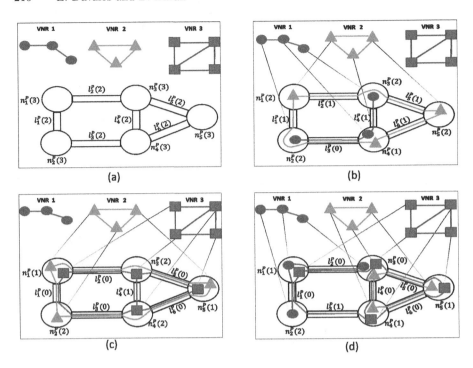

Fig. 1. (a) Initial situation; (b) Embedding of VNE Algorithm A; (c) Embedding of VNE Algorithm B; (d) Embedding of VNE Algorithm C.

Table 2. Values of performance metrics for the studied VNE algorithms

Performance Metric	Algorithm A	Algorithm B	Algorithm C
Accepted Ratio	0, 67	0, 67	**1,00**
Embedding Cost	**13,00**	18, 00	21, 00
Embedding Revenue	22, 00	30, 00	**40,00**
Rev./Cost Relation	1, 70	1, 67	**1,90**
VNE-NP	0, 23	0, 30	**0,48**

4.2   A Discussion of the Results

An initial and important observation is that Algorithm C reaches best values for 4 out of 5 metrics: *Accepted Ratio, Embedding Revenue, Revenue/Cost Relation* and *VNE-NP*. That was an expected result, since Algorithm C succedded in embedding the three VNRs, reaching the best revenue and revenue/cost relation in the process. Only *Embedding Cost* found Algorithm A as the best. This indicates that this metric can be strongly influenced by the diversity of resource demands for different VNRs and can fail in performing a good evaluation.

Now, we can obviate Algorithm C and compare only results for Algorithms A and B for the four remaining performance metrics. We can notice some important aspects:

- *Accepted Ratio* shows the same results for both algorithms A and B (0,67). Although these algorithms embedded two VNRs and blocked one, the potential revenue of VNR 2 is larger than VNR 1 given that VNR 2 needs more resources. This important aspect is not considered when using *Accepted Ratio* performance metric.
- *Revenue/Cost Relation* found better results for Algorithm A, while the two remaining metrics: *Embedding Revenue* and *VNE-NP* coincide in finding Algorithm B better than Algorithm A. The difference in complexity between blocked VNRs indicates that this is the expected result. That suggests that *Revenue/Cost Relation* fails in adequatly compare these two algorithms.

This analysis indicates that for the above example, *Embedding Revenue* and *VNE-NP* best express the economical benefit of the *InP* and the ability in embedding more complex VNRs, with a clear advantage in using VNE-NP given that it is normalized while *Embedding Revenue* is not.

5 Conclusion

Virtual Network Embedding (VNE) problem leads with the efficient allocation of physical network resources to virtual network requests. A VNE approach is evaluated with global, long-term performance metrics, that are computed at the end of a VNE process (or simulation).

Most used VNE performance metrics are related to economical profit of Infrastructure Provider (InP), being *"Embedding Cost"* and *"Accepted Ratio"* the most cited in the literature. However, they can loose objectivity when the resources requested by virtual network requests (VNRs) are heterogeneous, as shown in Sect. 4.

In this work, we propose a novel performance metric, named *Virtual Network Embedding-Normalized Profit* (VNE-NP), presenting an example where the proposed metric proved to give a better figure of merit than any other metric. The proposed performance metric offers a good, normalized representation of the profit reached by an *InP* in the VNE process, and considers both the savings in physical resources utilization as well as the ability of finding feasible efficient solutions for a maximum number of VNRs.

In future works, the authors plan to implement VNE-NP to network simulators, in order to evaluate VNE instances jointly with other performance metrics. Besides, it would be interesting to study real economical values of physical network resources (nodes and links resources) in cloud applications, aiming a more real evaluation of VNE-NP metric.

References

1. Alshaer, H.: An overview of network virtualization and cloud network as a service. Int. J. Netw. Manag. **25**, 1–30 (2015)
2. Nejabati, R., Peng, S., Simeonidou, D.: Role of optical network infrastructure virtualization in data center connectivity and cloud computing. In: Optical Fiber Communication Conference and Exposition and the National Fiber Optic Engineers Conference (OFC/NFOEC), pp. 1–3 (2013)
3. Fischer, A., Botero, J.F., Beck, M.T., De Meer, H., Hesselbach, X.: Virtual network embedding: a survey. IEEE Commun. Surv. Tutor. **15**, 1888–1906 (2013)
4. Belbekkouche, A., Hasan, M.M., Karmouch, A.: Resource discovery and allocation in network virtualization. IEEE Commun. Surv. Tutor. **144**, 1114–1128 (2012)
5. Chowdhury, N.M.M.K., Rahman, M.R., Boutaba, R.: Virtual network embedding with coordinated node and link mapping. In: IEEE INFOCOM, pp. 783–791 (2009)
6. Yu, H., Qiao, C., Anand, V., Liu, X., Di, H., Sun, G.: Survivable virtual infrastructure mapping in a federated computing and networking system under single regional failures. In: IEEE Global Telecommunications Conference GLOBECOM, pp. 1–6 (2010)
7. Chowdhury, M., Rahman, M.R., Boutaba, R.: Vineyard: virtual network embedding algorithms with coordinated node and link mapping. IEEE/ACM Trans. Netw. **20**, 206–219 (2012)
8. Lischka, J., Karl, H.: A virtual network mapping algorithm based on subgraph isomorphism detection. In: Proceedings of the 1st ACM Workshop on Virtualized Infrastructure Systems and Architectures, pp 81–88. ACM (2009)
9. Rahman, M.R., Boutaba, R.: SVNE: survivable virtual network embedding algorithms for network virtualization. IEEE Trans. Netw. Serv. Manag. **10**, 105–118 (2013)
10. Dávalos, E., Aceval, C., Franco, V., Barán, B.: A multi-objective approach for VNE problems using multiple ILP formulations. CLEI Electron. J. **19**, 1–15 (2016)

An Anomaly Detection Model in a LAN Using K-NN and High Performance Computing Techniques

Mercedes Barrionuevo[✉], Mariela Lopresti, Natalia Miranda, and Fabiana Piccoli

LIDIC, Universidad Nacional de San Luis, Ejército de los Andes - 950, 5700 San Luis, Argentina
{mdbarrio,omlopres,ncmiran,mpiccoli}@unsl.edu.ar

Abstract. Detecting unusual values from large volumes of information produced by network traffic has acquired considerable interest in the network security area. Having a system of detecting anomalous events in a time near their occurrence, it is important for all computer systems in a network. Detecting anomalous values can lead network administrators to identify system failures, take preventative actions and avoid a massive spread. Anomaly detection is a starting point to prevent attacks. In this article, we present a form of data pre-processing to identify anomalies using a supervised classification algorithm, image processing, parallel computing techniques and Graphical Processing Units.

Keywords: Network traffic · Anomaly · K-NN · High performance computing GPU

1 Introduction

Nowadays variety and complexity of internet traffic exceed everything imagined by Internet pioneers. We are currently immersed in a society dependent of computer systems, they are present in many areas such as: finances, industry, medicine and others aspects of everyday life. In order to protect or prevent these systems and their information (they can be important or relevant), it is necessary to implement technologies or models to avoid unauthorized or malicious access. This may be possible if valid access patterns are determined.

Threats to a data network are conformed by a set of frames with specific characteristics to look for vulnerabilities in a system. These vulnerabilities represent risks and can be used to perform future attacks.

When situations out of normal network profile are detected, administrators ask themselves questions such as What do they mean? Can such a situation be considered an attack? Does this deviation belong to traffic generated by new applications? Based on these, appear detection systems based on anomalies which report all unusual activity although they can be normal or not.

Generally, systems whose objective is to detect network attacks usually have a high error level, therefore it is necessary to have a semantic interpretation of their results. This feature together to multiplicity of network traffic generated by different applications and characteristics such as: bandwidth, time of connections, among others, determine a work of high computational cost.

© Springer International Publishing AG, part of Springer Nature 2018
A. E. De Giusti (Ed.): CACIC 2017, CCIS 790, pp. 219–228, 2018.
https://doi.org/10.1007/978-3-319-75214-3_21

The most of researches in this area tend to evaluate the deviation of new instances respect to the normal profile of network traffic. Convert these results into semantics reports for network administrators is a big challenge. Based on this, we propose a Parallel-Supervised Network Anomalies Detection System, P-SNADS.

In [1], we present a first non-supervised P-SNADS model, it detects anomalies through images (they represent the network traffic) comparison by SIFT (Scale Invariant Feature Transform) [5]. In this paper, we propose to combine traffic classification techniques and high-performance computation to obtain good results when we work with large data volumes and the shortest possible time. For this, we focus on the preprocessing stage of data obtained from the network. A parallel supervised classification algorithm K-NN (K-Nearest Neighboring) is used to obtain a smaller data set to process in the second stage.

This document is organized as follows: the next section describes the theoretical concepts involved in development. Section 3 details the characteristics of the first stage of P-SNADS and Sect. 4 shows the experimental results. Finally, the conclusions and future works are detailed.

2 Background

This work involves many concepts, among them we emphasize computers networks traffic and its anomalies, extraction methods of packages characteristics and supervised classification algorithms. In this section, we describe each one of them.

2.1 Computer Networks Data Traffic

Network traffic provides information about what travels by network. The most common data types are log data, such as Internet Protocol (TCP/IP) records, event logs, internet access data, Network Management Protocol (SNMP) data reporting, among others [10].

This information is necessary for network security, specifically for anomalous events detection. Figure 1 illustrates an example of TCP/IP traffic, the rows detail individual network traffic and the columns are specific characteristics of each traffic. In the example, the first column is a session index for each connection, and the second says when the connection has occurred [10].

Data traveling on network can provide important information about user and system behaviors. These data can be collected with some commercial products or specific software, for example TCP/IP data can be captured using different tools, called sniffers.

Network traffic is composed of packets, flows and sessions. A packet is a data unit exchanged between a source and a destination on the Internet or another TCP/IP-based network; a network flow is a one-way packets sequence between two endpoints; and the session data represents communication between computers. A communication involves the interchange of multiple flows.

Traditionally, an IP flow contains a set of attributes, for this work, the more important are: IP address of source and destination, source and destination port, and protocol type. The

```
1   06/24/1998 08:12:58 00:00:01 ntp/u 123 123 172.016.112.020 192.168.001.010 0 -
2   06/24/1998 08:12:58 00:00:01 ntp/u 123 123 172.016.112.020 192.168.001.010 0 -
3   06/24/1998 08:15:52 00:00:04 smtp 1024 25 172.016.114.169 195.115.218.108 0 -
4   06/24/1998 08:15:55 00:00:01 domain/u 53 53 192.168.001.010 172.016.112.020 0 -
5   06/24/1998 08:15:55 00:00:01 domain/u 53 53 192.168.001.010 172.016.112.020 0 -
6   06/24/1998 08:15:55 00:00:02 smtp 1025 25 172.016.114.169 196.227.033.189 0 -
7   06/24/1998 08:17:08 00:00:04 smtp 1026 25 172.016.113.084 195.115.218.108 0 -
8   06/24/1998 08:17:11 00:00:02 smtp 1027 25 172.016.113.084 196.227.033.189 0 -
9   06/24/1998 08:17:18 00:00:02 smtp 1028 25 172.016.112.149 195.115.218.108 0 -
10  06/24/1998 08:17:36 00:00:01 domain/u 53 53 192.168.001.010 192.168.001.020 0 -
11  06/24/1998 08:17:36 00:00:01 domain/u 53 53 192.168.001.010 192.168.001.020 0 -
12  06/24/1998 08:17:37 00:00:02 smtp 1029 25 172.016.114.169 194.027.251.021 0 -
13  06/24/1998 08:17:38 00:00:02 smtp 1048 25 172.016.114.169 194.007.248.153 0 -
14  06/24/1998 08:17:39 00:00:02 smtp 1049 25 172.016.114.169 197.182.091.233 0 -
15  06/24/1998 08:17:40 00:00:02 smtp 1051 25 172.016.114.169 195.115.218.108 0 -
16  06/24/1998 08:17:41 00:00:02 smtp 1052 25 172.016.114.169 196.227.033.189 0 -
17  06/24/1998 08:17:45 00:00:02 smtp 1104 25 172.016.114.169 135.008.060.182 0 -
19  06/24/1998 08:18:07 00:00:01 eco/i - - 192.168.001.005 192.168.001.001 0 -
20  06/24/1998 08:18:07 00:00:01 eco/i - - 192.168.001.005 192.168.001.001 0 -
```

Fig. 1. Example of TCP/IP Traffic.

protocol type, if you consider the 4-layer TCP/IP model, can be TCP or UDP (layer 3) or ICMP (layer 2).

This information allows to establish a behavior baseline or normal pattern of network traffic, and in consequence to identify unexpected or unwanted conduct, called anomalous traffic. Therefore, an analysis strategy by anomalies bases on the traffic description in normal conditions to classifies as anomaly all patterns that move away from it. In order to obtain this dataset, there are several techniques, some of which are mentioned in the following subsection.

Data Analysis of a Network Packet
Studying the particular aspects of network traffic, it is necessary to extract only information from data packets and then process them. There are different techniques of extraction and processing, some of them are:

- *Graphical representation of raw data*: Generally, the representations are 2D and 3D scatter graphics, time-based graphics, histograms, pie charts, or diagrams.
- *Statistical information and pattern extraction:* They are based on average calculations, time distributions and probability distribution functions.
- *Analysis based in rule (signatures), anomaly detection and policy:* All traffic inspection analyzer that look for coincidences with a particular rule or signature belong this category. Rules are defined as values for certain fields in the header or a combination of several of them. These techniques are used in intrusion detection systems (IDS), such as Snort.
- *Flow-based analysis:* It focus on network traffic management as flow. The most of network information exchanged is oriented to connection (and non-oriented to packet), the analysis can take advantage of this. A clear example of typical network flow is a TCP connection, where the data exchanged are governed by the TCP state machine [8].

Each of these techniques is suitable for specific situations, also it is possible combine them. This work is based on flow analysis and rule-based analysis.

Usual Attacks

One of the biggest challenges for network administrators is to detect attacks on computer networks. An attack implies to take advantage of a computer system vulnerability (operating system, application software, or user's system) for unknown purposes but, usually, causing damage. Therefore, it is impossible to make a complete classification of all the actual attacks and possible weaknesses of the networks, even more when networks are connected to Internet. The denial of service (DoS) and distributed denial of service (DDos) attacks are of great interest today.

A DoS attack comes from a single entity and its goal is to turn out unavailable the resources or services of a computer. There are different types, in particular this work has focused on the DoS attacks: Smurf, Fraggle and Land [3, 4], each one of them has the following characteristics:

- *Smurf:* This attack uses ICMP protocol (Control Management Protocol) to send a broadcast ping with a false source address. There are different ways to do a ping, they are:
    - *Normal Ping:* One or more ICMP echo requests are sent to a system, which responds with one or more ICMP echo replies. Thus, this operation verifies remote system.
    - *Broadcast Ping:* This ping sends an ICMP echo request to a broadcast address. Each system responds to sender, flooding it with ICMP echo replies.
    - *Broadcast ping with false source:* A broadcast ping is sent with victim's source address. Each system in network replies and floods the victim with answers. This operation is a combination of the two previous Ping.

    The pattern to recognize this attack type is to analyze to ICMP protocol, if source and destination IP addresses belong to the same network, and the destination address is a broadcast message.

- *Fraggle*: When you want to check if a system is working, you can use UDP-based tools instead of ICMP to inspect whether the system is listening by a specific port or not. This is commonly done with different types of vulnerability scans, that are used by attackers or security administrators. For example, if a system listens over Port 19 (TCP or UDP), when a connection is established, the system would respond with a constant character flow. Typically, the source system uses the TCP or UDP Port 7. When the source system begins to receive characters, it knows that the target system is operational and closes the connection. In a Fraggle attack, a broadcast packet is sent with a false address to the victim's port 19, if it has its port 19 open, it answers a constant flow of characters to victim. The pattern is similar to that of Smurf but in this case the protocol is UDP.

- *Land*: It's an attack using the TCP protocol. It creates an "infinite loop" which is caused by sending a SYN request with the same source and destination IP address. The victim computer responds to itself until a blocking state appears and it does not accept any new requests. Besides, as all processor resources are exhausted, the denial of service happens. To recognize this type of attack, it is necessary to analyze coincidence between the source and destination IP addresses, as well as the same ports.

As mentioned above, there are many other denial of service attacks, but the detection of patterns in them requires a deeper and detailed analysis that escapes this work.

2.2 Supervised Classification Algorithm K-NN

The classification process builds models capable of determining if an object, from its characteristics, is member or not of a category. The classification is supervised when, in advance, there is an already classified observations set, and it is known to which set belongs each observation. The algorithms dedicated to solve the supervised classification problems usually operate with information provided by a set of samples, patterns, examples or training prototypes that are assumed as representatives of each classes [9].

In particular, this paper uses a supervised classification algorithm based on neighborhood criteria. It is known as K nearest neighbor (K-NN). The method of the nearest neighbor and its variants are based on the intuitive idea: "Similar objects belong to the same class". The class can be determined by comparing the object against all elements in a class. The selected class is that holds the most similar objects.

The similarity idea is formally reflected in distance concept, usually the Euclidean distance is used [6]. The calculation of the nearest neighbor can be solved using parallel techniques, in [6] has been shown that the parallel implementation using GPU [7] obtains very good response times.

3 Parallel-Supervised Network Anomalies Detection System

The detecting task of possible packets with anomalous data in a computer network is very expensive. A good alternative can be combining classification techniques and high-performance computation (HPC) in a only one solution. P-SNADS is a system that combines HPC, supervised classification and image processing to detect possible attacks. In P-SNADS' architecture, we can distinguish two stages, the first one makes all necessary steps to capture and pre-classify traffic, while the second one is responsible to detect possible attacks. In this stage, the decision is based on images comparison all of them generated from data obtained in the previous stage. In this work, we focus on the first step of system, the second was presented in [1].

The stage 1 captures network traffic, pre-process and organizes it in data flows. From these flows, P-SNADS determines whether each one of them is normal or possibly anomalous. Figure 2 shows a P-SNADS graphical representation.

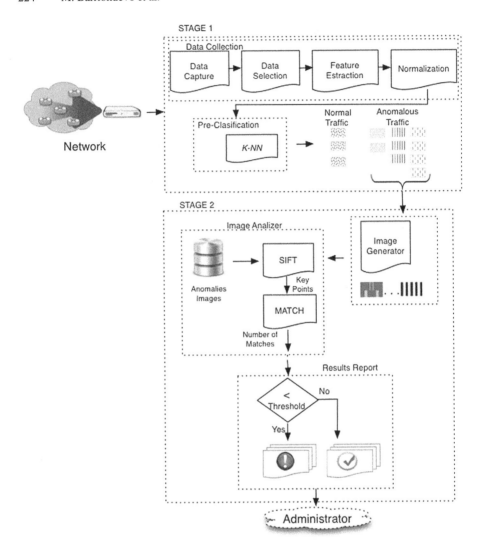

Fig. 2. P-SNADS' Architecture.

The stage 1 groups different tasks, we distinguish two tasks: data collection and data pre-classification, each has the following features and functions:

- *Data Collection:* Its objective is to obtain data to work, classify and reduce its volume for the Data Pre-classification. Data Collection implies the following subtasks:
  - *Data Capture:* This process catches network traffic. It uses a sniffer to do it, and it is activated at specific moments, for examples when there is more network traffic.
  - *Data Selection*: This step selects frames to be analyzed, according to the attacks considered, these are TCP, UDP and ICMP frames.

- *Feature Extraction:* In this step, we extract of each frame all interest fields to be analyzed. They are: source and destination IP address, source and destination port and protocol type (TCP, UDP or ICMP).

Figure 3 shows examples of tuples of normal traffic patterns (a) and anomalous traffic (b).

$$f_{normal1} = \{ 10.0.0.1, 212.48.72.19, 31215, 80, UDP\}$$
$$f_{normal2} = \{ 10.0.0.1, 13.29.10.199, 2233, 25, TCP\}$$
$$f_{normal3} = \{13.29.10.199, 10.0.0.1, , , ICMP\}$$

(a) Normal traffic patterns.

$$f_{Smurf} = \{ 10.0.0.1, 10.255.255.255, 31245, 80, ICMP\}$$
$$f_{Land} = \{ 10.0.0.1, 10.0.0.1, 80, 80, TCP\}$$
$$f_{Fraggle} = \{ 10.0.0.1, 10.255.255.255, 31245, 80, UDP\}$$

(b) Anomalous traffic patterns.

Fig. 3. Normal and anomalous traffic examples.

- *Normalization:* This step is fundamental, the tuples become an integer values vector. All address IP (IPv4) a.b.c.d are transformed according to Eq. (1).

$$\left(a \times 256^3\right) + \left(b \times 256^2\right) + \left(c \times 256^1\right) + \left(d \times 256^0\right) \tag{1}$$

- *Data Pre-classification:* Threats are not the only traffic on network, all packets generated in an attack coexist with regular traffic packets. This module classifies the frames obtained at Data Collection step as normal or anomalous traffic. To make this, we used the K-NN classification algorithm, it is implemented in parallel using GPU. Its work is to compare each vector (pre-processed flow), with every data flows recorded and representative of an anomaly. In consequence, a distance is computed to determine whether or not each new data flow can be considered an anomaly.

The following section analyses the performance of the P-SNADS, considering the effectiveness in anomalies detection.

4   Experimental Results Analysis

This section presents a experimental results analysis for the first stage of P-SNADS. T-Shark tool is used to catch data traffic. We work with several samples, each of them has approximately 2000 frames. These frames belong to a local area network (LAN) of Networks Laboratory of Universidad Nacional de San Luis. The three attacks are simulated in a server and they pretend to deny the HTTP service.

Once obtained the standard frames, we build different databases, all of them have normal and anomalous traffic. The Pre-classification module applies K-NN, it receives the databases as input data and performs an evaluation for different values of K. We consider four values of K, they are 5, 7, 10 and 12.

To compute K-NN, we use a computer with a GPU Tesla K20c (processors quantity = 2496, memory size = 4.6 GB, clock frequency = 706 MHz and processor memory clock = 2600 MHz).

When K-NN are computed for every different value, we evaluate the experimental results considering the following metrics: Positive Predictive Value (Precision - PPV), True Positive Rate (Recall - TPR), and F-measure (F) [2]. All of these measures can be calculated based in the next parameters:

- *True positive (TP):* It is the number of anomalous frames correctly detected.
- *False positive (FP):* It is the number of normal frames wrongly detected as anomalous frames.
- *False negative (FN)*: It is the number of anomalous frames not detected.
- *True negative (TN):* It is the number of normal frames correctly detected.

From these parameters, the metrics are defined as:

- *Positive Predictive Value or Precision:* it represents the possibility that a sample labeled as positive is indeed a true positive. It is the percentage of detected frames that are actually anomalies. Mathematically defined as:

$$PPV = \frac{TP}{(TP + FP)}$$

- *True Positive Rate or Recall:* It is the percentage of actual anomalous frames that are detected. It is calculated according to:

$$TPR = \frac{TP}{(TP + FN)}$$

- *F-measure (F):* It is a typical information retrieval metric, defined as the harmonic mean between the two-metrics explained above: Precision and Recall. Generally, F is used as a performance metric of K-NN in anomalies detection. Its formula is:

$$F = 2 \times \frac{(PPV \times TPR)}{(PPV + TPR)}$$

The results obtained with each metric are shown in Fig. 4. In it, each attack: Smurf (a), Land (b) and Fraggle (c) are considered.

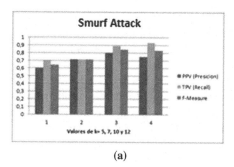

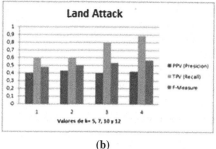

(a)   (b)

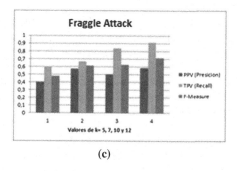

(c)

Fig. 4. Results obtained in attacks: *Smurf, Land, Fraggle*.

From observation of the above graphs, we can say that Smurf attack has an approximate accuracy of 72%, while for the others two are lower: Land = 41% and Fraggle = 52%.

Regarding Recall, more significant results are obtained, to Smurf is 80%, Land is 72% and Fraggle is 75%. In base of these values, we can infer that the detection rate of anomalous traffic is high, particularly when K = 12.

Finally, the F-measure also returns good results, particularly for K = 12 no matter which attack is. The values obtained are 0.83 for Smurf; 0.56 for Land and 0.71 for Fraggle. It means that our model performs well in detecting attacks.

Therefore, if we consider the metrics analyzed, we can conclude that P-SNADS satisfactorily achieves the objectives of this work.

5   Conclusions and Futures Works

Today, the anomalous traffic detection is a task of great interest, although there are several detection tools, there is a lot of work to be done. This obeys to large amount of circulating data on the Internet and constant change of traffic profile.

This work is focused on the traffic classification stage; we propose a model and analysis its feasibility for three known attacks, all of them are of kind of services denial: Smurf, Land and Fraggle. In order to accelerate the process and obtain results in less time, the implementation is solved using HPC techniques in GPU.

The proposal is evaluated according to different metrics, the proposed model shows an accuracy between 40% and 70%, and sensitivity between 60% and 83%. In addition, F-measure is used to measure the system performance, obtaining values between 0.5 and 0.83.

Although the results are satisfactory, as a future work it is necessary to analyze which factors affect and produce different performances according to attack. Another future job is to evaluate P-SNADS for others attack patterns. It is also intended to compare our development with those that use machine learning techniques or intelligent tools.

References

1. Barrionuevo, M., Lopresti, M., Miranda, N., Piccoli, M.: Un enfoque para la detección de anomalías en el tráfico de red usando imágenes y técnicas de computación de alto desempeño. In: XXII Congreso Argentino de Ciencias de la Computación, CACIC 2016, pp. 1166–1175 (2016)
2. Davis, J., Goadrich, M.: The relationship between precision-recall and ROC curves. In: ICML 2006: Proceedings of the 23rd International Conference on Machine Learning, New York, NY, USA, pp. 233–240. ACM (2006)
3. Gibson, D.: CompTIA Security+: Get Certified Get Ahead: SY0-201 Study Guide Createspace Independent Pub (2009). ISBN 9781439236369
4. Henao Ríos, J.L.: Definición De Un Modelo De Seguridad En Redes De Cómputo, Mediante El Uso De Técnicas De Inteligencia Artificial. Tesis presentada como requisito parcial para optar al título de Magíster en Ingeniería – Automatización Industrial, Universidad Nacional de Colombia (2012)
5. Lowe, D.: Distinctive image features from scale-invariant keypoints. Int. J. Comput. Vis. **60**, 91–110 (2004)
6. Miranda, N.: Cálculo en Tiempo Real de Identificadores Robustos para Objetos Multimedia Mediante una Arquitectura Paralela GPU-CPU, Tesis de Doctorado en Ciencias de la Computación, UNSL (2014)
7. Piccoli, M.F.: Computación de alto desempeño de GPU. 1era edic, La Plata Edulp (2011). ISBN 9789503407592
8. S. Institute: Transmission Control Protocol: DARPA Internet Program Protocol Specification. Defense Advanced Research Projects Agency, Information Processing Techniques Office (1981)
9. Tribak, H.: Análisis Estadístico de Distintas Técnicas de Inteligencia Artificial en Detección de Intrusos. Tesis Doctoral, Universidad de Granada (2012)
10. Wang, Y.: Statistical techniques for network security: modern statistically-based intrusion detection and protection. In: Network Traffic and Data, Information Science Reference - Imprint of: IGI Publishing (2008)

Innovation in Software Systems

Generation and Use of a Digest System by Integrating OCR and Smart Searches

Germán Cáseres[1,2(✉)], Lisandro Delía[1,2], Pablo Thomas[1,2], and Verónica Aguirre[1,2]

[1] Instituto de Investigación en Informática III-LIDI, Universidad Nacional de La Plata,
La Plata, Buenos Aires, Argentina
{gcaseres,ldelia,pthomas,vaguirre}@lidi.info.unlp.edu.ar
[2] Centro Asociado Comisión de Investigaciones Científicas de la Provincia de Buenos Aires,
La Plata, Argentina

Abstract. A digest can be defined as a regulations repository which is manipulated by organizations for extended time periods. The search for information in this repositories can be tedious without assistance from an ad-hoc software application. This work presents the development of a Digest Software System with its architecture and integration with other base tools. Finally, two study cases are presented where the developed product is used.

Keywords: Digest · Full text search · OCR · Solr · Tika

1 Introduction

Organizations usually have a vast set of pre-established regulations that have to be consulted regularly. Oftentimes, applicable laws defined in those standards are not known and searches must be done that result in tedious document reviews.

Clearly, it would be convenient to have some sort of repository where the entire legislation is stored. However, searching the regulatory framework in relation to any given issue may involve some time to collect and analyze current regulations.

In this context, there is a clear need to have a digest, i.e., a collection of all regulations applicable to a specific field. This digest should also be digital in nature, since it would not have a significant physical fingerprint, but it should also be integrated to a system that provides a certain level of intelligence to search for ordinances or resolutions on a specific topic.

Thus, there are two essential processes in a software system that acts as an institutional digest. First, regulations have to be digitized, considering that many of those might be available in printed format only, and which will therefore have to be converted to a digital format. Naturally, any dispositions or regulations issued today by institutions are already produced in digital format. All this constitutes a digital repository or database of regulations.

Secondly, such repository should include a feature to perform "smart" searches that consider the entire text of the regulations, showing results sorted by relevance (word

A. E. De Giusti (Ed.): CACIC 2017, CCIS 790, pp. 231–240, 2018.
https://doi.org/10.1007/978-3-319-75214-3_22

similarity, proximity, and so forth). These functionalities are available in current popular web search engines.

In this article, we introduce the development and use of a software system that is built as an institutional digest. The rest of this paper is organized as follows: in Sect. 2, the problem at hand is introduced. Then, in Sect. 3, the tools selected to solve the problem are described. Sections 4 and 5 deal with the digest system Digesto and its use. After that, study cases and the results obtained are detailed. Finally, conclusions and future lines of work are discussed.

2   Description of the Problem

The digitization process of a standard that is on paper support does not involve just obtaining a digital representation of its contents, but it also requires a mechanism that can interpret the textual information present in the digitized document. In general, this mechanism is not simple and requires applying image recognition algorithms capable of identifying language symbols.

Once this information is obtained, a mechanism that not only allows storing the text content of the regulations, but also ensures a fast response time for arbitrary content searches, has to be selected.

To achieve this, information search indexes must be generated based on the syntactic and semantic characteristics of the language used in the standards.

These mechanisms should be also integrated in a single system that can perform the necessary processes transparently to the user in charge of loading up the regulations or performing searches on them.

2.1   Digitization of Regulations

The digitization of a regulation is done using a device that is capable of capturing the content printed on the paper and saving it as a digital image. To do this task, a scanner or a digital photographic camera can be used.

Once a digital format image of the regulation is obtained, a recognition process has to be run to extract the text information that will be used as foundation for the searches. This process, called OCR (Optical Character Recognition) [1], emulates the ability of the human eye to recognize objects, identifying the symbols in an image that correspond to those of a specific alphabet.

Images enter the OCR process in a digital format (pixel matrix) and go through a number of stages that apply transformations on them to simplify the task of identifying the symbols in different contexts of colors, locations, designs, etc.

Process output information consists of the symbols extracted from the image in some character coding format (ASCII, UTF8, etc.). This output format is the most suitable to facilitate text processing and storage in any computer system.

The quality of the result depends on the quality of the digitization process and the characteristics of the algorithms used to carry out the process.

2.2   Storing Information for Content Searches

Storing the textual content of a regulation is a task that could be solved by simply storing the text as an attribute of a relational database table. However, solving this following such a simple method would involve leaving out search "smart" features, such as the ones that can be found in the most popular search engines.

To store text that is ready to allow quick searches and yields relevant results, different indexing techniques are required, which are usually not developed in the relational database engines [2] that are currently used (MySQL, PostgreSQL, SQL Server, and so forth).

3   Selecting the Right Tools

To solve the problems described above, specific knowledge is required in the field of image recognition as well as in relation to storing and indexing large volumes of information. For this reason, we decided to select tools that can solve these issues and can also be configured and integrated into a system at a specific domain, such as the Digesto system.

To perform the tasks related to text recognition on images, the TesseractOCR library [3] was used, which is an open source optical character recognition engine whose development began in 1995 and which has been optimized and improved by the Google organization since 2006 and up to the present time.

In the case of the search engine, an existing technology called Apache Solr [4] was selected; this technology makes the development, configuration and utilization of the various information indexing techniques easier, while providing a dynamic querying mechanism and ease of integration with other systems.

Solr is an open source search platform built on the Apache Lucene [5] project. Its main features are:

- Advanced text search capabilities (through Lucene)
- Optimization for large traffic volumes
- Based on standards (XML, JSON and HTTP) [6]
- Scalability and fault-tolerance
- Flexibilization and adaptability
- Extensible architecture through plug-ins

Solr uses the Lucene library to carry out indexation and text querying tasks. At the same time, it also presents an adaptable and extensible platform that can manage the different indexing or querying requirements, without affecting system stability.

Indexed information storage is also managed by Solr through its own implementation of a non-SQL database [7], which allows easily and quickly adapting to any data structure.

The use of standards such as XML, JSON and HTTP allows simple integration with other systems, since indexing the contents of a regulation or obtaining a set of results based on a search criterion simply involves running an HTTP requirement against the Solr server.

The plug-in extensible architecture allows integrating other components to extend tool capabilities. In this sense, one of the plug-ins available in the platform belongs to the same organization that develops Solr, and is called Apache Tika [8].

Tika is a plug-in that is independent from Solr and whose purpose is obtaining information from different popular file formats:

- Images (gif, png, bmp, etc.)
- Office packages (xls, doc, ppt, etc.)
- Compression and packing (zip, tar, gz, etc.)
- Structured text (xml, html, xaml, etc.)
- Portable document format (.pdf)
- Etc.

With Tika, metadata and text can be extracted from a wide variety of different file formats. Tika runs a parsing process on the different file formats to obtain all possible information from them.

In the case of image processing, Tika is integrated with TesseractOCR and it gives Solr all the information obtained from the optical character recognition process.

4 Developing the Digesto System

The Digesto system, the same as other information systems, has a relational database whose structure is related to basic system features:

- Administration of users with different access levels
- Regulation administration:
  - Metadata
    - Different visibility levels
    - Characterization by type or issuer
    - Identification number
    - Relation to other regulations and type of relation
  - Digitized contents of the paper print-out

For the Digesto system, paper-based regulations are digitized using a scanner and stored in PDF format (Portable Document Format). Initially, the process consists in just obtaining a digital representation of the paper-based regulation, and does not involve any type of text recognition.

In particular, the digitized content is not stored directly in the relational database, but in a folder within the file system, and a unique file name is assigned to each file. This helps avoid too large databases that could hinder backup tasks.

As regards the Digesto system, the storage scheme consists of a relational database and a file system, as shown in Fig. 1.

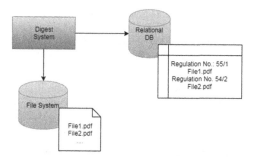

Fig. 1. Initial storage scheme.

4.1 Integration of the Digesto System with Solr

The storage scheme used in the Digesto system does not consider the textual contents of the regulations, but rather stores the information in PDF format together with the attributes defined for each of them as a set of metadata.

The content extraction work is managed by Solr and handled by Tika. Using Tika allows recognizing text information within each PDF file attached to each regulation, as well as any images present in the documents. These images can also be analyzed using Tika, so that they are also processed using optical character recognition (OCR) techniques to extract their textual content if possible. OCR tasks are processed by the TesseractOCR library.

The process of generating search indexes and returning search results is handled and run by Solr.

The communication between the Digesto system and Solr is done through HTTP requirements, with information being exchanged in XML or JSON format. Figure 2 depicts the storage scheme integrated with Solr.

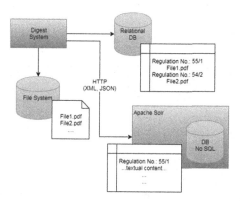

Fig. 2. Storage scheme integrated with Solr.

4.2 Synchronization Between the Digesto System and Solr

Synchronizing the information included in a regulation between the Digesto system and Solr is important to guarantee that the search results returned by the system are up to date.

When a new regulation is loaded to the Digesto system, it is stored in the relational database and sent to Solr to be indexed and stored in its own, search-oriented format.

When a regulation is modified, its information has to be totally or partially re-indexed.

Finally, if a regulation is removed, the corresponding information has to be removed from the index as well to prevent the outdated information to be included in future search results.

Even though both databases must be synchronized for the proper operation of the system, the indexed information can be automatically re-built from the relational database of the Digesto system.

4.3 Adding a Regulation to the Digesto System

With the storage infrastructure mounted and configured as shown in Fig. 3, the process for adding a regulation to Digesto involves the following steps:

1. Digitization of the paper-based regulation to PDF format using a scanner. (Manual process, external to the system).
2. Loading regulation metadata: date, number, issuer, attached digitized file, etc. (Manual process, in the system).
3. Storing regulation metadata in the relational database. (Automated process).
4. Storing the digitized file in server's file system. (Automated process).
5. Optical Character Recognition of the digitized file to obtain the textual content of the regulation. (Automated process in Solr through Tika and TesseractOCR).
6. Indexing recognized content to allow text searches. (Automated process in Solr).

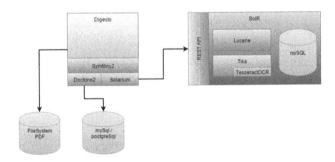

Fig. 3. Detailed structure of components in the integrated infrastructure.

Figure 4 shows a simplified diagram of the process for adding regulations.

Fig. 4. Process for adding regulations

5   Using the Digesto System

The integration of an ad hoc system to perform searches over a set of regulations opens up a number of possibilities that would be too expensive to develop.

The relevant aspects offered by Solr's search engine in the Digesto system are as follows:

Non-SQL storage - Flexibility. The storage method used by Solr is implemented through a non relational database (non-SQL). This type of databases allows indexing entirely heterogeneous documents as regards their structure.

In the case of the Digesto system, each regulation has a number of attributes that are specific to the domain and have to be indexed in the search engine together with the textual information of the regulation.

Some of these attributes should not be treated as text, since they represent dates or numeric values and must allow carrying out comparative searches using mathematical operators such as greater than, less than, not equal to, and so forth. Solr can handle this situation through the specification of a scheme that defines the type of data that each attribute will contain.

The search engine easily adapts to the specific data structure of the regulations and is tolerant to changes that occur with time due to its non-SQL nature.

Non-SQL storage - Scalability. The non-relational database model presents advantages when it comes to escalating in terms of performance through the use of computer clusters for distributed query processing [9]. Solr can work with clusters, so it can provide mechanisms to improve response speed with large volumes of information.

Query Language. Through Lucene, Solr provides a powerful query language that is easy to understand for the end user. It has many similarities with the searches that can be done with the most popular engines nowadays.

Through Solr, Digesto allows searching for regulations that meet complex conditions, while for the person using Digesto, finding regulations is as easy as finding a page on the Internet.

Plug-In Expansible Architecture. Solr provides an expansible architecture that allows modifying or adding new information indexing methods.

The Digesto system uses this advantage to improve national identification number indexation so that searches can be done either using thousand separators or omitting them.

This is a specific requirement from one of the institutions that is currently using the system, and it was solved through the development of a specific plug-in.

Deferred Indexing. Since the Digesto system and the search engine are separate, when users add regulations to the system, they do not have to wait until the OCR +indexation process ends; they can keep working while the necessary tasks to ready the regulation for inclusion on search results are run in the background.

6 Study Cases

The development of the Digesto system was originally aimed at addressing the requirements of the School of Computer Science of the National University of La Plata (UNLP). It went into production during the second half of 2015.

The second application case for the system was at the School of Economic Sciences of the UNLP, where specific changes were implemented as required by the institution and an automated import and indexation feature to add digitized regulations was implemented. The system went live in the first half of 2016.

Both instances of the system, Digesto Info (School of Computer Science) and Digesto Econo (School of Economic Sciences), are currently running on stable versions and available for everyday use at both institutions. Figure 5 shows a screenshot of the main screen for searching regulations, which is common to all instances.

Fig. 5. Screenshot of the regulations search screen, Digesto Econo.

7   Results Obtained

Both the School of Computer Science and the School of Computer Sciences are currently using the system. The Digesto Econo instance currently holds more than 7200 loaded regulations that can be queried.

Response times for searches on regulation contents are comparable to those of any search process done at popular Internet portals such as Google, Yahoo! or Bing, and they meet the expectations of the users working with the system.

Finding a specific regulation or a set of regulations in relation to specific content is as simple and familiar as searching for a website in a web browser. More advanced queries respond to the same syntax used by Google, and results are presented sorted by relevance.

8   Conclusions

A study was carried out aimed at finding a feasible alternative for the development of a system with requirements that are strongly related to image recognition and agile information search.

The tools selected during this study were analyzed and the Digesto system was developed, which streamlines tasks related to loading and parsing historic and current regulations.

The use of a specific tool such as Solr to carry out the searches provides an added value to the Digesto system that would have been very difficult to achieve if a new tool had been developed from scratch.

Even though the configuration, synchronization and adaptation of Solr is not a trivial process, and specific knowledge of the subject area on which it is going to be used is required, the time invested doing this is negligible compared to the benefits obtained.

The Digesto system that was developed, as well as each of its instances (Info and Econo) meet the requirements and expectations of the end users, since they have a familiar and user-friendly tool that not only makes regulation querying easy, it also simplifies regulation digitization.

9   Future Lines of Work

Since the generic nature of Solr can be applied to different subject areas, in the future we are considering analyzing, configuring and optimizing the tool to improve both metadata extraction and the relevance of the search results returned by Digesto.

Additionally, the regulation digitization process will be improved through the development of a mechanism that will make digital information to remain available after the digitization of paper-based regulations to allow the automated extraction and load of metadata with no user interaction. This would allow users to only carry out the digitization process during the initial load stage; indexation in the Digesto system would be automated.

References

1. Shalin, A., Chopra, A., Ghadge, A.: Optical character recognition. IJARCCE, **3,** January 2014
2. Thomas, P., Bertone, R.: Introducción a las bases de datos. Prentice Hall - Pearson Education, Upper Saddle River (2011). ISBN 9789876153515
3. Tesseract OCR. https://github.com/tesseract-ocr/tesseract. Accessed 21 July
4. Apache Solr. http://lucene.apache.org/solr/. Accessed 21 July
5. Apache Lucene. http://lucene.apache.org/. Accessed 21 July
6. Richardson, L., Ruby, S.: RESTful Web Services, 1st edn. O'Reilly Media, California (2007). ISBN 9780596529260
7. Sadalage, P.J., Fowler, M.: NoSQL Distilled: A Brief Guide to the Emerging World of Polyglot Persistence, 1st edn. Addison-Wesley Professional, Reading (2012). ISBN 9780321826626
8. Apache Tika. https://tika.apache.org/. Accessed 21 July
9. Buyya, R.: High Performance Cluster Computing: Architectures and Systems, 1st edn. Prentice Hall, Upper Saddle River (1999). ISBN 9780130137845

Signal Processing and Real-Time Systems

Excluding Ionospherically Unsafe Satellite Geometries in GBAS CAT-I

Oscar Bria[✉], Javier Giacomantone, and Luciano Lorenti

School of Computer Science, Research Institute in Computer Science (III-LIDI),
National University of La Plata, La Plata, Argentina
onb@info.unlp.edu.ar

Abstract. We show the results of the implementation of a preliminary algorithm for excluding ionospherically unsafe satellite geometries in Ground-Based Augmentation Systems Category I. Minimum knowledge of the ionospheric threat model is assumed and the assistance of the code-carrier divergence monitor is not considered. All the satellites in view above 5° in elevation are included in the computations. The inflation of the standard deviation of the vertical ionospheric gradient implements the exclusion. Full availability remains for a typical day in the site of La Plata Airport.

Keywords: GBAS Category I · Ionospheric threat
Parameter inflation

1 Introduction to GBAS

Ground-Based Augmentation System (GBAS) is a system that provides differential corrections and integrity monitoring of Global Navigation Satellite Systems (GNSS) signals for navigation and precision approach service in the vicinity of the host airport. GBAS yields the accuracy, integrity, continuity and availability necessary for Category I, and eventually Category II, and III precision approach operations [1,2].

The system consists of three parts: (1) the satellite signal in space (SIS) coming from one or several GNSS constellations; (2) the local Ground Facility (GGF) equipped normally with four satellite receivers, processing equipment and a VHF data broadcast (VDB) transmitter; and (3) the aircraft devices related to the multi-mode receiver (MMR).

The GGF provides the aircraft with approach path data and, for each satellite in view, geo-referenced range corrections and integrity information. The corrections enable the aircraft to determine its position relative to the approach path more accurately. Under nominal conditions these corrections are considered practically the same for the ground station and for the aircraft. That is, the basic assumption of GBAS is that errors have a high local correlation.

Integrity is the function of a system that warns users in a timely manner when the system or some part of it should not be used. The integrity function

© Springer International Publishing AG, part of Springer Nature 2018
A. E. De Giusti (Ed.): CACIC 2017, CCIS 790, pp. 243–252, 2018.
https://doi.org/10.1007/978-3-319-75214-3_23

prevents severe risks, eventually affecting system continuity and availability [3]. In GBAS Category I (CAT-I) the responsibility for integrity resides exclusively in the GGF. Verification and certification of GBAS integrity is based on the analysis of extremely rare events which can lead to large positioning errors. These events are generally only dealt theoretically or by simulation [4,5]. The most important of these rare effects are strong ionospheric gradients, which are not directly recognized by the GGF by any intended means. Hence the importance of being able to foresee and mitigate the effects of this anomalies in some way [6]. Excluding unsafe geometries is one of such ways; ionospheric field monitor is other alternative [7].

2   Protection Levels, Alert Limits and Position Errors

As mentioned, for GBAS CAT-I the GGF is designed to guarantee the integrity of each broadcasted correction by monitoring, in diverse ways, each related satellite measure to ensure that the correction error is bounded. If that is not the case the satellite is declared unsafe. The nominal correction error standard deviation for each satellite $\sigma_{\mathrm{pr_{gnd}},i}$ $[m]$ as seen from ground, and the nominal standard deviation of the vertical ionospheric gradient σ_{vig} $[m/m]$ coming from site studies, are also broadcasted.

Based on the information received from the GGF and also based in own data, the aircraft computes horizontal and vertical protection levels (HPL and VPL) for the measurements for each epoch (every 0.5 s). Particularly VPL are safe if they are bellow the vertical alert limit (VAL). For GBAS CAT-I precision approach operations VAL = 10 m at the minimum decision height of 200 ft that occurs at 6 km from the runway during landing.

If VPL is larger than VAL an integrity alert is generated. VPL is supposed to exceed the real unknown vertical position error (VPE). If VPE is larger than VPL but smaller than VAL the information is misleading. If VPE is larger than VPL and also larger than VAL the information is hazardously misleading.

The aircraft computes VPL as follow (see [8] for details):

$$\mathrm{VPL} = K_{\mathrm{ffmd}}\sqrt{\sum_{i}^{N} S_{\mathrm{vert},i}^2 \sigma_i^2}. \tag{1}$$

$$\sigma_i^2 = \sigma_{\mathrm{pr_{gnd}},i}^2 + \sigma_{\mathrm{iono},i}^2 + \sigma_{\mathrm{air},i}^2 + \sigma_{\mathrm{tropo},i}^2, \tag{2}$$

$$\sigma_{\mathrm{iono},i} = F_i \sigma_{\mathrm{vig}}(x_{\mathrm{aircraft}} + 2\tau v_{\mathrm{aircraft}}), \tag{3}$$

$$\sigma_{\mathrm{air},i}^2 = \sigma_{\mathrm{multipath},i}^2 + \sigma_{\mathrm{noise},i}^2. \tag{4}$$

$S_{\mathrm{vert},i}$ is the vertical position component of the weighted-least-squares projections matrix for satellite i (see Eq. (8)). N is the number of satellite in-view for the present epoch.

K_{ffmd} is the multiplier that determines the required probability of fault-free missed detection.

σ_i^2 is the variance of a normal distribution overbounding the range domain error distribution for satellite i for the fault-free hypothesis H_0 (see [9]).

$\sigma_{\text{pr}_{\text{gnd}},i}^2$ is the fault-free variance of the ground error term associated with the correction for satellite i.

$\sigma_{\text{iono},i}$ is the ground residual ionospheric uncertainty for satellite i. F_i is the vertical-to-slam obliquity factor for satellite i. σ_{vig} is the standard deviation of a normal distribution of the residual ionospheric uncertainty due to nominal spatial decorrelation (a typical value is $4\,\text{mm/km}$). The following factor has two components, the horizontal distance from GGF to aircraft (x_{aircraft}), and a synthetic distance produced by a smoothing filter used to mitigate multipath and noise with a time constant τ of $100\,\text{s}$. v_{aircraft} is the velocity of the aircraft in the direction of the airport.

For details on $\sigma_{\text{air},i}^2$ and $\sigma_{\text{tropo},i}^2$ see the above last references.

In the above set of equations is not included the vertical protection level under a single-satellite (satellite i) ephemeris fault, however it is considered in the computations. Failures of the hypothesis H_1 [10] are not relevant to excluding geometries [11].

3   Ionospheric Threat and Tolerable Error Limit

GPS satellites fly in medium Earth orbits (MEO) at an altitude of approximately $20200\,\text{km}$. The ionosphere is a region of the atmosphere located about $50 - 1000\,\text{km}$ above the Earth's surface. In this region, solar radiation produces free electrons and ions that cause phase advances and group delays to GPS radio waves.

Ionospheric fronts (also called ionospheric storms) pose a significant threat to single frequency ground based augmentation systems (GBAS) for airplane precision approach because they can produce differential delays between the aircrafts and the GGF that are not detected in time to generate an integrity alert [12]. That is, uncorrelated delays could produce misleading and hazardously misleading situations. Ionospheric fronts are recommended [13] to be modeled by a moving wedge form with four parameters[1], including the maximum ionospheric spatial gradient for a particular region [14].

The first wedge model has been parameterized for the conterminous U.S. (CONUS) where ionospheric delay gradients as large as $435\,\text{mm/km}$ have been observed [15]. In the Brazil ionosphere the largest gradient of about $850\,\text{mm/km}$ has been registered [16]. There are not known developments of ionospheric threat wedge model for Argentina.

The development and utilization of the ionospheric threat model occurs in two stages [17]. The first stage is observation, in which data accumulated over a

---

[1] The four paramenters are: spatial gradient, front moving speed, width and maximum delay [11].

lengthy period (usually including the greatest activity of a solar cycle) is collected to describe and cover the features of ionosphere impact on GBAS [18]. The results of observation are used to estimate the bounding parameters of the threat model. The second stage is simulation, in which the completed threat model is used in a simulation including the GGF and user operation. The simulations provide estimations of the integrity risk (particularly the hazardously misleading information (HMI) analyses [19]), the availability, and the impact to the ground and airborne monitors.

Equation (3) gives the magnitude of ionospheric range error in slant direction under steady-state conditions. The distance for decision height (DH) for CAT-I is 6 km away from the GGF. For a nominal σ_{vig} of 4 mm/km the error is bounded by 0.24 m, in about 99.8% of the cases. Meanwhile an anomalous large ionospheric delay gradient of 425 mm/km could produce certainly a range error as large as 8.5 m.

The maximum vertical position error due to the worst-case user error induced by an ionosphere anomaly (as estimated by the ground subsystem) need only be bounded by a tolerable error limit (TEL) that luckily is greater than VAL [11,15,20,21].

Several criteria have been proposed to establish a value for TEL. In [21] the obstacle clearance surface (OCS) concept is used to assess the safety of a CAT-I approach if an ionospheric anomaly produces vertical navigation errors. A maximum vertical error of about 29 m would be allowable at the nominal DH of 200 ft.

4   Algorithm Description

We followed [11,15,22,23] as references for the algorithm implementation. The algorithm produces an inflation factor that depends of current satellite geometry. Inflation factors larger than 1 are applied to σ_{vig} when it nominal value do not produce a VPL that exceeds VAL when the possible error is not bounded by TEL. This mechanism excludes unsafe geometries for been considered by the aircraft.

The algorithm has four principal computational steps: 1. *GGF and Subset Geometries*, 2. *Ionosphere-Induced Range Error*, 3. *Ionosphere-Induced Vertical Error* and 4. *Parameter Inflation*.

4.1   GGF and Subset Geometries

Satellites that are visible to the GGF may not be included in the positioning solution of an approaching airplane. It is assumed that up to two satellites from the all-in-view satellite at the ground facility are not used by the airborne[2]. If there are N satellites visible to the GBAS ground facility, there are

$$\sum_{k=N-2}^{N} \binom{N}{k} \tag{5}$$

---

[2] The minimum number of satellites to be used by the airborne is four.

subset satellite geometries from the set of N of. Figure 1 shows the evolution for the number of satellites in view. Figure 2 shows an example with nine satellites in view at a given epoch, the total number of subset geometries to consider in this case is, $\sum_{k=7}^{9}\binom{9}{k} = 46$.

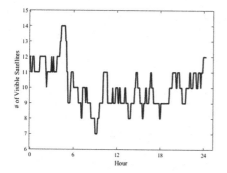

Fig. 1. Evolution of the number of visible satellites above 5° during a 24 h typical period for a GBAS ground facility as if it was located at La Plata airport (34.9655° S, 57.8954° W).

Fig. 2. Diagram of satellite positions over the sky above 5° (actually above 30° in this case) from the GBAS ground facility point of view. Nine satellite are in view for the current epoch.

4.2 Ionosphere-Induced Range Error

The closed-form approximation of the ionosphere-induced differential range error is:

$$\varepsilon = g \times (x_{\text{aircraft}} + 2\tau v_{\text{aircraft}}). \tag{6}$$

ε is the ionosphere-induced differential range error $[m]$.
g is the ionospheric gradient $[mm/km]$.
x_{aircraft} is the separation between the GGF and the approaching airplane $[km]$.
τ is the time constant of the carrier-smoother filter $[s]$.
v_{aircraft} is the velocity of the approaching airplane $[km/s]$.

Given an airplane at a certain distance and with certain velocity equation (6) represents the worse case for a given g. In the bibliography (e.g., [24]) considerations are taken about the relative velocity between the ionospheric front and the particular satellite, and the preventive action of the code-carrier divergence (CCD) monitor is considered [25]. Neither of those advantages are taken here to possible reduce the range error ε for every satellite for a particular geometry.

4.3 Ionosphere-Induced Vertical Error

Given airplane and ionosphere front movement geometries, a large ionospheric gradient may be unobservable to the GGF and meanwhile affecting the airplane that is not conveniently prevented of the integrity risk. While an airplane is approaching a runway, an ionospheric front can impact the SIS of two satellites ($k1$ and $k2$) simultaneously. Hence the worst case ionospheric error in vertical (IEV) for any pair of satellite of a given geometry for a particular epoch can be expressed as follows[3],

$$\text{IEV}_{k1,k2} = |S_{\text{vert},k1}\varepsilon_{k1}| + |S_{\text{vert},k2}\varepsilon_{k2}|. \tag{7}$$

$$S = (G^T W G)^{-1} G^T W. \tag{8}$$

$$G_i = [-\cos \text{El}_i \cos \text{Az}_i \quad -\cos \text{El}_i \sin \text{Az}_i \quad -\sin \text{El}_i \quad 1]. \tag{9}$$

$$W^{-1} = \begin{bmatrix} \sigma_1^2 & 0 & \cdots & 0 \\ 0 & \sigma_2^2 & \cdots & 0 \\ \vdots & \vdots & \ddots & \vdots \\ 0 & 0 & \cdots & \sigma_N^2 \end{bmatrix}. \tag{10}$$

where $S_{\text{vert},ki}$ is the vertical position component of the weighted-least-squares projection matrix S for satellite ki (see [8]), this component is dependent of satellite geometry (number of satellite in view and their spatial distribution referred to the GBAS local ground station) at each epoch; G_i is the row of the observation matrix G for satellite i; Az_i and El_i are the azimuth and elevation of satellite i (see Fig. 2); W^{-1} is the inverse of the least square weighting matrix; and σ_i is the variance of a normal distribution that overbounds the true VPE distribution for satellite i under the fault-free hypothesis.

The IEV for every pair of each subset geometry considered for the approaching airplane is calculated and compared to obtain the maximum IEV (MIEV) for each geometry in a particular epoch. The number of pairs to be compared for each subset geometry with k satellites is

$$\binom{k}{2}. \tag{11}$$

Figure 3 shows and example of MIEVs compared with TEL.

Figure 4 shows the nominal VPLs at the same epoch as Fig. 3. The subset geometries with VPL exceeding VAL are not approved by the airplane and they can not cause integrity failures even though their MIEVs a greater than TEL.

4.4   Parameter Inflation

From Figs. 3 and 4 can be observed that some geometries exceeding TEL does not exceed VAL. In those cases exist potentially hazardous geometries not excluded by the integrity mechanism supported by the VPL computated with the nominal σ_{vig} broadcasted (see Eqs. (1) and (3)).

---

[3] A less constrained expression for IEV is presented in [22].

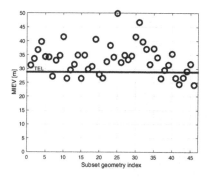 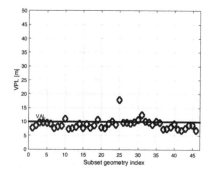

Fig. 3. MIEV for 46 subset geometries given 9 satellites in view. The subset geometries exceeding TEL are potentially hazardous for this epoch.

Fig. 4. Nominal VPL at the same epoch as Fig. 3. The subset geometries with VPL exceeding VAL can not cause integrity failures.

If the GGF inflates the broadcasted parameters above their nominal values the airborne VPL increase as well. The most effective parameter to inflate is σ_{vig} which increase σ_i^2.

To obtain the minimum σ_{vig} needed for an epoch, VPLs are pre-computed by the GGF iteratively increasing a inflation factor I_{vig} until all hazardous geometries are properly removed. Some particular considerations have to be made to make the computation but exceed the limits of this explanation (see [22, 24]). The new inflated σ_{vig} is broadcasted to the airplane. As Fig. 5 shows, all hazardous geometries exceeding TEL are excluded after inflation.

5   Algorithm Test

The algorithm implementation was tested for the location coordinates of La Plata Airport taken samples of recorded ephemeris every minute of a typical day. The assumed position of the aircraft is the decision point at 200 ft of elevation. An effective separation of 20 km results from the sum of the actual distance of 6 km between the reference station and the user, and the 14 km of synthetic separation generated by the memory of the code-carrier smoothing filter used to mitigate multipath error and code noise [8][4]. The nominal value of $\sigma_{\text{vig}} = 4.0$ mm/km. VAL = 10 m for approaching operations. The only parameter of the threat model to be considered is the maximum ionospheric gradient $g = 400$ mm/km.

Figure 6 shows the inflation factor I_{vig}. The inflated σ_{vig} can not exceed the maximum allowed broadcast value of 25.5 mm/km [26], meaning that in this case the maximum permitted value of $I_{\text{vig}} = 6.375$.

---

[4] A contant velocity of 0.07 km/s is assumed during the approach. The time constant of the carrier-smothing filter is $\tau = 100$ s.

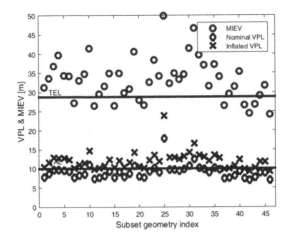

Fig. 5. Satellite geometry exclusion by σ_{vig} inflation. All hazardous geometries exceeding TEL are excluded after inflation.

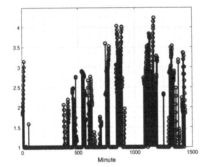

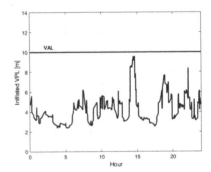

Fig. 6. Inflation factor I_{vig} for a 24 h period. The broadcasted σ_{vig} is the inflation factor times the nominal $\sigma_{vig} = 4\,mm/km$.

Fig. 7. Inflated VPL at La Plata airport for a typical day. Availability is 100% for a DH at 6 km using all the satellite in view.

By applying inflation factors to σ_{vig} all potentially hazardous geometries (and many more acceptable geometries) are eliminated from the approved set of geometries. Hence, system integrity is guaranteed by reducing system availability. Figure 7 shows the inflated VPL for the conditions of the test. The availability in this case remains 100%.

6   Conclusions

It is difficult to improve integrity into existing systems while retaining sufficient availability to make the applications viable. As Pullen stated, these challenges are more than mathematical and require more than simply adding redundancy to mitigate the effects of individual failures [27].

Most of the anomalies affecting GBAS can be detected by the monitors founded in the CAT-I ground facility. Even moderate ionospheric anomalies are detected by the CCD and the clock acceleration monitors [12]. However, the worst-case ionospheric anomalies require additional mitigation techniques. The technique used here excludes possible hazardous geometries.

Equations (1) and (7) generate bounds too conservative to represent the wedge threat model and to accurately model the more realistic geometry and monitoring conditions found in practice. Nevertheless, the implementation shows that the availability is optimal for the site of La Plata Airport. This is due to the well suited geometry conditions, particularly the relatively large number of satellite always in view above 5° in elevation, as is observed in Fig. 1.

References

1. International Civil Aviation Organization (ICAO): International Standards, Recommended Practices and Procedures for Air Navigation Services Annex 10 (1985)
2. U S Federal Aviation Administration (FAA): Specificaction Performance Type One Local Area Augmentation System Ground Facility. FAA-E-2937A (2002)
3. Rinnan, A., Gundersen, N., Sigmond, M., Nilsen, J.: Operational GNSS Integrity. In: Dynamic Positioning Conference (2011)
4. Dautermann, T., Sgammini, M., Pullen, S.: GBAS ionospheric threat analysis using DLRs hardware signal simulator. In: 2010 5th ESA Workshop on Satellite Navigation Technologies and European Workshop on GNSS Signals and Signal Processing (NAVITEC), pp. 1–7. IEEE (2010)
5. Gunawardena, S., Zhu, Z., De Haag, M., Graas, F.: Remote-controlled, continuously operating GPS anomalous event monitor. J. Inst. Navig. **56**, 97–113 (2009)
6. Park, Y., Pullen, S., Enge P.: Enabling LAAS airport surface movement: mitigating the anomalous ionospheric threat. In: IEEE/ION, Position, Location, and Navigation Symposium (2010)
7. Suzuki, S., Nozaki, Y., Ono, T., Yosihara, T., Saitoh, S., Fukushima, S.: CAT-I GBAS availability improvement through ionosphere field monitor (IFM). In: Proceedings of the 24th International Technical Meeting of the Satellite Division of the Institute of Navigation (2011)
8. Radio Technical Commission for Aeronautics (RTCA): Minimum Operational Performance Standards for GPS Local Area Augmentation Systm Airborne Equipment. Tecnical report DO253C (2008)
9. Radio Technical Commission for Aeronautics (RTCA): Minimum Aviation System Performance for the Local Area Augmentation System. Technical report DO245A (2004)
10. Elias, P., Saotome, O.: System architecture-based design methodology for monitoring the ground-based augmentatiom system, category I - integrity risk. J. Aerosp. Technol. Manag. **4**, 205–218 (2012). São José dos Campos
11. Lee, J., Pullen, S., Park, Y., Enge P., Brenner, M.: Position-domain geometry screening to maximize LAAS availability in the presence of ionosphere anomalies. In: Proceedings of the 19th International Technical Meeting of the Satellite Division of the Institute of Navigation ION GNSS (2006)
12. Luo, M., Pullen, S., Akos, D., Xie, G., Datta-Barua, S., Walter, T., Enge P.: Assessment of ionospheric impact on LAAS using WAAS supertruth data. In: Proceedings of the ION 58th Annual Meeting (2002)

13. International Civil Aviation Orgaanization South American Office (ICAO-SAM): Guide for Ground Based Augmentation System Implementation (2013)
14. Pullen, S. Park Y., Enge, P.: The IMpact and Mitigation of ionspheric anomalies on ground-based augmentation of GNSS. Radio Sci. 44 (2009)
15. Pullen, S., Enge, P.: An overview of GBAS integrity monitoring with a focus on ionspheric spatial anomalies. Indian J. Radio Space Phys. (2007)
16. Lee, J., Yoon, M., Pullen, S., Gillespie, J., Mather, N., Cole, R., Rodrigues de Souza, J., Doherty, P., Pradipta, R.: Preliminary results from ionospheric threat model development to support GBAS operations in the Brazilian region. In: Proceedings of the 28th International Technical Meeting of the Satellite Division of the Institute of Navigation (2015)
17. International Civil Aviation Orgaanization Asia and Pacific Office (ICAO-APAC): GBAS Safety Assesment Guidance Related to Anomalous Ionospheric Conditions (2016)
18. Kim, M., Lee, J., Pullen, S., Gillespie, J.: Data quality improvement and applications of long-term monitoring of ionospheric anomalies for GBAS. In: Proceedings of ION GNSS (2012)
19. U.S. Federal Aviation Administration (FAA): Ground Based Augmentation System Performance Analysis and Activities Report. First Quarter Report (2017)
20. Murphy, T., Harris, M., Park, Y., Pullen, S.: GBAS differentially corrected positioning service ionospheric anomaly errors evaluated in an operational context. In: Proceedings of the 2010 International Technical Meeting of the Institute of Navigation (2010)
21. Shively, C., Niles, R.: Safety concepts for mitigation of ionospheric anomaly errors in GBAS. In: Proceedings of the 2008 International Technical Meeting of the Institute of Navigation (2008)
22. Lee, J., Seo, J., Park, Y., Pullen, S., Enge, P.: Ionospheric threat mitigation by geometry screening in ground-based augmentation systems. J. Aircr. **48**, 1422–1433 (2011)
23. Vemuri, S., Sarma, A., Redd, A., Reddy, D.: Investigation of the effect of ionospheric gradient on GPS signals in the context of LAAS. Prog. Electromagn. Res. B **57**, 191–205 (2014)
24. Seo, J., Lee, J., Pullen, S., Enge, P., Close, S.: Trageted parameter inflation within ground-based augmentation systems to minimizw anomalous ionospheric impact. J. Aircr. **49**, 587–599 (2012)
25. Simili, D., Pervan, B.: Code-carrier divergence monitor for the GPS local area augmentation system. In: IEEE/ION, Position, Location, and Navigation Symposium (2006)
26. Radio Technical Commission for Aeronautics (RTCA): Minimum Operational Performance Standards for GPS Local Area Augmentation Systm Airborne Equipment. Tecnical report DO246D (2008)
27. Pullen, S.: Lessons learned from the development of GNSS integrity augmentations. In: Coordinates (2016). http://mycoordinates.org

CAN Bus Experiments of Real-Time Communications

Fernando G. Tinetti[✉], Fernando L. Romero, and Alejandro D. Pérez

Facultad de Informática, Instituto de Investigación en Informática LIDI (III-LIDI),
UNLP, 50 y 120, La Plata, Argentina
{fernando,fromero}@lidi.info.unlp.edu.ar,
perez.alejandrodaniel@gmail.com

Abstract. This paper presents a benchmark development and the analysis of communication times in a CAN (Controller Area Network) bus. Preemptive and fixed priority scheduling is taken as departure point for the initial experiments and analysis. This method would be adapted for programming CAN messages without preemption of the shared communications channel. It is also complemented by a specific priority assignment algorithm, suitable for non-preemptive systems. A real CAN network is used for the experiments, and results are analyzed from the point of view of real-time performance and CAN specification. We have found well known, deterministic, and correct performance communication times. Messages and signals are delivered within deadlines, a fundamental requirement for a real-time system.

Keywords: CAN bus implementation · Real-time experiments
Instrumentation and monitoring · Real-time schedulability

1 Introduction

The initial development of a CAN time analysis is based on [6], which defines a preemptive and fixed priority task scheduling (mainly) for single-processor systems. This method is adapted for the programming of CAN messages and several enhancements defined in [2]. Basically, an optimal prioritization algorithm introduced in [1] is applicable to non-proprietary systems. Enhancements and optimizations can be experimentally verified (at least in part) by building a real CAN network where specific communication time measurements can be made. Time measurements/sampling can be then used for evaluating the fulfillment of CAN real time requirements.

A CAN bus is arbitrated using priorities, and once the bus access is obtained, the message is transmitted in full. Thus, the bus appropriative policy prevents another message from gaining access to the bus while a message is being transmitted. The priority inversion problem allowed by the CAN appropriateness should be addressed. Regardless of priority inversion, every message has its own

---

F. G. Tinetti—Comisión de Investigaciones Científicas, Prov. de Bs. As.

© Springer International Publishing AG, part of Springer Nature 2018
A. E. De Giusti (Ed.): CACIC 2017, CCIS 790, pp. 253–262, 2018.
https://doi.org/10.1007/978-3-319-75214-3_24

deadline, and the bus arbitration will impose some delay that should be minimized in order to avoid real-time deadline violations. This work will be focused on the behavior of the Data Frames transmission of the CAN standard.

Messages in the CAN bus are handled by controllers, and a single controller may handle several CAN nodes. Also, each controller implements the bus arbitration while it maintains a queue of pending messages. The controller queue is managed according to fixed priority and non-preemptive scheduling. Controllers are synchronized at the start of a message with the clock of the sending node (rising edge). A transmission is allowed to start after the bus is idle for a 3-bit (interframe) period. A controller begins to transmit with a dominant bit ("0"), which causes the rest of the controllers to synchronize with the rising edge of this bit and become receivers. Any message that is ready to be transmitted must wait for another arbitration cycle to start when the bus is again idle. The CAN protocol requires the transmitter to insert a bit with opposite polarity every 5 bits of the same polarity, a technique known as "bit stuffing". Thus, a stuffing bit may be added every 4 bits of the message. Taking into account the message bit length, mbl, the constant number of bits k needed for the node identification, the maximum number of bits added for stuffing, and the bit transmission time, τ_{bit}, the maximum transmission time of the message would be given by Mt_m in (1).

$$Mt_m = \left(mbl + k + \left\lfloor \frac{mbl + k - 1}{4} \right\rfloor \right) \tau_{bit} \tag{1}$$

2   Waiting, Errors, and Maximum Time

Given a specific application or experiment, the message types are predefined, i.e. each message m has a unique and fixed identifier and priority. Messages are queued in controllers by a software routine. Message queueing needs a run time between 0 and Jm, known as queuing the message jitter, and is inherited from the response time of the task, including the delay by polling [6]. The message time period Tm is considered for events that trigger the message queueing. There are three types of events associated with Tm: (a) Events with exact period Tm, (b) Events that occur sporadically with a minimum separation time Tm, and (c) Events that occur only when the system starts. Each message has a hard deadline Dm, the maximum time from the initial event that generates the message to be queued to the actual message arrival at destination.

The worst case for response time Rm of a message can be defined as the longest time since the start event occurs until the message begins to be received by the node/s that require it. A message can be called "schedulable" if and only if its worst case response time is less than or equal to Dm: $Rm \leq Dm$. The whole system is "schedulable" if and only if all the messages are schedulable. Rm is basically the aggregation of: (1) The delay time Wm (also called Window time), which is the longest message waiting time in the CAN controller, and (2) The worst message transmission time, Mt_m. In turn, Wm is a function of: (1) Blocking time, Bm, given by messages of lower priority in the transmission process, and (2) Interference time, where a message with higher priority is transmitted earlier than m. The message blocking time can be calculated as $Bm = max(C_k)$ with $k \in lp(m)$, and $lp(m)$ is the set of messages with lower priority than m. The interference time is closely related to the concept of "busy period" introduced in [5], where a busy period of *level i* is defined as the time interval [a, b] within which the tasks with priority i or greater are processed within this interval and there are no tasks with priority i in the intervals $(a - t, a)$ and $(b, b + t)$ with $t > 0$. Adapting this definition to the CAN protocol, we have a busy period of priority m. The period starts at a time Ts where a message of priority m or greater is queued to transmit, and there are no queued messages of priority m or greater than m. It is a continuous interval of time, during which any priority message less than m is not transmitted. Finally, the period ends at time Te, when the bus becomes ready for the next transmission and arbitration cycle and there are no messages with priority greater than m.

The key characteristic of the busy period is that all messages of priority m or higher are transmitted within the period. In mathematical terms, the busy periods can be seen as intervals $[Ts, Te)$. Furthermore, the end of a busy period may coincide with the beginning of another busy period [5]. The busy period elapsed time can be calculated as the maximum of t_m^{n+1} given in Eq. 2, where $gep(m)$ is the set of messages with priority greater than or equal to m, and $f(t_m^n, t_j)$ is the function that combines t_m^n with the times related to message j: J_j (jitter) and T_j (time period).

$$t_m^{n+1} = B_m + \sum_{j \in gep(m)} \lceil f(t_m^n, tr_j) \rceil C_j \tag{2}$$

The busy period time given by the recurrence in Eq. 2 monotonically grows from B_m up to one of the following values: (a) $t_m^n + C_m > D_m$, which makes the message non-schedulable or unschedulable, or (b) $t_m^{n+1} = t_m^n$, where the worst response time of the first instance of the message is reached in the busy period determined by $t_m^n + C_m$

Errors and their related recovery times have to be taken into account when dealing with noisy environments. Each controller detecting an error starts a recovery process by transmitting an error signal. The resynchronization process takes at Least 29 bit transmission times. Furthermore, resynchronization is only the first step of the error recovery process. Other tasks (and their corresponding times) involved in the recovery process are those required to the retransmission of the message affected by errors. The equation including errors and their associated times in noisy environments is given in Eq. 3, where E_m involves at least the 29-bit resynchronization and message retransmission, which is usually considered in the analysis as the worst case overhead time as given in Eq. 4.

$$t_m = B_m + E_m + \sum_{j \in gep(m)} \lceil f(t_m^n, tr_j) \rceil C_j \tag{3}$$

$$Over_m = \max_{j \in gep(m)} (C_j) + 29\tau_{bit} \tag{4}$$

There are other details (and their corresponding times) involved in dealing with errors, but the current work is focused on the basic analysis of CAN bus messages and delay times. Thus, we will focus on a real CAN network and experimentation in the next section without taking into account errors and error recovery time/s.

3   Specific Benchmark

The Society of Automotive Engineers (SAE) provides a set of test data to evaluate communication technologies handling the seven different subsystems in an electric car prototype [6]. Signal data details are used to show a case of "real" use for the timing model of the previous section, with the 53 signals given by the SAE and explained in [4]. The seven subsystems that generate signals include the brakes, the driver himself, the engine, etc. In total there are 53 signals, characterized not only by the subsystem that generates them but by other important details, such as the amount of information bits, if they are periodic or sporadic, jitter, etc. Every signal implies handling a message with specific real-time latency/deadline.

The order in which the messages in a controller queue are transmitted will be determined by their priorities, so priority definition will determine the schedulability of a system with specific signal periods. Also, priority assignment will be directly related to the robustness of the communication system when facing errors. Priority assignment "by deadline" (deadline monotonic priority assignment) is proposed in [6], i.e. those messages in the queue nearer their deadline will be assigned greater priority. This priority assignment policy is optimal for systems with preemptive and fixed priority task scheduling, assuming deadlines are no longer than message periods. A non-optimal policy does not mean it is useless, it actually means that another option should be chosen under (more) critical times/deadlines. Table 1 shows an example similar to that found in [2] in which an unschedulable system is generated by: (a) assuming no jitter, 0 jitter time, (b) the channel is already being used by 1 ms by a lower priority message, LM, that gained access to the bus before messages M1, M2, and M3 arrive at the controller, and (c) deadline monotonic priority assignment. Given that priorities assignment determine the order M1, M2, M3, if the channel is (already) busy by 1 ms, then messages M1 and M2 use the channel by a total amount of 2.2 ms. Thus, while message M2 is being transmitted, a new instance of message M1, is queued and this new instance is the one with highest priority. Then, while

Table 1. Timing example

Message	Period & Deadline	Trans. time
LM	N/A	1 ms
M1	3.0 ms	1.1 ms
M2	4.0 ms	1.1 ms
M3	4.5 ms	0.5 ms

the new instance of message M1 is being transmitted a new instance of message M2 is queued, and message M3 is delayed beyond its deadline. The sequence of messages in the channel would be

$$LM => M1, \text{ after } 1\,ms => M2, \text{ after } 2.1\,ms => M1', \text{ after } 3.2\,ms$$

because the channel is not initially preempted from the lower priority message/s (represented by LM in the sequence above) and priorities are fixed and determined by deadline/s. However, if the order of messages is determined as M1, M3, and M2 the worst response times are $R_{M1} = 2.1\,ms$, $R_{M2} = 2.6\,ms$, and $R_{M3} = 3.7\,ms$. Thus, this *new* priority assignment determines a schedulable system, where response times $R_m < D_m$, $\forall m$. The new *priority assignment* imply the following sequence of messages in the communication channel

$$LM => M1, \text{ after } 1\,ms => M3, \text{ after } 2.1\,ms => M2, \text{ after } 2.6\,ms$$

and no new instances of messages M1 and M2 will generate any delay on message M3. In this context, the priority assignment algorithm given in [1] is claimed to be optimal in non-preemptive systems in [3]. In general, the algorithm given in [1] is useful as long as the worst case of response time of a message: (a) does not depend on an ordering of the highest priority messages, and (b) does not change its length (it is not made longer, in particular) when having a higher priority.

The length of the delay queue and the length of the busy period do not depend on a specific order of the high priority messages. The blocking time, B_m, can be made longer by changing the priority, but at the same time the interference is decreased. The priority assignment algorithm given in [1] performs a maximum of $n(n - 1)/2$ evaluations for n messages, and guarantees message scheduling when possible. It should be borne in mind that the algorithm does not specify an order in which messages should be analyzed at each priority level. This order greatly influences the priority assignment if there is more than one scheduling, and a *poor* choice of initial order may result in a non-optimal scheduling.

Given a set of CAN messages, it is possible to assign the corresponding priorities by following a sequence of simple steps

1. Define the message characteristics: size, identifier, bus speed, etc.
2. Sort messages by some criterion, whether those given in [6] or [1].
3. Apply the timing model to each message. Usually, it is possible to analyze the minimum transmission rate at which the system is schedulable.

In the case of the SAE signals and data, the "D - J" method given in [6] will be used as a guide, in which higher priority is assigned to signals with lower waiting time, (that is, a smaller D - J value, being D and J Deadline time and Waiting time, respectively). Once signals have their priorities, it is possible to analyze the system's schedulability with the timing model given above and considering the data rate of the communication channel. Besides, the channel utilization is may be enhanced with a technique referred to as *"piggyback"*. Basically, the piggyback technique takes advantage of periodic signals that can be grouped in a single message. Table 2 shows the first 10 signals defined by the SAE, all of them of a single-byte periodic signals with deadline time (D) equal to period (P), and jitter time given as J, where it is possible to identify 4 signals with the same period from the same source. More specifically, signals 1, 2, 4 and 6 from the Battery subsystem are sent every 100 ms. Instead of sending 4 one-byte messages, a single message is sent with 4 bytes using the piggyback technique. Piggybacking reduces bus overhead of three messages. The transmission of a data byte can require the transmission of up to 63 bits. This technique can be extended to periodic signals that have different periods, as long as the minimum time period is a divisor of the other period times. For example, signals 29, 30, and 32 have the same source subsystem, with periods 10 ms, 10 ms, and 5 ms respectively. Thus, every 2 messages of signal 32, the signals 29 and 30 can be added to the same message with piggybacking.

Table 2. First 10 SAE signals

#S	Signal	From	D = P	J
1	Hi&Lo contactor open/close	Battery	100 ms	0.6 ms
2	Brake pressure, line	Battery	100 ms	0.7 ms
3	Processed motor speed	Battery	1000 ms	1.0 ms
4	Torque command	Battery	100 ms	0.8 ms
5	Brake pressure, master cylinder	Battery	1000 ms	1.1 ms
6	Accelerator position	Battery	100 ms	0.9 ms
7	Torque measured	Driver	5 ms	0.1 ms
8	Transaction clutch line pressure	Brakes	5 ms	0.1 ms
9	Clutch pressure control	Brakes	5 ms	0.2 ms
10	High contactor control	Trans	100 ms	0.2 ms

The piggyback technique can also be applied to sporadic signals. These signals can be sent in a "server" message where the station sending the message checks for the occurrence of the sporadic signal before queuing the message. With this approach, a sporadic signal can be delayed no longer than the polling period time, plus the worst latency time of the "server" message. For a message with deadline of 20 ms, a server message with a 15 ms polling period and 5 ms worst case latency the technique would be good enough. Combining piggybacking with "server" messages for the sporadic signals the SAE benchmark/system is schedulable with a data rate of 125 Kb/s. Piggybacking provides most of the optimization, making possible channel utilization below 100%.

4   Experiments on a Real CAN Network

Figure 1(a) schematically shows the CAN network we built to validate the previous analysis in a real network, specifically for experimentation. Real-time generation signals/messages generation is achieved by using Arduino development cards (UNO and Mega). Figure 1(b) shows several runtime network data, in particular the Arduino output with timestamped events. The timestamped events are received in the PC at runtime from the Arduino Mega. Data shown on the screen is only for visual monitoring, the real-time and precise timing calculations are made in a spreadsheet after each specific experiment.

Figure 2 follows the same construction scheme of the experimental CAN network, including the Kinetis K70 development card. The Kinetis K70 includes a CAN interface, so it was immediately available to interoperate with the Arduino-based CAN network.

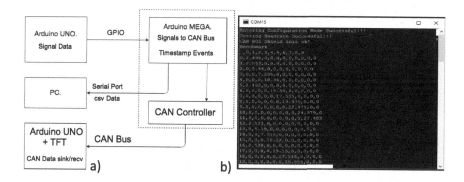

Fig. 1. CAN network: schematic and monitoring

Fig. 2. CAN network including a Kinetis K70 node

Although the data presented in Table 3 corresponds to a very short elapsed time of the experiments it is possible to verify that messages in the real network are sent sequentially, each one adding its transmission time to the waiting time of the next messages to be transmitted. Thus, it resembles the incremental sequence of message times as in Eq. 2 of the timing model given in a previous section. Experimentation on the real network allows us to verify that:

- The timing model is accurate in the sense that it represents the actual behavior of a real network, i.e. there is a *busy period* in which messages with low priority have to wait for a message with high priority, implying monotonically increasing waiting times.
- The actual writing time of a specific sequence of messages, where the waiting time is not always the maximum possible, because messages are delivered as soon as the communication channel is available.

Table 3. Timing measurements in a real CAN network

	0	1	2	3	4	5	6	7	8	9
0	2.576	0	0	0	0	0	0	0	0	0
1	2.579	0	0	0	0	0	0	0	0	0
2	2.584	0	0	0	0	0	0	0	0	0
3	0	2.66	0	0	0	0	0	0	0	0
4	0	0	5.248	0	0	0	0	0	0	0
5	0	0	0	7.84	0	0	0	0	0	0
6	0	0	0	0	10.432	0	0	0	0	0
7	0	0	0	0	0	13.27	0	0	0	0
8	0	0	0	0	0	0	15.564	0	0	0
9	0	0	0	0	0	0	0	18.163	0	0
10	0	0	0	0	0	0	0	0	0	20.752

Figure 3 shows the sequence of message arrivals to the CAN controller, and waiting times calculated from the measurements taken in the real CAN network while processing the SAE benchmark data. As schematically shown in Fig. 1, the Arduino UNO generated the signal data (those defined by the SAE benchmark), which the Arduino Mega handles for

- Message transmission to the CAN Bus, i.e. queueing and the real transmission.
- Message time instrumentation and monitoring, i.e. timestamping events and sending monitoring data to an external data analyzer (a PC in this case).

Each vertical bar in Fig. 3 identifies a particular message or message instance (where the signal type is identified by a color or gray level) numbering them from 0 onwards (on the x-axis). The height of each bar is directly proportional to the message elapsed time from the event of reaching the CAN controller until it is received at destination. Looking in detail at the first 10 bars of Fig. 3, it is possible to identify that:

- The CAN messages 0 to 2 belong to the same signal, 0, which has a period of 30 ms, so the sender can send the 3 messages before the arrival of signal 1, which has a period of 100 ms.

– After sending the first 3 messages, in the same instant (at 100 ms) data from signals 1 to 8 arrive. These all enter at the same time, so there are incremental times of messages 3 to 10 in the graph, depending on the CAN behavior: messages are sent taking into account the corresponding priorities.
– Messages that arrived at the same instant are sent in less than 30 ms and then a new message of signal 0 arrives. It is important to note that none of the messages had a latency higher than the worst time previously calculated with the timing model. Thus, it can be said that the model, as well as its implementation have been successfully tested.

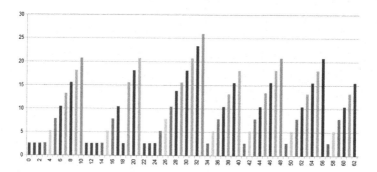

Fig. 3. Busy periods in the CAN network

5   Conclusions and Further Work

It has been possible to carry out the experimental corroboration of the timing model analysis proposed in previous works regarding latency and response times in the transmission of messages using the CAN protocol. The mathematical representation of each of the phenomena present on the bus has been analyzed with a set of signals of a hypothetical system, based on the SAE benchmark. This approach has been extensively used by automobile and machinery manufacturers when considering their CAN-based systems. Thus the analysis in this work is useful in itself and allows for new research and approaches. A real CAN network has been implemented and validated, building not only the hardware on which to carry out the experimentation but also including the necessary instrumentation for the collection of data to verify with the mathematical model.

As part of the future work, a careful study should be considered to increase the experimentation hardware environment, mainly in terms of having a CAN network closer to the real ones regarding the number of controllers. Analogously, the bus bandwidth and the number of message sources (types of signals involved) that each CAN controller must handle when accessing the CAN bus must be carefully determined.

References

1. Audsley, N.: Optimal priority assignment and feasibility of static priority tasks with arbitrary start times (1991)
2. Davis, R.I., Burns, A., Bril, R.J., Lukkien, J.J.: Controller area network (CAN) schedulability analysis: refuted, revisited and revised. Real-Time Syst. **35**(3), 239–272 (2007). https://doi.org/10.1007/s11241-007-9012-7
3. George, L., Rivierre, N., Spuri, M.: Preemptive and non-preemptive real-time uniprocessor scheduling. Research Report RR-2966. INRIA (1996). https://hal.inria.fr/inria-00073732. projet REFLECS
4. Kopetz, H.: A solution to an automotive control system benchmark. In: 1994 Proceedings Real-Time Systems Symposium, pp. 154–158, December 1994
5. Lehoczky, J.P.: Fixed priority scheduling of periodic task sets with arbitrary deadlines. In: 1990 Proceedings 11th Real-Time Systems Symposium, pp. 201–209, December 1990
6. Tindell, K., Burns, A., Wellings, A.: Calculating controller area network (CAN) message response times. Control Eng. Pract. **3**(8), 1163–1169 (1995). http://www.sciencedirect.com/science/article/pii/0967066195001128

Computer Security

Analysis of Methodologies of Digital Data Collection in Web Servers

Mónica D. Tugnarelli[1(✉)], Mauro F. Fornaroli[1], Sonia R. Santana[1], Eduardo Jacobo[1], and Javier Díaz[2]

[1] Facultad de Ciencias de la Administración, Universidad Nacional de Entre Ríos, Av. Tavella 1400, 3200 Concordia, Entre Ríos, Argentina
{montug,maufor}@fcad.uner.edu.ar
[2] Facultad de Informática, Universidad Nacional de La Plata, 50 y 120, 1900 La Plata, Buenos Aires, Argentina

Abstract. When an incident or security threat occurs, in which a system resource is compromised or potentially exposed to unauthorized access, computer forensics techniques and methodologies must ensure that it is possible to adequately determine what, who, when and how the incident occurred, as well as to ensure and preserve the evidence collected. This paper explore two methodologies of digital data collection, the first called Preventive Approach-Data Collection a priori or Forensic Readiness and the second called Reactive Approach - Post-Collection of a security event to comparatively analyze its performance based on certain criteria and control points established over HTTP and HTTP/2 web servers.

Keywords: Security · Incident · Forensia · Methodologies · HTTP

1 Introduction

If an IT security architecture is correctly defined, it must provide a plan and set of policies that describe both the security services offered to users and the system components required to deploy those services. These security policies are applied to the information assets identified for their relevance to the organization's goals, knowing how they are managed and what are their risks to implement strategies and mechanisms that ensure confidentiality, integrity and availability of those information assets [1].

When a security incident or threat occurs, in which a system resource is compromised or potentially exposed to unauthorized access, this security architecture is violated. Generally speaking, as environmental threats, aspects ranging from administrative security, communications security, environmental security to physical security can be considered. Therefore, the security architecture must be able to deal with both intentional and accidental threats. The implementation of a systematic incident monitoring and management program, based on the use of methodologies, can provide a structured and organized approach to minimize the impact of the security incident and help to deliver a rapid and adequate response.

© Springer International Publishing AG, part of Springer Nature 2018
A. E. De Giusti (Ed.): CACIC 2017, CCIS 790, pp. 265–271, 2018.
https://doi.org/10.1007/978-3-319-75214-3_25

Every day hundreds of teams are exposed to potential incidents, consider as an example the advance of Internet of Things (IoT) and its working characteristics emission of possibilities and risks of an incident and its consequent impact [2, 3].

Computer forensics methodologies must ensure that it is possible to determine adequately what, who, when and how happened in relation to that security incident, as well as to take care of the preservation and traceability of the collected data.

The definition offered by the first Digital Forensics Research Workshop (DFRWS), states that the digital forensic analysis or computer forensics is *"The use of scientifically proven and derived methods towards the preservation, collection, validation, identification, analysis, interpretation, documentation, and presentation of digital evidence derived from digital sources in order to facilitate or promote the reconstruction of facts, which may constitute legal evidence, or helping to anticipate unauthorized actions shown to be disruptive to planned operations"* [4].

The data sources are numerous, ranging from computers, cell phones, digital camera cards, embedded chips, drones, memories snapshots, to game consoles, that is to say, any device that produce digital data.

Computer forensics therefore requires a correct application of scientific methods, technique and tools to complete the stages related to the identification, preservation and analysis of digital evidence which, if necessary, can be considered legally in a judicial process, so in addition needs to ensure the quality and traceability of these data.

Given this panorama, this PID 7052 [5] seeks to advance in the comparative study of data collection methodologies related to security incidents and, particularly, to analyze the performance of these methodologies in web server environments.

2 Data Collection Methodologies

Currently, and generally speaking, data collection methodologies can be classified into two approaches:

2.1 Preventive Approach: Data Collection a Priori from a Security Event

Also known as *Forensic Readiness* [6–8]. This approach introduces the concept of guarding the possible evidence before an incident occurs to primarily cover two objectives: maximize the environment's ability to gather reliable digital evidence and minimizing the forensic cost during the response to an incident. The premise is that such data can be used not only as an input for the analysis of potential security incidents and recovery for business continuity, but also as legal evidence which involves the assurance of the evidence as the data is actively collected. On the other hand, it is fundamental to have the ability to process data effectively and to have properly trained staff who know how to ensure that the potential digital evidence is rightly preserved. This approach further states that being prepared to gather and use evidence can also have benefits acting as a deterrent against the high rates of violation of internal security policies. Some of the key activities in Forensic Readiness planning are

- define the scenarios or assets than may require digital evidences;
- identify the available sources and different types of possible evidence;
- establish a safe way of collecting evidence to meet the legal admissibility requirements;
- establish a policy for safe storage and safe handling of evidence;
- ensure monitoring to detect and prevent major incidents;
- train staff so that everyone understand their role in the digital evidence process and the legal sensitivity evidence;
- ensure legal control to facilitate action for incident response.

In summary, an organization's ability to exploit these data and anticipate the response to an incident is the focus of Forensic Availability.

2.2 Reactive Approach - Post-collection of a Security Event

This approach attempts to recover the evidence after the security incident is detected in order to perform a forensic analysis to determine what happened. The examination must be conducted in such a way as to ensure the admissibility of evidence. Piccirilli [9] provides in his doctoral thesis a description of the stages that can be applied in cases recollection of digital evidence involving computer-related elements, which include:

- the study and analysis of the environment, to identify the digital evidence to be obtained;
- the analysis claims subject to expert examination, which establishes the objective that the digital evidence must meet;
- the acquisition of digital evidence;
- the analysis of the evidence obtained, in accordance with the guidelines of the request forensic examination;
- the way of presenting the digital evidence obtained from the performed investigation;
- the preservation of the treated digital evidence (for eventual future stages of investigation, whose source would be the digital evidence itself).

Likewise, an exploratory analysis has been carried out on the most widely considered protocol standards and models, such as RFC 3227 [10] and ISO/IEC 27037 [11], where a set of common points are observed for correct forensic analysis. Among them we can summarize the importance of preserving the testing environment, how and where evidence is stored, how it is analyzed for maximum outcome, and finally the importance of reports that are clear and concise [12, 13].

In this paper, both methodological approaches applied to web servers will be analyzed, specifically analyzing HTTP protocol information in versions 1.1 and 2.

3   HTTP Protocol

Hypertext Transfer Protocol (HTTP) is an application level protocol with defined characteristics for use in distributed, collaborative and hypermedia information systems. It is characterized by being a simple and widely accepted client/server protocol, which defines the structure of the request/response messages as well as the way in which these messages are exchanged between clients and web servers. Improvements have been introduced in its different versions, mainly aimed at improving its performance, reducing resource consumption and latency, and resolving some of the problems of communication through TCP [14, 15].

The latest version HTTP/2 [16], presents a binary protocol that incorporates multiplexing and the mandatory use of TLS keeping the same semantics and compatibility with versions 1.0 and 1.1.1. The protocol is implemented if the client and server have support and if either of them do not have it, in the protocol negotiation, it is agreed to use the previous versions. Currently, most browsers and server environments have official implementations for the new version.

The following Table 1 summarizes the main differences between the versions:

Table 1. Main differences between HTTP versions.

	HTTP/1.0 (1996) RFC 1945	HTTP/1.1 (2000) RFC 2616	HTTP/2 (2015) RFC 7540
Requirements management	A requirement delivered at a time, over a connection	HTTP Keep Alive Mechanism: several requirements can use multiple connections with the server to reduce latency	Multiple request/ response messages on the same connection. Allows you to assign priorities to the requirements
Header field	Text format. HTTP messages: ASCII encoding sent as plain text over the connection	Text format. HTTP messages: ASCII encoding sent as plain text over the connection	Binary format. HTTP messages are converted into encrypted binary frames Compression of header (HPACK Algorithm)
Multiplexing	Does not allow simultaneous connections using the same TCP connection	Does not allow simultaneous connections using the same TCP connection	Allows multiple requests and responses in parallel using the same (a single) TCP connection, sending each request in a different stream
Server side	Download of resources at the client's request (first HTML, then CSS, JS, images, links)	Download of resources at the client's request (first HTML, then CSS, JS, images, links)	Server Push Technology: allows files (CSS, JS, images) to be uploaded from the server to the client without the client asking for it

4   Referring to Testing and Control Points

As it has been expressed in previous paragraphs, the analysis proposed in this work is based on the need to reach general and comparative conclusions about the performance of the two methodological approaches considering aspects such as: the quality of the collected data, the traceability of the data, the level of responsibility of the data, analysis of incidents response answer times, conservation of the evidence and volume of the collected data.

In order to develop the activities and tests, a work group has been configured in a LAN Ethernet web which is made of an Operative Ubuntu Server version 15.10 and a Web Apache Server version 2.4.12. This net is completed by six workstations connected to both, the wired and wireless net.

For the execution of tests and the acquisition of data, free distribution computing forensics tools have been analyzed [17, 18], such as CAINE [19], Black Arch Linux [20] and Kali Linux [21]. Kali Linux version 64 bit 2017.1, which has more than 300 tools and applications related with the audit and the computer forensics was chosen.

The following documents have been selected as general guides for the proofs and the frame of the work:

- RFC 3227: published by the Internet Engineering Task Force (IETF) which set guidelines to collect and store evidences without putting them on risk.
- ISO/IEC 27037:2012 which gives guidelines for the proper handling of the digital evidence governed by three essential principles: the relevance, the reliability and the sufficiency.
- OSSTMM (Open Source Security Testing Methodology Manual) [22]. It is one of the most complete professional standards used to audit systems security.

The project's scheduled first activities originated some results, which are detailed as follows. The first activity consisted on identifying the control points in the protocols HTTP 1.1 and HTTP/2. In order to do this, the capture, analysis and guard of the following have been selected.

a. Incoming and outgoing traffic of the ports 80 and 443 TCP, to get information about the possible kinds of attacks and the origin of them.
b. Condition of the established connections in the 80 and 443 ports.
c. Log files (/var/log/):
    - *messages.log*: general system of messages record.
    - *auth.log*: authentication record.
    - *secure*: authentication record.
    - *utmp/wtmp*: logins record.
d. *httpd*: log record of Apache: error.log and access.log. The former gives diagnostic information and records any that could occur in the processing requirements. The latter stores all the processed requirements by the server.
e. configuration files from Apache server: with the purpose of determining no authorized modifications in the server configuration altering its function.

The second activity focuses on the identification of comparative points among the gathering methodologies of digital evidence, for which data are being collected. These data will be analyzed in the following stages taking into account the particularities of each approaching.

a. Preventive approach
   - Monitoring and recompilation of data according to the established points detailed in the activity 1.
   - Two daily copies of the collected data are stored on external storage with integrity protection of hash (MD5).
b. Reactive approach
   - Standard monitoring and recompilation a data according to the points detailed in the activity 1.

These data will allow to build a comparative matrix with quantitative and qualitative data, which will try to answer about some main issues such as:

- Which methodology does offer a better answer in case of a security incident?
- Which will be the infrastructure cost of any of them?
- Which approach does offer better times of operative recovery?
- Which approach does offer the most suitable environment to realize computer forensics after an incident?
- Can the quality, traceability and inviolability of the collected data be secured in the preventive approach?

5   Conclusions and Future Work

This article presents the first findings of PID 7052-UNER called Analysis of methodologies of digital data collection.

With regard to the collection methodologies proposed for the analysis, an exploratory study of related material and publications was carried out, identifying the main characteristics, objectives and reasons why an organization can adopt a preventive or reactive approach to security incidents. In this sense, the team intends to build a comparative matrix that presents the relevant aspects in terms of quality, traceability and data availability, the incident's response time in both cases and last but not least, the volume and way of storing the gathered information.

The new version of the HTTP protocol called HTTP/2 has been analyzed in order to know its implications for data traffic capture. From the point of view of interest to this work, no major changes were detected at the application level, but progress should be made in the future in the analysis of its relationship with TCP and security restrictions with the use of TLS.

First results show that: (a) The Forensic Readiness methodology provides an active mechanism for anticipating incidents in contrast to security incident response methodologies; (b) Digital continuity, risk management and forensic preparedness support each other; (c) Maximizing the exploitation of potential evidence: preserved, unpolluted or damaged evidence; (d) The integrity of the data is ensured with a digital hash strip.

The next stages of the PID, which are under development, include the simulation of a Denial of Service (DoS) attack for the purpose of analyzing the various aspects already mentioned related to the performance of the methodologies.

References

1. ISACA: Incident Management and Response. http://www.isaca.org/. Accessed 23 July 2017
2. Internet Crime Complaint Center (IC3): Annual Report (2015). http://www.ic3.gov/media/annualreports.aspx. Accessed 14 Mar 2017
3. Ministerio Público Fiscal de la Ciudad Autónoma de Buenos Aires. CyberCrime Informe Final 2013 - Delitos Informáticos. http://delitosinformaticos.fiscalias.gob.ar/wp-content/uploads/2014/02/CyberCrime-Informe-Final-2013-flip.pdf. Accessed 14 Feb 2017
4. Digital Forensic Research Workshop (DFRWS). http://www.dfrws.org/. Accessed 14 Feb 2017
5. Tugnarelli, M., Fornaroli, M., Santana, S., Jacobo, E., Díaz, J.: Análisis de Metodologías de Recolección de Datos Digitales. In: Libro de Actas Workshop de Investigadores en Ciencias de la Computación, pp. 1000–1004 (2017). ISBN 978-987-42-5143-5
6. Tan, J.: Forensic Readiness. http://isis.poly.edu/kulesh/forensics/forensic_readiness.pdf. Accessed 30 Sept 2016
7. Rowlingson, R.: A ten step for forensic readiness. Int. J. Digit. Evid. **2**, 1–28 (2004)
8. Pooe, A., Labuschagne, L.: A conceptual model for digital forensic readiness. http://ieeexplore.ieee.org/document/6320452/. Accessed 7 Oct 2017
9. Piccirilli, D.: Protocolos a aplicar en la forensia informática en el marco de las nuevas tecnologías (pericia – forensia y cibercrimen). Tesis de doctorado. Facultad de Informática. Universidad Nacional de La Plata (2016). http://hdl.handle.net/10915/52212
10. IETF: RFC 3227 Guidelines for Evidence Collection and Archiving. https://www.ietf.org/rfc/rfc3227.txt. Accessed 30 Aug 2016
11. Guidelines for identification, collection, acquisition and preservation of digital evidence ISO/IEC 27037:2012
12. U.S. Department of Justice: Electronic Crime Scene Investigation: A Guide for First Responders, 2nd Edn. https://www.ncjrs.gov/pdffiles1/nij/219941.pdf. Accessed 30 Aug 2017
13. Forte, D.: Principles of digital evidence collection. Netw. Secur. **2003**(12), 6–7 (2003). https://doi.org/10.1016/S1353-4858(03)00006-0
14. IETF: RFC 1945 Hypertext Transfer Protocol - HTTP/1.0. http://tools.ietf.org/html/rfc1945. Accessed 30 June 2017
15. IETF: RFC 2616 Hypertext Transfer Protocol - HTTP/1.1. http://tools.ietf.org/html/rfc2616. Accessed 30 June 2017
16. IETF: RFC 7540 Hypertext Transfer Protocol Version 2 (HTTP/2). https://tools.ietf.org/html/rfc7540. Accessed 30 July 2017
17. Altheide, C., Carvey, H.: Digital Forensics with Open Source Tools, pp. 1–8 (2011). https://doi.org/10.1016/b978-1-59749-586-8.00001-7
18. Tugnarelli, M., Fornaroli, M., Pacifico, C.: Análisis de prestaciones de herramientas de software libre para la recolección a priori de evidencia digital en servidores web. In: Libro de Actas Workshop de Investigadores en Ciencias de la Computación, pp. 985–990 (2015). ISBN 978-987-633-134-0
19. Computer Aided Investigative Environment. http://www.caine-live.net/. Accessed 30 Sept 2017
20. BlackArch Linux. https://blackarch.org/. Accessed 30 Aug 2017
21. KALI Linux. https://www.kali.org. Accessed 30 Aug 2017
22. ISECOM: Open Source Security Testing Methodology Manual (OSSTMM). http://www.isecom.org/mirror/OSSTMM.3.pdf. Accessed 30 Mar 2017

Observer Effect: How Intercepting HTTPS Traffic Forces Malware to Change Their Behavior

María José Erquiaga[1,2,3(✉)], Sebastián García[4], and Carlos García Garino[1,3]

[1] ITIC, UNCuyo, Mendoza, Argentina
merquiaga@uncu.edu.ar, cgarcia@itu.uncu.edu.ar
[2] Facultad de Ciencias Exactas y Naturales, UNCuyo, Mendoza, Argentina
[3] Facultad de Ingeniería, UNCuyo, Mendoza, Argentina
[4] CTU University, Prague, Czech Republic
sebastian.garcia@agents.fel.cvut.cz

Abstract. During the last couple of years there has been an important surge on the use of HTTPs by malware. The reason for this increase is not completely understood yet, but it is hypothesized that it was forced by organizations only allowing web traffic to the Internet. Using HTTPs makes malware behavior similar to normal connections. Therefore, there has been a growing interest in understanding the usage of HTTPs by malware. This paper describes our research to obtain large quantities of real malware traffic using HTTPs, our use of man-in-the-middle HTTPs interceptor proxies to open and study the content, and our analysis of how the behavior of the malware changes after being intercepted. The research goal is to understand how malware uses HTTPs and the impact of intercepting its traffic. We conclude that the use of an interceptor proxy forces the malware to change its behavior and therefore should be carefully considered before being implemented.

Keywords: Malware · Botnets · HTTPs · Malware traffic · Network security
MITM · Proxy · Malware behavior

1 Introduction

In physics, the observer effect alludes to the influence of the observer on the phenomenon under observation. In most areas, this influence is often caused by instruments and modifies the behavior of what is being measured in some important manner. However, the observer effect can also appear in other contexts, such as malware execution and analysis for network security. Unfortunately, the impact of capturing techniques on the behavior of malware in the network was often overlooked. In this work, we study the observer effect in regard to the use of web TLS (Transport Layer Security) interceptor proxies for network malware analysis. The usage of web proxies TLS interceptors allows companies to view the content of its employee's encrypted connections. This technology is nowadays widely implemented in large companies and it is supposedly used to protect the employees from infections. However, the inflicted changes upon the behavior of

© Springer International Publishing AG, part of Springer Nature 2018
A. E. De Giusti (Ed.): CACIC 2017, CCIS 790, pp. 272–281, 2018.
https://doi.org/10.1007/978-3-319-75214-3_26

malware, the invasion of employee's privacy and the implementation costs can be an inconvenience for some companies.

This research focuses on understanding the influence of web proxies TLS interceptors during the execution of malware. To achieve the analysis, we created a new and large TLS dataset of real malware samples extending for more than one year. The malware was run in a special infrastructure for selective interception and with complete access to the Internet. The average execution time of each malware is one week, with some executions lasting two months. The main goal of this work is to find how malware changed its behavior due to the filtering, blocking and interception of its web TLS connections. The most important factor of our research was the verification process, which consisted in executing the malware twice and simultaneously: once using the interceptor proxy and once without it.

The contributions of this work are: (1) The creation of a dataset. The dataset created is a large and modern one, it includes more than 80 malware were carefully captured with a methodology explained in this article. (2) Malware interception using https or port 443. The malware selected to be captured was the one using encrypted communication or port 443 (the port assigned to encrypt the communication). Also, two scenarios were considered; with proxy and without proxy interception. (3) Publication of the dataset in the stratosphere web site and twitter in order to be available for the research community. (4) An analysis of the implications of intercepting the traffic of malware, described in this paper.

The remainder of this work is organized as follows. Section 2 describes the background concepts, definitions and the previous work. Section 3 describes the dataset creation and features. This section also includes a description of the laboratory infrastructure and the methodology to obtain the dataset. Section 4 shows an analysis of the malware captures and a comparison of the same malware with and without using proxy. Finally, Sect. 5 presents the conclusions and future work.

2   Background and Previous Work

TLS is the standard security protocol for encrypting information in a network. It establishes an encrypted link using asymmetric and symmetric encryption algorithms. TLS is the widest used encryption protocol because it uses a trust chain to verify that the service is trustable and it doesn't require the client to have any special password. Recently, there seems to be a rise in the use of TLS by malware, causing new difficulties for the analysts and rising several new questions about what the malware is doing inside the encrypted channel, and how its attack strategy changes.

The study of TLS interception in the network and its impact on the users has been analyzed before from the perspective of privacy [1]. The practice of using TLS interceptor proxies is common inside companies, even when employees are unaware. The most important impact of this practice is that users get used to being intercepted and their general security protection measures decrease. The authors concluded that approximately 0.6% of all users inside companies are subject to interception.

The analysis of TLS usage by malware was previously studied by Cisco in an attempt to find their actions without decrypting the traffic [5]. The authors used 18 malware families that usually encrypt their traffic to understand the motivations behind encryption. The research found that 98.4% of the encrypted malware traffic used port 443/TCP for this purpose. However, there is no analysis of the malware using port 443/TCP with other protocols that are not TLS. Therefore, they mainly focused on TLS protocol on port 443/TCP.

Furthermore, Carné de Carnavalet and Mannan [2], conduct investigations into the risks introduced by TLS interception tools, by analyzing the risks of using antivirus and parental control tools with a proxy.

Cisco researchers have found that the amount of malware using TLS has grown in the last years. Their analysis reveals that malware uses TLS differently than normal traffic [6]. The author proposed to augment the common 5-tuple structure source and destination IP address, source and destination port number and protocol ID) with TLS-based features. Among the additional features are the list of offered cipher suites, the selected cipher suite, the sequence of lengths and type codes of TLS records, and the time between TLS records in milliseconds [7].

Most of the analysis of malware using TLS protocol focuses on malware detection. In [3], the authors propose to detect malware using HTTPS traffic, by using k-NN classification. Another recent approach was to detect the malware by studying its encrypted HTTPs communication [4]. The goal of the authors was to detect HTTPS malware connections by extracting new features and using data from the Bro IDS program.

3   HTTPs Malware Dataset

The most important challenge of analyzing malware using HTTPs is the lack of a good public dataset. As part of our work we spent almost one year collecting real, and long term, malware traffic. Our dataset consists of more than 80 network malware traffic captures. It has been created as an activity of our Nomad Project [9]. One of the goals of the dataset is to study the behavior of malware and how it changes in time. To obtain this type of data we executed the malware for long terms, up to 3 weeks or even months. The dataset contains malware capture of different types of malware (such as Trojans, Adware, Botnets, etc.). For each capture, we generated several files to improve future analyses.

The process of creating the dataset can be described in four phases, (1) design and creation of the laboratory, (2) design of the capture methodology, (3) generation of experiments and (4) output of information. The following subsections describe these phases in detail.

3.1   Malware Laboratory Infrastructure

The malware laboratory infrastructure consisted in a host Linux computer running more than 30 VirtualBox Windows 7 virtual machines. The host computer also ran a separate mitmproxy[1] implementation for each malware, allowing the complete isolation of results. The malware had unrestricted access to the Internet except for a limited bandwidth and an SMTP redirection to an e-mail honeypot, as it is shown in Fig. 1. It can be seen how all most common ports for the web connections were redirected through the web TLS interceptor.

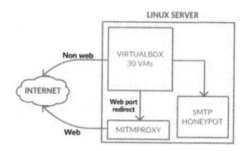

Fig. 1. Malware capture laboratory infrastructure

3.2 Capture Methodology

The methodology implemented to capture malware traffic is based on the analysis of known malware that we use to infect machines in our laboratory. The steps to capture malware traffic are: (1) find the malware binary (2) copy the binary to the server (3) start the virtual machine and infect it (4) compute the start date and the infection date and monitoring the machine (5) Stop and publish the capture. To find the malware binaries we search in web sites specialized in malware samples such as virus total, hybrid analysis, and SSL blacklist. We monitor each machine using tcpdump, mitmproxy outputs and cacti[2]. Thought those tools it was possible to detect if the machines were infected or not and if the communication was still alive. Once we considered we had enough information, we stopped the capture, generate the output of the dataset and published it in with the corresponding ID in the stratosphere website, blog and twitter.

3.3 Experiments and Output Files

The dataset consists of 80 different malware captures [8]. The malware captured includes botnet, trojans, backdoors, and adware, among other ones. Approximately 90% of these captures used port 443/TCP for communicating. However, only 83% of the captures used the TLS protocol over port 443/TCP. This means that at least 17% of malware used port 443/TCP for their own custom encryption protocol. Regarding the usage of these connections, from the complete set of captures, approximately 30% used the port 443/TCP (both with and without TLS) for their Command and Control channels. This means that most of the TLS connections generated by malware were not directly related to its remote control.

---

[1] https://mitmproxy.org/.
[2] https://www.cacti.net/.

Each malware has assigned a unique ID in order to be identified. If we execute the malware twice, we add a number to the ID. For instance, for a 260 malware ID, the first capture will be coded 260-1, the second one 260-2, and so on. The URL format to access to the capture information contains this ID. For example: https://mcfp.felk.cvut.cz/publicDatasets/CTU-Malware-Capture-Botnet-260-1.

4   Comparison and Evaluation of the Behavior of Malware with Intercepting TLS Proxies

In this section, we analyze the network behavior of malware captures when they are being intercepted by a TLS proxy. We analyzed each malware traffic capture to evaluate its behavior in the two previously defined scenarios (with proxy interception and no proxy interception). The goal is to detect the behavior differences for a given malware. Seven different malware captures identified as 169-1, 169-2, 169-3, 192-1, 192-2, 219-1 and 219-2 were analyzed.

4.1   Miuref Capture (169)

This malware belongs to the Miuref family. It was executed three times, twice with an interceptor proxy (captures 169-1 and 169-2) and once without proxy (capture 169-3).

Miuref capture with TLS Proxy (169-1[3] and 169-2[4])

In this capture, Miuref first resolves the domains; service8.org, 1. web-counter.info, timeservice24.com, 2. web-counter.info, 3. web-counter.info, 4. web-counter.info, and 5. web-counter.info. These are the main Command and Control channels of the malware. All the domains have one or more IP addresses and the malware starts to connect to them on port 443/TCP. Given that the protocol spoken by the malware on port 443/TCP is not TLS, the MITM proxy generates the follow error:

502 Bad Gateway. SSL handshake error: The client may not trust the proxy's certificate.

This is the first important conflict between the malware and the proxy, since the proxy does not allow the traffic to connect to Internet. Therefore, the C&C servers are not reached properly. After the unsuccessful connections, the malware contacts an IP address that is hardcoded in the binary: 185.118.67.195. This IP is contacted on port 80/TCP and the protocol spoken is correct HTTP. This backup C&C mechanism worked well and allowed the malware to download a possible binary update.

The second most important conflict of the malware and the MITM proxy is that the malware keeps trying to connect to the 443/TCP ports in the C&C servers, generating a large amount of very suspicious traffic.

As the malware is related with ClickFraud and advertising, it also connects to twitter.com, youtube.com, google.com, facebook.com, bing.com, etc. These requests

---

[3] https://mcfp.felk.cvut.cz/publicDatasets/CTU-Malware-Capture-Botnet-169-1/.

[4] https://mcfp.felk.cvut.cz/publicDatasets/CTU-Malware-Capture-Botnet-169-2/.

were done because certain webpages had links to them and not because the malware was abusing their services. We were able to verify this claim because it was possible to observe the HTTPs traffic and distinguish the real requests.

Then, the malware resolves the domain bam.nr-data.net, obtaining the following IPs 50.31.164.175, 162.247.242.18, 50.31.164.173, 50.31.164.166, 50.31.164.174, 162.247.242.19. It uses port 80 to contact the IP 50.31.164.175 and establishes a CC channel. For example, an unsuccessful connection to port 443 that were not SSL is the one to the IP 138.201.125.95.

Miuref capture without Proxy (169-3)

This is a capture of the Miuref malware but without using any MITM proxy. In this case, the malware tries to connect to its C&C servers using the port 443/TCP with its custom encryption protocols and it is successful. After contacting the C&C servers the malware also contacts its hardcoded IP address 185.118.67.195 and downloads a binary update. The operation of the malware remains similar to the capture with the proxy and it connects to several ClickFrauds and advertising sites, such as platform.twitter.com, connect.facebook.net, google.com and bing.com.

In this capture the behavior is similar to the previous capture (it resolves the same domains, contacts the same IPs). However, the main difference is that the TLS connection is established.

Regarding the capture without MITM, from the 206 unique domains requested, 30% were unique to this capture. From all the traffic in the capture with the MITM proxy, 18% was sent to port 443/TCP, while only 8% of the traffic in the capture without the MITM proxy was sent to the same port. This difference is due to the use of an interceptor HTTPs proxy.

4.2   Remote Admin.Ammyy Capture (ID 192)

This malware is a remote admin tool called Ammyy. This is a possible legitimate application, but it is usually abused for its remote administration capabilities. This malware was executed twice; with proxy, and without proxy.

Remote Admin.Ammyy capture with proxy (192-2[5])

This malware first resolves the domain rl.ammyy.com and contacts the IP 176.56.184.37 in port 80/tcp. Then, it contacts four different IPs in the ports 443/TCP, 80/TCP and 8080/TCP in sequence. The IP address are 88.198.6.56, 88.198.6.55, 95.211.242.83 and 95.211.191.142. Those IPs could be hardcoded in the binary file, or they may be delivered in the communication C&C channel with the server from the IP 176.56.184.37. The malware does not connect successfully to the IPs 88.198.6.56, 88.198.6.55, 95.211.242.83 and 95.211.191.142. This happens because the MITM proxy cannot recognize the protocols used in those ports. It means that the malware is using the protocol in an unconventional manner.

---

[5] https://mcfp.felk.cvut.cz/publicDatasets/CTU-Malware-Capture-Botnet-192-2/.

Remote Admin.Ammyy capture without proxy (192-1[6] and 192-3[7])

The malware resolves the domain rl.ammyy.com and connects to its IP, 176.56.184.37, in the port 80/tcp. This CC channel works fine and receives a string of binary data. The malware then connects to a group of four IPs: 95.211.191.142, 95.211.242.83, 88.198.6.56, 88.198.6.54. The IPs are connected in an endless loop. In each loop, each IP is contacted on port 443/tcp, 80/tcp and 8080/tcp, in that order mostly. These IPs could be sent in the binary answer from the first CC server or they could have been hardcoded in the malware binary. None of the looping servers were correctly executing the CC. This resulted in the malware not being able to activate of further receive orders.

Regarding capture 192-3, we observed; first, it resolves www.msftncsi.com and contacts the remote server in port 80. Then, it contacts the same IP (217.182.53.102) on port 443. It resolves the domain rl.ammyy.com, and contacts the domain in port 80 and exchange binary information. Then it contacts the IP 95.211.191.142, port 443 tcp (it sends some binary information). Repeating this process in an endless loop.

4.3   Capture Kover.B (ID 219)

The malware executed is probably a trojan called Kover.B, it was executed with proxy and without proxy. In both cases, the malware contacted the remote Command and Control server in port 443/TCP and established an encrypted channel.

Capture Kover.B with proxy (ID 219-1[8])

First, the malware tries to establishes a Command and Control channel with the IP 42.2.231.204 on port 80/TCP, with 149.80.126.178 on port 8080/TCP and with 119.116.67.233 on port 443/TCP. Most of them used an unknown encryption protocol. These connections failed because the proxy could not understand them. The only connection that is successful with the IP 42.2.231.204 because it used real HTTP. Then, the malware attempts to create C&C channels on port 8080/TCP and 443/TCP with several IP addresses. Most of these also failed for the same reason. When all these connections failed, the malware establish a C&C channel with the IP 185.117.72.90 on port 80/TCP using HTTP protocol. The malware contacted 5,130 IP addresses using port 80/TCP, but only 4 of them were successful. This is in huge contrast with the execution of this malware without proxy, were approximately 560 were successful.

Capture Kover.B without proxy (ID 219-2[9])

The malware starts by creating a C&C channel with the IP addresses 179.13.161.66 on port 80/TCP, with 143.241.134.70 on port 443/TCP and with 214.146.130.191 on port 443/TCP. These IP do not answer any more.

Then, the infected computer establishes a connection to www.microsoft.com, which is odd for any malware. Since the Windows computer is configured not to update, this

---

[6] https://mcfp.felk.cvut.cz/publicDatasets/CTU-Malware-Capture-Botnet-192-1/.

[7] https://mcfp.felk.cvut.cz/publicDatasets/CTU-Malware-Capture-Botnet-192-3/.

[8] https://mcfp.felk.cvut.cz/publicDatasets/CTU-Malware-Capture-Botnet-219-1/.

[9] https://mcfp.felk.cvut.cz/publicDatasets/CTU-Malware-Capture-Botnet-219-2/.

may be a result of the malware opening another process. There are also connections to www.download.windowsupdate.com.

At the same time, the malware tries to connect to at least 20 different IP addresses on port 443/TCP. Most of them do not respond. The IP that answers is 198.144.30.128 on port 443/TCP, related with the domain store.korfx.com. It is clear that these IP are hardcoded in the malware. During the operation of the malware several IPs addresses were contacted on ports 80 and 443/TCP, trying to find C&C servers. With most of them the protocol is a custom encryption. With others, such as 189.241.104.183 on port 80/TCP, the communication uses HTTP and the data uses a custom encryption. The malware contacted 5,334 different IP addresses on port 80/TCP trying to reach different C&C servers. However, 4.767 of them were not working. Only 4 IP addresses were contacted on port 443/TCP as C&C servers.

4.4   Capture Trojanized BitTorrent with Open Candy (ID 208)

This malware is probable a BitTorrent client that was trojanized with the adware Open Candy. It was executed twice; with and without proxy. In the two scenarios, the malware contacted the port 443/TCP and established a communication with a remote server. However, it was not an encrypted communication.

This capture is shown as an example of how there may be situations where the use of MITM proxy does not have an impact in the traffic. Since this malware does not have a Command and Control channel, it did not have any issue with the proxy.

Trojanized BitTorrent with Open Candy capture with proxy (ID 208-1[10])

During this execution, the malware resolved different domains (i-50.b-000.xyz.bench.utorrent.com, i-21.b-42606.ut.bench.utorrent.com and bittorrent.vo.llnwd.net) related with the operation of BitTorrent. Most of the connections and updates are done using port 80/TCP. Some IP addresses are also contacted using UDP packets, due to the operation of the P2P protocol. Finally, it contacts other domains (previously contacted using the port 80), using the port 443/TCP. This process is repeated several times during the capture.

Capture Trojanized BitTorrent with Open Candy without proxy (ID 208-2[11])

This capture has the same behavior as the previous capture (208-1, with proxy). It contacts some domains on port 80, and then it establishes an SSL communication with those IPs on port 443.

4.5   Discussion

After executing the malware with and without the web TLS proxy interception we discover a very important characteristic of the problem studied: the behavior of most malware changed when it was executed with a proxy. The most important findings are three. First, while using the interceptor proxy, certain amount of malware, was not able

---

[10] https://mcfp.felk.cvut.cz/publicDatasets/CTU-Malware-Capture-Botnet-208-1/.

[11] https://mcfp.felk.cvut.cz/publicDatasets/CTU-Malware-Capture-Botnet-208-2/.

to communicate with the Internet at all, because the protocol used on port 443/TCP was not TLS. Therefore, the proxy refused to establish the connection. This forced the malware to new actions. Second, when the malware didn't achieve the connection to its remote servers, two new behaviors were observed: (1) the malware tried to reconnect continually to its C&C server, generating huge noise in the network, and (2) the malware seek another way to connect (choosing a different port, or looking for others servers). An example of this difference can be seen in Figs. 2 and 3. In particular, Fig. 2 describes the behavior of the malware when was captured with mitmproxy and Fig. 3 illustrates the behavior of the same malware without using a proxy. Third, some malware running with the web interceptor was not able to establish the C&C channel, while the capture without the web interceptor was able to do it. In these cases, the intercepted malware sent more than three times the amount of traffic compared with the not intercepted malware.

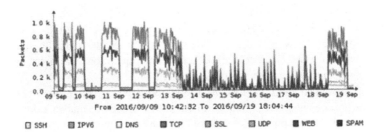

Fig. 2. Malware captured with mitmproxy

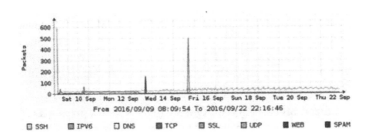

Fig. 3. Malware captured without mitmproxy

5 Conclusion and Future Work

The analysis of the behavior of malware inside an encrypted connection is difficult. For this reason, we consider our malware dataset and analysis of encrypted behavior a step forward in this topic. There are two main conclusions regarding the impact of using a proxy for malware analysis. First, we observed a large amount of malware using a custom protocol on ports reserved for the HTTPs/HTTP protocols (ports 80, 8080 and 443). Blocking these connections forced the malware to generate new behaviors.

Second, we noticed that malware's behavior can change in undefined ways when an intercepting proxy is used. Therefore, the implementation of a proxy should be carefully considered to detect malware in the network.

As future work, we will analyze more in detail other features in the captures. First, to detect which malware we are executing and second, to identify which version of the protocol the malware is using. When we executed the malware samples, we were provided of information from virus total and hybrid analysis. Even though this site is the more important virus database, it provides information from the possible name of the malware. For that reason, we consider that it is essential to verify which malware we are really executing. Second, we compared the differences between the malware that was using encrypted communication and not, but we did not analyze the version of the encryption protocol it was using.

References

1. O'Neill, M., Ruoti, S., Seamons, K., Zappala, D.: TLS inspection: how often and who cares? IEEE Internet Comput. **21**(3), 22–29 (2017). https://doi.org/10.1109/MIC.2017.58
2. de Carné de Carnavalet, X., Mannan, M.: Killed by Proxy: Analyzing Client-end TLS Interception Software, 21–24 February 2016, San Diego, CA, USA. Copyright 2016 Internet Society, ISBN 1-891562-41-X. https://doi.org/10.14722/ndss.2016.2337
3. Lokoč, J., Kohout, J., Čech, P., Skopal, T., Pevný, T.: k-NN classification of Malware in HTTPS traffic using the metric space approach. In: Chau, M., Wang, G.Alan, Chen, H. (eds.) PAISI 2016. LNCS, vol. 9650, pp. 131–145. Springer, Cham (2016). https://doi.org/10.1007/978-3-319-31863-9_10
4. Střasák, F.: Detection of HTTPS Malware Traffic. Open Informatics, Computer and Information Science, May 2017. https://dspace.cvut.cz/bitstream/handle/10467/68528/F3-BP-2017-Strasak-Frantisek-strasak_thesis_2017.pdf?sequence=-1
5. Anderson, B., Paul, S., McGrew, D.: Deciphering Malware's use of TLS (without Decryption) (2016). http://arxiv.org/abs/1607.01639
6. Anderson, B.: Hiding in Plain Sight: Malware's Use of TLS and Encryption, 25 January 2016. http://blogs.cisco.com/security/malwares-use-of-tls-and-encryption
7. Anderson, B., McGrew, D., Kendler, A.: Cisco Systems, Inc. Classifying Encrypted Traffic with TLS-Aware Telemetry, January 2016. http://resources.sei.cmu.edu/library/asset-view.cfm?assetID=449962
8. Stratosphere Dataset. https://stratosphereips.org/category/dataset.html
9. Nomad Project. https://stratosphereips.org/category/Nomad.html

Innovation in Computer Science Education

ECMRE: Extended Concurrent Multi Robot Environment

Juan Castro[1(✉)], Laura De Giusti[1,2], Gladys Gorga[1],
Mariano Sánchez[1], and Marcelo Naiouf[1]

[1] School of Computer Science, Computer Science Research Institute LIDI (III-LIDI),
UNLP, La Plata, Argentina
camaju_25@hotmail.com,
{ldgiusti,ggorga,msanchez,mnaiouf}@lidi.info.unlp.edu.ar
[2] Scientific Research Agency of the Province of Buenos Aires (CICPBA), La Plata, Argentina

Abstract. ECMRE is an extension of CMRE (Concurrent Multi Robot Environment) that adds features related to current parallel architectures: processor heterogeneity, energy consumption, processor speed change techniques in relation to temperature and/or energy consumption.

ECMRE allows incorporating the topics of concurrency and parallelism in a simple and entertaining manner in beginner classes in the courses of Computer Science by means of a graphic and interactive environment.

An initial test was carried out in a course with 42 students to analyze how they adapt to this new environment and how they can use it.

Keywords: Concurrency · Parallelism · Heterogeneous processors
Parallel algorithms · Energy consumption

1 Introduction

Concurrency has been a central issue in the development of Computer Science, and the mechanisms used to express concurrent processes that cooperate and compete for resources have been in the core curriculum of Computer Science studies since the seventies, in particular after the foundational works of Hoare, Dijkstra and Hansen [1–3]. On the other hand, parallelism, understood as "real concurrency" in which multiple processors can operate simultaneously on multiple control threads at the same point in time, was for many years a possibility that was limited by available hardware technology [4]. Classic Computer Science curricula [5–7] included the concepts of concurrency in various areas (Languages, Paradigms, Operating Systems), but parallelism was almost entirely omitted, except to present the concepts of distributed systems.

Changes in technology have produced an evolution of the major topics in Computer Science, mainly due to the new applications being developed from having access to more powerful and less expensive architectures and communications networks [8]. For this reason, international curricular recommendations mention the need to include the topics of concurrency and parallelism from the early stages of student education, since all architectures and real systems with which they will work in the future will be essentially parallel [9]. However, parallel programming (and the essential concepts of concurrency)

© Springer International Publishing AG, part of Springer Nature 2018
A. E. De Giusti (Ed.): CACIC 2017, CCIS 790, pp. 285–294, 2018.
https://doi.org/10.1007/978-3-319-75214-3_27

is more complex for students who are starting their studies, and new strategies are required to teach the topic.

Given the stimuli to which students are exposed from an early age, be it through video games, computers, mobile phones, tablets, or any other electronic device, the use of interactive tools to teach core concepts to students in a CS1 course [9–11] has become essential [12]. In this sense, the possibility to take the initial steps in the world of programming through a graphic and interactive environment allows reducing the gap that traditionally existed between abstraction and the possibility of seeing a graphic representation of how the concepts being learned are applied in an environment that is conceptually similar to those used in everyday life [8, 13].

CMRE is a graphic environment that has a set of robots that move within a city, and it has allowed teaching the basic concepts of concurrency and parallelism in a beginner's course in Computer Science. In a previous article [14], the idea of adding advanced features commonly found in current parallel architectures (such as heterogeneity, energy consumption, temperature generated) to the environment was discussed. As a continuation of that work, we have implemented such an extension and created ECMRE (Extended Concurrent Multi Robot Environment), which is presented here.

This article is organized as follows: Sect. 2 details the advanced features present in modern parallel architectures that have been included in the environment; Sect. 3 describes the original version of CMRE; Sect. 4 discusses the extensions developed to create ECMRE; and Sect. 5 presents a test carried out with the new environment in a first-year course. Section 6 discusses the conclusions.

2   Advanced Features of Parallel Architectures

Current parallel architectures come with advanced features that should be included when teaching the basic concepts of concurrency and parallelism. In particular, architecture heterogeneity and energy consumption.

2.1   Heterogeneity in Parallel Architectures

Since the early computers, there has been an ever-present desire to increase machine computational power. However, it is currently hard to increase processor speed by increasing their clock rate. Hardware architects face two issues: heat generation and energy consumption. The solution to this problem introduced by designers has been integrating two or more computational cores within a single chip, which is known as multicore processor. Multicore processors improve application performance by distributing work among the available cores [15, 16].

Currently, research is focusing mainly on heterogeneous multicore architectures (i.e., architectures whose cores have different performance and energy consumption characteristics and which may or may not use different sets of instructions), since having different types of cores allows optimizing performance and, when tasks are appropriately distributed among cores, higher performance/energy ratio efficiencies are achieved.

In this type of architectures, heterogeneity is present in various aspects, most significantly in core computational power (computation speed), memory access time, and communication speed among cores. These three aspects determine the time required to execute the instructions in each core, and thus, the same sentence executed by two different cores can take different times. On the other hand, since there is a certain degree of independence of the features that cause heterogeneity, not all instructions are affected in the same proportion. That is, a floating point operation that is run in core A, may take a fourth of the time it takes when run in core B, while a writing operation may take half the time when run in it.

2.2 Energy Consumption in Parallel Applications

Energy consumption is a key aspect of current processors. In general, the performance of a parallel algorithm is not measured only in its execution time, but also in energy consumed. Thus, there will be Flops/Watt or Flops/Joule ratios corresponding to a relation between computation and instant power or total energy [17, 18].

It is important to teach Computer Science students to always use consumption metrics as an indicator of algorithm quality. Additionally, they should also understand the automatic mechanisms developed by processors according to the temperature reached (which is a direct function of the energy consumed in a period of time) [17].

There are performance adjustment techniques used in current processors that consider energy consumption, temperature and other values as indicators for decision-making. Overclocking and underclocking are two of the most widely used techniques to increase or decrease processor clock rate in order to increase performance or standardizing consumption and temperature values when the processor is overloaded.

3 Current Version of CMRE

The main features of CMRE can be summarized as follows [15, 19]:

- There are multiple processors (robots) that carry out tasks and that can co-operate and/or compete. They represent the cores of a real multiprocessor architecture. These virtual robots can have their own clock, and different times for carrying out their specific tasks.
- The environment model ("city") where the robots carry out their tasks supports exclusive areas, partially shared areas and fully shared areas. An exclusive area allows only one robot to move in it, a partially shared area specifies the set of robots that can move in it, and a fully shared area allows all robots defined in the program to move in it.
- If only one robot is used in an area that encompasses the entire city, the scheme used in Visual Da Vinci is repeated [20, 21].
- When two or more robots are in a (partially or fully) shared area, they compete for access to the corners on their runs, and the resources found there. For this, they must be synchronized.

- When two or more robots (in a common area or not) wish to exchange information (data or control), they must use explicit messages.
- Synchronization is done through a mechanism that is equivalent to a binary semaphore.
- Mutual exclusion can be generated by stating the areas reached by each robot. Entering other areas in the city, as well as exiting them, is not allowed.
- The entire execution model is synchronous and allows the existence of a cycle virtual clock which, in turn, allows assigning specific times for the operations, simulating the existence of a heterogeneous architecture.
- The environment allows executing the program in a traditional manner or with step-by-step instructions, giving the user detailed control over program execution to allow them controlling typical concurrency situations such as conflicts (collisions) or deadlocks.
- In the step-by-step mode, the effect of the operations can be reflected on physical robots, communicated through Wi-Fi. The physical robots have Linux as operating system, which allows running an http server implemented on NodeJS [22]. Thus, the environment communicates with the robots (each physical robot corresponds to a virtual one in the environment). These are point-to-point, two-way communications, i.e., the environment sends instructions to the physical robot and then the robot sends its response to the environment stating that the instruction given has been fulfilled.

4   CMRE Extension

ECMRE (Extended Concurrent Multi Robot Environment) is an extended version of its predecessor (CMRE) and, as such, it adds the concepts of heterogeneous multicore architectures, energy consumption, processor temperature, and overclocking and underclocking techniques to it.

Students can work on ECMRE by representing different types of multicore architectures and watch in a graphic and interactive manner the information related to operation time for each robot and variations in consumption and temperature values corresponding to algorithm runs. By analyzing this information, students can modify their algorithms (for example, they can balance workloads) to obtain solutions that are efficient as regards energy consumption and temperatures reached.

4.1   Representing Parallel Architecture Heterogeneity

In this section, the main adaptations made to CMRE to address speed and energy consumption aspects in ECMRE are described.

Processor Performance. In ECMRE there is a *Details* area (Fig. 1(a)) to adjust the general parameters for the application and for each robot in particular. It includes a table called ROBOTS that has a column that allows defining the speed for each robot. This simplifies working with the robots, which could present variations in their performance because they will execute algorithm instructions at different speeds. There are 3 speeds that can be selected, and they are related as follows:

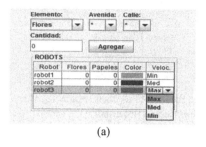
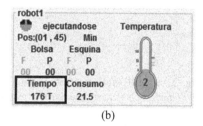

(a)   (b)

Fig. 1. Areas in ECMRE: (a) *Details*, where each robot is configured, (b) *Execution Information*, where the execution time for the robot is displayed.

- *Max* is the maximum speed available.
- *Med* is half the maximum speed.
- *Min* is half the medium speed.

In ECMRE, T is defined as a unit of time (equivalent to 100 ms) to measure robot/processor performance. We decided to use a subset of 10 primitive instructions (*block-Corner, put-downFlower, put-downPaper, right, sendMessage, freeCorner, move, receiveMessage, pick-upFlower* and *pick-upPaper*) classified based on their complexity, and an execution time consistent with robot speed was assigned to them.

Also, ECMRE has an *Execution Information* area that displays updated information for each robot during the execution of the algorithm (Fig. 1(b)). One of the entries there corresponds to the execution time measured in T units. This information is extremely useful to assess algorithm performance.

The ability of controlling the speed for each robot combined with the assignment of times to primitive instructions in ECMRE allows working with robots/processors with different performances, simulating one of the features of heterogeneous multicore architectures.

Energy Consumption. ECMRE adds a new section called Robot/Processor where energy consumption options can be set (in Joules) for a set of primitive instructions (Fig. 2(a)). Based on this, each robot stores its own consumption information and updates it during algorithm execution, which is displayed in the Execution Information area (Fig. 2(b)).

Processor speed is a factor that affects consumption (as speed increases, so does consumption). In ECMRE, the consumption generated by robot r to execute instruction i is given by the consumption of i previously specified multiplied by a coefficient that represents the speed of r at that moment (0.25 for *Min*, 0.5 for *Med* and 1 for *Max*).

Fig. 2. ECMRE (a) Energy consumption by instruction in the Robot/Processor section, (b) *Execution Information* area, where robot energy consumption information is displayed

4.2 Temperature Representation

In the Robot/Processor section mentioned above, the temperature (in Celsius) produced when executing each instruction of the set of primitives can also be set for each robot (Fig. 3(a)).

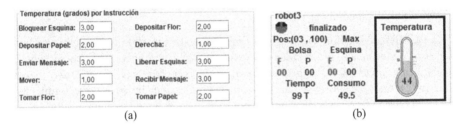

Fig. 3. ECMRE (a) Temperature by instruction in the Robot/Processor section, (b) *Execution Information*, where robot temperature information is displayed. (Color figure online)

The required logic has been implemented so that each robot records and updates its temperature and then this information can be viewed while the algorithm is being executed. To this end, a thermometer was added to the *Execution Information* area of the robot (Fig. 3(b)) to display the temperature with a numeric value. The thermometer changes its color (gray, green, orange and red) as temperature increases or decreases, where gray represents the minimum temperature and red, the maximum.

This feature is also affected by robot speed (as speed increases, so does temperature). In ECMRE, the temperature of robot r after executing instruction i is given by its previous temperature plus the temperature generated by instruction i previously specified, and this total is multiplied by a coefficient that represents the speed of r at that moment (0.92 for *Min*, 0.95 for *Med* and 0.98 for *Max*).

4.3 Representation of Overclocking and Underclocking Techniques

On the other hand, ECMRE allows for the possibility of robots using *overclocking* and *underclocking* techniques while the algorithm is being run. In the *Robot/Processor* section in ECMRE, the following parameters that enable this functionality are set (Fig. 4):

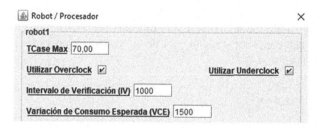

Fig. 4. ECMRE - Performance adjustment parameters in the Robot/Processor section

- *TCase Max:* maximum processor temperature. If this value is exceeded:

- An underclock condition will be attempted to help decrease processor temperature.
- If underclock is not admitted, or if the current speed is already the minimum speed, the robot will stop until its temperature goes back to normal.

- *Use Overclock:* this enables the use of an overclocking operation in the robot.
- *Use Underclock:* this enables the use of an underclocking operation in the robot.
- *Verification Interval (VI):* this indicates how often the increase in energy consumption should be checked and, if necessary, the corresponding overclocking/underclocking operation applied. The value is expressed in units of time T.
- *Expected Consumption Variation (ECV):* this indicates the variation in energy consumption (in joules) expected for the time defined in *VI*. This value is used to apply overclocking/underclocking operations.

The performance adjustment algorithm in each robot works as follows: For each instruction that is executed, it assesses the following:

- If robot temperature is higher than the specified maximum temperature (TCase Max):

- If the robot supports underclocking and its current speed is not the minimum speed, an underclock operation is applied to help decrease temperature. Note that if robot speed is already Min, it cannot be further reduced.
- Otherwise, the robot stops until its temperature cools down to 25°C and then resumes processing.

- If the increased consumption recorded during the verification interval (VI) exceeds the expected consumption variation (ECV):

- If the robot supports underclocking and its current speed is not the minimum speed, an underclock operation is applied to help decrease energy consumption and temperature. Note that if robot speed is already Min, it cannot be further reduced.

- If the increased consumption recorded during the verification interval (VI) is lower than the expected consumption variation (ECV):

- If the robot supports overclocking and its current speed is not the maximum speed, an overclock operation is applied to increase performance. Note that if robot speed is already Max, it cannot be further increased.

Overclock and underclock operations are not applied while consumption variation time is lower than the value set for *VI*. Every time an overclock or underclock operation is applied, or when the robot stops to cool down, consumption variation and elapsed time values are reset to 0.

4.4 Processor Logs

The new functionalities added to ECMRE may require an analysis after the algorithm is run to assess if the result obtained meets expectations. If execution time or energy consumption are higher than expected, modifications to the implemented solution may be proposed, or tasks could be reassigned among participating processors to achieve better results. To facilitate this analysis, ECMRE includes a new section called *Processor Log* that shows a user-friendly summary (through tables and charts) of the execution of an algorithm.

ECMRE records processor information while the algorithm is being run. In the *Robot/Processor* section, the option *Log Frequency* can be set to define how often (number of instructions) this information is recorded for each robot at runtime.

Recorded events include: processor stopped due to overload, overclock, and underclock. For each recorded log entry, the following robot information is stored: event (LOG, STOPPED, OVERCLOCK and UNDERCLOCK), speed before and after the event, temperature, and energy consumption.

The *Processor Log* section includes the following 5 subsections: Temperature, Temperature Chart, Consumption, Consumption Chart, and Consumption by Instruction Chart. For each of these, the user can select the robot to be analyzed.

5   Test Session with Students

ECMRE was presented in the course Programming Workshop of the School of Computer Science of the UNLP. This is a first-year course that consists of 3 modules. The third of these modules deals with the introduction to basic concurrent programming concepts, which is done through the use of CMRE.

The class started with a brief review of the concepts of concurrency and parallelism addressed by the environment, such as multicore architectures (both homogeneous and heterogeneous), energy consumption, temperature, performance adjustment techniques in processors, and load balancing. For each item, the concept and its significance in relation to current computer architectures were reviewed, and the new elements added to CMRE (temperature, consumption and speed) to create ECMRE, were introduced.

Once the theoretical review was completed, a practical activity was presented to be carried out under the supervision of the educator and the group of students. The students did not interact directly with the environment because it was still under development. The practical activity consisted in solving a model problem using ECMRE so that students could see how execution time, energy consumption and temperature changed based on different robot configurations. To this end, the tables, charts and logs described in the previous section were used.

At the end of the practical activity, each student answered a brief, anonymous survey intended as a first feedback from students, who will be the end users of the tool. This survey consisted of 5 questions answered on a Likert scale that goes from 1 (fully disagree) to 5 (fully agree). The survey was taken by the 42 students who attended the class on the day of the experience; the results obtained are listed in Table 1.

Table 1. Results of the survey taken by students of the Programming Workshop.

Question	Results obtained				
	Fully agree	Agree	Neither agree nor disagree	Disagree	Fully disagree
ECMRE helps learning the concepts presented	36%	57%	7%	0%	0%
Having a practical tool that allows viewing the theoretical content learned during the class through specific examples is useful	55%	38%	7%	0%	0%
The contents in ECMRE are organized and its use is intuitive	24%	52%	24%	0%	0%
The icons and charts used in the application are of the right size and match their associated function	48%	38%	14%	0%	0%
Having this application as a supplement to theoretical classes is beneficial	52%	36%	12%	0%	0%

6   Conclusions

The concepts of heterogeneity, energy consumption and temperature in parallel architectures are highly relevant, and we have presented an extension of CMRE (ECMRE) that allows including them.

ECMRE appears as a very useful tool to introduce these concepts in beginner classes in Computer Science courses of studies. To achieve this, two stages have been carried out. On the one hand, CMRE was modified to allow including these features in robots and, on the other, graphical tools were added to allow students view and then analyze this information in an easy and entertaining manner.

Thus, the complexity level of possible scenarios is increased, which poses a much more ambitious challenge that matches the technological reality of current processors.

References

1. Hoare, C.: Communicating Sequential Processes. Prentice Hall, Upper Saddle River (1985)
2. Dijkstra, Edsger W.: Finding the correctness proof of a concurrent program. In: Bauer, Friedrich L., et al. (eds.) Program Construction. LNCS, vol. 69, pp. 24–34. Springer, Heidelberg (1979). https://doi.org/10.1007/BFb0014652
3. Hansen, P.B.: The Architecture of Concurrent Processes. Prentice Hall, Upper Saddle River (1977)
4. Dasgupta, S.: Computer Architecture: A Modern Synthesis, Vol. 2: Advanced Topics, vol. 2. John Wiley & Sons, New York (1989)

5. ACM Curriculum Committee on Computer Science: Curriculum 1968: recommendations for the undergraduate program in computer science. Commun. ACM **11**(3), 151–197 (1968)
6. ACM Curriculum Committee on Computer Science: Curriculum 1978: recommendations for the undergraduate program in computer science. Commun. ACM **22**(3), 147–166 (1979)
7. ACM Two-Year College Education Committee: Guidelines for associate-degree and certificate programs to support computing in a networked environment. The Association for Computing Machinery, New York (1999)
8. Hoonlor, A., Szymanski, B.K., Zaki, M.J., Thompson, J.: An evolution of computer science research. Commun. ACM **56**, 74–83 (2013)
9. ACM/IEEE-CS Joint Task Force on Computing Curricula: Computer Science Curricula 2013. Report from the Task Force (2013)
10. ACM/IEEE-CS Joint Task Force on Computing Curricula: Computer Engineering 2004: Curriculum Guidelines for Undergraduate Degree Programs in Computer Engineering. Report in the Computing Curricula Series (2004)
11. ACM/IEEE-CS Joint Interim Review Task Force: Computer Science Curriculum 2008: An Interim Revision of CS 2001. Report from the Interim Review Task Force (2008)
12. De Giusti, L., Leibovich, F., Sanchez, M., Chichizola, F., Naiouf, M., De Giusti, A.: Desafíos y herramientas para la enseñanza temprana de Concurrencia y Paralelismo. In: Congreso Argentino de Ciencias de la Computación (CACIC), pp. 1585–1595. Fundación de Altos Estudios en Ciencias Exactas, Mar del Plata (2013)
13. AMD: Evolución de la tecnología de múltiple núcleo. http://multicore.amd.com/es-ES/AMD-Multi-Core/resources/Technology-Evolution (2009)
14. De Giusti, L., Leibovich, F., Chichizola, F., Naiouf, M., De Giusti, A.: Incorporando conceptos en la enseñanza de Concurrencia y Paralelismo utilizando el entorno CMRE. In: Congreso Argentino de Ciencias de la Computación (CACIC), pp. 1212–1221. Red de Universidades con Carreras en Informática (RedUNCI), Junín (2015)
15. Gepner, P., Kowalik, M.F.: Multi-core processors: new way to achieve high system performance. In: Proceeding of International Symposium on Parallel Computing in Electrical Engineering 2006 (PAR ELEC 2006), pp. 9–13 (2006)
16. Cool, M.M.: Programming models for scalable multicore programming (2007). http://www.hpcwire.com/features/17902939.html
17. Balladini, J., Rucci, E., De Giusti, A., Naiouf, M., Suppi, R., Rexachs, D., Luque, E.: Power characterisation of shared-memory HPC systems. Computer Science & Technology Series–XVIII Argentine Congress of Computer Science Selected Papers, pp. 53–65 (2013)
18. Brown, D.J.: Toward energy-efficient computing. Mag. Commun. ACM **53**(3), 50–58 (2010)
19. De Giusti, A., De Giusti L., Leibovich, F., Sanchez, M., Rodriguez Eguren, S.: Entorno interactivo multirobot para el aprendizaje de conceptos de Concurrencia y Paralelismo. In: IX Congreso de Tecnología en Educación y Educación en Tecnología, pp. 74–81. TE&ET, Chilecito Argentina (2014)
20. Champredonde R., De Giusti A. "Herramienta visual para la enseñanza de programación". Congreso Argentino de Ciencias de la Computación (CACIC), pp. 520–531. Red de Universidades con Carreras en Informática (REDUNCI), San Luis (1996)
21. Champredonde, R., De Giusti A.: Design and implementation of the visual DaVinci language. In: Congreso Argentino de Ciencias de la Computación (CACIC), pp. 980–992. Red de Universidades con Carreras en Informática (REDUNCI), La Plata (1997)
22. Nodejs page: https://nodejs.org/api/http.html. Accessed 21 July 2017

Inverting the Class or Investing in the Class? Flipped Classroom in Teaching Technology for Multimedia Production

Mirta G. Fernández[1,2(✉)] 📵, María V. Godoy Guglielmone[2] 📵,
Sonia I. Mariño[2] 📵, and Walter G. Barrios[2] 📵

[1] Facultad de Artes, Diseño y Ciencias de la Cultura (FADyC),
Universidad Nacional del Nordeste (UNNE), Corrientes, Argentina
mirtagf@hotmail.com
[2] Facultad de Ciencias Exactas y Naturales y Agrimensura (FaCENA),
Universidad Nacional del Nordeste (UNNE), Corrientes, Argentina
mvgg2001@yahoo.com, simarinio@yahoo.com,
waltergbarrios@yahoo.com.ar

Abstract. In reference to the approaches that have prevailed in education in general-and in artistic education in particular- this paper promotes the introduction of applicable methods in order to generate interest among young students and to train them through the Flipped Classroom. This is an active approach, focused on the student which derives from the premise of extending the time of an activity in order to favor critical thinking and autonomy in learning. In this regard, some of the linked learning theories are highlighted; the proposal is outlined; the didactic, curricular and technological decisions are detailed. Results of its implementation are reflected in a first year subject of the School of Arts of the Northeast National University in order to promote the teaching of a software tool in an interactive multimedia narrative realization. Finally, conclusions are drawn and synthesized in the significant impact of learning for the realization of the productions in question and underlying derivations.

Keywords: Flipped classroom · Ubiquitous learning · TPACK model application
Active learning methodologies · Flipped classroom method evaluation

1 Introduction

Recent advances in technology and ideology have opened new directions for educational research in order to eliminate spatial-temporal barriers [1]. Encouraged by the increase of materials and distributed resources in the WWW, discussion and changes in the physical classroom are being generated.

On the other hand, according to the approaches that have prevailed in education in general and in artistic education in particular, Aguirre and Giráldez [2] promote the introduction of applicable methods with the aim of generating interest among young students and train them through the flipped classroom. It consists of an active approach

© Springer International Publishing AG, part of Springer Nature 2018
A. E. De Giusti (Ed.): CACIC 2017, CCIS 790, pp. 295–307, 2018.
https://doi.org/10.1007/978-3-319-75214-3_28

centered on the student and which derives from the premise of extending the time of an activity in order to favor critical thinking and autonomy in learning.

Flipped Classroom refers to a teaching approach in which traditional classroom and self-learning activities are reversed or "overturned". It is presented as a pedagogical approach which uses - in general - pre-recorded conferences or readings, and guided activities. Thus, class time is used for interactive discussion, problem solving, and other activities developed with the teacher presence [3–5].

The Flipped Classroom changes the role of the teacher from being the "wise character on the stage" to being a "guide" in the process. In [3, 6, 7] some advantages and disadvantages of the Flipped Classroom are mentioned.

Some advantages are:

– an increase in the interaction between students and teachers;
– a change about the responsibility to learn upon students;
– the student's ability to study at the right time, and as many times as necessary;
– a collection of teaching resources available at any time and place;
– collaborative work among students;
– an increase in student's participation and a change from passive listening to active learning.

And some possible disadvantages are:

– time and resources investment to develop the courses;
– the possible need for technological investment;
– the time for teachers and students to adapt themselves and to acquire the new skills in order to apply the Flipped Classroom foundations;
– required for this more active and self-directed approach to learning.

For this reason, it is stated that the key to success is that students take responsibility for their learning and that they go prepared to class. This can be seen both as an advantage and as a disadvantage.

As mentioned before, this work reflects an experience based on the advantages provided implementing the Flipped Classroom as a strategy of active learning and to recognize the different learning rhythms in a large group of students from first year of the subject Introduction to Applied Technologies to Art of the Bachelor's Degree in Combined Arts from FADYCC (School of Arts, Design and Cultural Science) which belongs to the Northeast National University[1] (UNNE) (Chaco).

The proposal is part of the development of a practical work, in which the main purpose is the development of a multimedia narrative through the integration of multiple resources (graphics, images in movement, sound, buttons, among others) which were deployed in partial phases such as: analysis and interpretation, and application.

The tasks were monitored through tutoring in the Virtual classroom and the experience was recorded through a questionnaire that reflected the participants' perception. Based on this, the incorporation of some improvements in the approach is projected.

---

[1] http://www.unne.edu.ar/.

1.1   Theoretical Basis and Linked Terminology to the Flipped Classroom

In their study Bishop and Verleger [1] explain how the Flipped or Inverted Classroom methodology represents a combination of theories of learning: based on a constructivist ideology and instruction activities derived from methods under the behavioral principles. It is possible to adhere to these principles returning to Vygotsky's theory of the Proximal Development Zone (ZPD) [8], which explains how the students' learning depends on their previous knowledge in the area and how they are articulated, explaining that they require the help of the educator to reach their full potential, as well as highlighting the importance of the interaction with their peers, a scaffolding and an appropriate feedback.

Meanwhile, their spreaders and promoters Sams and Bergmann [4] point out that it is simply to turn the traditional method in which the educational content is presented in the classroom and the practice activities are carried out at home as it is shown in Fig. 1. In this case students receive the "master class" at home and they do the previously thought and planned homework in the classroom.

Fig. 1. General mechanism flipped classroom

In 2014, the Flipped Learning Network (FLN) [9] provided a universal definition as well as four widespread pillars of which are synthesized and translated in Fig. 2. These are intended to provide guidance for their implementation.

Fig. 2. The four pillars of F-L-I-P [9].

Even with the numerous existing experiences, one of the main criticisms to this model is that inverting a classroom may not necessarily lead to Inverted Learning [9]. This is related to the adequate preparation and the use of technological tools in activities "outside the classroom" [10], i.e., it is required to use the class time appropriately and with the intention that the model promotes [4, 11].

1.2 Evaluation of the Methodology

Following Acuña [6], Fernandez et al. [7] the dimensions that can be considered to be the most accepted when assessing the effects of inverting the classroom, are:

– experiential (of the learning process),
– regarding the use of video (as a mechanism of instruction).

It is also possible to predict that the combination of new teaching technologies with interactive classroom activities may result in better learning, but it may be unsatisfactory for the students [12]. In this sense Persky [13], shares some of his findings which are linked to the resistance to change that students have, and according to his experience, although the students learn more, they do not like the course and he says that the more he used inverted learning in his classes, the more his assessment as teacher lowered. Considering that the discontent and unfavorable reaction of the students could be due to the inherent inheritance of the traditional teaching model in which the teacher is responsible for "teaching" and "transmitting" the knowledge, thus the expectation of the traditional student is to deposit in the teacher the responsibility of acquiring new learnings and knowledge [14].

1.3 To Summarize, What Is Flipped Classroom?

The existing literature agrees that one creates an environment of inverted learning, when teachers develop or select lessons available, whenever and wherever it is convenient for the student, at home, in class, during the study room, on the bus to a game or even from a hospital bed [5]; aspects that according to Burbules [15] define ubiquity in teaching. Teachers can deliver this instruction recording and narrating presentations, creating videos of themselves teaching or selecting tutorials of reliable Internet sites. Students can see the videos or screenshots as many times as they need it, allowing them to improve their productivity in the classroom.

As described in this paper, the class goes from being of passive reception to one of more active participation. The teacher, by freeing himself from the class time he uses for the instruction of the students, can focus on attending to the specific needs of learning and on responding to the diversity and the different paces of learning.

1.4 Motivation in the Selection of the Method

A hypothesis that gives rise to a paradigm shift in the classroom is the time it takes for first-year students to become familiar with some computer technologies, in which particular skills and sensitivities are put into play. An experience closely linked to such inference is presented at Algonquin College [16] in a video production class, in which Inverted Classroom was used to teach the operation of editing software, a cumbersome procedure to explain in a conventional class.

The afore-mentioned among other factors, promotes the introduction of variations in the approach to a didactic proposal in the subject Introduction to Applied Technologies to Art, in 2016 in order to achieve a more meaningful learning taking advantage of "inverting" the classroom. As Fig. 3 illustrates the roles and responsibilities of the participants become more proactive.

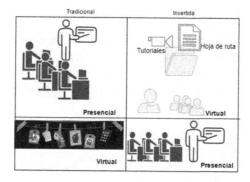

Fig. 3. Migration to the Flipped Classroom in the experience

The metaphor illustrates on the left the components incorporated for the traditional strategy and on the right the resources deployed to provide the necessary scaffolding to the tasks.

1.5 Think Before Innovating: Use of the TPACK Model in the Didactic Redesign

In a continuous process of decision making around the different elements of the curriculum, an alternative is to resort to the TPACK (Technological Pedagogical Content Knowledge) model [17]. The model allows emphasizing the creative-constructive dimension of the preparation and development of teaching processes, the role of the teacher as a facilitator of environments, the explicitness and discussion around these elements to integrate TIC in an effective way [18, 19]. As illustrated in Fig. 4, the orientations give rise to a series of decisions for such purposes.

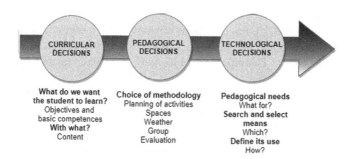

Fig. 4. Implications in the use of ICT according to TPACK [17]

The TPACK framework, and following Harris and Hofer [20], contributed to the present work orientations for the redesign of tasks according to the activities with TIC or Learning Activity Types. Those related to the Visual Arts1 from them: Build up Knowledge/Conceptualize and Apply, in the curricular context [21].

2   Method

In the didactic and pedagogical development for the integration of technology in teaching, the guidelines proposed by TPACK were followed. So, curricular and pedagogical decisions as well as the selection of technological resources were made. Subsequently, the results were analyzed, and the pedagogical proposal was validated in order to obtain retrospective views from the students.

3   Results

The subject belongs to the first year. In the curriculum, the selected theme was designed to develop exercises in the IT (information technology) classroom, using a software tool to perform an applied work.

The disparity of previous knowledge or the preparation of the students to learn in the same way was identified as the main weakness of the traditional methodology. The time it takes students to become familiar with some technologies is heterogeneous, mainly in the first University years. In addition, other factors were identified:

– students who are not familiar with technology in academic environments,
– high rate of non-attendance,
– lack of time and space for the development of customized computer classes.

Furthermore, it was admitted that students were overwhelmed with the infinity of material available on the Internet. For that reason, they formed social networks in which they shared videos and resources to give specific answers to each group of work outside the class. The described situation influenced the teacher's activities due to the impossibility of knowing all the materials available and of giving an adequate response to the enquiries.

The above-mentioned factors contributed to the decision of rethinking the mechanisms used, so during 2016, the curricular objectives were revised, and the didactic strategy was redesigned, through guidelines that are described below.

Curricular decisions: Definition of objectives, competences and content to be addressed

The curricular decisions consisted in the definition of an integrating practical work, which allowed to reach a dual objective of the stages:

– *Analysis and interpretation:* Identify vocabulary, concepts, meanings and metaphors present in a narrative by the author Jorge Luis Borges "The Garden of Forking Paths".

– **Application:** To develop artistic representations, individually or collaboratively, using different media to develop an interactive multimedia narrative (texts, still and moving images, buttons, sound, graphics, etc.)

These objectives were defined through activities that challenge students to transfer their knowledge using a variety of resources and techniques. They also develop the competencies required in the subject that contribute to the professional profile outlined in the career.

3.1 Pedagogical Decisions: Planning of Activities

The Flipped Classroom's planning consisted of a series of face-to-face classes in which specific guidelines were established through a roadmap. This was subsequently arranged in the virtual classroom to carry out the programmed activities:

• *Activities in classes.*

It began with a brief exposition of the study dynamics, objectives, implicit tasks, including dates of deliveries according to the partial stages of:

– Navigation map of the narrative to be treated.
– Interactive narrative in the recommended software.

Next, the text to be addressed was analyzed in a preliminary way, in order to anticipate the work outside the classroom; the remaining classes were destined to carry out group productions.

• *Post-class activity.*

These activities consisted of a set of tasks, each one consisting of at least three tutorials.

They were defined with the purpose of recognizing the work environment, carrying out individual practices, developing skills in handling the tool and advancing in the achievement of the particular objectives.

The evaluation of the work was oriented to achieve partial deliveries, in accordance with the proposed objectives and the stipulated times.

3.2 Technological Decisions: Selection of Tools and Resources

Technological decisions focused on the preparation of a roadmap, the use of virtual space, the selection of tutorials and the implementation of the tool.

The objectives and tasks were projected in detail in the roadmap.

The use of the draw.io on-line tool was recommended in order to prepare the navigation map, which allows it to be edited collaboratively.

The virtual classroom was used as support for the planned activities, and materials, links and resources were available. To achieve the students' follow-up, the configuration of Groups (of students), Grouping (by tutors) and Tasks or Delivery Spaces was mainly used as shown in Fig. 5. The possibility of making partial presentations was also established and in this way the student could get to know the teacher's assessment quickly.

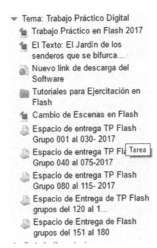

▼ Tema: Trabajo Práctico Digital

🐦 Trabajo Práctico en Flash 2017

🐦 El Texto: El Jardín de los
senderos que se bifurca...

📄 Nuevo link de descarga del
Software

📁 Tutoriales para Ejercitación en
Flash

🐦 Cambio de Escenas en Flash

📄 Espacio de entrega TP Flash
Grupo 001 al 030- 2017

📄 Espacio de entrega TP Fl Tarea
Grupo 040 al 075-2017

📄 Espacio de entrega TP Flash
Grupo 080 al 115- 2017

📄 Espacio de Entrega de TP Flash
grupos del 120 al 1...

📄 Espacio de Entrega de Flash
grupos del 151 al 180

Fig. 5. Materials, task configurations and groups in the virtual classroom

Basically, the students had to exercise three tutorials available on the Web, consisting of a series of intermediate instructions. The material advantage prevails among others:

– It is an interactive website designed as a material with illustrations and the possibility of reproducing small fragments of the instructions, as shown in Fig. 6.

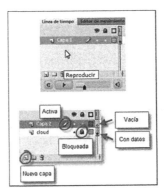

Fig. 6. Interactive Web material selected for use in Flipped Classroom (http://mosaic.uoc.edu/FlashCS5/cast/index.html)

– Instructions can be obtained and printed in text format (.pdf).
– The first three tutorials provide scaffolding for the accomplishment of the tasks, with the possibility of extending with other tutorials and resources of the same Web site.

– The published texts and images of the designed material are created using a license[2] which allows them to be copied, distributed and publicly transmitted, making sure the author and the source were cited.

For the implementation of the tutorial in the selected tool, the same one as in previous courses was used (Adobe Flash CS 5). In the elaboration of the perception survey applied at the end of the study, a Google Form was set up, in order to collect the opinions, and then process them.

The already mentioned advantages -among others- offered the teachers the possibility of unifying the materials destined to the students, in order to facilitate the access online or the downloads.

3.3 Evaluation of Flipped Classroom Proposal

As regards the learning process evaluation, two dimensions were proposed: progress and students' achievements.

In the progress evaluation, the students presented difficulties of a higher level of complexity that exceeded the content of the material. For example, difficulties associated with: the use of certain sound format, the incorporation of codes or "script" applied to the interaction of buttons and scenes, or others problems of a "technical" nature.

In partial stages, a diversity of production with satisfactory results was observed.

This was linked to the abilities and interests of the students and the nature of the curriculum. Some highlights are: the recording and editing of sounds with tools different from the ones proposed, the introduction of a script to generate random scenes, the application of playful approaches to narrative, and others.

In relation to deadlines, the virtual classroom of the subject and the spaces allocated for such purposes, contributed to the delivery in an organized manner and on the stipulated dates.

3.4 Validation of the Proposal. A Case Study in 2016

In order to validate the proposal, in 2016 an online form was prepared and implemented. The survey was applied in order to recognize the perspectives and expectations of 60 participants -chosen randomly- in relation to the methodology and tutorials used. It consisted of five (5) questions.

A scale of 1 to 4 was defined, in which one (1) represented "in disagreement", two (2) "neutral", three (3) "in agreement" and in the other extreme, four (4) "very much agreed". The results are the following:

The students were inquired about "I liked the possibility of doing a tutorial/watching a video instead of attending a traditional class (exposition) of the program's tools". As shown in Fig. 7, 75% responded between the 2 and 4 scales; while 25% responded option 1 or in "disagreement".

---

[2] http://creativecommons.org/licenses/by/3.0/es/legalcode.es.

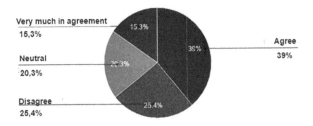

Fig. 7. Perception of the student as regards the use of video and the methodology used.

In reference to the statement "I prefer to have the traditional class (exposition) of the teacher instead of doing active and group work in classes such as those carried out", the 32.2% were "in disagreement", while the rest was concentrated in the remaining scales as shown in Fig. 8.

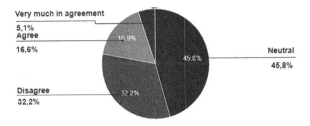

Fig. 8. The preference of traditional teaching method

Regarding the question "the use of videos allowed me to learn the study material more effectively than doing the readings alone"; more than 80% responded to options 3 and 4, as illustrated in Fig. 9. So, the students consider the material greatly facilitated their productions.

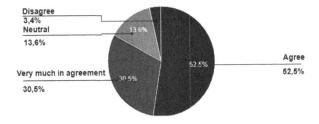

Fig. 9. Evaluation about the use of video.

About the question "Did I learn more when I used videos, short readings and active learning activities in class compared to the traditional method (teacher's exposition)?" Only 10.2% disagreed (Fig. 10).

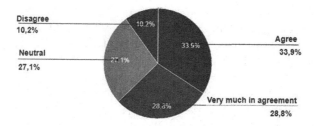

Fig. 10. Level of learning obtained with the tutorials from the student's perspective

Enquiring about the teaching accompaniment (Fig. 11), and asking specifically about "I felt disconnected without a teacher present during videos or virtual activities", 40% answered affirmatively. So, the tutorial system must be revised and optimized.

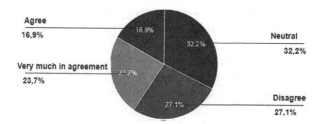

Fig. 11. Evaluation of tutoring.

It was also requested to indicate (in the form) the tutor of the tasks, in order to obtain a tutoring retrospective and introduce improvements in the mechanisms designed to future courses.

4   Conclusions and Future Work

The exposed results demonstrate that it is possible to infer that the advantages of the flipped classroom as an active learning strategy have been exploited.

This paper explained the redefinition of the activities in the subject Introduction to Applied Technologies to Art in the first year of the Bachelor's Degree in combined Arts, applying the Flipped Classroom as a methodology strategy and following the Model TPACK. Thus, this paper focused on achieving the learning objectives expressed in two instances: outside the classroom to access information and didactic content and, in the classroom, to carry out productions.

The described experience was originated in 2012 as a conventional attending class activity, and in 2016 part of the proposal migrated and it was supported in the subject's virtual classroom for tutoring and access to materials.

In addition, the learning process was monitored and once it finished provided feedback data. The results showed that a significant proportion of students prefer the traditional methodology, although they recognize that they learn more, the flipped classroom promotes autonomous work and contributes to adequate management of time.

On the other hand, from the point of view of the teacher, some advantages are: the ease to develop personalized group learning, the productive use of the time in the classroom, the promotion of ubiquitous learning, the possibility of improving continuous learning and establishing a link between formal and non-formal education through Web available resources. In short, it plays a vital role in the creation of students, in the consequence of a deeper learning and in the appropriation of content, which is why the Inverted Classroom model is of interest in the teaching of technology.

The results allow to assume that the dissemination of practices focused on active learning in the university classrooms implemented since the early years is essential to achieve educational innovations. Identifying those strategies that work leads to encourage the different education protagonists in their search for new ways to improve teaching in the various scenarios which the knowledge society presents, and in response to the diversity of study rhythms.

In particular, the design of the Flipped Classroom proposal and its validation have made it possible to corroborate the initial interpellation that originated this work: the inversion of the class contributes to the investment in the class. This is supported by the fact that teachers:

- Generated new formats in order to promote the student´s interaction, defining the content, the task of monitoring and evaluating accordingly.
- Facilitated experiences of autonomous access to content, critical and constructive work in attending class time.
- Contributed to research practices development, which are different from the traditional
- Followed up personal and group advances of the students in relation to the fidelity of authorship in the productions.

On the other hand, the investment in the class is illustrated by equipping students with some of the competencies required for 21st century society such as to work with accessible content in different formats, in virtual spaces and the cooperative work among others.

In 2017 a similar implementation in the systematization process was carried out, thus the analysis of both situations will provide data in order to improve the proposed design.

In addition, validating students' learning through intermediate questionnaires or online activities will be investigated in order to achieve a more effective follow-up.

Acknowledgements. The authors are part of the Project accredited by the General Secretariat of Science and Technology by Resol. 241/17 of the Northeast National University, PI 16F019, whose title is "IT in Information Systems: Models, methods and tools". Director of the same Prof. Mariño, Sonia I. and Co-Director, Prof. Godoy Guglielmone, Maria V. The support of the Secretariat is appreciated.

References

1. Bishop, J.L., Verleger, M.A.: The flipped classroom: a survey of the research. In: Proceedings of ASEE National Conference, GA, Atlanta, vol. 30, no. 9, pp. 1–18 (2013)
2. Jiménez, L., Aguirre, I., Pimentel, L.G.: Educación artística, cultura y ciudadanía, OEI, Fundación Santillana, Madrid, España (2009)
3. Halili, S.H., Zainuddin, Z.: Flipping the classroom: What we know and what. Online J. Distance Educ. e-Learning **3**(1), 28–35 (2015)
4. Bergmann, J., Sams, A.: Flip Your Classroom: Reach Every Student in Every Class Every Day, 1st edn. International Society for Technology in Education, Washington, D.C. (2012)
5. Hamdan, N., McKnight, P., McKnight, K., Arfstrom, K.M.: The flipped learning model: a white paper based on the literature review titled a review of flipped learning. Flipped Learning Network/Pearson/George Mason University (2013)
6. Peña, A.B.: Vectores de la Pedagogía Docente Actual. ACCI, Madrid (2014)
7. Fernández, D.A., Tabasso, E.: Humanizar la utilización de las TIC en educación. Revista de Investigación en Educación **15**(1), 80–82 (2016). Dykinson, Madrid
8. Vigotsky, L.S.: Interacción entre enseñanza y desarrollo. In: Colectivo de Autores del Departamento de Psicología Infantil y de la Educación. Selección de Lecturas de Psicología de las Edades I (tomo III), La Habana, pp. 25–46 (1988)
9. Flipped Learning Network (FLN): The Four Pillars of F-L-I-P (2014)
10. Domínguez, L.C., Vega, N.V., Espitia, E.L., Sanabria, Á.E., Corso, C., Serna, A.M., Osorio, C.: Impact of the flipped classroom strategy in the learning environment in surgery: a comparison with the lectures. Biomédica **35**(4), 513–521 (2015)
11. Perdomo Rodríguez, W.: Estudio de evidencias de aprendizaje significativo en un aula bajo el modelo flipped classroom. EDUTEC, Revista Electrónica de Tecnología Educativa **55**, 1–17 (2016)
12. Missildine, K., Fountain, R., Summers, L., Gosselin, K.: Flipping the classroom to improve student performance and satisfaction. J. Nurs. Educ. **52**(10), 597–599 (2013)
13. UNMC Newsroom. http://www.unmc.edu/news.cfm?match=12626. Accessed 20 Nov 2017
14. Observatorio de Innovación Educativa: Aprendizaje Invertido. Edu Trends Reporte. Tecnológico de Monterrey, Monterrey, México (2014)
15. Burbules, N.C.: Meanings of "ubiquitous learning". Educ. Policy Anal. Arch. **22**(104), 1–10 (2014)
16. Alshahrani, K., Ally, M.: Transforming Education in the Gulf Region: Emerging Learning Technologies and Innovative Pedagogy for the 21st Century. Routledge Research in Education. Taylor & Francis, New York (2016)
17. Koehler, M., Mishra, P.: What is technological pedagogical content knowledge (TPACK)? Contemp. Issues Technol. Teach. Educ. **9**(1), 60–70 (2009)
18. Cabero Almenara, J.: Reflexiones educativas sobre las tecnologías de la información y la comunicación (TIC). Tecnología, Ciencia y Educación **1**, 19–27 (2015)
19. Cabero, J.: La formación del profesorado en TIC: modelo TPACK, Ed. Universidad de Sevilla (2014)
20. Harris, J., Mishra, P., Koehler, M.: Teachers' technological pedagogical content knowledge and learning activity types: curriculum-based technology integration reframed. J. Res. Technol. Educ. **41**(4), 393–416 (2009)
21. Fernández, M., Barrios, W., Godoy, M., Gendin, G.: Art and ICT: initial experiences with software tools in the training of Bachelors Degree in Combined Arts. In: XIX Argentine Congress of Computer Science Selected Papers. Computer Science and Technology Series, pp. 121–130. EdUNLP, La Plata (2014)

Author Index

Printed in the United States
By Bookmasters